Thomas Ryba

The Essence of Phenomenology and Its Meaning for the Scientific Study of Religion

PETER LANG

New York • Bern • Frankfurt am Main • Paris

Library of Congress Cataloging-in-Publication Data

Ryba, Thomas
    The essence of phenomenology and its meaning
for the scientific study of religion / Thomas Ryba.
        p. cm. — (Toronto studies in religion ; vol. 7)
        Bibliography: p.
        Includes indexes.
        1. Religion—Study and teaching.   2. Phenomenology.
    I. Title.   II. Series.
    BL41.R93   1991   142'.7—dc20   89-32373
    ISBN 0-8204-0742-9   CIP
    ISSN 8756-7385

Selections from "Gilson vs. Maritain: the Start of Thomistic Metaphysics," © Copyright 1990, *Doctor Communis,* Vaticano, Italy. Reprinted by permission.

Selections from "Thomistic Existentialism and the Silence of the Quinque Viae," © Copyright 1986, *The Modern Schoolman,* St. Louis. Reprinted by permission.

Selections from "Ad Mentem Thomae: Does Natural Philosophy Prove God?," © Copyright 1990, *Divus Thomas,* Piacenza, Italy. Reprinted by permission.

Selections from "Transcendental Thomism and Thomistic Texts," © Copyright 1990, *The Thomist,* Washington, D.C. Reprinted by permission.

Selections from "Immateriality and Metaphysics," © Copyright 1988, *Angelicum,* Rome Italy. Reprinted by permission.

The Essence of Phenomenology
and Its Meaning for the
Scientific Study of Religion

Toronto Studies in Religion

Donald Wiebe, General Editor
Trinity College
University of Toronto

Vol. 7

Published in association with
the Centre for Religious Studies
at the University of Toronto

PETER LANG
New York • Bern • Frankfurt am Main • Paris

DEDICATION

For my mother,

Judith,

and in memory of my father,

Frank

All that you have spoken you have spoken with a sincere heart, and there is
no one who would gainsay your words. For this is not the first day in which
your wisdom is manifested; but from the beginning of your days, all the
people have known your shrewdness because the disposition of your heart is
good.

Book of Judith, 8: 28-30.

Come, then, dear father, mount upon my neck;
I'll bear you on my shoulders. That is not
Too much for me. Whatever waits for us,
We shall share one danger, one salvation.
You, father, take up our household gods and their symbols;
I cannot touch them, just come from such war and fresh slaughter,
Until I shall wash my pollution away in a Living Stream of Water.

Aeneid, 2: 707-720
(*mutatis mutandis*)

TABLE OF CONTENTS

LIST OF FIGURES

ACKNOWLEDGEMENTS

A book is like a physical event in that it is the result of forces and influences which, though not always manifest in the final product, are nevertheless responsible for its emergence. In the case of this particular book, hidden influences have collaborated to make it a better work than it would have been, had I been left to my own resources. For this reason, I would like to thank the many people who made it possible.

First and foremost, I owe a profound debt of gratitude to my mentor, Professor Edmund Perry (Northwestern University), who was instrumental in the inception of this book's central idea and has been this work's keenest critic and kindest advocate during its lengthy period of composition. I would also like to thank the scholars who read the manuscript in its various stages of development and made many positive suggestions to improve its contents. Especially, I would like to thank Dr. Donald Wiebe (University of Toronto), Dr. Ursula King (University of Bristol) and Dr. N. Ross Reat (University of Queensland) each of whom read the manuscript in its entirety and were very encouraging about the value of its publication.

Also, I would be remiss if I did not thank my good friends for the numerous and sometimes intangible, contributions they made toward this book's completion. To Dr. Robert Hughes (Harry S. Truman College), who read portions of an earlier incarnation of the manuscript, and his wife Ellen, I owe thanks not only for points of style but also for warm, intelligent friendship. To Dr. James Deaville (McMaster University) I am indebted both for a fine translation of the phenomenological portions of the *New Organon* and for the hours he and I spent working it into intelligible philosophical English. To Dr. Leslie Clifford McTighe (Loyola University, Chicago), an *alter ego* in the most precise sense, I owe an almost endless list of debts. Among his contributions to this work were: license to use his house on Cape Cod (where I wrote chapters 2, 4, and 5 of this manuscript), his meticulous editing of the penultimate version of the manuscript and his long-suffering friendship. I would also like to thank my new friend and colleague, Dr. Paul Eduardo Muller-Ortega (Michigan State), whose gentlemanly and scholarly qualities testify to his noble heritage and continue to be a source of encouragement to me, a stranger in a strange land. Special mention and thanks also to Ms. Wendy McDaniel and Ms. Carey Draeger, who patiently word-processed this text and worked out the significant technical details necessary to make it photo-ready.

Finally, I would like to thank my wife, Christine, who, because of her grace and steadfastness during the interminable writing of this book, has supercharged the words "sport," "trooper," and "beauty" each with a new surplus of meaning.

PREFACE

The idea of phenomenology has had a complex and often confusing history. Since its original conceptualization by Johann Lambert in 1764, it has undergone a variagated evolution which has given rise to many competing phenomenologies, particularly during the 20th century. In spite of its great variety--and, most likely, *because* of it--phenomenology has achieved a place as one of the dominant philosophical and methodological ideas in the latter half of this century. Philosophers, religionists, sociologists, economists, anthropologists, aestheticians, theologians and many other specialists have claimed it as their *métier*.[1] The wide interest in the phenomenological method as a technique for presuppositionless description may be construed, in part, as a response to one of the needs of science under the current *Zeitgeist*: the need for a scientific method which will rigorously satisfy an objective criteriology.[2] That relativism which taints the social, religious, and theological sciences by assailing propositional truth makes phenomenology, or a rigorously descriptive method like phenomenology, a *sine qua non* for the restoration of scientific certainty. But the proliferation of meanings associated with the word 'phenomenology' threatens to introduce so much obscurity into the search for a single descriptive method that the goal of this search may be abandoned as unachieveable. It is in the area of religious studies that the frustration concerning the phenomenological method is particularly acute. The general problem may be stated as follows: although the phenomenological method seems to gain in attractiveness with the publication of every new article employing it, the very equivocity in what 'phenomenology' means for different practitioners threatens ultimately to undermine its generalizability. To rephrase an epigram of G. K. Chesterton, if phenomenology is everything, then phenomenology is nothing. It is this problem which this book is specifically designed to address.

Phenomenology's harmony with the current *Zeitgeist* can be measured, in an impressionistic way, both by its efficacy in capturing the imagination of conservative religious organizations as well as by its efficacy in capturing the popular consciousness. An example of the former is the Roman Catholic interest in phenomenology as a method of theological analysis. The thought of Roman Catholic theologians and philosophers

---

[1] The philosophical, theological and sociological phenomenologists are well known. Less famous are those who have applied phenomenological methods to economics, thinkers such as Murray Rothbard and Ludwig von Mises. The fact that phenomenology is becoming an accepted method in the "hardest" of the social sciences, economics, also says something about its spreading influence.

[2] Both the Lambertian and Husserlian phenomenologies, for example, were conceived as methods of apodictic description which would allow true appearance to be distinguished from false appearance. Interpreted in this way phenomenology is a prerequisite to criteriology (theory of judgment).

such as Karl Rahner, Bernard Lonergan, Emerich Coreth, Otto Muck and David Tracy demonstrates either a marked dependence upon, or adjustment to, phenomenological concepts. Even the current pontiff, John Paul II, has laid claim to the title "phenomenologist" with the publication of his two books, *The Acting Person* and *Sources of Renewal*.[3] For phenomenologically inclined Roman Catholics, the importance of these two works remained unparalleled until the Jesuit John Kobler, who with a penchant for revisionism often typical of church historians, published his book *Vatican II and Phenomenology*.[4] Its central thesis is not only that the documents of Vatican II are susceptible to phenomenological analysis but that the council itself was *self-consciously* an exercise in the application of the phenomenological method to church doctrine. In other words, the council fathers were *de facto* phenomenologists! Because of these three works, as well as the general tenor of Roman Catholic theology, many observers both inside and outside the Roman Catholic Church make the inference that its theology may be on the verge of another grand synthesis, one which might, with equal probability, alter, rival or supplant Thomism. Before phenomenology can result in such a grand synthesis in this epoch of the democracy of knowledge, however, it must first capture the popular consciousness.

Although there is no evidence of a widespread awareness of what phenomenology is and what it promises, there is some evidence that phenomenology is slowly becoming known to those outside of the academic community through a sort of intellectual "trickle down" effect. As more courses on the phenomenological method are taught at the collegiate level, more college students become familiar with phenomenological esoterica. Of course, phenomenology has a long way to come before it is the chief topic of barbers' conversation as the Hegelian dialectic was in Copenhagen at the time of Kierkegaard. Phenomenology still awaits its great popularizers. Nevertheless, there are signs that the swell in academic interest is about to break upon the popular consciousness.

Recently, Mike Royko, the cranky, syndicated Chicago journalist, devoted one of his columns to a humorously scathing indictment of phenomenological terminology in educational theory.[5] Though an isolated incident, this article was significant for two reasons. First, it demonstrated that the idea of phenomenology has found a path to the mass media and, thus, to mass consciousness. Second, it demonstrated that the phenomenological method was being taught in at least one American college as a viable

---

[3]The first, published in the series *Analecta Husserliana*, is a phenomenological anthropology which combines elements of Aristotelian-Thomistic metaphysics, anthropology and ethics as well as Scheler's phenomenological method to produce a description of "man's constitutive tendencies and strivings, . . . his status in the world, the meaning of freedom and of human fulfillment." [Anna-Teresa Tymieniecka in the Editorial Introduction to *The Acting Person* (Dordrecht: D. Reidel, 1979) xxii]. The second, an attempt to define those precepts of Vatican II which require urgent implementation, employs categories of existential phenomenology as a hermeneutic both to interpret how the Vatican II documents shape official church doctrine as well as to explain how they speak to the Catholic believer in his *Sitz im Leben*. See Karol Wojtyla, *Sources of Renewal* (San Francisco: Harper and Row, 1980) iv.

[4]John F. Kobler, *Vatican II and Phenomenology* (Dordrecht: Martinus Nijhoff, 1985).

[5]Mike Royko, "Educt, Reduct and Other Muck," *Chicago Tribune* 6 August, 1985.

approach to educational theory, and it is a truism that the vocables of today's educational theory become the buzzwords of tomorrow's educational bureaucracy. Couple the significance of this newspaper article with the fact that the phenomenology is being presented as a tool for marketing research at the university level--and, in a thinly veiled form, in some marketing textbooks--and one reaches the conclusion that phenomenology may, before long, become another one of the stock methodologies which have broad interdisciplinary application, methodologies such as content analysis, sampling theory, time-series analysis, and decision theory.[6]

As suggestive as the signs are that phenomenology is waxing in methodological popularity, this interest will be ultimately fruitless unless the many different definitions of phenomenology are brought together according to their points of agreement. Just as there are neither many varieties of induction nor many varieties of deduction--but a single general paradigm for each method--so too phenomenology, if it is to be a practicable method, must be brought to the normalization which characterizes practicable methods. At present, however, there is no single paradigm for phenomenology because no one definition of phenomenology distinguishes itself from all others by its extraordinary clarity, precision, depth and utility. Indeed, the variety, turgidity, imprecision, shallowness and impracticality of the various meanings of phenomenology obfuscate whatever happy methodological features the different phenomenologies share. It is the popularity of phenomenology which intensifies the multiplication of phenomenologies, and this multiplication, in turn, further frustrates consensus about what phenomenology is. But perhaps the most banal threat to phenomenology comes from those specialists who adopt it as a method *because* it is both fashionable and ambiguous.

Because there is confusion about what 'phenomenology' means, and because the popularity of the method grows despite this confusion, it is possible for specialists to assume the title "phenomenologist," improve their chances of publication and gain an *entrée* into a fashionable methodological circle, all without having to adopt a clearly defined methodological program. However, to adopt the title "phenomenologist" because it is fashionable, and to do so without a clear understanding of what phenomenology *ought to be*, is risky. Intellectual fashions share the same capriciousness as sartorial fashions: both are outlandish, superficial and ephemeral. Moreover, whatever a fashion hides, distorts or disguises is generally more tantalizing than what it reveals. To be a follower of phenomenology in the same way one is a follower of fashion is to write phenomenology's death writ. It is to be inauthentic to the intellectual spirit which pursues a method for the sake of truth; it is also to ignore the more interesting issues of method in favor of superficial solutions to methodological difficulties.

In light of the threats and prospects which currently characterize the interpretation of phenomenology, now would seem a propitious time to reexamine the history of phenomenology in the hope that such a reexamination will lead to a path out of the mire of ambiguity in which the idea of phenomenology is imbued. The purpose of this book is to reexamine the history of phenomenology in order to find this path.

---

[6]The chief barrier to phenomenology's becoming an interdisciplinary technique is its lack of a specific method. At present, it is too many things to too many people for it to be grouped in the same class with these techniques. The purpose of this work is to aid in the crystalization of a definition which will unify phenomenology's method.

The *general* utility of this book is as a historical prolegomenon to the normalization of phenomenology's meaning. In other words, its utility lies in its persuasiveness as a historical argument for a single phenomenological method. It has general relevance for any specialist who is willing to set aside preconceptions about what 'phenomenology' means and who is willing to consider the problem of phenomenology's meaning as a problem in semantic synthesis. This work, thus, speaks to anyone who wishes to understand the common semantic core to the various philosophical meanings of 'phenomenology.'

The proximate purpose of this work circumscribes a much narrower utility, however. Specifically, this book is an attempt to disclose the essential meaning behind the philosophical definitions of phenomenology and to explain what, if anything, this meaning tells us about how better to do phenomenology of religion. This proximate purpose is merely the first step toward the accomplishment of the tacit agenda behind this work, that of completing a full-blown phenomenological analysis of a particular religious tradition. The historical prolegomenon, it is hoped, will be followed by a manual on the rules of phenomenological method for religious studies and, later, by an application of the prescribed method to a world religion. Even if neither of the projected works is ever accomplished, the present work can stand on its own merits as a significant, revisionist contribution to the history of phenomenology and, as such, a significant departure from the approaches of its predecessors. The independent value of this historical prolegomenon derives from the way it defies convention.

First, this work takes seriously the Husserlian methodological imperative, "Back to the things themselves!" It ignores conventional wisdom about what 'phenomenology' does or does not mean and attempts to reopen the question, and then answer it, by going back to each of the significant historical manifestations of philosphical phenomenology. In short, this work is a phenomenology of phenomenology.

Second, although the primary aim of this work is descriptive, its secondary aim is prescriptive. Unlike previous works which describe the multiplicity of meanings associated with 'phenomenology' but do not offer a generalizable meaning expressive of all, this work proposes a definition of 'phenomenology' which encompasses shared meanings and resolves conflicting meanings, when these opposing meanings can be resolved under definitive philosophical presuppositions. The result is what might be called the semantic essence of the word 'phenomenology.'

Third, this work is directed to the reconciliation of the various meanings of 'phenomenology' and not, as in the majority of its predecessors, to its fragmentation. The intentionality operative in this work is one which looks self-consciously for identities and analogies between the various meanings of 'phenomenology.' Its aim is to learn from all by neglecting none, its method being ultimately synthetic and only secondarily analytic. The governing motif of this semantic investigation of phenomenology, is synonymy and not equivocity or disparity.

Fourth, this work does not recognize the complete legitimacy of religious phenomenology's claim to methodological and theoretical autonomy. Rather, it recognizes the fact that however religious studies have transformed the meaning of 'phenomenology,' the original matrix in which that meaning grew up was philosophical. Therefore, to render the primordial meaning of phenomenology is necessarily to return to its philosophical meanings. It is from just a such a *reditus* that a new vitality can be injected into those religious conceptualizations of phenomenology which, in their insularity, have grown incestuous, sterile and boring. The descriptions and analyses provided in this work are designed to contribute to this revitalization.

INTRODUCTION

The Thesis of This Work

Simply put, the thesis of this work is that behind the multiple definitions of 'philosophical phenomenology' lies a normative semantic nucleus which can be employed to augment the phenomenological method in religious studies. A number of corollaries follow self-evidently from this thesis: first, that there is a normative nucleus of meaning behind the wide variety of philosophical phenomenologies; second, that the phenomenology of religion is in need of augmentation; and, third, that the normative meaning of 'philosophical phenomenology' and the various meanings of 'phenomenology of religion' are sufficiently similar to allow the commerce of meaning from one to the other.

1. The Equivocity of 'Phenomenology' as a Problem

For those unacquainted with the history of phenomenology, the above thesis and corollaries may seem to be perplexing. One would expect that all methods going by the name of 'phenomenology' would share a common meaning. This is prescribed by the conventions of the art of definition which demand that definitions should precisely specify those features common to the class of objects covered by that definition. If a definition is represented by a single technical term (as in the case of the word 'phenomenology'), that word's signification should be coextensive with its definition's signification. Conversely, if a word is used to denote two things which are radically different, then it has no technical utility. A word is usually chosen to describe a class of things which falls under a typology of characteristics. This is true even in the case of proper names. To use a word meaningfully to denote a class of objects presupposes that the members of this class share sufficient similarities to be covered by the typology implicit in the definition with which that word is associated.

When one examines the historical evolution of those disciplines which go by the name 'phenomenology,' one discovers that the definitional task is not as simple as one might expect. In fact, it is quite difficult to produce a single general definition of 'phenomenology' to which even a small number of phenomenologists will assent. Either the expected commonalities of meaning are obscured by methodological squabbles and infighting or by the desire to narrow the meaning of 'phenomenology' so drastically that it has little intradisciplinary, and no interdisciplinary applicability. Not only is the shared meaning of 'philosophical phenomenology' and 'phenomenology of religion' occluded, but the more specific shared meanings of 'Husserlian phenomenology' and 'Lambertian phenomenology,' on one hand, and the shared meanings of 'the phenomenology of Chantepie de la Saussaye' and the 'phenomenology of Smart,' on the other, are occluded, as well.

Some (Spiegelberg and Oxtoby) would argue that it is equally difficult to say what 'phenomenology' means within a discipline as it is to say what 'phenomenology' means across disciplines.[1] According to this semantically nominalistic line of thought, there is no general meaning of 'phenomenology'; there are only individual, idiosyncratic methods which capitalize upon the word 'phenomenology.' When methodologists use this term they use it according to a private meaning and not according to a semantic consensus. 'Phenomenology' is, according to this interpretation, a *flatus vocis*, an empty utterance, a general term with no precise signification. From this, it follows that no semantic assignment or rules of usage exist by which a common set of properties are denoted. A general meaning of 'phenomenology' does not, therefore, exist.

1.1. Historical Approaches to the Ambiguity of 'Phenomenology of Religion'

Until very recently, historians of phenomenology such as Spiegelberg, Sharpe, Oxtoby, Hultkrantz, Bleeker and Pummer were content to report the equivocity of 'phenomenology' in minute detail, thus reinforcing the common perception that there was no general meaning of the term.[2] This tendency was particularly pronounced in religious studies, where there was no dominant paradigm of phenomenology to set the field in some order. Though less pronounced, the tendency of historians of philosophical phenomenology to emphasize the differences between extra-Husserlian phenomenologies achieved both the programmatic effect of demonstrating that the Husserlian phenomenology was preferable in its methodological precision as well as the semantic effect of occluding the common meaning of 'phenomenology' as it existed outside of the Husserlian conceptualization. Although the problem of the apparent ambiguity of 'phenomenology' was recognized, the attitude of both camps was *laissez-faire*.

Historians of philosophical phenomenology and historians of religious phenomenology were alike in their complacency. Both groups refrained from positive suggestions. Historians of philosophical phenomenology believed that the ambiguity in the meaning of 'philosophical phenomenology' would eventually be resolved by the dominance of the Husserlian method. Historians of religious phenomenology believed that the ambiguity of the meaning of 'religious phenomenology' would eventually be

---

[1]See, for example, Herbert Spiegelberg's discussion in *The Phenomenological Movement* (The Hague: Martinus Nijhoff, 1982), 1-24, as well as Willard G. Oxtoby's curt assessment of the general meaning of 'phenomenology of religion' in "*Religionswissenschaft* Revisited," in *Religions in Antiquity: Essays in Memory of E.R. Goodenough* (Leiden: E.J. Brill, 1968) 597.

[2]See Spiegelberg, *The Phenomenological Movement*, 1-24; Oxtoby, "*Religionswissenschaft* Revisited," 590-608; Eric Sharpe, *Comparative Religion: A History* (London: Duckworth, 1975), 220-250; Ake Hultkrantz, "The Phenomenology of Religion: Aims and Methods," *Temenos* 6 (1970): 68-88; C. J. Bleeker, "The Phenomenology Method," *Numen* 6 (1959): 1-15; and Reinhard Pummer, "Recent Publications on the Methodology of the Science of Religion," *Numen* 22 (1975): 161-182.

resolved when a religionist, actually working with religious data, discovered a combination of procedures capable of producing useful results. The eventual hegemony of the Husserlian method was seen to be the solution to the ambiguity of 'philosophical phenomenology,' and it was supposed that the solution to the problem of the ambiguity of 'phenomenology' in religious studies would be the hegemony of a method which did not yet exist.

In these first chroniclers of phenomenology, one finds a pervasive indifference about the causes of the proliferation of phenomenologies. They were not concerned, for the most part, with the *legitimacy* of this proliferation but accepted the methodological situation as given. This meant that they were unconcerned with whether or not it was possible to approach the ambiguity of 'phenomenology' unpragmatically as a critical-historical problem capable of theoretical solution. In short, they did not ask the question whether the various historical manifestations of phenomenology concealed a transcendental project and whether this project, if it existed, might hold the key to the solution of the ambiguity of 'phenomenology.'

1.2. A Recent Re-evaluation

Most recently, however, the equivocity of 'phenomenology' has begun to emerge as a critical methodological problem within the study of religion. This has come about both because the ambiguity of 'phenomenology' has failed practical resolution across disciplines and because the proliferation of the varieties of religious phenomenology has been accompanied by the sterility of its sports.

In a recent article on the historical relations between phenomenology of religion and philosophical phenomenology, George James provided a shrewd discussion of the dependence of religious phenomenology on extra-Husserlian philosophical phenomenology. In this article, James characterized the semantic confusion which prevails about the phenomenology of religion as follows:

> The meaning of phenomenology for such areas of study as psychology, sociology, history, law, political science, art, *et cetera* is far from established. Yet among persons within each of these disciplines, there seems to be at least a degree of agreement on the presumption that the philosophical insights of Husserl and his successors do have a bearing on their work and that the relation between the two is to be sought in the study of and reflection on the works of Husserl, his followers and their critics. . . . Such is not the case with the academic study of religion. But a look at the use made of so-called phenomenology within the field of religion suggests that the phenomenology of religion . . . entails a level of confusion that exceeds that of other fields. Within the field of religion the term is employed in a sense that not only does not square with its meaning for Husserl, but it seems also to have connotations that it could not possibly have had for him or any of his followers. If we assume that the academic study of religion does not normally appropriate terms to which it assigns a variety of ambiguous meanings, it seems that these connotations, and thus the confusion they have engendered, must have some historical source.[3]

Within this passage are a number of observations which, when transposed into questions of research, can lead to a definition of 'phenomenology' with which both

---

[3]George A. James, "Phenomenology and the Study of Religion," *The Journal of Religion* 65, number 3 (July 1985): 311.

philosophers and religionists can live. These questions are: (1) Why is Husserlian phenomenology the dominant model of phenomenology in every discipline *except* religious studies? (2) What are the theoretical and historical relations between philosophical phenomenology and the phenomenology of religion? (3) Why can the Husserlian phenomenology claim exclusive rights to the title 'philosophical phenomenology'? (4) Is it possible to discover a common method behind Husserlian phenomenology, its philosophical antecedents and the phenomenologies of religion? James provides partial answers to the first and second of these questions. He takes the *philosophical* supremacy of the Husserlian method for granted and discusses the non-Husserlian philosophical origins of the phenomenology of religion apologetically. Unfortunately, his analysis is not complete; it never approaches the heart of the question about Husserlian phenomenology's claim to supremacy. Instead, it focuses on the reasons the phenomenology of religion is not Husserlian.

James' approach to explaining the equivocity of 'phenomenology' is twofold: first, he describes the extra-Husserlian philosophical meanings of 'phenomenology' which have influenced the phenomenology of religion; second, he describes those aspects of these philosophical phenomenologies which the phenomenology of religion has co-opted. In the course of this discussion, James makes it very clear that the commerce of meaning between philosophical and religious phenomenology has been unidirectional: phenomenology of religion borrows its methods from extra-Husserlian philosophical phenomenology, but philosophical phenomenology borrows no methods from the phenomenology of religion. This discussion has important implications for those in religious studies who believe they can forge a method in a vacuum; it conclusively establishes that religious phenomenology depends upon philosophy both for method-ological refinements and the presuppositional analysis which is the guarantor of logical rigor.

Though James' article represents a real advance over the works of his predecessors, it advances the cause of univocity in the definition of religious phenomenology but little. Because he is unwilling to challenge the crucial presupposition that Husserlian phenomenology has exclusive rights as a phenomenological paradigm, he inadvertently consigns the phenomenology of religion to the scrapheap of outmoded methods along with the *apparently* obsolete philosophical phenomenologies upon which it depends.

Moreover, James' analysis does nothing to clarify the common meaning of 'phenomenology' for religious studies and philosophy, unless one considers surrender to the equation between 'Husserlian phenomenology' and 'philosophical phenomenology' a resolution of the meaning of 'phenomenology' and not an unjustifiable narrowing of it. If one makes the problem of the ambiguity of 'phenomenology' a matter of its dependence upon philosophical, but equally ambiguous, definitions of 'phenomenology,' one has simply pushed the problem of religious phenomenology's definition a step further back toward its historical foundation: the ambiguity of 'philosophical phenomenology.' One must still contend with the problem of the definition of 'philosophical phenomenology.' To resolve the ambiguity of 'religious phenomenology,' what is needed is a conclusive demonstration that philosophical phenomenologies do resemble one another. If a resemblance can be demonstrated, then (and only then) will it be possible to establish the full extent of resemblances between philosophical and religious phenomenologies.[4] Because James stops short of the required demonstration--a demonstration which proves the resemblance between Husserlian and extra-Husserlian phenomenology--the result is that his discussion of philosophical influences upon religious phenomenology advances our understanding of the similarities between religious and philosophical phenomenologies only slightly.

1.3. Summary of the Definitional Problem

Based upon a reading of the various histories of phenomenology, it is possible to summarize the problem of the ambiguity of phenomenology as follows. One can maintain that the equivocity of 'philosophical phenomenology' is *not* a problem, only if one accepts Husserlian phenomenology's claim to methodological superiority. For one to do so, however, is for one to accept a meaning so narrow as to exclude any phenomenology not squarely in the Husserlian camp. Since, as James demonstrates, religious phenomenology does not depend upon Husserlian phenomenology, the acceptance of Husserlian phenomenology as the normative denotation of 'philosophical phenomenology' does nothing to clarify the general meaning of 'religious phenomenology.' And insofar as the definitions of 'religious phenomenology' are conditioned exclusively by extra-Husserlian phenomenologies, they share the apparent obsolescence of the extra-Husserlian philosophical methods as well as the ambiguity of meaning which derives from the variety of these methods. If one does not assume, *a priori*, that extra-Husserlian phenomenologies are obsolete, then the resolution of the ambiguity behind the description 'phenomenology of religion' depends upon the resolution of the ambiguity behind the description 'philosophical phenomenology.' The resolution of the latter must precede the resolution of the former.

2. The Purpose and Methodological Approach of This Work

Unlike the historical approaches which precede it, the purpose of this work is to determine the *general* meaning of 'phenomenology.' And insofar as philosophy has always been the font of meaning for 'religious phenomenology,' the approach of this work is to disclose the general meaning of 'philosophical phenomenology' in order to resolve the alienation between Husserlian phenomenology, extra-Husserlian phenomenologies and religious phenomenology and, in the process, provide an augmentation of the latter.

Unlike the histories of the phenomenology which have been concerned with the variety and ambiguity of definitions, the purpose of this work is *synthetic* and *hortatory*. It is synthetic because it is directed to the commonalities of meaning shared by philosophical and religious phenomenologies and not exclusively to their differences.

---

[4]One might be tempted to infer, *a priori*, that any resemblance between philosophical phenomenologies means a resemblance between these and religious phenomenologies since an order of dependence has already been established. However, this inference is not formally valid but is a species of the fallacy of undistributed middle. (If some Xs are Ys and some Ys are Rs, it does not follow that some Xs are Rs because it is possible for some Ys which are Xs to be other than the Ys which are Rs.)

It is hortatory because it is directed to *suggesting* what a complete definition of 'phenomenology' must entail.[5] Though it arrives at this hortatory definition by way of an examination of the historical manifestations of philosophical phenomenology, the definition it proposes is more than the greatest common denominator of these phenomenologies. Unlike its predecessors, this work is directed to the prescription of an *essential* definition of phenomenology. It is not only concerned with the common aspects of the historical manifestations of phenomenology--what phenomenology has been--but it is also concerned with those aspects of phenomenology which, if not present in a particular manifestation, ought to be.

In order to accomplish the purpose of this work, it is convenient to adapt semantic field analysis as a tool for the description of philosophical phenomenology. Though primarily a technique of linguistic research, semantic field analysis (appropriately adapted) has wide application in any discipline where questions of meaning are important.

2.1. *The Notion of the Semantic Field*

The key concept behind semantic field theory is, obviously enough, that of the semantic field. This concept's ancestry can be discovered in the Humboldtian linguistics and the philosophy of Husserl, though Jost Trier gave it its first explicit formulation. In his article, "Linguistic Fields, Conceptual Systems and the *Weltbild*," N. C. W. Spence provides a brief description of the Trierian notion of semantic field.

> The theory has a [grand] . . . sweep about it: language is no conglomerate of single words, but a whole with meaningful division, a super-*Gestalt*: conceptual fields shape the raw material of experience and divide it up without overlapping, like the pieces in a completed jig-saw puzzle. The individual field, in its turn, is a mosaic of related words or concepts, the individual word getting its meaning only through distinguishing itself from its neighbors, and the field again being divided up completely and without overlapping. The concepts in a field, in short, form a structure of independent elements. A word-form may change without there being any change in the structure of the field, in *Sprachinhalte*. . . . Any change in the limits of a concept, on the other hand, will involve a modification of the value of the other concepts in the same field, and of the words which express those concepts.[6]

---

[5]Henry S. Leonard provides the description of "hortatory definition" which is presupposed by this work:

> "Generally speaking, hortatory definitions reflect an advance in human knowledge. A word or phrase came into use at a time when knowledge of the subject matter roughly indicated by the word or phrase was less reliable or less extensive than at the time when the hortatory definition is proposed. On other occasions, the proposal of hortatory definition is less a reflection of past gains in human knowledge . . . than it is a prediction that change in conventions will stimulate or facilitate a rapid future extension of human knowledge."

A hortatory definition is designed as a recommendation that others change the intension and extension of a word in such a way that the knowledge it conveys becomes more systematic and productive. See Henry S. Leonard, *Principles of Reasoning* (New York: Dover, 1967) 284-285.

[6]N.C.W. Spence, "Linguistic Fields, Conceptual Systems and the *Weltbild*," *Transactions of The Philological Society* (New York, 1961) 90.

According to Trier, any language's vocabulary segments the world into classes of things, each of which delimits an "integrated conceptual domain."[7] Within this domain, "conceptual space is differentiated into elementary regions whose boundaries delimit and are delimited by the boundaries of others."[8] Corresponding to these elementary regions are words which signify the region. Although different languages segment the world in different ways, all languages segment a shared world. It is the grounding of language in the world which makes communication between different linguistic communities possible. According to Katz, translation within the context of linguistic field theory can be likened to comparing "different maps of the same geographic terrain drawn according to different cartographical interests."[9]

With the formulation of linguistic field theory, Trier initiated something of a Copernican revolution in linguistics. Language was no longer to be conceptualized as a set of linguistic atoms whose grammatical relations and functions were formal and unchanging, rather language was a field of dynamic relations, a "high level abstraction which is accessible to us only when clothed in particular utterances."[10] To understand the meaning of a word, a lexicon was no longer sufficient, it was necessary instead to grasp a word in its full significance according to its occurrence, context "and, ultimately, within the framework of the whole culture of which it form[ed] a part."[11]

Though the Trierian semantic field represented a great innovation in linguistic theory, linguists were quick to point out its defects. Dynamic as was its understanding of language, it unjustifiably postulated a rigidity in the meaning of words; they could be distinguished only because of the opposition in their meanings. However, the postulate of the rigidity of meaning did not square with the linguistic data and became the chief bone of contention in discussions of Trier's theory. Since Trier's original formulation, linguists such as Ipsen, Jolles and Porzig have labored to remove the defects of the Trierian semantic field and to make the claims of semantic field theory more modest in scope and not quite as pretentious in promise. Against Trier, they have demonstrated the following. First, vocabularies do not always fit into "closely-articulated fields which fit into each other and delimit each other . . . without overlapping."[12] Second, single words do not acquire their meanings only through opposition; synonymy plays an important a role in defining the meanings of words. And, third, conceptual

---

[7]Jerold Katz, *Semantic Theory* (Evanston: Harper & Row, 1972) 346.

[8]Katz 346.

[9]Katz 346.

[10]Stephen Ullman, *The Principles of Semantics* (Oxford: Basil Blackwell, 1963) 25.

[11]Spence, "Linguistic Fields Conceptual Systems and the *Weltbild*," 98.

[12]Spence 98.

fields are not identical to lexical fields. Language structure determines thought as much as--if not more than--thought determines language structure.[13]

Based upon the augmentations of the Trierian semantic field, a new model of semantic field theory has been proposed. Though including the basic Trierian conceptualization of language as an articulated field, it is sensitive to many characteristics of language neglected by Trierian theory: (a) it recognizes the fluidity and ambiguity of words and their related concepts; (b) it recognizes that the meanings of words are shaped by the subfields of other words; (c) it recognizes the diachronic development of concepts, associated words and their relationships; (d) it recognizes that any semantic field may be sectioned according to all relevant associations of sense (including its associated speech community, its associated social stratum, its associated geographical region, its associated age group, etc.); (e) it recognizes the necessity of amply documented, empirical studies of linguistic use; and (f) it recognizes the need for descriptions which, though based on simplifications and omissions, accurately reflect the tenor of the studied linguistic field.[14]

It is the above description of semantic field theory which shall guide this work. However, the particular synthetic intention of this work--to look for commonalities of meaning behind the word 'phenomenology'--and its prescriptive program make it necessary to introduce two additional methodological refinements: the notion of semantic potential and the notion of semantic kernel or nucleus.

2.2. The Notion of the Semantic Potential of a Word

If one considers language a dynamic field defined by the diachronic and synchronic relations between words, concepts and realities, then the causality which is operative in the evolution of a word and its related meaning is twofold: it is historical and it is contemporaneous. The historical meaning of a word is what one discovers when one consults a good etymology; it consists of the past meanings of the word arranged in chronological order and generally bears some resemblance to the contemporary meaning of the word either through an extension of synonymy or by a transformation of associations which is intelligible once one understands the word's history. If the word is not preceded by an *etumon* then the historical meanings of a word are associated with that particular word's form as they both changed through time. If the word has an *etumon* (or *etuma*), then the earliest historical meaning is that which is associated with a word from another, usually ancient, language. In the latter case, the historical meaning of the word may stretch back in time millennia and even be conditioned by the linguistic world of an extinct culture.

The contemporaneous meaning of a word is the meaning a word has now and has had for some time. It is this meaning which is primarily efficacious in determining its future use.

---

[13]Spence 98.

[14]Spence 87-106.

The notion of semantic potential allows us to postulate the potential meaning of a word, or the limits within which a word's meaning may change, as these are predictable upon the basis of its contemporaneous and historical meanings. It is related to the semantic field in much the same way that the event horizon of a physical thing is related to the physical field of which it is a part.[15] Just as the future of a physical event is determined by past and present physical relations (those relations being equivalent to the physical field of which the event is a part), so too the future meaning of a word (its semantic potential) is partially determined by its past uses and their relations to the accompanying *Weltbilder* as well as by its present relations to a conceptual field expressive of a contemporaneous *Weltbild*.

It also is possible to describe the limits within which a word's meaning may evolve because of the semantic "inertia" which is characteristic of most linguistic fields. Because human culture evolves at a relatively slow rate--at least with respect to its *Weltbild* and general conceptual structure--words and their associated meanings, when defined adequately, resist change. One discovers the semantic potential of a word by investigating its past and present meanings and how these are related to the regions of discourse with which they are associated. To investigate the semantic potential of 'phenomenology,' for example, is to investigate: (a) the meanings of its *etuma* and their relations to their respective *Weltbilder* and (b) the meanings of phenomenology as it is employed contemporaneously as this is expressive of a contemporary *Weltbild*. The semantic potential which results is a hypothesis about the admissible variation of the meaning of a word under a prevailing *Weltanschauung*.

The semantic potential can be constructed for words either in the past or present. If constructed for past words, its chief use is as a test by which one's understanding of the admissible variation in a word's meaning can be tested against its actual historical variation. Any great difference between the postulated semantic potential and the actual historical change in the meaning of the word forces one to change one's model of the semantic field of the word's meaning. If postulated for current words and their meanings, its chief use is in the construction of semantic nuclei, the stuff of which dictionaries, definitions and typologies are made.

2.3. The Notion of the Semantic Nucleus of a Word

The notion of the semantic nucleus of a word is suggested by the Husserlian concept of nuclear meaning as "the sheer 'objective meaning,' . . . which could be everywhere described in purely identical objective terms."[16] The semantic nucleus of a word is its objective definition which everywhere applies to the denotation of the word. The semantic nucleus is related to the semantic field and semantic potential of a word as the meaning which covers the past meanings of the word as well as its possible future meanings. The semantic nucleus of a word is thus the common meaning

---

[15]For a description of the notion of 'event horizon' (or, as it is sometimes called, 'prior cone of an event') see Chapter G in "Axiomatic Systems of Physics" in Rudolf Carnap's *Introduction to Symbolic Logic and Its Applications* (New York: Dover, 1958) 197-212.

[16]Edmund Husserl, *Ideas*, trans. W.R. Boyce Gibson (New York: Humanities Press, 1976) 266.

of a word *through* time. It is not, however, the simple definition of all *past* consistent meanings but also includes consistent possible future meanings insofar as these are discernable. Thus, the semantic nucleus of a term has a normative and a prescriptive aspect. It is prescriptive in that it proposes a finer technical meaning of the word than the word would have on the basis of its past meanings alone. It contains within it all of the consistent meanings of a word's semantic potential because it covers the consistent meanings a word might assume in the future along with those common consistent meanings it has assumed in the past.

Since it is the purpose of this work to produce a definition of 'phenomenology' which is equivalent to this word's semantic nucleus, this definition will be primarily prescriptive. Since ambiguity characterizes the meaning of the word 'phenomenology,' and since most efforts have been directed to explaining the differences between the various phenomenologies instead of their similarities, any definition which captures the semantic nucleus of 'phenomenology' must prescribe rules of usage. It is presumed that such a definition will be of value in augmenting that collection of methodologies which goes by the name of 'phenomenology of religion'--at least insofar as the phenomenology of religion resembles the disclosed essence of phenomenology.

3. The Organization of this Work

The organization of this study reflects the order in which the significant examples of philosophical phenomenology emerged. By 'significant examples of philosophical phenomenology' is meant those philosophies which demonstrate an awareness that phenomenology is a discipline or method with a unique field of objects and ends as well as a unique methodology and placement in the architectonic of the sciences. Necessarily excluded from consideration are those quasi-phenomenologies which employ the terms 'phenomenological,' 'phenomena,' etc. without using the word 'phenomenology.' The absence of this last word has been sufficient to exclude these phenomenologies from consideration because it is one thing to be cognizant that there is a logic to phenomena and another to be cognizant of the possibility that a science might be constructed along new methodological lines to study that logic. It is the presupposition of this study that works which make no mention of the term 'phenomenology' do not demonstrate sufficient awareness of that intentionality which is directed to the formulation of a science of phenomena to be included as phenomenologies. This presupposition also frees this work from involvement in controversies about whether some philosophical system is essentially a phenomenology when it does not describe itself as such.

In the first chapter, the semantic potential of the *etuma* '*phainomena*' and '*logos*' are discussed as the background for the succeeding chapters. Chapters two through eight are descriptions of the semantic fields associated with the various definitions of 'philosophical phenomenology' from Lambert to Husserl. Chapter nine is a discussion of the meaning of the semantic nucleus of 'philosophical phenomenology' and the various methodological steps it entails. Chapter ten contains the conclusions which can be drawn about the relevance of the nuclear meaning of 'philosophical phenomenology' for the study of religion.

CHAPTER I

THE SEMANTIC POTENTIAL OF 'PHENOMENOLOGY'

1. Semantic Preliminaries

In order to understand the intentionality operative behind the "will to phenomenology" which is the efficient cause behind the six philosophical notions of phenomenology prior to Husserl, it is necessary to examine each in turn with as much precision as considerations of space will allow.[1] To prepare for these examinations, a brief treatment of the etymology and the semantic history of the word elements 'phenomena' (*phainomena*) and 'ology' ('*o*' + '*logos*') is necessary as a propaedeutic to the synthetic definition which will follow the seven descriptions of philosophical phenomenology. Such a treatment is required because the meanings of the Greek etymological antecedents establish the *semantic potentials* for these terms in their later philosophical synthesis.

The phrase 'semantic potential' is a neologism coined to describe the comprehensive limits within which a word may develop meaning. In relation to the notion of semantic field, the semantic potential may be defined as a set of latent possibilities of meaning, any one of which may be actualized and established as central to a historically emergent semantic field.[2] The semantic potential of any given word is not always present in the earliest meaning of the etymological antecedent to the word. In fact, in semantic history curious reversals often occur in which the same word may, at a later time, mean the exact opposite of what it meant at some earlier period. In such cases, the semantic potential of the later meaning is established at the time the reversal of the earlier meaning occurs.[3]

If the usefulness of the notion of 'semantic potential' is granted, then one can say that the tenor of phenomenology was set in the ancient meanings of '*phainomena*'

---

[1] I use the phrase 'will to phenomenology' to denote the general intention to create a science of phenomena shared by those thinkers from Lambert to Peirce.

[2] The notion of semantic potential has the Husserlian concept of internal noematic horizon as its correlate. See Chapter VIII.

[3] The semantic potential is not an absolute property of the meaning of a word. Rather, it is a property relative to the way a word demarcates a region of the world. As such it can be relative to any *Sitz im Leben*.

and '*logos*.' From a discussion of these meanings, it will become clear how the Greek interpretations of these word elements prepared the way for the development of both the science of phenomena as well as the "will to phenomenology" which gave this science its origin.

2. The Etymology of 'Phainomenon'

The word '*phainomenon*' ('phenomenon') is the noun formed from the passive inflection '*phainomai*,' of the verb '*phainô*.' '*Phainô*' is formed from the Greek root '*pha-*' which is the cognate of the Sanskrit '*bhâ*,' '*bhâ*' meaning "to shine, be bright or luminous, . . . to be splendid, or beautiful or eminent, . . . to appear as, seem, look like, pass for, . . . to show exhibit, manifest."[4] '*Pha-*', in its earliest form, is found in the noun '*phaos*' (or interchangeably '*phôs*'), meaning "light" or especially "daylight." The presence of the root '*pha-*' in '*phainomenon*' suggests that this word's meaning is tied to notions of things which come to light, things illuminated or revealed. In fact, the verb '*phainô*' has as its primary meaning "to bring to light, to bring to sight, make to appear, . . . to make a sign appear to one, . . . to show, to make known," etc.[5] The various inflections of the verb '*phainô*', however, have ambiguous significations much like those of the English verb 'appear.' On one hand, '*phainô*' suggests a veridical revelation, an appearing which manifests the true inner nature of its object; but, on the other hand, it also suggests a revelation which is deceptive or probable, a mere seeming, an illusory manifestation of a partially hidden nature.[6] Owen Barfield lends support to this etymology when, in his anthroposophical phenomenology *Saving the Appearances*, he argues that the middle voice of '*phainô*' ('*phainomai*') is most representative of this verb's kernel of ambiguity: "The middle voice of the Greek verb suggests neither wholly 'what is perceived, from within themselves, by men' nor wholly 'what, from without, forces itself on men's senses' but something between the two."[7] Indeed, the middle voice of '*phainô*' generally takes a reflexive pronoun in the dative case; in taking a pronoun it relativizes the subject of the verb to the indirect object as in the English example: "The moon appeared to him as nothing more than a white balloon suspended in the stygian darkness."

Martin Heidegger, in his etymological exposition which appears in the second chapter of *Being and Time*, attempts to make a point opposite to that proposed above:

---

[4]See: Henry George Liddell and Robert Scott, *A Greek-English Lexicon Based on the German Work of Francis Fassow* (New York: Harper and Brothers, 1846) 1589 and Sir Monier Monier-Williams, *A Sanskrit-English Dictionary* (Oxford: Clarendon Press, 1976) 750.

[5]Liddell and Scott, *A Greek-English Lexicon* 1589.

[6]Liddell and Scott 1589.

[7]Owen Barfield, *Saving the Appearances: A Study in Idolatry* (New York: Harcourt, Brace & World, Inc., 1976) 48.

he argues that the objective and veridical signification of '*phainô*' is semantically primordial and that it is in the light of this primordiality that the other inflections should be interpreted.[8]   However, the full meaning of this word allows us to follow his argument only as far as to admit that the veridical meaning of this word may, indeed, be historically primordial but it is not semantically primordial. Heidegger's etymology is colored by the desire make the meaning which '*phainô*' held for the pre-Socratics its essential meaning, a meaning from which all the later meanings have strayed. The idea that the pre-Socratics lived in a "golden age of consciousness" characterized by a privileged insight into the nature of being, and that their language reflected this insight, cannot be taken seriously. The evolution of the meaning of '*phainô*' is, in fact, characterized by a progressive unfolding of the ambiguity in the states-of-affairs which this verb denotes. To put it another way: the Greeks came to realize that appearances are not identical with reality. This debt they chiefly owed Plato. Ultimately, the association of epistemologically ambiguous objects with the noun '*phainomenon*' charged this word with meanings reflecting an awareness of man's subjectivity. This association is carried directly down to our own time in meanings associated with the English words 'appearance' and 'phenomenon.'

Though we may discount the importance Heidegger attributes to the veridical meaning of '*phainomena*' he does provide a valuable insight into the scope of this word's denotation: "[T]he *phainomena* or 'phenomena' are the totality of what lies in the light of day or can be brought to light--what the Greeks sometimes identified simply with *ta onta* (entities)."[9]   The operative phrase in this passage is "the totality of what . . . can be brought to light." For the ancient Greeks, '*phainomena*' is a word which denotes all possible objects of experience, particularly as they can seem or be seen. '*Phainomena*' signifies an expansive domain of everything which appears or can appear.

3. The Etymology of 'Logos'

The word elements '*o*' and '*logos*' are combined with other Greek nouns, by ancient writers, to form compound words meaning "a field of discourse about a particular subject" as in the word '*theologia*' which means "speaking . . . or . . . writing on God and the divine nature."[10]   The word element '*o*' is the suffix of combination used to represent the thematic vowel to join a consonant stem in order to link Greek words to form compounds.[11]   '*Logos*' is the Greek noun having the primary meaning of "the word or outward sign by which inward thought is expressed and made known," but it also

---

[8]Martin Heidegger, *Being and Time* (New York: Harper & Row, 1962) 51.

[9]Heidegger 51.

[10]Liddell and Scott 630.

[11]*Compact Edition of the Oxford English Dictionary* (Oxford: Oxford University Press, 1979) 1960.

16

means "the inward thought or reason itself."[12] It is never used to denote a word in its mere grammatical sense--as in the name of a thing, for example--but it is used in the sense of intentional meaning or concept.[13] In this respect, it resembles the Latin word 'ratio.'[14] Many specific meanings of 'logos' are encompassed in its primary signification, but they lend this signification various connotations. Thus, 'logos' also connotes language, discourse, dialogue, discussion, reports, authentic narrative, history, prose, proposition, principle, essence, definition, reason, examination by reason, reflection, evaluation, relation, proportion, analogy, ratio, reasonable ground, arrangement.[15]

Taking its primary meaning as his starting point, Martin Heidegger emphasizes, as particularly important to an understanding of phenomenology, those connotations of 'logos' which make it discourse which reveals or displays the hidden or partially hidden by words (that is, logos as apophainesthai).[16] If the rigor of such discourse is great, then discourse becomes proof and logos (as apophainesthai) becomes apophansis or apodeixis.[17] These last two Greek words hold particular significance for an understanding of the semantic potential of 'logos' because they are adopted by Husserl to express the rigor he intends for his science of phenomena. Husserlian science, like Greek science, is to be apophantisch (apophantic) and apodiktisch (apodictic), which is to say it is to be a science of appearance based upon incontrovertible judgments and demonstrations.

Logos (discourse) as apophainesthai (revelation through argument) gains both importance and precision in the writings of the Greek philosophers, particularly in the works of Plato and Aristotle. There, 'logos' functions as a shared term in the two fields of meaning, fields defined by terms, concepts, semantic affinities and polarities, all centered around the shared axial term epistêmê (science). 'Epistêmê,' 'logos,' and the Platonic and Aristotelian semantic fields which are their loci, comprise two constellations of meaning which determine much of the semantic potential of the word element '-ology.' Appreciation of this semantic potential presupposes some familiarity with the semantic fields which condition it.

3.1. Logos as Science in Plato's Thought.

The semantic field circumscribed by Plato's thought about 'epistêmê' is complex and dynamic: it paces the maturation of Plato's philosophical thinking, and the dynamism in the meaning of 'logos' follows Plato's deepening understanding of

---

[12]Liddell and Scott, A Greek-English Lexicon 862-863.

[13]Liddell and Scott 862-863.

[14]Liddell and Scott 862-863.

[15]Liddell and Scott 862-863.

[16]Heidegger 56.

[17]Heidegger 56.

'*epistêmê*' (science). Initially, Plato lends '*logos*' a common non-technical meaning by setting it in opposition to '*muthos*.' '*Logos*,' according to this meaning, "signifies a true, analytical account," and '*muthos*' a fanciful story or allegory which expresses an aspect of the Greek's *Weltanschauung*.[18] But to describe its philosophically specific meanings, Plato links '*logos*' more directly with '*epistêmê*.' In the *Phaedo*, for example, Plato describes '*epistêmê*,' as that which is made possible by giving an explanation (*logos*) of what is known, but this definition of science is inconclusive and provisional, at best. In the *Theaetetus*, the meaning of science is broadened by making it equivalent to true opinion about and description (*logos*) of the distinguishing features of a thing or a matter.[19] But this definition is rejected at the end of the dialogue as fraught with tacit difficulties, first, because it is a definition which can equally well apply to phenomenal experience as to knowledge of the forms--something Plato does not wish to admit--and, second, because it is a definition which harbors a vicious circularity: it defines knowledge by including explanation which, itself, presupposes knowledge. As Socrates is made to say: "[W]hen we are inquiring after the nature of knowledge, nothing could be sillier than to say it is correct belief [*doxa*] together with a *knowledge* of differentness or of anything whatever."[20]

In the *Republic*, the semantic relations between '*epistêmê*' and '*logos*' become most clearly defined. There, Plato sets '*epistêmê*' (science or certain knowledge) and the *eidê* (ideas or forms) in opposition to *doxa* (opinion) and *aisthêta* (sensibles) much in the way Parmenides contrasts *noêta* (thoughts) and *alêtheia* (truth) with *doxa* (opinion).[21] The sensibles (*aisthêta*) and phenomena (*phainomena*) cannot be objects of science. Rather, the proper objects of science are the forms (*eidê*) and being (*ousia*). In the *Republic*, the Platonic notion of *epistêmê* reaches its completion--if not its clearest elaboration--in a series of analogies which suggest that the dialectical method (*dialektikê*) is the sure path to science:

> . . . [A]s essence is to generation, so is intellection to opinion, so is science to belief, and understanding to image thinking or surmise. . . . And do you not . . . give the name dialectician to the man which is able to exact an account [*ton logon*] of the essence [*tês ousias*] of each thing? [Then] . . . we have set dialectic above all other studies to be as it were the coping stone---and . . . no other higher kind of study would rightly be placed above it. . . .[22]

---

[18]See: F.E. Peters, *Greek Philosophical Terms: A Historical Lexicon* (New York: New York University Press, 1967)111, Liddel and Scott, *A Greek-English Lexicon* 862 and Plato, *Phaedo* 61b.

[19]Plato, *Theaetetus* 201c-208c.

[20]Plato, *Theaetetus* 210a.

[21]Plato, *Republic* V: 476a-480a and Paremenides, *Fragments* 8: 34-35, 50-51.

[22]Plato, *Republic* 8: 534a-534e.

Here, the doctrine which emerges in the *Sophist* is reaffirmed: certain knowledge is knowledge of being and the forms, and the method which allows us access to both is dialectic.[23] The equation of *dialektikê* with *epistêmê* does not entirely abrogate the earlier definition of *epistêmê* provided in the *Theaetetus*. Plato makes this clear, negatively, by making Socrates give an account of the traits which prevent men from grasping essential truths, where in the *Republic* he makes Socrates say:

> . . . [T]he man who is unable to define his discourse [*tô logô*] and distinguish and abstract from all other things the aspect or idea of the good and who cannot, as it were in the battle, running the gauntlet of all tests, and striving to examine everything by essential reality and not by opinion, hold on his way through all this without tripping on his reasoning--the man who lacks this particular good, but if he apprehends any adumbration of it, his contact with it is by opinion [*doxê*] not by knowledge [*epistêmê*]. . . . [24]

The exact account the philosopher is to provide of the essence of a thing is an account not of sensible distinguishing features, as stated provisionally in the *Theaetetus*, but an account of the synoptic ascension (*dialektikê*) which leads to a comprehension of the forms which transcend sensible particulars.[25] This synoptic ascension (or dialectic) possesses two methodological steps: (1) collection (*sunagôgê*) and (2) division (*diairesis*), as we learn in the *Phaedrus*.[26] There, the difference between these two steps is described by Socrates as follows:

> . . . [W]e did casually allude to a certain pair of procedures, and it would be very agreeable if we could seize their significance in a scientific fashion. . . . The first is that in which we bring a dispersed plurality under a single form, seeing it all together--the purpose being to define so-and-so, and thus to make plain whatever may be chosen as the topic for exposition. . . . The reverse of the other, where by we are enabled to divide into forms, [follows] . . . the objective articulation; we are not to attempt to hack off parts like a clumsy butcher, but to take example from our two recent speeches. The single general form which they postulated was irrationality; next, on the analogy of a single natural body with its pair of like-named members . . . they conceived of madness as a single objective form existing in human beings. Wherefore the first speech divided off a part on the left, and continuing to make divisions, never desisting until it discovered one particular part bearing the name of 'sinister' love, on which it very properly poured abuse. The other speech conducted us to the forms of madness which lay on the right-hand side, and upon discovering a type of love that shares its name with the other but was divine. . . . Believe me, Phaedrus, I am myself a lover of these divisions and collections, that I may gain the power to speak and to think, and whenever I deem another man able to discern an objective plurality and unity, I follow '. . . where he leadeth as a god.' Furthermore . . . it is those that have this ability whom for the present I call dialecticians.[27]

---

[23]Plato, *Sophist* 253c-253e.

[24]Plato, *Republic*, 8: 534c.

[25]Plato, *Republic* 8: 537c.

[26]Plato, *Phaedrus* 265d-266a.

[27]Plato, *Phaedrus* 265c-266a.

What the stranger tells Socrates about *diairesis* in the *Politicus* serves as a gloss on the vague explanation provided in the *Phaedrus.*

> We must beware lest we break off one small fragment of a class and then contrast it with all the important sections left behind. We must only divide where there is real cleavage between specific forms. The section must always possess a specific form. It is splendid if one really can divide off the class sought for immediately from all the rest--that is, if the structures of reality authorizes such immediate division. . . . But, it is dangerous, Socrates, to chop reality into small portions. It is always safer to go down the middle to make cuts. The real cleavages among the forms are more likely to be found thus, and the whole art of these definitions consists in finding these cleavages.[28]

Later, the stranger further explains the method of real divisions with reference to affinity and difference.

> Now the following would be the right method [of division]. Whenever it is the essential *affinity* between a group of forms which the philosopher perceives upon first inspection, he ought not to forsake his task until he sees clearly as many true differences as exist within the whole complex unity--the differences which exist in reality and constitute the several species. Conversely, when he begins by contemplating all *unlikenesses* of one kind or another which are to be found in various groups of forms, the philosopher must not . . . give up in disgust, until he has gathered together all the forms which are in fact cognate and has penned them safely in their common fold by comprehending them all in their real general group.[29]

For Plato, *logos* as *epistêmê* is ultimately *dialektikê.* It is discourse which renders an account scientific by describing the synoptic process of, first, the colligation of all the particulars through which a form is dimly perceived, and, second, the separation of the (provisional) specific forms which allows one to ascend to the perfect contemplation of the primordial form which originally was only dimly apprehended through the colligation. Moreover, the *diairesis* by which the philosopher accomplishes this second step must follow the natural divisions in the things themselves and must proceed by way of comparison and contrast.

3.2. Logos as Science in Aristotle's Thought

In Aristotle's philosophy, '*logos*' and '*epistêmê*' have their loci in a semantic field which, in fundamental respects, is quite different from that described by Plato. Aristotle does agree with Plato that sensibles (*aisthêta*) and phenomena (*phainomena*) cannot be objects of science (*epistêmê*). However, he rejects Plato's equation of dialectic and science because dialectic is not strict demonstration (*apodeixis*) founded upon the apophantic intuition of first principles; dialectic is a weaker form of

---

[28]Plato, *Politicus* 262a-262b.

[29]Plato, *Politicus* 285b.

knowledge dependent upon "opinions [*doxa*] that are accepted by the majority of the wise."[30]

For Aristotle, *logos* is *epistêmê* when the premises from which this form of discourse proceeds "are true and primary, or such that our knowledge of them has originally come through premises which are primary, universal and true."[31]   One recognizes the truth, universality and primacy of a premise by a direct intuition into the judgment which it contains, a judgment whose object is an intelligible essence. An essence is made intelligible by virtue of our understanding *why* it is what it is, and one successfully understands what an essence is when one is capable of subjecting it to an analysis in terms of the Aristotelian four causes.[32]   One might say that Aristotle's conception of science stands to Plato's conception of science as deduction stands to induction.   Aristotelian science begins with indubitable judgments of being and by means of infallible syllogistic forms is able, deductively, to produce apodictic certainties. In contrast, Platonic science begins with a mass of regularities and differences and, by means of the colligation and analysis of these regularities, is able to arrive at the form which is responsible for their intelligibility.   For Aristotle, however, any variety of thought founded upon induction is founded upon a syllogism which is not universal and which is, thus, imperfect.   It is the hypothetical nature of the Platonic dialectic about which Aristotle is critical because, by definition, a hypothesis is antithetical to a perfectly intuitive insight into being.

Through an intensification of the meaning of essential intuition, Aristotle--as it were--stands the Platonic dialectical method on its head. Instead of beginning with a dialectical induction of a form--that is, a colligation of particular instantiations which are mere adumbrations of an essence--Aristotle presupposes the existence of intuitive first principles and abstractable forms (*eidê*) which are the objects of contemplation (*theôria*) and found all the branches of science.   All knowledge, when it is not the direct contemplation of the intelligibles, is either rigorous deduction (*apodeixis*), which follows directly from a judgment of the intelligible, or rigorous deduction, which follows from other valid deductions which, in turn, mediate the original judgments.[33]   Aristotle's epistemology is, thus, the cradle of modern axiomatics.

Logos as Aristotelian *apodeixis* and *epistêmê* has a definite architectonic.   At the head of this structure are the axioms or indemonstrable, intuitive first principles. The axioms are of two varieties: (a) those which are common to all the sciences and (b) those which are peculiar to a particular science.   The former are transcendental judgments which range over every science--the principles of logic, for example--the latter are determined by the genus of the science: those essences it takes as its specific subject matter. For example, though arithmetic and geometry both employ many of the

---

[30]Aristotle, *Prior Analytics* I:I:24a-24b.

[31]Aristotle, *Topics* I: I: 100a.

[32]Aristotle, *Posterior Analytics* I: I: 71b. 10, II: 94a. 20-25, Aristotle, *Physics* II: 194b-195a.

[33]Aristotle, *Posterior Analytics* I: 3: 5-24.

same logical axioms, the object of geometry is magnitude and extension, but the object of arithmetic is the unit.[34]

On the basis of this model of science, Aristotle is able to characterize the Platonic dialectic as little more than a series of hypotheses lacking an intuitive foundation since a hypothesis (*hupothesis*) is nothing more than a proposition "from the truth of which, if assumed, a conclusion can be established."[35] The *assumption* of the truth of a hypothesis is not what lends it its logical efficacy. Indeed, no hypothesis is actually true or false, but by assuming it to be true, one is freed to accomplish a valid deduction. A hypothesis, then, is an instrument, a logical fiction of sorts, which allows one to put forward a proposition which, when treated as an axiom, enables one to close a lacuna in a chain of deductions. It is a device for closing the rent in the fabric of the epistemological architectonic, thus enabling a particular science to patch, what would otherwise be, a syllogistic hiatus. The only variety of science which is relatively devoid of such fictions is *theologia* because it, alone among the theoretical sciences, deals with axioms which are the most transcendental. All other sciences are ranked under *theologia* according to the number of hypotheses which must be imported into them in order to give them the rigor of *apodeixis*.

The more a science is colored by the adventitious and the phenomenal, the more hypotheses must be imported into it to make it rigorous. Because phenomena can never be made the subject of universal propositions, phenomena cannot be made the subject-matter of any of the sciences. Though all of the sciences have being as their subject-matter, phenomena do not have being apart from the substrates in which they inhere. Therefore, phenomena are not, properly, the subject-matter of any of the sciences. Although phenomena (as *aisthêta*) convey the essences of beings to the intellect, in themselves they are mere surds with no particular intelligiblity. Though Plato and Aristotle are at odds about what methodology constitutes science, they are in agreement that phenomena are not a proper subject-matter for science. *Phainomenologia* could never have been *epistêmê* for either Plato or Aristotle.

4. Oppositions Between the Ancient and Modern Concepts of Science

Perhaps, the most striking way to illustrate the difference in the ancient Greek and modern Western understandings of the relationship between phenomena and science is to cite the passage from Simplicius' *Commentary on the Physics of Aristotle*, where the difference between certain knowledge and hypothetical knowledge is explained.

> It happens frequently that the astronomer and the physicist take up the same subject. . . . But in such a case they do not proceed in the same way: the physicist must demonstrate every single one of his propositions by deriving it from the essences of bodies, or from their power, or from what best accords with their

---

[34]Aristotle, *Posterior Analytics* I: V.

[35]Aristotle translated and quoted in Sir Thomas L. Heath, *The Thirteen Books of Euclid's Elements*, vol. 1 (New York: Dover Publications, 1956) 120.

perfection, or from their generation and their transformation. The astronomer, on the other hand, establishes his propositions by means of "what goes with" magnitudes and figures, or by means of the magnitude of the motion in question, or the time that corresponds to it. Often the physicist will fasten on the cause and direct his attention to the power that produces the effect he is studying, while the astronomer is not equipped to contemplate causes. . . . At other times he feels obliged to posit certain hypothetical modes of being which are such that, once considered, the phenomena are saved. . . .[36]

This passage, though misinterpreted by some modern commentators, clearly distinguishes physics from astronomy by describing physics as leading to greater certainty than astronomy. According to Simplicius, physics is based upon contemplation (*theôria*) of the essences of beings, but astronomy is based upon the circumstantial and incidental properties of beings.[37] It is the astronomer--because his concern is primarily the adventitious properties of beings--who formulates hypotheses to save appearances. But this is considered an inferior form of knowledge in comparison with physics which is apophantic in its principles and apodictic in its conclusions. For the ancient Greeks, hypothetical reasoning has value only as being productive of fictions which explain phenomena when no essential knowledge is forthcoming. If, for example, three fictions were in contention to explain a single astronomical phenomenon, and no one had an advantage over the others, then, according to the ancient Greek understanding of '*hupothesis*,' none of these competing models could be considered true or false without the criterion of essential judgment.

This notion of science is the exact opposite of the notion of science which prevails after the Galilean revolution and which is interpreted as normative, today. Galileo identifies certain knowledge (*scientia*) with those hypotheses which are more mathematically effective at saving the relevant appearances than others. In the Galilean notion of science, experimental knowledge is exemplary, and the possibility that one can come to contemplative knowledge of physical essences is no longer taken seriously. But it is this abandonment of essential knowledge which, paradoxically, opens the way for the possibility of a science of phenomena because it frees the investigation of phenomena from the strictures of the old equation of knowledge and essential insight.

---

[36]Simplicius translated and quoted in Pierre Duhem, *To Save the Phenomena* (Chicago: University of Chicago Press, 1969) 10.

[37]Insofar as the astronomer is concerned with the phenomenal properties of heavenly bodies he can have no apodictic knowledge of them. Aristotle describes the general principle behind this belief as follows: "[No] attribute can be demonstrated or known by strictly scientific knowledge to inhere in perishable things. The proof can only be accidental, because the attribute's connexion with its perishable subject is not commensurately universal but temporary and special." Aristotle, *Posterior Analytics* I: VIII: 75b. 25.

Simplicius applies this Aristotelian understanding in a non-Aristotelian fashion. Aristotle's explicit purpose in the *Physics* is to propose scientific explanations for the motion of heavenly bodies. The explanations he arrives at he does not construe as mere hypotheses but as certainties. The difference between Simplicius and Aristotle on this point may thus be summarized as a difference in their understanding of the nature of heavenly bodies. Aristotle bases his discussion upon the physicists' certainty about nature, Simplicius does not. Both Aristotle and Simplicius are not in agreement that scientific knowledge comes only from attributes of imperishable things. They do not always agree about which things are imperishable, however.

Since one can mathematically describe the behavior of phenomena, one can--according to the Galilean model--have positive knowledge of their regular behavior.

It is no wonder, then, that when Husserl attempts to create a phenomenology which is to be both a science based upon *essential* insights into the objects of consciousness as well as a science which is the genetic heir to the Western scientific tradition, he makes use of notions which come form both the pre-Galilean and post-Galilean models of knowledge. Indeed, the philosophical phenomenologies discussed in the following pages contain descriptions of phenomenological method which owe much to both the Platonic and Aristotelian models of science, to the semantic potentials of the Greek words '*phainomena*' and '*logos*' and to the subsequent development of scientific method in the West.

CHAPTER II

LAMBERT: PHENOMENOLOGY AS TRANSCENDENTAL OPTICS

1. The Lambertian Phenomenology in Context

According to both the *Oxford English Dictionary* and Herbert Spiegelberg in his book, *The Phenomenological Movement*, the first philosopher to use the noun 'phenomenology' in a published work was Johann Heinrich Lambert, a follower of Christian Wolff and a formative influence upon Kant and his *Critique of Pure Reason*.[1] In Spiegelberg's estimation, however, neither Lambert's origination of the term 'phenomenology' nor his conceptualization of the science of phenomena legitimates the inclusion of the Lambertian phenomenology as one of the precursors of the phenomenological movement founded by Husserl. As Spiegelberg succinctly puts it, "Interesting though this theory [Lambert's phenomenology] is even for later phenomenology, it is obvious that it has nothing to do with an intuitive method for achieving insights into essential structure."[2] In light of the different methodological approach of the present work, as well as upon the basis of a more exhaustive investigation of the textual site of Lambert's use of 'phenomenology' than is evidenced in *The Phenomenological Movement*, Spiegelberg's judgment will be demonstrated to be incorrect. It will be shown that Lambert's phenomenology is indeed concerned with the intuition of essential structures. It will be shown, moreover, that Lambert's transcendental optics, in important ways, anticipates Husserl's method of perspectival variation. In the course of this work, it will become clear that Lambert's anticipation of the Husserlian method makes transcendental optics, if not Husserlian phenomenology's ancestor, at least its prophet. For the moment, however, the issue is not whether Lambert anticipated Husserl's phenomenology but exactly what Lambert understood phenomenology to be.

The textual site of the first use of 'phenomenology' is Lambert's work *Neues Organon oder Gedanken über die Erforschung und Bezeichnung des Wahren und der Unterscheidung von Irrtum und Schein* (*The New Instrument or Thoughts about the*

---

[1]See the letter from J.H. Lambert to Kant, Nov. 13, 1765, in Kant's *Collected Works*, ed. Karl Rosenkranz and Friedrich Schubert, 10 vols. (Leipzig: Leopold Voss, 1838) 1: 347.

[2]Herbert Spiegelberg, *The Phenomenological Movement* (The Hague: Martinus Nijhoff, 1982) 11.

Exploration and Designation of the True and the Discrimination of Error and Appearance), published in 1764. The first two words of this rather lengthy title reflect the intention of the author to develop a 'new organon' (or 'new instrument') of phenomenological analysis--a philosophical method designed to supercede the empirical method of Bacon and the logical method of Aristotle. The remainder of the title reflects the author's fundamental concern about the distinctions between truth, appearance and error, as well as his intention to describe the instrument for arriving at this distinction. Because appearance is the medium by which whatever we know of truth or error is revealed to us, Lambert thinks that the analysis of appearance holds radical significance for the development of the physical sciences, psychology and moral philosophy. As a part of this new organon, phenomenology becomes the chief method for separating truth from appearance in each discipline.

2. Lambertian Phenomenology

It is impossible to begin a discussion of the Lambertian phenomenology without, first, describing Lambert's understanding of appearance and truth. This description is presupposed because it would be impossible to discuss phenomenology without first describing its object and its product.

2.1. Truth, Appearance and Error

Lambert defines the true first because, although it is almost never experienced as unmediated by appearance, it is, nevertheless, the regulative concept against which appearance and error are distinguished. Truth, simply put, is what is actually left when appearance and error have been eliminated. Truth is the conformity of thought with what actually exists.[3] Appearance, in contradistinction, is not the true but neither is it completely deception. In its most general meaning, appearance is the jumble of phenomena which mediates truth but which also veils and distorts it. When reduced by phenomenological analysis, appearance gives way to truth and to *mere appearance*, the latter being mere illusion, unrelated to anything real at bottom. Mere appearance is chimerical and the residue of scientific investigation.[4] It is appearance, in the first sense, which is the object of phenomenology because it provides the undifferentiated field from which all judgments about the world derive. What we know of error and truth are discovered there. Appearance, in the general sense, thus occupies a position midway between truth and falsity.

Lambert defines the problem, and the method for the solution of the problem, of appearance in the following passage.

> This thing [appearance] causes us very often to conceive of things in a different form, and also that we take that, what they appear to be, for that which they really are, or

---

[3]Johann Lambert, *Neues Organon* 2 vols. (Leipzig: Johann Wendler, 1764) 2: 31: 235. [Deaville translation].

[4]Lambert 2: 1: 217-218.

conversely confuse the latter with the former. This means to avoid the deception and to penetrate through the appearance to the true are accordingly . . . essential to a philosopher, who . . . seeks to recognize the true in itself, the more numerous the sources are, from which the deceptions flow. The theory of appearance and its influence upon the correctness and incorrectness of human cognition comprises accordingly that part of basic general science, which we call phenomenology. . . ."[5]

Appearance, as a general concept, originates from the descriptions of phenomena within the modality of sight, but as Lambert intends it this notion must be extended broadly so as to become multifarious in its application to other sense modalities and conscious faculties including imagination, memory, habit and the passions.[6]   In extension, appearance is marked by the distinction of three genera representing the three different realms of experience.   Within these genera, however, appearance may be further distinguished according to characteristics which are common, no matter which realm of experience they characterize.

2.2. The Three Realms of Experience

According to Lambert, experience may be trichotomized into physical experience, psychological experience, and moral experience.   Physical experience is the form of experience most closely related to physical processes and is caused by the impinging of matter upon the sensory nerves.   In its most primitive form, it is without interpretation or conceptualization.   Psychological experience is the experience which results from the workings of imagination, memory, passion and habit upon concepts formed from sense data.   Finally, moral experience is experience having to do with the moral imperative, possible courses of behavior and duty as these are related to good, evil, and the end of man.   Moral experience depends upon physical and psychological experience for its foundation but transcends them both.[7]

Corresponding to each experiential realm is a form of appearance: physical appearance corresponds to physical experience; psychological appearance corresponds to psychological experience and moral appearance corresponds to moral experience.   Each of the three classes of experience can be further dichotomized according to whether the experience is subjective or objective.   The former represents the forms of consciousness constituted by the contributions of the experiencing subject, alone.   But the latter represents the forms of consciousness which are co-constituted by the object and subject but mediated by subjective experience.   Thus, physical, psychological and moral experience each have their subjective and objective sides.   These sides are quite clearly discernable in physical experience because physical experience always presumes, apart from the experiencing subject, an external object which is mediated by objective appearance and which contributes to the constitution of concepts.

---

[5]Lambert 2: 1: 217-218.

[6]Lambert 2: 10: 223.

[7]Lambert 2: 20-22: 229-230.

28

With respect to psychological experience, the relation is somewhat more subtle. In psychological experience, the subject often plays the role of both subject and object; thus, the forms of appearance associated with psychological experience are often much more deceptive. This is because psychological observation is prey to the confusion which results when it is impossible to tell whether the observing subject has, in some manner, altered the experience of the observed object. Since both observer and observed find their locus within the same consciousness, it is often difficult to distinguish the objective appearance of psychological acts and structures from their subjective appearance.

In moral experience, the difficulty in distinguishing the objective and subjective sides of experience is greater, since this variety of experience presupposes both physical and psychological experience but transcends them by way of its involvement with value. Inasmuch as values or moral norms are community property and are not purely subjective phenomena, it is possible to distinguish an objective component in moral experience. However, any sustained argumentation about which moral norms are preferable, which good is supreme, or which course of action is most noble cannot be divorced from examination of constitutive operations of psychological and physical experience and always runs the risk that it might be hampered by the varieties of objective and subjective appearance typical of these realms.[8]

Finally, since human consciousness never operates in a void disconnected from a community of conceptualization and speech, Lambert recognizes that experience (and appearance) can be yet further divided into semiotic and hermeneutic experience. Discourse about the physical, the psychological and the moral worlds presupposes the conventional association of signs, words and meanings as instruments for the representation of experience. However, these signs, words and meanings are susceptible to the same vagaries as other varieties of experience and can actually be constitutive of them. Our experience of each world is a conglomerate of intentional relations involving interpretations of signs and words as well as interpretations of sensations and feelings. In the field of experience, meaning and signification and sensorial and psychological processes co-condition one another. This means that subjective and objective experience can be further dichotomized into semiotic experience (and appearance) and hermeneutic experience (and appearance). Semiotic appearance is characterized by a turgidity in the signification of a symbol, event, thing, etc. Hermeneutic appearance is characterized by a turgidity in the taken meaning of a word, sentence, paragraph, text, etc.[9]

The various realms of appearance and their attendant forms of experience are represented in Chart 1. According to Lambert, there are twelve possible varieties of appearance, beginning with physical objective semiotic appearance and continuing through moral subjective hermeneutic appearance. Each provides a possible objective

---

[8]Lambert 2: 20-22: 229-230.

[9]Lambert 2: 32: 236.

CHART 1

The Varieties of Experience According to Lambert

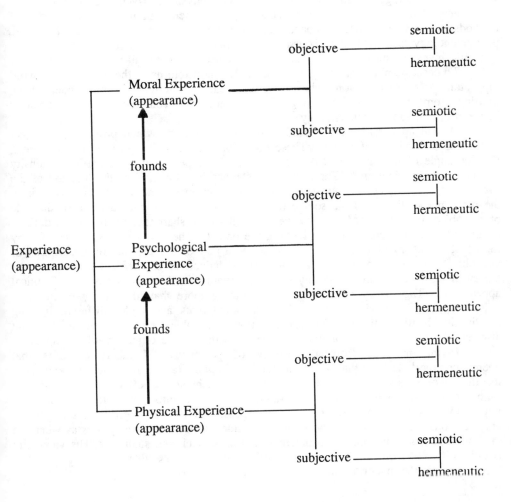

for the phenomenological method but the correct order of phenomenological investigation is an ascension from the most concrete form of appearance--physical appearance--through psychological appearance to moral appearance.

2.3. Phenomenology and the Analogy of Optics

Having delimited the realms of appearance, Lambert provides an explanation of what phenomenology is and how it investigates physical, psychological and moral experience. On the one hand, phenomenology is a science of phenomena, a body of methods and certain knowledge concerning the nature of appearance; on the other hand, phenomenology is a field of discourse about appearance, a language founded upon the scientific investigation of phenomena but with a peculiar vocabulary and extension.

To describe phenomenological method, Lambert returns to the origin of the word 'appearance' (schein), a word whose original meaning referred to optical phenomena. Starting from this original meaning of appearance, he constructs a grand analogy between optics and phenomenology.

Optical appearance is the product of four conditions which provide the subject matter for the science of optics. These conditions are: (1) The position of the object, (2) The angle of illumination, (3) The position of the percipient, and (4) The intensity and color of illumination.[10] The optical appearance is a function of the location of the eye viewing the object, or how distant it is from the object and whether or not it is in the plane perpendicular to the source of illumination. It is also a function of the side of the object turned toward the observer as well as the sharpness of the object defined by the intensity and color of light bathing the object. The science of optics is able, by means of its theory of perspective, to prescribe a method for the faithful description of any object because through the employment of deductive, geometrical proofs and the theory of light, it can anticipate any possible variation in the four conditions of optical appearance. The theory of perspective is nothing more than the theory of the way objects appear when viewed from different standpoints and under different lighting conditions. It allows the faithful representation of an object under a specific view but also enables the optician to picture or understand the visible object in all its aspects.[11]

Taking his cue from the theory of perspective, Lambert proposes that phenomenology's task be that of a 'transcendental optics,' a science which, by extending the theory of perspectives to all experience, will achieve the effect of distinguishing truth from falsity within appearance and, thus, come into possession of the total impression that a thing makes upon consciousness. Already, in referring to thought, we are accustomed to the use of concepts such as sides, aspects and viewpoints as when we say "Viewed from this side the problem seems to be such and such," or "His viewpoint is quite different from mine." In metaphorical speech we are also quite accustomed to "give *eyes* to the understanding, and extend the concept of seeing also to abstract

---

[10]Lambert 2: 24: 231-232.

[11]Lambert 2: 4: 220.

things."[12] In these sorts of speech acts, we unconsciously demonstrate that we recognize an analogy between intellectual acts and sensory acts. What the optical theory of perspective is able to accomplish in interpreting the visual mode of experience, a phenomenological theory of transcendental perspective should be able to accomplish for *all* conscious experience. The construction of such a transcendental perspective is a matter of seeking those analogues in consciousness which are transpositions of the four conditions of optical appearance.

Lambert does not facilely discount the difficulty of this undertaking. He admits that there is no necessarily isomorphic relationship between the four conditions governing visual appearance and those governing other varieties of conscious appearance. Conditions are likely to vary as one moves through the various realms of experience and examines the associated varieties of appearance and objects. What is required to distinguish the truth of conscious objects from their mere appearance is a technique of altering the field of consciousness in such a way that any conscious object will be revealed in its apparent multiplicity. That this is necessary is clear from what Lambert says of a visual appearance viewed from a limited perspective.

> . . . [E]very single viewpoint makes the same [viewpoint] known . . . only by means of the relationships belonging to it as it is in itself, and as a result [is] neither complete nor immediate and hence shows only the visible form of the same.[13]

The same is true for conscious appearance. To view a conscious object from one perspective is to know only one side of that object; to know only one side is to know incompletely, mediately and apparently. When we say, "From this side it seems to me such and such," we qualify our assertion by the word 'seems' because by the very nature of our limited perspective, we are aware that we have insufficient knowledge of the thing to distinguish its true character from its appearance.[14] To view from a transcendental perspective, in contrast, implies that we have a view which transcends a single conscious way of conceptualizing an object; it implies that we have a view which is the intersection of all possible conscious appearances of an object.

2.4. Phenomenology and Perspectival Variation

The construction of a transcendental view of a visible experience is easy enough. One simply walks around the visible object until one has examined and measured the object from enough sides to distinguish the real relationships between its various parts from apparent relationships. Applying the various axioms and constructions of Euclidean geometry, one draws a line figure showing all relations between sides. Then, applying the rules of projective geometry, one can represent the object according to any view

---

[12]Lambert 2: 27: 232-233.

[13]Lambert 2: 28: 233.

[14]Lambert 2: 60: 253.

because the object's geometrical shape prescribes a regular series of relations which hold between it and any point in space.

In order to construct a transcendental view of an object of consciousness, such as an opinion, a concept, etc., it is necessary to discover a series of conscious alterations which serve the same function for concepts as movements in space do for visual objects. One must be able to alter consciousness' relation to an object's mediating appearance in order to view the appearance from all perspectives and reveal the underlying substrate which is the object. How this is to be done, is intimated by Lambert in two different passages. The first is more general.

> In order to discover the relative part of the appearance of things, it is good to vary the condition of things in all manners. One prescribes the rule not only for appearance but also for true characteristics if one wants to separate the essential from the incidental.[15]

In the second passage, he is more specific.

> . . . [T]o regard . . . an intention from all sides means to look at the causes, means, hindrances, particular difficulties, results, etc., and to examine everything that is connected with it, that is dependent on it, etc. In as many regards as a thing can be considered, so many individual *viewpoints* it has also. And the expression to consider a thing more closely, likewise indicates that one imagines a distance between the viewpoint and the thing, which all the smaller is, when the more precisely the thing is considered in all its parts.[16]

Imaginative variation of the ways of considering a thing is the method by which it is possible to separate the mere appearance of a thing from its true presence, but this method is valuable for ascertaining the essential nature of a thing, as well. In the second application, one varies the conceptualization of the actual qualities of the present object so as to distinguish its adventitious properties from its essential attributes. One's dexterity in altering the conditioning factors of consciousness leads to the revelation of the essential nature of the conscious object by bringing the subject to an awareness of the "disharmonies and incompletenesses which are found in the deceiving appearance."[17]

Although the infancy of phenomenology makes unfeasible the creation of a geometry of consciousness by which conscious alterations are related to their objects by apodictic, deductively formal relations--like those in the optical theory of perspective--there are, nevertheless, identifiable alterations of consciousness which can be used to control the formation of conceptualization.[18] The recognition of these conscious acts and their utility in distinguishing mere appearance from truth make a Lambertian phenomenology practical. Among the many conscious distortions of

---

[15]Lambert 2: 60: 253.

[16]Lambert 2: 27: 233.

[17]Lambert 2: 15-17: 226-227.

[18]Lambert 2: 272: 425-426.

conception, Lambert includes: who the percipient is, whether the experience of the object is old or new, whether the percipient is biased or not, whether the percipient experiences the object deeply or superficially, and so on.[19] All such conditions contribute to the distortion of an object by creating appearances which mediate its presence.[20] However, the fact that these distortions can be identified through an act of reflection about their influence upon the cognition of an object means that they can be described and controlled. By imaginatively varying these conditions, one can sequentially rehearse the perspectives of all possible subjects. One, then, can distinguish the regularities which characterize the substrate from all views and separate these from the distortions of consciousness which provide the thing's variable appearances, once one has arrived at truth. It is the Lambertian method of conscious variation which Husserl, over 150 years later, adopts, modifies and renames 'perspectival variation.' Contrary to Spiegelberg's opinion, there is sufficient evidence to indicate that the Lambertian method clearly anticipates Husserl's most important technique for bringing essences to intuition.[21]

Although transcendental optics, in the general sense described, has application to each of the three realms of experience, its mode of operation with respect to each varies with the difference in its objects. Thus, 'transcendental optics' means something slightly different for physical, psychological and moral experience.

The way Lambert understands physical sensation governs his explanation of the way transcendental optics may be used to distinguish the truth of sensation from its appearance. For Lambert, sensation operates mechanistically, a perfect causality obtaining between the properties of the sensed object and the excitation of nerves in the sensing subject. However, many conditions qualify this causality and result in ambiguities and deceptions which contribute to the origination of physical appearance. The two divisions of such qualifying conditions are: (1) conditions affecting the object, conditions which produce variations in the properties and accidents of an object, conditions such as position, temperature, lighting, distance, motion, etc. and (2) conditions affecting the subject's sensation of the object, conditions such as morbidity of the subject's body, variation in attention, variation in thresholds of sensation, etc.[22]

In the case of physical sensations, the method of sensorial variation which Lambert proposes involves, first, fixing the position of the sensing subject, second, controlling the conscious alterations within the subject's mind to keep them minimal, third, varying those external physical conditions which initially distort the object one by

---

[19]Lambert 2: 29: 233-234.

[20]Lambert 2: 29: 234.

[21]That Lambert consistently refers to his phenomenology as a "transcendental optics" and its results as "transcendental perspective" seems to indicate an anticipation of the scientific transcendence toward the object which Husserlian phenomenology is designed to effect. Moreover, the Lambertian technique of the imaginative variation of phenomenal data is a direct anticipation of the Husserlian method of eidetic variation. The only thing lacking in the Lambertian technique of perspectival variation is the systematic focus which Husserl provides in his rich descriptions of conscious structure.

[22]Lambert 2: 23: 231.

one and then in all possible combinations.[23]   All the while these operations are performed, the resultant changes in the appearance of the object should be duly noted and recorded.   Finally, the alterations in the object which emerge as a result of the physical variations should be organized in a form so that a specific operation (or group of operations) can be linked to a particular change in appearance.   After all of the perspectives of the appearance have been exhausted, the true appearance of the thing emerges as the sensorial description which is invariant through all transformations relative to the percipient.[24]   According to Lambert, all physical objects are invariant according to three general categories of language which describe any physical object's primordial sensory characteristics (characteristics unmediated by any intervening objects or causality).   These categories are dimension, solidity, and mobility.[25]   All other physical characteristics are not essential to physical bodies qua physical bodies but, nevertheless, can be of considerable assistance in defining the individual essences of physical things.   These remaining phenomenal properties correspond to Locke's complex ideas in the relation they hold to the real things behind the appearance.[26]

Thus, transcendental optics, when applied to the objects of sensation, is concerned with mere immediate appearance and simple sensorial efficacy.   When transcendental optics is applied to psychological appearance, however, its intent and method become more complex.

Psychological appearance, like physical appearance, has its origins in the physical world outside of consciousness.[27]   But unlike physical appearance, psychological appearance is co-founded by many other mental operations (as was mentioned earlier).

The physical ground of psychological appearance, according to Lambert, is the motion of the sensory nerves which, induced by an external object, is transmitted to the brain, where, by the branching of the nerve endings, this motion is transmitted to adjacent parts, and so on, until many portions of the brain are each, in turn, set in motion.[28]   Limiting the transmission of sympathetic vibrations to the various parts of the brain are the various minimum motive thresholds (necessary to awaken concepts), the distance between brain regions and the arborescent neuronal trunks.   Both distance and neuronal arborescence cooperate to diminish the strength of the original neural transmissions, thus, preventing some concepts from being awakened by sensory stimulation alone.   The variation in the forms of physical appearance for any one object may

---

[23]Lambert 2: 47-49: 244-246.

[24]Lambert 2: 58: 251.

[25]Lambert 2: 60: 253, 2: 85: 269.

[26]See John Locke, *An Essay Concerning Human Understanding*, 2 vols. (London: J.M. Dents & Sons, 1974) 1: 2: 1-3: 90 and 1: 12: 1-8: 129-132.

[27]Lambert 2: 286-288: 435.

[28]Lambert 2: 98: 278.

result in an object's misconceptualization because changes in lighting, distance, or other conditions may influence the strength of neuronal transmission. But neuronal branching may cause misconceptualization in another way. Since every sensorial excitation results in a branching cascade of nerve stimulations, every physical appearance affects a whole series of regions in the brain. Since so many regions are affected by any given excitation, it is inevitable that disparate appearances awaken common concepts. This sort of brain activity results in conceptual ambiguity when similar concepts are formed from very different varieties of experience. The linguistic term for this confusion of concepts (or objects under the same concept) is 'metaphor.'[29]

Even though a whole class of psychological appearances may seem to be explained with reference to the purely mechanical distortion of concepts, Lambert actually believes that even in these cases habit is also a deciding influence. The most vivid concept awakened by a particular physical appearance is that which has been associated with that particular configuration of neuronal excitation by a *habitus*. A *habitus* makes the cause and effect relationship between nerve stimulation and concept certain. It is that concept which is particularly susceptible to excitation which has priority over other potential concepts. The habitual concept is the concept which the mind takes as the primary signification of an appearance. But even this habitual concept can be distorted by mechanical dysfunctions as well as by the spontaneous activities of both imagination and memory.[30]

Imagination distorts awakened concepts by causing the concept emergent from sensation to become the "intermingling of prior conceptions and influences."[31] The imagination, being an active agency of mind, is awakened by sensation and contributes extraneous, remembered data to the conceptualization of the external object. These conceptual distortions Lambert calls "mistakes of surreption" because they occur secretly, as it were, when the memory confuses the conceptual distinction between true appearance and mere appearance by assembling images which are false but not disharmonious with respect to the true appearance.[32] The mind is, then, tricked into believing that the images are part of the original appearance and thus, error is introduced into the forming concept.[33]

Memory, too, interferes with conceptualization when a memory fault results in the alteration of an awakened concept making it incommensurate with a concept produced by an identical sensory stimulation. Memory may sometimes be unable to reawaken a sensation or concept in the form it was experienced because the concept associated with the original sensation is attenuated with respect to some of its sensorial

---

[29]Lambert 2: 90: 272-273.

[30]Lambert 2: 11-15: 224-226.

[31]Lambert 2: 287-288: 435.

[32]Lambert 2: 14: 225.

[33]Lambert 2: 14: 225.

contents and not others. In such cases, judgments of predication involving two concepts, the concept of the remembered appearance and the concept of the present appearance, will not correspond and the awakened conceptualization of appearance and the present appearance will seem to contradict one another.[34]

2.5. *Phenomenology and the Method of Isochronisms*

All of these possible forms of distortion greatly complicate the phenomenology of psychological appearance. Chiefly, however, there are two separate areas for the phenomenological investigation of psychological appearance: first, the realm of external phenomena and, second, the realm of internal phenomena. The definition of psychological appearance and the way in which the transcendental optician (or phenomenologist) should approach both varieties of psychological appearance are described in the following passage.

> Psychological, empty appearance occurs, whenever the side [aspect] which one imagines to be on the thing is not. The real on the other hand, [occurs] where the side [aspect], which one imagines is on the thing. . . . The empty in appearance consists . . . of the subjective part of the same, in which the imagination, prejudices and affections mingle with the objective part, and which as a result must be deduced from the thought and special disposition of a person. If one knows what the thing essentially is, and at the same time how someone imagines the same, many subjective sources of opinion can be deduced from the difference, and through several of the same experiences one attains to that which is general in such sources, which apply to several things because of the 'isochronism' that occurs thereby, and hence determine more precisely the sides of the thing which he imagines. . . .[35]

For discovering the true in psychological appearance, Lambert prescribes the use of isochronisms in conjunction with the variation of observational perspectives. Lambert borrows the term 'isochronism' from astronomy where it is used to describe identical observations made simultaneously at two equidistant points. Its utility in astronomy derives from the fact that it enables the astronomer to distinguish the apparent behavior of heavenly bodies from their real behavior. Lambert intends this term in a somewhat more general sense as the common observation of a phenomenon by multiple observers at the same time. The use of multiple observers is necessitated by Lambert's intention to homogenize the conscious distortion of the appearance: the more observers the more easily will they reach a consensus about the invariant aspects of the appearance and the less likely will they be to make the same observational mistakes. Once notes about the observations are compared, the objective or true aspects of the appearance should emerge as easily separable from the parallax or subjective part of each appearance, providing all the observers do not share the same prejudices.[36] It would, presumably, be a part of the selection process to insure that the observers were not similarly biased.

---

[34]Lambert 2: 11-12: 224.

[35]Lambert 2: 287: 435.

[36]Lambert 2: 56: 250.

This, then, is the transcendental perspective which Lambert proposes for external appearances, but what of appearances that occur internally, that are accessible only indirectly through communication with subjects about their delusive imaginings?[37]

The method which Lambert proposes for the investigation of internal psychological appearances is a variation on that proposed for external appearances. To differentiate the true from the false in memory, for example, one must consult others who have experienced the same event and compare one's memory against their recollections.[38] The greater the variety in the interests and numbers of these individuals, the greater the precision which will be obtained in distinguishing fancy from consensus. Truthfulness of psychological appearance is, thus, a matter of the completeness and harmony of concepts in a community of observers. To be truthful is to be possible, conceivable, correct, and complete.[39] Anomalies between multiple viewpoints provide the means to attain knowledge of appearance *qua* appearance and lead "if not to the discovery of the true, at least to the conclusion, that it must be differently constituted."[40] If one discovers disharmonies in the descriptions of isochronic observers then these disharmonies should be able to lead deductively to the anticipation of further disharmonies or at least to the description of irregularities which are the characteristic marks of particular viewpoints. In the case that one is unable to discover disharmonies, but one is aware that the number of observers is too small to constitute a consensus, then an appearance is to be judged provisionally true. The provisionally true is that to which we refer as having the appearance of truth.[41]

Although Lambert discusses the application of transcendental optics almost solely in terms of physical and psychological appearance (and their rather simple mechanisms), the techniques of isochronism and perspectival variation have application to speculative, moral and empiriological thought, as well. Scholarly truth is reached when the community of workers in a field come to an agreement, about the truth (or appearance of truth) of a body of judgments concerning their field's common object of study as well as about the methods which are successful in revealing this truth. This is the minimal definition of a field of common scholarly concern. Everything beyond these agreed upon judgments constitutes an object for further study, later disagreement and, ultimately, consensus. In speculative thought, both the method of isochronism and perspectival variation promise to make the separation of truth from mere appearance possible. Transcendental optics, thus, stands as a generalizable method for all scientific investigation.

---

[37]Lambert 2: 271: 424.

[38]This is by extension of what Lambert says about astronomical isochronisms and memory.

[39]Lambert 2: 104: 282-283.

[40]Lambert 2: 52: 247-248.

[41]Lambert 2: 52: 247-248.

2.6. Phenomenology and the New Realm of Discourse

Though phenomenological analyses may be carried out at the physical, psychological, and moral levels, the foundedness of moral experience upon psychological experiences, and the foundedness of psychological experience--in turn--on physical experience, makes the development of physical phenomenology of primary importance. Even in the loftiest intellectual pursuits, the origin of abstract concepts lies in the phenomenal world of sensation and of concrete concepts which are fleshed in by sensations. It is for this reason that a transcendental optics must ultimately return to the level of sensation to develop a language of appearance whose purpose will be to provide a rigorous description of sensations and to build upon these descriptions a scientific discourse suitable for the description of all conscious activities. Because sensations act as primordial signs of the regular relationship between our bodies, brains and the surrounding world, they can be read as effects which convey knowledge of external causes. The ultimate goal of phenomenology (or transcendental optics), according to Lambert, is to construct a model of consciousness which, employing a very precise, but technical observation language, would allow the perfect description of every conscious event as well as its relations to the properties of external objects. In effect, Lambert is proposing a theory of transcendental optics which would be every bit as formal and rigorous as the optical theory of perspective. Lambert sees his own attempt at phenomenology in the *New Organon* as only the faintest shadow of what a true science of phenomena might be. The phenomenological language of Lambertian transcendental optics is:

> . . . only an approximate outline of the true language, for which we should completely name every fiber, determine its communication with the adjoining ones, and be able to indicate the clear concept which they specially stimulate, and which is an image of sensation, in order to make complete in this way the correction of the true language and the language of appearance.[42]

It is with this intention that Lambert's notion of a transcendental optics intersects with the Husserlian notion of phenomenological reduction. Although Lambert believes that phenomenology must lead back to a language of neuronal events and not to a language of pure phenomenological description from within consciousness--as with Husserl--both he and Husserl seek the foundation of phenomenological description in a language about the ultimate elements of experience. Nevertheless, any further commentary on the similarities between these thinkers must wait for a later chapter.

---

[42]Lambert 2: 101: 280.

3. The Objects of Lambertian Phenomenology

For Lambert, *anything* which can possess a false aspect, a seeming-so-but-not-actually-being-so, may be a phenomenon. *Specifically*, however, this encompasses sensations, perceptions, imaginings, memories, passions, habits as well as those possible forms of moral behavior which have reference to good, evil and the destiny of man. Though he is the first philosopher to use the term 'phenomenology,' he is fully aware of its semantic potential with respect to both the ambiguity and comprehensiveness of phenomenology's objects. Like the ancient Greek notion of phenomena, Lambert's phenomena encompass many objects in both the natural world and the world of consciousness, and they depend upon nature and consciousness for their co-constitution. Unfortunately, both the varieties and the constitution of phenomena are conceived of by Lambert in a particularly crude, materialistic fashion. Lambert describes phenomena as classifiable on the basis of a series of levels of foundedness, each level being determined to a greater or lesser extent by a group of corresponding neuronal events. The physiological determination of phenomena decreases as the number of mediating levels of phenomena increases. Therefore, sensations found perceptions; perceptions found memories, passions, habits and ideas; and all of these found moral concepts. Sensations are most directly determined by brain mechanisms, perception less so; by the time one reaches the level of moral concepts, the material determination of thought is superceded by its social determination in an intersubjective community. In order to remove the deceptive appearance from a phenomenon, one must understand its cause, but the efficacy of neuronal causation differs from level to phenomenal level.

In his desire to make phenomenology a science for distinguishing error from true appearance, Lambert settles upon a physiological foundation for the *a priori* structures of consciousness. In doing this, he substitutes an unproven theoretical model of consciousness, a model based upon a primitive understanding of neuronal events, for a presuppositionless analysis of the phenomenological objects in question. In this respect, he violates the demand--a demand that only became clearly incumbent upon later phenomenologists--that phenomenology must let the objects condition their conceptual descriptions and not *vice versa*. Moreover, his procedure of reducing phenomena to mechanistic events, in many respects, seems a mere accidental appendage to both of his enduring discoveries: his positive description of phenomena (as susceptible to classification in a serial hierarchy of foundedness) and his description of the method of perspectival variation. The value of Lambert's hierarchical interpretation of phenomena is demonstrated in that the remaining six philosophical phenomenologists assume it in one form or another, but in no other thinker is it linked to a similar, materialistic interpretation. None of those phenomenologists who recognize the necessity of positing an *a priori* principle of constitution (Hamilton, Hegel, Whewell, Peirce, and Husserl) find it necessary to seek it in a theoretical artifact of consciousness, a materialistic model of the brain's operations.

4. The Ends of Lambertian Phenomenology

The proximate end of Lambert's phenomenology is to separate truth from error, but this end is actually polythematic and corresponds to Lambert's distinction between the three varieties of phenomenal experience. More specifically, the proximate end of the Lambertian phenomenology is (a) to separate physical truth from physical appearance, (b) to separate psychological truth from psychological appearance and (c) to separate moral truth from moral appearance. These mediate ends may again be analyzed into sub-themes based upon whether the physical, psychological and moral phenomena are objective or subjective and whether they are semiotic or hermeneutic appearances.

The fact that these ends can be described as proximate implies that they are the nearest ends on the way to some ultimate end or achievement. In Lambert's phenomenology this is borne out in that the above ends do not exhaust the phenomenological project. The ultimate end of Lambertian phenomenology is to construct a model and language of conscious experience which will allow the precise description of every mental event (and its corresponding relations) to its conscious objects.

The only defect of either the proximate or ultimate ends of the Lambertian phenomenology is that Lambert conceives his model of consciousness as one which is physiological: it presumes the differentiation of truth from error to be expressible in the vocabulary of the language of neuronal events. The particular naiveté of his conception of phenomenology lies not so much in its reductionistic intent as in his wedding of what is actually an independent phenomenological method to a very primitive understanding of brain events. It is presumptuous to hope that an examination of brain mechanisms, alone, will explain consciousness, and it is futile to hope that physiology, alone, can explain the difference between truth and falsity.[43]

5. The Lambertian Phenomenological Technique

The technique of Lambertian phenomenology is conditioned by Lambert's understanding of phenomenology as a transcendental optics, "a science which by extending the theory of perspectives to all experience, . . . achieve[s] the effect of distinguishing truth from falsity" while bringing consciousness into possession of the complete object.[44] The definition of phenomenology as transcendental optics presupposes a basic analogy between the levels of consciousness which makes these levels susceptible to similar conscious alterations. Just as one comes to complete visualization of a perceived object by varying one's perspectives of that object, one comes to a complete conceptualization of any idea by varying one's perspectives of that idea. One comes to a true concept of any object by altering the conscious viewpoints of an object

[43]See Sir John Eccles, *The Understanding of the Brain* (New York: McGraw Hill, 1977) 192-228.

[44]Lambert 2: 266: 421.

so that its constant structure emerges against a backdrop of its rehearsed adventitious features, features such as causes, obstructions, qualities, accidents, etc. The point of this variation is to be able to separate the actual properties from the deceptive appearances by discovering those disharmonies between perspectives which are sufficient to disqualify certain apprehensions as illusory. Once one has completed the perspectival alterations of the experience of the object, it is possible to consider the effects of all conditionings of the percipient upon the underlying reality which is the object. This means that it will be possible to identify both the conditions affecting the object and the conditions affecting the subject. By separating conditions from the underlying substratum (or substance) the object will stand denuded.

Lambert prescribes an orderly sequence for the accomplishment of this technique for physical appearances, and one can only presume that it applies analogically to higher conscious experiences of objects. The method of physical perspectival variation has these six steps: (1) fixing the position of the percipient, (2) willfully varying all possible conscious alterations of the object from a fixed viewpoint, (3) varying the objective properties of the object according to a single conscious alteration, then, according to another, and so on, until all conscious alterations discovered in the second step are exhausted, (4) collecting the regularities, constants or harmonies behind these alterations into a description of the object, (5) collecting the apparent variations into a series of descriptions expressive of the causality obtaining between consciousness, physical alterations and appearance, (6) the comparison of the descriptions produced in steps four and five in order to distinguish false appearance from true appearance.

The chief difficulty with the Lambertian technique is that Lambert is far from clear in providing any rules of thumb for the perspectival variations of objects belonging to a higher conscious level than physical perception. Although the technique described for distinguishing false physical appearance from true physical appearance is relatively clear, and indeed seems a species of experimental technique employed by the inductive sciences, he leaves the method of ideational variation undescribed. This lack of description means great difficulty for those seeking to apply perspectival variation to conceptual appearances. How, for example, is one to subject a religious idea to such an analysis? In what way can a concept which is the product of a particular historical milieu be subjected to the method of perspectival variation? What alterations are to be induced in such an object? The Lambertian phenomenology, as suggestive as it is, does not provide a means for addressing any of these questions with enough specificity for it to be considered a mature method. Therein lies its chief defect.

CHAPTER III

ROBISON:
THE ROLE OF PHENOMENOLOGY
IN TAXONOMIC PHILOSOPHY

1. The Robisonian Phenomenology in Context

In the English literature, the first mention of 'phenomenology' occurs in John Robison's article "Philosophy" written for the third edition of the *Encyclopaedia Britannica*.[1] Though writing in 1798--some fifteen years after the publication of the *Critique of Pure Reason*--Robison reveals no awareness of either the Kantian distinction between noumena and phenomena or of its significance to the development of phenomenological science. Of the immediately preceding continental philosophies, only Johann Lambert's bears any resemblance to that of Robison, but in the case of Lambert's philosophy, the resemblance is either accidental or a matter of common primal sources, not a matter of direct lineage. The only philosophical system which Robison explicitly claims as a direct ancestor of his own is that of Francis Bacon, and Bacon's philosophy is far older than the thought which is of prominence on the Continent at the time Robison wrote his article on philosophy for *Encyclopaedia Britannica*.[2]

Explicitly, Robison fancies himself a Baconian because Bacon's works provide the rich stock from which he draws his principles of philosophical practice. For Robison, Bacon's empirical method represents the paradigm of philosophical investigation.[3] Implicitly, and despite his protestations to the contrary, Robison also evidences a significant Aristotelian influence. This influence is merely indirect, however, because it appears in Robison's philosophy only by way of its being first in Bacon. It consists of those Aristotelian elements which were so much a part of the intellectual atmosphere which Bacon breathed that even he could not recognize, and thus repudiate, them.

Arguing from Bacon's philosophy, against that of Aristotle, Robison posits the phenomenal world as the origin and limit of all meaningful knowledge. He accepts

---

[1] *Encyclopaedia Britannica*, 3rd ed., s.v. "Philosophy," by John Robison, 1798.

[2] This is evidenced in Robison's strong empiricist bent.

[3] This is particularly obvious with respect to Robison's skeptical phenomenalism.

the empiricist inversion of the Aristotelian dictum regarding "the saving of appearances" and derivatively maintains both that theory is strictly produced by observation and that there is only one theory which best explains any given set of phenomena. But, in consonance with the Aristotelian understanding of science, Robison interprets the proper business of philosophy to be taxonomy. Phenomenology exists within his schema for the sciences as the necessary, initial step which makes taxonomic philosophy possible.

Though we may easily discover and characterize the Aristotelian and Baconian influences upon Robison's philosophy, a *more careful* examination of the literary site of Robison's article suggests another philosophical influence. It is an influence which is neither as personal, nor directly significant, nor as easy to discover as those of Bacon and Aristotle. Paradoxically, it is elusive precisely because it is obvious: it is the Encylopedists' influence upon Robison.

In its early history, the *Encyclopaedia Britannica* was composed--like all encyclopedias emergent during or after the French Enlightenment--according to a particular philosophy of science, a view which gained currency among the French Encylopedists and continued to exercise influence even upon a philosopher of the stature of Hegel.[4] The roots of this philosophy of science stretch back to Francis Bacon who had proposed a complex geography of the sciences as well as a universal method for the observation of phenomena.[5] At the hands of the French Encyclopedists, however, the complex Baconian method became naively simplified. The Encylopedists' simplification of Baconian method made the synopsis and structuring of all knowledge the first step to a universal science. They believed that the concentration of all man's knowledge, if properly schematized and catalogued, would lead to an ultimate taxonomy of science and to an ultimate, but scientifically founded, worldview. The reason why such a unification had not before been accomplished, so the Encylopedists argued, was that it had never before been possible to view the whole, properly structured, culture of man in one place. The Encylopedists--as their name indicates--wished to rectify the fragmentary character of previous science by bringing the whole of man's knowledge under a single methodological and textual compass.[6] They searched, therefore, for essential descriptions and a taxonomy which would bring all the different sciences into a single architechtonic of knowledge.

Robison's article on philosophy demonstrates a kindred outlook, as do the works of his mentors. Both Bacon and Aristotle shared affinities toward aspects of the encyclopedic structuring of knowledge because the science of their time--particularly the natural science of their time--was taxonomic. Where they differed with the Encylopedists was over the difficulty and compactness of the task. Though Robison

---

[4]Hegel's philosophy, despite the esteem it is held in by Marxists, was the product of a bourgeois Encyclopedist milieu. This can be clearly seen by the way Hegel formulates his intention of creating a universal system of the sciences. This intention was one with the synoptic approaches to knowledge which emerged during the Enlightenment.

[5]The Baconian method, from which Robison borrows considerably, is most clearly outlined in the *Novum Organum*.

[6]Francis Bacon's attempt to reduce all knowledge to sensations influenced the synoptic program of the Encyclopedicists and particularly the development of Diderot's *Système figuré des connaissances humaines*.

at no point overtly proclaims the Encylopedists' project to be identical with his own, it is hardly an accident that a man who shares so many particulars with the Encylopedists should be chosen to write the explanatory piece on philosophy. It is a piece of writing which aggrandized the very end to which the encyclopedias were directed.

2. Robisonian Phenomenology

Robison entertained the meaning of phenomenology only inasmuch as it was possible to consider it a part of philosophy, and for Robison the tasks and ends of philosophy were *scientific*. A simpler, but more insensitive, way of putting this is that he virtually equated the methods of natural science and philosophy. In part, his freedom to make this equation was inherited from the Encyclopedicist and Baconian approaches to philosophy, but, in part, it was also due to the amazing practical success which Sir Isaac Newton achieved in applying an empirical method, not unlike Robison's own, to physical phenomena. At the time that Robison wrote, the Newtonian method was the paradigm of certain knowledge. However, since Newton expressed his principles in a form which was neither popular with philosophers, nor general enough to be applicable to all studies, Robison was forced to look to Bacon as the philosophical mentor to give *general expression* to the practical, natural-scientific method which Sir Isaac employed.

2.1. The Robisonian Definition of 'Philosophy'

Arguing from sketchy discussions of the Baconian and Newtonian methods, Robison concludes that philosophy--science in the broadest sense--is found neither upon the "scientific superiority" of the objects philosophers study, nor upon the scientific superiority of the method philosophers employ.[7] There is only one scientific method and it is in use in all the departments of human knowledge. Furthermore, Robison rejects the traditional, thematically Aristotelian, concern with causation. The philosopher must not indulge in causal explanations which posit an occult force behind the regularities of phenomena. The philosopher's

> . . . discoveries are nothing but the discovery of general facts, the discovery of physical laws: and his employment is the same with that of the descriptive historian. He observes and describes with care and accuracy the events of nature; and then he groups them into classes, in consequence of resembing circumstances, detected in the midst of many others which are dissimilar and occasional.[8]

The classes that the philosopher discovers can be further generalized and ordered. By comparing classes with respect to their similarities, he can create super-classes of objects possessing a type of resemblance. By comparing classes with respect to their

---

[7]*Encyclopaedia Britannica*, 3rd ed., s.v. "Philosophy," by John Robison, 1798, 587.

[8]Robison 587.

dissimilarities, he can characterize class differences based upon varying properties. Depending upon to what extent he attenuates his generalizations, the philosopher can establish a hierarchy of classes structured according to the relations of domination, subordination or alternation. The architectonic that one arrives at is a map of the structure of natural law in the universe. It is the ultimate task of the philosopher to provide this taxonomy of natural laws and forces for

> . . . when the philosopher proceeds farther to the arrangement of events, according to the various degrees of complication, he is, *ipso facto*, making an arrangement of all natural powers according to their various degrees of subordinate influence. And thus his occupation is perfectly similar to the descriptive historian, classification and arrangement; and this constitutes all the science attainable by both.[9]

With this last statement, Robison might seem to confuse the substances of philosophy and science, or philosophy and descriptive history. If the historian, scientist and philosopher are all engaged in the arrangement of taxonomies, what difference has Robison left between them? Robison's answer to this question is subtle. Though two people may employ similar methods to attain a similar sort of certainty, the extent and objects of their application, the domains of fact which they hope to classify, may vary greatly. The difference which separates philosophy from natural science or descriptive history is the difference between the portions of the phenomenal world for which the philosopher develops his taxonomies. Natural science, which is limited to physical processes operative in the world, and descriptive history, which is limited to the behavior of man through time, mark off limited sectors of man's possible field of investigation. Philosophers alone address all the phenomena of the world, because philosophy is directed to the taxonomic description of all things.

The precise definition of philosophy that Robison arrives at is the following:

> Philosophy may therefore be defined, as the study of the phenomena of the universe with a view to discover the general laws which indicate the powers of natural substances, to explain subordinate phenomena and to improve art: Or in compliance with the natural instinct much spoken of, Philosophy is the study of the phenomena of the universe with a view to discover their causes, to explain subordinate phenomena and to improve art.[10]

Robison includes the latter half of this definition as a concession to those who believe in causation. He himself rejects all varieties of causation but argues plausibly against only that variety termed *necessary causation.*

Robison's argument proceeds in much the same manner as Hume's. Causes, taken as necessary bonds of union between concomitant objects or events, "are not only perceived *by means* of events alone, but are perceived solely in the events and cannot be distinguished from the conjunctions themselves."[11] No matter what experience we

---

[9]Robison 587.

[10]Robison 587.

[11]Robison 586.

reflect upon we will not discover causes in it. Causes can not be isolated from events at hand, nor can they be found in memory or any agency of it. Neither can they be deduced from other perception or from the general laws operative in consciousness. The necessity of terror at the sight of a ferocious animal is not connected with that animal in the same way we may say that the diagonal of a square is necessarily connected with its incommensurability to that square's sides. Necessity has its proper application only in the case of logical truths, for necessity is only properly predicable of those propositions whose contraries are not only false "but incapable of being distinctly conceived."[12] Matters of fact, the objects often associated with necessary causation, do not present a parallel instance. Neither historical events nor the phenomena of nature can be said to be related to their conditions necessarily because they may be imagined to be different than they are.

The effect of Robison's rejection of necessary causation is to split the objects of knowledge into two groups: necessary truths (which are of an analytic nature and have no reality in the phenomenal world) and contingent events (which are of a tychastic nature and have real existence in the phenomenal world). Natural science progresses because it is possible to construct abstractive generalizations based upon experience. These abstractions, however, have no assured connection with the realities they represent. Particularly in the lowest stages of abstraction, there is no necessary relation between phenomena and concepts. There simply are no necessary chains of causation to assure us that our generalizations are valid. The validity of our generalizations, thus, must depend upon some other principle. Robison makes the validity of abstractive reasoning dependent upon the sobriety of the philosophical descriptions designed to produce them. The sounder the method for arriving at these descriptions, the more plausible the abstractions, inferences or deductions based upon them. Because Robison rejects a necessary connection between phenomena and conceptualization--one of the means for insuring the certainty of knowledge about the world--a rigorous method of description becomes the *sine qua non*.

The method which Robison arrives at for establishing the validity of philosophical investigation he believes to have had its origin in Bacon's empiricism and to have been practiced by scientists ever since. It is a method tractable to the assumption that causation is not about occult forces hiding from observation but has meaning only as a postulate about the regularity of concomitant phenomena. It is a method which maintains that the rigor of the sciences is derivative from deductions based upon accurate descriptions of phenomena and taxonomic abstractions. This method "like that of the natural historian is threefold; *DESCRIPTION, ARRANGEMENT* AND *REFERENCE*; while the objects are not *things* but *events*."[13]

---

[12]Robison 586.

[13]Robison 587.

48

2.2. Phenomenology as Description

The significance of the last clause in this definition is great. So committed to a phenomenalistic interpretation is Robison that he wishes to exclude even things from his ontology. This exclusion is possible precisely because there is no principle of necessary connection between phenomena. Things are defined as such because a belief exists that certain traits belong together, that the properties which make a horse a horse, a dog a dog, a man a man, are necessarily connected. But to accept things would be to reintroduce necessary connection at the lowest level of philosophical ontology. Therefore, to be consistent with his rejection of necessary causation, Robison must make the starting point of his philosophy uninterpreted phenomena, and he must make the method for the study of these events a science of pure description, phenomenology.

According to Robison, phenomenology has been a part of the empirical sciences since their inception. In a passage reminiscent of Aristotle's illustration of the principle of "saving appearances," Robison traces the origins of phenomenology back to the Alexandrian school of astronomy.[14] He considers astronomical description the paradigm of phenomenology because of the "prodigious," and seemingly insurmountable, difficulty of its task as well as because of the amazing precision of its predictions. Commonplace description is inferior to such scientific description not because our senses usually give us false information--Robison is too much of an empiricist ever to admit this--but because the mind possesses a proclivity towards hasty, false judgments. Descriptive astronomy leads to the scrutiny of heavenly phenomena with the goal of producing accurate judgments not based upon foregone hypotheses. Because astronomical bodies have appearances which, without accurate measurement, make it easy to attribute contradictory motions to them, a presuppositionless science of astronomical description is necessary for astronomy's development. Though astronomy suggests itself to Robison as a concrete example of the singular development of phenomenological measures, phenomenology--abstracted from any particular natural science--is best termed *history*. In its application to astronomy, this is not at all apparent because the objects of astronomical description manifest a regular, cyclical motion. When phenomenology is applied to events which do not possess rhythms or cycles, it is easier to assent to its function as history. Phenomenology, of the astronomical variety, enables the astronomer to predict the position of a heavenly body at any moment, whether that moment be past, present or future. But such a function is often alien to the phenomenology of unique human events.

Though Robison may indiscriminately apply the term 'history' to astronomy, the type of phenomena astronomers study are more limited than the affairs of man; they lose their thematically historical significance as soon as the astronomer discovers a regularity which dissolves their uniqueness. What distinguishes human history, as history *par excellence*, from natural history, as its mere reflection, is the significance

---

[14]Robison 587.

of *discontinuities* in the affairs of men.[15] Discontinuities are at the heart of investigation into the history of man for they make the measurement of change, regression and progress possible. As valuable as it is to astronomy, phenomenology, as the "complete or copious narration of facts, properly selected, cleared of all unnecessary and extraneous circumstances, and accurately narrated," holds more promise for the scientific history of man than for the scientific history of stellar phenomena.[16] To put it simply, those cultural sciences which study phenomena characterized by irregularity, novelty and high orders of complexity will find a precise science of description even more valuable than those natural sciences which study the regular, relatively simple, processes of the physical world.[17]

2.3. Taxonomy

Once he has described the phenomena at hand, the philosopher must proceed to the next methodological step, that of arrangement and investigation. A second step is necessary at all because regulative principles for the construction of a taxonomy do not exist in the science of description. Phenomenology, in itself, is directed to the unique and individual. As such, principles governing the validity of abstractions and comparisons are outside of its purview. Thus, a second, taxonomic method must be engaged to place the phenomenologically pure descriptions "into a compendious and perspicuous form, so that a general knowledge of the universe may be easily acquired and firmly retained."[18]

A taxonomy is constructed on the basis of groupings of resemblances and distinctions. Objects sharing the greatest number of similarities constitute the lowest abstractive levels. Included in these classes are all objects which are termed 'individual.' These consist of momentary occurrences of simple, phenomenal individuals: a rectangular patch of the color brilliant red at the time t_1, for example. Next come classes of objects--at different levels of abstraction--which share class designations: apples and the various types of apples, race, and the various types of race, and so on. Finally, at the highest abstractive levels are universal designations, terms which are different from one another but which, in combination, constitute whole classes of objects: universals such as extension, color, animality, and so on. The relations which hold between the various abstractive levels of a taxonomy Robison terms '*general*

---

[15]The discontinuities of human history, because history is a unique series of events, is sufficient to make a rigorous science of history founded upon induction difficult, if not impossible.

[16]Robison 587.

[17]We find them more valuable indeed, because they are too difficult to come by owing to the unique nature of human history and the complexity of human nature and society.

[18]Robison 588.

50

facts' or 'natural' and 'physical laws'; he is careful to point out, however, that these facts are only constructs of consciousness. In reality, only individual phenomena exist.[19]

In Robison's schema of philosophic method, phenomenology is distinguished from arrangement because, as the first step, phenomenology is directed towards the rendering of accurate descriptions of phenomena, but arrangement, as the methodological second step, is directed towards the systematization of the differences and similarities between phenomena and abstractions. As its Latin origins suggest, 'investigation' means the "tracking down" or the "tracing out" of taxonomic regularities.[20]

2.4. Aitiology

Even including both phenomenology and investigation, philosophy would be a sterile endeavor were it not for one further methodological step. Were philosophers only concerned with description and its regular arrangement they would be unable to predict the behavior of things; they would be unable to discover "that natural bond of union between concomitant facts which is conceived by us as the cause of this concomitancy."[21] The required third methodological step or discipline required is the explanation of the possible relations between phenomena. This part of philosophy is called '*aitiology.*' [Robison, following the Greek etymology, prefers the spelling 'aitiology.' We will follow this convention throughout this chapter to denote the Robisonian notion of a science which seeks correlations between phenomena but not hypostatized causes.]

In philosophy, aitiology has the function of investigating general facts or physical laws inasmuch as these represent the regularities which hold between taxonomic classes. Aitiology seeks no new entities; it is concerned only with regular correlations between classes of phenomena. Causes, interpreted as correlations, have no existence beyond the circumstances within which they are discovered. Though we may speak of gravitation, magnetism, elasticity or sensibility as if they were principles greater than their constituent appearances, such locutions merely denote high-level abstractions based upon a regular concomitance between phenomena. When we consider any two massive objects, if we say that they attract one another *because of graviation*, we do not postulate some third entity which accounts for their attraction. Rather, we describe a relation of physics which holds between all bodies possessing mass. As individual massive bodies they gravitate towards one another; it is not because an occult force is interposed between them that they are invested with motion.

Robison's interpretation of causation--if it may be called causation at all--is thorough-goingly anti-metaphysical. The discovery of principles of regularity derives from our capacity to group phenomena into classes and then to postulate super-orders of correlation between these classes. Our ability to predict comes not from some force

---

[19]Robison 588.

[20]This is literally the association of a mark or track with a thing. Thus, to track down an animal is to make inductions about its path because of a visible mark left behind. This process naturally involves the establishment of a causal relationship between the animal and the tracks it leaves.

[21]Robison 587.

operating efficaciously as the nexus between events but from the mind's capacity to weigh the probability that certain features will attend change. Aitiology is the science of prediction based upon abstractions of real experience. Because its objects may be eventualities which have never before been experienced, aitiology cannot be considered as *scientific* a discipline as either phenomenology or investigation. However, what aitiology lacks in certainty it makes up in creativity. The laws it uncovers enable philosophers to predict possibilities which would, otherwise, remain undisclosed until their moment of appearance. Aitiology enables the philosopher and scientist to predict the future on the basis of observations which occurred in the past.

3. The Objects of Robisonian Phenomenology

Robison defines phenomena as events, not things, unconnected by causality, since--according to his interpretation--causality is a conscious construct of mind unrelated to data in the events which it presumes to connect. In describing phenomena as events, Robison intends a field of objects which are discrete, perceivable wholes but which are not identifiable as functional parts of things. Events are to be understood, by the application of common sense, as the qualitative spatio-temporal parts of things, but if one understands by 'spatio-temporal parts' the functional constituents of things--their organs, mechanisms, physical structure, etc.--then one's understanding of 'parts' is a misapprehension. Interest in the functional parts of things is a characteristic of the sciences of taxonomy or aitiology, sciences which presuppose the phenomenological description of events, but it is out of place in phenomenology itself, a science which is concerned with the pure description of *qualia*.

According to Robison, to render phenomena descriptively means simply to describe what appears without deductions or inferences. Thus, there is no role for the constitutive function of consciousness in phenomenology either explicitly--as a creative force in making sense of the uninterpreted data--or implicitly--as the creative force underlying the phenomena as they are known. Robison ignores the problem of whether all experience is the result of consciousness' categorical construction of reality. For him, the examination of phenomena is conceived, quite naively, as a presuppositionless analysis of an external (but faithfully transmitted) reality but without any recourse to analytic or synthetic *a priori* truths. This understanding of consciousness (and its relationship to phenomena) is one which makes consciousness passive with respect to observation. It implies a diremption, at the level of observed events, between the world of thought and the world external to consciousness, which makes the latter efficacious in determining the former. Robison never considers the possibility that, even at the level of sensorial attention, consciousness constructs its objects: he has no interest in phenomena except as external objects given without an interpretation.

Nevertheless, in supporting the possibility that there can be uninterpreted perceptions, Robison tacitly presupposes that consciousness can effect a willful alteration in its field of experience in order to bring an uninterpreted event (phenomenon) into resolution. This means that Robison's notion of observation is an early anticipation of the Husserlian *epoché*. Robison's is the more primitive notion, however, because he sees consciousness' role only as that of a suspension of conceptual importations which leads back to the qualia of an event, where Husserl's *epochê* is more radical in that it seeks the constitution of the phenomenon, itself, *in consciousness*. Even so, the goal of phenomenological analysis in Robison and Husserl intersect at this point: for both of them, the starting point of science is that description of phenomena which allows phenomena to dictate their own terms. From this--the only legitimate foundation of empirical science--classifications and laws can be derived. In Robison's phenomenology, this means that when consciousness is made to be most passive--that is, when the constructive importations of consciousness are suspended by willful control--then unbiased description results. When conscious operations are let loose again to order the phenomena according to their qualities, then one has taxonomy and aitiology.

4. The Ends of Robisonian Phenomenology

The ends of the Robisonian phenomenology are best understood as examples of a typically Baconian concern to construct a science founded upon empirical observation without theoretical importations. To characterize the Robisonian project in this fashion, however, is not to negate its validity. In general, the method which results from this intent bears strong resemblances to the methods of other phenomenologists before Husserl--particularly those of Hamilton and Whewell. This would seems a significant argument in favor of both the Robisonian intent and method.

The proximate end of the Robisonian phenomenology is to provide a foundation of descriptions upon which a taxonomy and aitiology can be presuppositionlessly based. The way in which Robison conceives phenomena as uninterpreted events makes phenomenological descriptions the thematically neutral material from which schemas of order and explanation are built up. Of course, by limiting phenomenological events to external physical objects Robison implies that there are limits to the materials ordered by taxonomy and explained by aitiology. This is the chief defect in the proximate ends of Robisonian phenomenology.

The ultimate end of the Robisonian phenomenology is to lead to the description of phenomena of the universe in order to discover causes, explain nature and improve art. Following the analogy of proximate ends, the ultimate end of the Robisonian phenomenology is defective in limiting the range of phenomenological objects to phenomena exterior to consciousness. However, if one ignores the peculiar restrictions placed upon the intent behind this ultimate end, then it becomes obvious that, in all other respects, this end is notable for its universality.

5. The Robisonian Phenomenological Technique

If Lambert's phenomenological technique can be faulted for its vagueness, then this accusation applies doubly to the phenomenological technique of Robison. The technique of Robisonian phenomenology is a technique directed to the description of general facts, but Robison provides virtually no explanation of how this description is to proceed. He does say, however, that this description must not add theoretical terms to the observational data. He carries this stipulation so far, in fact, as to prevent the phenomenologist from accepting things as they are given in nature. Thus, the proper objects of phenomenology are not naturally given wholes such as a man, a horse, or an atom but the concomitant data which compose these wholes. The concern of the Robisonian phenomenology is the description of these data in their individuality and combination but without reference to causal principles. This sort of description of phenomena includes a record of phenomenal concomitants, regularities, irregularities and discontinuities in all of their complexity and narrated, at least initially, using the vocabulary of perceptions. Robison leaves us no better description of phenomenological technique than that it is to be the "complete or copious narration of facts, properly selected, cleared of all unnecessary and extraneous circumstances, and accurately narrated."[22]   How one is to insure the completeness, the selection, the purity and accuracy of this narration, Robison never clearly explains.

---

[22]Robison 587.

CHAPTER IV

HEGEL: PHENOMENOLOGY
AND THE DIALECTIC OF SPIRIT

1. The Hegelian Phenomenology in Context

Since its inception, the Hegelian philosophical project has been of such significance to sociology, political science, philosophy and economics as to have been the subject of numerous interpretations and expositions. To produce a novel interpretation of it--even if this were the purpose of this chapter, which it manifestly is not--would be well nigh impossible. Even to describe the historical emergence of the Hegelian phenomenology would be to belabor a task accomplished repeatedly and better by others. The present examination of the Hegelian phenomenology will, therefore, circumvent any discussion of the historical placement of the Hegelian philosophy to attend directly to the Hegelian phenomenological project.

Also purposefully omitted from this examination of the Hegelian phenomenological project is an exhaustive scrutiny of the schematization of the dialectical evolution of consciousness, a schematization which constitutes the largest, and the most involved part, of the *Phenomenology of Spirit*. Though many of Hegel's general observations about the evolution of consciousness bear directly upon the Husserlian phenomenological method, the specific evolutionary sequence Hegel prescribes is capricious and idiosyncratic. Although he asserts that the prescribed sequence is the necessary product of Spirit's dialectical rebounding from itself, upon close examination the necessity of this interplay is far from self-evident. This chapter omits the concrete schematization of consciousness' evolution provided by Hegel in order to avoid a philosophical imbroglio which would only impede the descriptive task. This, initially, may seem to be a vitiation of one of the guiding principles of Hegelian philosophy, because examining those aspects of the Hegelian system which anticipate Husserlian phenomenology while, at the same time, divorcing those aspects from their logical placement in the Hegelian dialectic may seem antithetical to an axiom about which Hegel is adamant: that to extract purposes, concepts, or results from the organic process which gives rise to them is to misconstrue them.[1] However, the flirting with this danger is only apparent. Since the concrete contents of the various evolutionary states of consciousness have little relevance as foreshadowings of the Husserlian phenomenology, little violence will be

---

[1] G.W.F. Hegel, *The Phenomenology of Mind*, translated by J.B. Baillie (New York: Harper & Row, 1967) 69.

done to the Hegelian system by their omission. This is not to say that a description of Hegel's dialectical method will be ignored. Indeed, it will be described in general terms and tribute will be paid to it for what it is: a legitimate philosophical method among many others--not the be-all and end-all of philosophical method. Because the description of the Hegelian phenomenology will be limited in this fashion, the present discussion will center on the introduction of the *Phenomenology of Spirit*, an introduction which Hegel considers an honest--and, presumably organic--encapsulation of his understanding of the purpose, objects and method of phenomenology.[2]

2. Hegelian Phenomenology

Hegel's discussion of phenomenology emerges as a part of his general intention to create a complete system of the sciences, an encyclopedia which will encompass and explain the origin, progress, structure and end of the cosmos as a whole. An absolute idealist, Hegel believes his intention to be achievable on the basis of *spirit* (or mind) alone. His philosophical quest is, like many German philosophers of the 19th century, a quest for categories of being which will instrumentally reduce experience to a manageable number of ideas, forms, or contents of thought. Once he discovers these categories and their relations, rules of combination, oppositions and dialectic, then he is able to construct a *mathesis universalis*, a formal system for the rigorous description and prediction of cosmic evolution, an evolution he equates with the life of absolute spirit.[3]

The Hegelian search for a *mathesis universalis* is a search for an alethiology, a science of truth, because Hegel makes no ultimate distinction between the inside of consciousness and the world outside, between epistemology and ontology. What is true is what is revealed by consciousness, but what consciousness is is not separable from

---

[2]To place these limitations on an exposition of Hegel's phenomenology does not do away with all expository difficulties, however. The obscurity of the Hegelian terminology and the tortuousness of the Hegelian argumentative style still remain. For the former, a philosophical dictionary provides some relief, but a dictionary is of no help in tracing the contours of argument in the *Phenomenology of Spirit*.

A chief barrier to interpretation, the Hegelian argumentative style is extremely problematic for anyone interested in concisely summarizing the *Phenomenology of Spirit*. Instead of presenting his arguments sequentially, progressively developing one theme, bringing it to completion, and then, using this theme to develop subsequent themes, Hegel discusses themes simultaneously and in spirals. Typically, he selects a field of related themes, discusses the interconnection, expands these interconnections to include yet other related themes, once again examines the interconnections between these new themes and the old and then, returns to the old themes to expand them even further on the basis of the newly discovered relations. The character of this argumentative style may be likened to a swelling prolation of thought which sweeps back in on itself. In this prolation, propositions flow and ebb, each ambiguously shading into one another, without discernable first principles nor deductions. Most characteristic of Hegel's argumentation--if argumentation it may be called--is that it is given to repetitions; Hegel returns to a theme as often as he thinks necessary to develop it. It is this characteristic which makes his thought so tedious and, paradoxically, so convincing. Convincing as it may well be, Hegel's argumentative style--with its tendency to sacrifice lucidity on the altar of profundity--only imperils the descriptive task. Thus, at the risk of compromising Hegel's profundity by altering the style of his thought, this chapter is an attempt to straighten the circuitous path of his argumentation and to translate his insights into language a bit more homely than that of the *Phenomenology of Spirit*. It is hoped that the resultant gain in clarity will more than recompense the loss of stylistic texture which must be the unavoidable result.

[3]Hegel 85. Hegel does not use the phrase '*mathesis universalis*,' but it seems an apt description for his dialectic and philosophical architectonic considered according to its formal features.

what the world is except through forms of consciousness. It is only through the forms of consciousness that the identity of mind and the world is both obscured and revealed.

The equation of absolute spirit and the cosmos (with all that it includes) is both the fundamental axiom and point of departure for the Hegelian system. Hegel asserts a grand analogy between the evolution of human consciousness and the evolution of the universe because both obey identical laws of spirit, this compliance indicating their common grounding in spirit and, thus, a common nature. Human consciousness, in general, and human consciousness, in particular, instantiate a larger *psuchê* in which all beings hold a common share. It follows from this that the comparison of physical evolution and the evolution of man's consciousness produces certain permissible equivocations. These, indeed, are demanded because absolute spirit is active within each evolutionary sequence to the same ultimate end (perfect self-consciousness) and with many identical results. Moreover, it is the interaction between the sequences of physical and conscious evolution which, in a sort of dialectical *perichôrêsis*, conditions the evolution of the cosmos at large by awakening absolute spirit to itself. Thus, the Hegelian system trades upon an equivocation between the cosmos and absolute spirit while justifying this equation by maintaining the instrumentality of man's consciousness to be the chief means by which the identity of both can be proven.[4] Human consciousness, as a part of the world and an instantiation of spirit, is the medium by which the cosmos knows itself as spirit. Because it acts upon the world, consciousness effects alterations in the world and concomitantly in itself. Its alteration of the world and itself, and the knowledge thereby gained, are the revelations of spirit to itself in the guise of man's conscious life. Thus, to seek to understand the laws which govern the physical universe is to be turned, quite unaccidentally, toward an understanding of human consciousness. Seek ontology and one discovers *psychic* laws which prescribe the possible relations of consciousness to itself, to other things and to other selves.

Though these philosophical preliminaries give rise to the Hegelian notion of phenomenology, they are merely its most primitive foundation. They, in themselves, explain neither the need for the science of phenomena nor the form which such a science ought assume. To understand the *raison d'être* of phenomenology, we must look to the Hegelian interpretation of philosophy, truth and subjectivity.

2.1. Philosophy, Truth and Subjectivity in Hegel's Thought

Hegel's understanding of the relationship between philosophy, truth and subjectivity is expressed in the course of his critique of philosophy, which constitutes a portion of the introduction to the *Phenomenology of Spirit*. This critique is programmatic; it is a critique with a philosophical method waiting in the wings.

Beginning as he does with an absolute monism which equates the cosmos, thought and the process of becoming (as well as many other things), Hegel finds it impossible to sanction other philosophical methods which make unique claims to truth while evidencing only the narrowest awareness of reality's complexity. He finds particularly suspect those philosophies which present their first principles as verities which are eter-

---

[4]Hegel 85-86.

58

nal, ahistorical, univocal, and systemically necessary and sufficient. Hegel presumes to know better. Philosophies do not spontaneously emerge in a vacuum. They are rigorous, but fragmentary, models of reality emergent from adversarial relations to other philosophies or worldviews. There is no justification in supposing that principles posited intra-systemically are less conditioned by their adversarial relations to other philosophies than in supposing the system (as a whole which is greater than the sum of its principles) is, thus, conditioned.[5] To presuppose that a concept, as it functions within a particular philosophy, adequately captures reality strikes Hegel as naive. Truth is never facile. Rather, truth is an evolutionary product, the result of the encompassment, resolution and fulfillment of all competing views of existence. It is simply impossible to arrive at truth by ignoring the historical, physical and supernatural struggles of which it is the meaning.

Hegel concludes that the only philosophical system worthy of the name is the one which interprets, encompasses, and synthesizes all philosophical oppositions. It is a system which treats its first principles as tentative, as mere starting points, as inherently incomplete themes which self-critically lead to their own perfection.[6] The variety of philosophical self-criticism Hegel has in mind is that which emerges from a completely self-contained, intra-systemic *problématique*. According to Hegel's analysis, such self-criticism is impossible in any naive philosophical system, because in such systems philosophical problems emerge only in reaction to other, already extant, philosophical adversaries. In a limited philosophical system, a perfectly self-sufficient critique is impossible because it cannot be completely derived from contained themes. The only criticism possible within it takes place contextualized by themes which transcend the system. In responding to exterior themes, a limited (or naive) philosophical system immediately betrays its dependence upon alien principles. It is only in a system which comprehends all other systems that alien themes do not exist and an intra-systemic critique is possible. An intra-systemic critique is possible only in a philosophy which is thematically comprehensive, a philosophy which in its breadth encompasses all legitimate philosophical themes. According to Hegel's assurances, it is his philosophy alone which is susceptible to a reflexive intra-systemic critique because it is the systematic resolution, and culmination, of all philosophies.[7]

Nevertheless, not even comprehensiveness and critical self-reflexivity are sufficient, by themselves, to make a philosophical system veracious. A philosophical system must also be scientific. Indeed, it could not even be a philosophical system were it not scientific, though by "scientific" Hegel means something quite different from the connotations associated with this word as it is used in the natural sciences.[8] For a philosophical system to be scientific in the Hegelian sense, it must be an "abandonment

---

[5]Hegel 68-69.

[6]Hegel 85.

[7]Hegel 111.

[8]Hegel 111.

to the very life of the object" and it must reveal "the inner necessity controlling the object, and express this only."[9]

For Hegel, the inner necessity controlling any object does not merely have its locus in the object as a thing in itself, but it is mediated by the alterations consciousness effects in the perception and conceptualization of the object. A scientific study of an object, a study which reveals the life and internal necessity of an object, is an examination of the subjecthood of the subject and the objectivity of the object, in their specificity, as these are produced in conscious experience. Specificity is the operative word here.

The philosopher who constructs a scientific philosophical system does not begin with a survey of being and a generalization of the conscious experience of it. Rather, he steeps his mind in the perceptual experience of the object's concrete qualities. He then returns from this perceptual baptism, having taken the content of these experiences into himself, and reduces this content to a series of fixed descriptions. Later, when he chooses to reactivate these descriptions, conceptually, he reactivates them not as mere descriptions unrelated to anything in the world but as ideas transcending the surface meaning of the description, as concepts which transcendentally signify their original objects. Thus, the perceptual complexity--or wealth--which attends extant objects is reconstituted mnemonically and intentionally but not actually. To insure that a concept captures reality, it is of the utmost importance that the concept which awakens the description be precise, but it is also important that the description give some indication that it is founded upon real experience and not lifeless definition. Without such description, the accurate communication of philosophical concepts from the scientific philosopher to his audience will be impossible. Scientific philosophy, according to the Hegelian style, must begin with the experience of *onta*; vital and productive philosophy can result only from precise descriptions which capture the vitality and motion of reality.[10]

Recognizing, as he does, that careful description is the *sine qua non* of philosophy, Hegel contradicts the common estimate of his philosophy, an estimate which makes the Hegelian system intentionally incomprehensible. Contrary to critical consensus, the Hegelian system is (at least in intention) a system founded upon precise, though very subtle, descriptive distinctions. Hegel accurately observes that without the precise determination and arrangement of distinctions "science has not general intelligibility."[11] Apparently incognizant of his writings' turgidity, he goes further to prescribe that scientific philosophy must comply with the following principle: "Only what is perfectly determinate in form is at the same time exoteric, comprehensible, and capable of being possessed by everybody."[12] Though most readers of Hegel would find this an uncon-

---

[9]Hegel 112.

[10]Hegel 112.

[11]Hegel 76.

[12]Hegel 76.

scionable description of his philosophical style, his advocacy of this principle does, at least, indicate that Hegel aspires to an aesthetics of philosophy which falls within the mainstream of the Western tradition. Indeed, scientific thought, and philosophy in particular, ought to be formally determinate, clear in meaning and a tool accessible to all, even if the Hegelian system does not, by any stretch of the imagination, fulfill these criteria.

The point of the perspicacity of scientific description is that it should extend so completely as to reveal the polarity in the experience of any object as well as this polarity's resolution. Such description must reveal the object as a thing both conditioned and unaffected by consciousness. The purpose of scientific observation and description does not, primarily, lie in the revelation of objects but, rather, in what they disclose about human consciousness and absolute spirit. Its purpose is not the study of objects for their own sake nor for any utilitarian knowledge such investigation might produce. Scientific philosophy, for Hegel, is the study of objects for the purpose of revealing truth about the interdependence of subjectivity and objectivity and the structures of consciousness necessary to the construction of objects. In the scientific study of objects, consciousness is presented to itself as an object of scientific investigation itself. It is in this dialectic in which consciousness is, first, taken as a subject with an external object, and then, as an object to itself in its own reflexivity, that what Hegel calls the "inner life of the object" and the "inner necessity controlling the object" are made clear and describable in terms of conscious operations, alone.

Now it follows from what Hegel thinks about the universe, its evolution and its relation to consciousness and absolute spirit that he does not presume the object of scientific philosophy to be an ahistorical, unchanging and generalizable consciousness but, instead, consciousness evolving. Once the scope of scientific philosophy has been described this broadly all of man's mental life--and, along with it, all conscious experience and all sedimentations of consciousness--become possible objects of study. Anything which can be made an object can be studied with respect to consciousness and subjecthood. In fact, Hegel believes the wider philosophy's territory is, the deeper the conclusions that will be reached. Hegel indicates the expansiveness of philosophy's field of objects as follows:

> Science lays before us the morphogenetic process of . . . cultural development in all its detailed fullness and necessity, and at the same time shows it to be something that has sunk into the human mind as a moment of its being and become a possession of mind. The goal to be reached is the mind's insight into what knowing is.[13]

Scientific philosophy can, thus, be a conscious reactivation of the sedimented meanings (or conscious moments) through which consciousness has passed in its evolution. This means that culture, history, art, religion and even science, itself, have all left accretions of meaning which have transformed the nature of consciousness, and because they have done this, they are all possible objects for scientific philosophy.

---

[13]Hegel 90.

Nevertheless, they are proper objects of scientific philosophy only if they can be alienated from consciousness and, then, brought back into comprehension within it.

2.2. The Meaning of 'Appearance' in Hegel's Thought

The process of conscious reactivation of meaning is a complex theme which comprises the greater part of *Phenomenology of Spirit*. This work is, in fact, one long demonstration that such conscious reactivation can be accomplished, starting with primordial sensory experiences and continuing until the highest cultural forms are phenomenologically reconstituted in their historical necessity. But before one can hope to understand what this phenomenological reconstitution involves, one must understand the fundamental character of consciousness which grounds the possibility of phenomenology as scientific philosophy. This ground, a ground which can neither be distinguished as exterior to consciousness nor interior to consciousness, as neither subsistent nor nonsubsistent, as neither determinate nor indeterminate, as neither conscious movement nor stasis, is called by Hegel "appearance."[14]

By "appearance," Hegel intends the conscious state resulting from the suspension of that operation of consciousness which Husserl would call intentionality but which might more neutrally be referred to as "object-constituting consciousness." The realm of consciousness thus defined is the mental state in which no conscious moments are discriminated. It is experience unburdened by clear and distinct conceptualizations, experience in which the distinctions between subject and object and mental activity and inactivity are meaningless. It is the unconstructed--or deconstructed--field of experience, as it is in itself. The cryptic nature of appearance, thus defined, is noteworthy:

> Appearance is the process of arising into being and passing away, a process that does not itself arise and pass away, but is *per se*, and constitutes reality and the life-movement of truth. The truth is thus like the bacchanalian revel, where not a member is sober; and because every member no sooner becomes detached than it *eo ipso* collapses straightaway, the revel is just as much a state of transparent unbroken calm. Judged by that movement, the particular shapes which the mind assumes do not indeed subsist any more than do determinate thoughts or ideas; but they are, all the same, as much positive necessary moments, as negative and transitory. In the entirety of the movement, taken as an unbroken quiescent whole, that which obtains distinction in the course of its process and secures specific existence, is preserved in the form of self-recollection, in which existence is self-knowledge, and self-knowledge, again, is immediate existence.[15]

Viewed as unconstructed (or deconstructed), appearance is radically unintelligible: it is but in what sense *it is* cannot be described. Only as structured by consciousness through distinction does it give rise to intelligible experience. Yet, it is not as though either its structured or unconstructed states perfectly represent its nature. This is the paradox of appearance in Hegel. Of course, should phenomenology take as its object of study appearance in its formless homogeneity without bothering to investigate conscious distinctions, self-recollection and self-knowledge, then phenomenology would be

---

[14]Hegel 105-106.

[15]Hegel 94.

a science of experience in only the emptiest sense. It would be a science in which nothing is learned. No, it is precisely because phenomenology takes as its task "the scientific statement of the course of this [conscious] development" and through the accomplishment of this task the resultant "breaking down and superseding" of "fixed and determinate thoughts" that phenomenology ultimately reconciles being, appearance, and knowledge.[16] It must be underscored that no reconciliation between being, appearance and understanding has value unless it is intelligible. The net effect of a phenomenology of spirit (mind) must be the return of being and knowing to a single quiescent whole, but it must be a return which is grasped as an "organically connected whole" and not as a whole in which the various moments of conscious evolution are homogenized and without meaning.[17]

2.3. Hegelian Phenomenology and Consciousness

Hegelian phenomenological analysis begins with appearance and its various objective and subjective manifestations. Most important, for analysis, are the emergent structures of appearance because these provide the relatively stable forms which make the interpretation of appearance as essence, self-knowledge and immediate existence possible. However, Hegel denies any absolute reality to these structures, except as they are founded upon and indicate the ultimate unity which is disclosed through consciousness' dialectical operation upon them. Hence, it is a major task of phenomenology to trace this dialectic, and through a description of its various moments, disclose the unity and completeness of the absolute which underlies it. Phenomenology is to show that, no matter what form they take, subjectivity and objectivity are nothing more than developments in consciousness, life movements which reveal its being and the being of spirit (mind) with which it is identical. Hegel argues phenomenology must demonstrate, with respect to consciousness, that "[w]hat seems to take place outside it, to be an activity directed against it, is its own doing, its own activity; and substance shows that it is in reality subject."[18] The completion of this demonstration is the completion of human knowledge, and this completion can only occur when one has shown completely that "mind has made its existence adequate to and one with its own essential nature."[19]

2.4. Dialectics and Phenomenology

The tool for effecting this phenomenological demonstration (or reunification) is not like the logical tools generally associated with philosophy. The Hegelian dialectic does not proceed by way of logical proofs. Logical proofs require grounds which are

---

[16]Hegel 97.

[17]Hegel 96-97.

[18]Hegel 97.

[19]Hegel 123.

themselves subject to proofs and so on *ad infinitum*.[20]   Moreover, logical proofs presuppose a certain relationship between consciousness and its objects. The conscious subject, in logic, is fixed as an objective self, it is a substratum in which predicative judgments occur but in which the predicates and subjects of these judgments are not identified as moments of the substratum. The conscious subject retains the contents of these predicates and subjects--as well as their identity in the judgment--but does not transcend them by seeing them as moments of its own consciousness. In the logically thinking consciousness, there is a naive acceptance of the meaning of words as well as a total lack of awareness about the role consciousness plays in the constitution of that meaning. The ego, thus, exists along side the various judgments, subjects and predicates and does not see itself as the agent for their constitution.[21]   Deduction proceeds as a bare formalism in which the meanings of the logical predicates and subjects are presupposed and in which valid reasoning is based upon propositional form alone. Logical deductions are valid so long as a certain protocol of substitution is followed and the propositions and conclusion of the deduction are well formed.

Dialectics, on the contrary, has a different focus. Its concern is not with logical form but with the construction and deconstruction of the constituent meanings themselves. It begins with the supposition ignored by traditional logic: that the relation between a logical subject and predicate can be explored entirely within consciousness. The bare concept in dialectics is analyzed into a form and content which are both "through and through [conscious] subject *impliciter* and *per se*."[22]   The movement of dialectics is, therefore, away from a barren logical formalism, from a mere recipe for the kinds of valid deductions, and toward an exploration of the conscious life of constituent meanings and concepts. As Hegel puts it:

> There is to be found, therefore, no sort of content standing in a relation, as it were to an underlying subject, and getting its significance by being attached to this as a predicate. The proposition as it appears is a mere empty form.[23]

2.5. *The Criteriology Presupposed by Hegelian Dialectics*

But once phenomenological dialectics has reduced everything to an aspect of consciousness what is to prevent it from losing its purpose? Where is such a method to begin its analysis? What can be the criterion which measures the veracity of the phenomenological method? Hegel's response is that consciousness, within itself, provides the criterion for its own veracious self-investigation. This is consciousness' comparison of its own moments.

---

[20]Hegel 123.

[21]Hegel 123.

[22]Hegel 123.

[23]Hegel 141-142.

Two moments of the dialectic of consciousness are of particular importance in understanding how it proceeds dependably. One is the moment of negativity whereby the ego distinguishes itself from object-constituting subjectivity as a form of negativity, a moment which consists of the experience of objects as not-subject or not-I. The second, is the moment of inequality of the object-as-conceived-within- consciousness and the object-intended-outside-of-consciousness, a moment which, because everything is at base spirit, is really an inequality of one conscious content and another. The first of these moments occurs whenever one reflects upon conscious experience, and it is, thus, a prelude to the second moment which is considerably more involved. It is the second moment which takes us to the heart of the Hegelian dialectic.

By saying that the comparison of consciousness with itself is the criterion for judging the meaning of a proposition, Hegel intends the following. Since any comparison made by consciousness is made within consciousness, consciousness differentiates itself into three movements: a movement which represents the object as a concept, a movement which represents the object as apart from conscious conceptualization of it (as another being *in itself*) and a movement which is the comparison of the object for consciousness and the object in itself. The criterion employed in testing the veracity of a judgment about a concept is internal to consciousness and consists of the adequacy of a concept in representing its intended object. We know when a judgment is false, or a concept inadequate, when we see that the meaning of the judgment (or concept) is inadequate to exhaust the being of an intended object. This is, merely, a matter of evaluating the correspondence between a notion (essence, being, truth) of an object and the object as it exists or, in other words, evaluating the correspondence between the notion of the object *qua* object and the notion of the inner nature of the object.[24] Whenever the correspondence is great, we say the concept of an object is adequate. All of this takes place, according to Hegel, completely within consciousness.

There is, however, a curious redoubling of consciousness which takes place when such comparisons are made but frustrated. This redoubling is part and parcel of consciousness' historical evolution and a most intriguing part of phenomenological investigation. Hegel refers to this occurrence as the dialectic of negativity. The dialectic of negativity occurs when one seems unable to be certain about whether or not a concept correctly comprehends an object or when one makes a positive judgment that a concept inadequately represents an object. Either circumstance necessarily results in an alteration of the object. That this is so can be seen quite easily. To make a comparison between concept and intended object implies that one has knowledge of both. But the inability to get behind the intended object by means of the grasped concept is tantamount to admitting either (a) that the concept is imperfectly constructed or (b) that the object itself is not, in fact, clearly known. Should the concept remain inadequate even after further development, then it must be assumed that the object intended has not been properly clarified. What was once thought to be clear and distinct is recognized as confusing because of the dissonance between the mind's

---

[24]Hegel 141-142.

conceptualization of an object and intended object. At this point, both the mind's intention of the object and its conceptualization of the object change. The result is that the very experience of the object both in being and for consciousness is immutably altered and one comes, by way of negation, to new positive knowledge of what the object is and what the concept should be.[25]

This dialectical movement has traditionally been described through the use of the (deceptively simple) schema described in Chart 2. However, this leaves out the movements of thought which give rise to the dialectic. A better representation would be the one described in Chart 3. This diagram better represents the Hegelian intention because it indicates the provisional nature of any concept or intended object. All concepts are, when first constructed, thought to represent their objects veraciously. It is only through the passage of time (t_1, t_2, t_3, t_4, etc.) that the dissonance between them and their objects becomes apparent. At first, this dissonance is sufficient to change only the conception, which--again--for a time, is sufficient to represent the intended object. It is only after the alternative conceptualizations are exhausted that a new object may be conceived and the process begun again.[26]

2.6. Hegelian Dialectics and the Recovery of the Past

As it stands, the Hegelian dialectic seems to be a promising tool for the reconstruction of conscious evolution, a sort of *mathesis universalis* for the discovery of the laws of world history. But before a reconstruction of consciousness' history can be undertaken it must be preceded by a dialectical deconstruction. It makes no sense to begin, axiomatically as it were, with a fundamental thesis and then to reconstruct the antitheses, syntheses, and theses which lead to the present epoch deductively, without first asking oneself whether these deductions have any bearing on world history as it actually occurred. Better to begin with the present as the most recent synthesis and, then, deconstruct its constitutive antitheses, theses, and preceding syntheses working backwards until a first undifferentiated thesis is discovered. A philosophy which takes history seriously must begin with this latter method; the inescapability of the historically actual necessitates an empiriological method which does not discount reality. A phenomenological method which is designed to reveal the lives of its objects cannot, except at its own peril, ignore the *haecceity* and actuality of historical objects.

---

[25]Fichte, not Hegel, introduced the triad thesis, antithesis, synthesis but did not posit the same relations between each term as did Hegel. For Fichte, the antithesis did not arise from the thesis. Moreover, he conceived the synthesis as a simple union of thesis and antithesis not their sublation. Hegel never used the technical terms 'thesis,' 'antithesis,' 'synthesis' but portions of the *Phenomenology of Spirit* contain arguments which implicitly make use of this schema. See the article "Fichte" in *The Encyclopedia of Philosophy*, 8 vols. (New York: Macmillan Publishing Co., 1967) 3: 192-196 and also, J. G. Fichte, *The Science of Knowledge*, ed. and trans. Peter Heath and John Lachs (Cambridge: Cambridge University Press, 1982) 93-217.

[26]A note of caution: one must take care not to follow the represented schema too slavishly for it is an open question as to how many conceptions must be proposed and rejected before the comprehension of the object itself is changed. In addition, one must remember that Hegel believes that the appeal to experience is one of the chief means by which knowledge increases. The dialectic (theseis, antithesis, synthesis) occurs with regularity only when the addition of data is at a minimum, otherwise, the evolution of consciousness would seem to be considerably more complicated.

CHART 2

The Conventional Schematization of the
Hegelian Dialectic

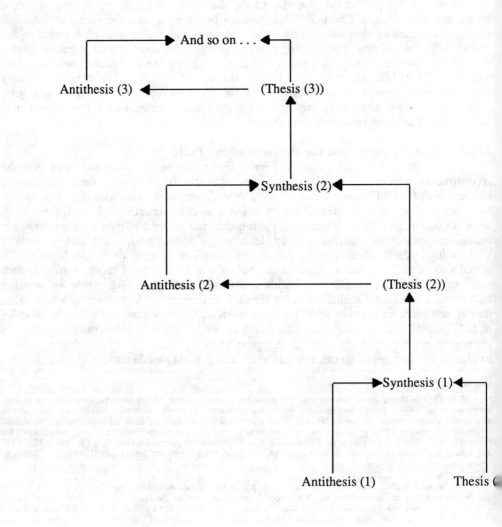

CHART 3

The Suggested Schematization of the Hegelian Dialectic

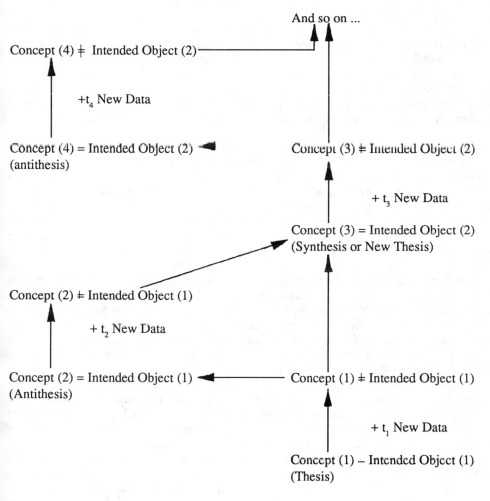

And so on . . .

It is a serious indictment of the Hegelian system that it, inauthentically, ignores historical actuality and in so doing stands the empiriological approach on its head. Instead of beginning in the present and working backwards through history, Hegel in the *Phenomenology of Spirit* begins with an axiomatic first thesis--sense certainty--and proceeds to construct its resultant differentiations freely, at will and without apparent necessity. Schematically resembling the deductive model of philosophical systems, this approach effectively contradicts Hegel's critique of deductive logic and axiomatic philosophical systems. This contradiction is indicative of perhaps, the fundamental lapse in the Hegelian phenomenological method: Hegel's phenomenology is inauthentic with respect to the real significance of the dialectic. Despite his protestations to the contrary, Hegel is unable to extricate himself from a philosophical approach which is primarily prescriptive and constructive and not descriptive and analytical. In his desire to prove that the Prussian state is the *eschaton* (the dialectical result of spirit's development), Hegel blinds himself to an opportunity to be led by the dialectic to the discovery of moments of conscious evolution which he can neither anticipate nor imagine.[27]

2.7. Hegelian Dialectics and the Anticipation of the Future

One final point ought to be made before leaving the discussion of the Hegelian phenomenology. It has to do with Hegel's application of the negative dialectic and his hope for phenomenology as a whole. For Hegel, the negative dialectic is not only a method for reawakening bygone modes of consciousness but it can also be employed as a means to discern the future and the forms of consciousness the future will bring. By considering a notion one can--Hegel does not tell us how--reveal the contradictions in its very life, propose antitheses, reveal further contradictions, and finally, discover a synthesis which transcends and resolves the various contradictions. It is this claim, the claim that by analyzing the contradictions in things one can discern the future, that is taken over and modified by Karl Marx. At Marx's hands, what is a phenomenological method becomes a method of revolution by substitution of human political activity for human contemplative activity. The result is the creation of one of the most powerful, and insidious, impetuses for political and social change the world has seen. But to be fair to Marx, it must be recognized that he might never have been able to use the Hegelian phenomenological method had Hegel not claimed for it a stricter necessity than it was due. Hegel's fault--if one may be allowed to criticize instead of merely describe--is in discounting historical possibility and emphasizing the certainty and necessity of a particular historical direction. Thus, the flaw in the Hegelian system does not lie in his formulation of phenomenology nor its method but in Hegel's personal predisposition to focus upon one possible future for consciousness and to argue that it must necessarily result. This defect is no barrier to an appreciation of Hegel's phenomenology but it is certainly a barrier to the application of his method to the study of religion. Any religionist using the Hegelian method will have to modify it to

---

[27]That Hegel did equate the Prussian state with Spirit's highest political realization is more apparent in the *Philosophy of Right* than in the *Phenomenology of Spirit*.

accommodate the aleatory nature of his historical objects; he must not suppose the Hegelian analysis to be complete or finished.

3. The Objects of Hegelian Phenomenology

In contrast to Robisonian phenomena, Hegelian phenomena are deeply subjective in their constitution. Because Hegel equates phenomena with spirit (as it is embodied in the forms of consciousness corresponding to the stages of the cosmos' evolution), anything in the world which is the product of objective or subjective consciousness is a phenomenon. Hegel, thus, broadens the notion of phenomena to the greatest extent which can be permitted in an idealistic system: phenomena are identical with all possible ideas in the world. But in broadening the notion of phenomena in this way, he eliminates their materiality and ultimate otherness because both matter and otherness are presumably reducible within the categories of Hegelian idealism. For Hegel, the phenomenon proves an undepletably rich field which one can mine for the rational structures of spirit. Objects such as sensorial content are concepts. Thus, the content of sensation is not a mere given, a mere hyletic component from which sensations are built. Rather, it is an intelligible manifestation of spirit.

While investigating its intelligibility, Hegel does not leave the field of phenomena disorganized but, in general, accepts the hierarchical arrangement of consciousness evident in the order of foundedness which Lambert prescribes for sensation, perception, and ideation. Much of the structure of the *Phenomenology of Spirit* corresponds to a conceptual climb up a scaffolding which is artificially attached to the edifice of spirit. At the foundation of spirit is *the* crucial understanding of phenomena. There lies what Hegel designates appearance, in its most fundamental sense, as the unconstructed (or deconstructed) experience from which the world of conceptualization is raised. As such, it is both the point of origin and the terminus of phenomenological investigation, for in the course of examining the development of consciousness through the "inner life" and "inner necessity" controlling the object, Hegel is really seeking knowledge which will make the irrationality of deconstructed appearance intelligible. The tool for accomplishing the reconciliation between the adventitious and necessary aspects of appearance is the dialectical analysis of concepts (about which more will be said later).

Though it is difficult to criticize the breadth of the Hegelian conception of phenomena, the fact that it presupposes the forms of consciousness to operate by necessary laws of development seems to ignore the *a posteriori* constituents of experience and to make of the phenomenal world one vast clockwork of Spirit. Since Hegel has left us no (intelligible) discussion about how the hyletic components of experience are to be made rational and since he completely ignored the role the adventitious plays in the conscious constitution of the world, the necessity he assigns to his idealistic explanation of the world is, perhaps, his phenomenology's weakest feature. Because he maintains these aspects to be dictated by the objects of phenomenology themselves, his notion of phenomena transitivity shares the same defects.

Therefore, the Hegelian phenomena seem to be prejudiced constructs; they are objects whose nature is conditioned by some unjustified Hegelian presuppositions.

4. The Ends of the Hegelian Phenomenology

To describe the ultimate end of the Hegelian phenomenology it is most convenient to resort to the description which Hegel provides himself. According to Hegel, the ultimate end of the phenomenology of Spirit is to disclose

> . . . the morphogenetic process of . . . cultural development in all its detailed fullness and necessity, and at the same time . . . [to show] it to be something that has sunk into the human mind as a moment of its being and become a possession of mind.[28]

In other words, the Hegelian phenomenology is directed to the reconstitution of the mental (and spiritual) development of man by examining the successive sedimentations or accretions of meaning which are stratified in human cultural history. Because Hegel believes that conscious development occurs by a series of necessary sublations which preserve something of the content of an evolving thesis while identifying it with the new synthesis, he believes the structure of these sublations can, as it were, be read backwards, thereby making the reconstitution of the cultural life of man possible.

There are, however, at least four proximate ends which must be accomplished before Hegel's ultimate intention can be achieved. They are related to one another serially, the accomplishment of the fourth presupposing the accomplishment of the third, the third presupposing the accomplishment of the second and the second presupposing the accomplishment of the first.

Hegel's first proximate intention is the development of a scientific method by which it will be possible to abandon oneself to the inner life and necessity controlling the object. Hegel limits the denotation of the word 'scientific' only to those methods which are able to describe the internal logic of their objects as that logic mirrors their morphogenetic complexity. This means that Hegel, first, seeks a science which is capable of disclosing its objects as the necessary products of their history. The method he proposes is the Hegelian dialectic.

Hegel's second proximate intention is, on the basis of the first proximate end, to construct a schema for the categories of being (a *mathesis universalis*) which will allow the instrumental reduction of reality's complexity to a philosophical shorthand. The categories which are to constitute this schema are not to be mere constructions of thought but must take their meaning from distinctions actually existing in the world.

Hegel's third proximate intention is to develop his philosophical system according to the actual forms of consciousness which have historically emerged in dialectical interaction with one another. In other words, Hegel attempts to construct his schema,

---

[28]Hegel 90.

diachronically as well as synchronically, from the conceptual products of the dialectic between subjecthood and objecthood.

Hegel's fourth and final intention is to construct a complete system of the sciences which will explain the origin, progress and structure of the cosmos in its necessity and movement. With respect to this proximate end, the phenomenology of Spirit is the foundation science of the Hegelian architectonic. Upon it are built logic, the philosophy of nature and the philosophy of mind.

Little can be said in the way of criticism of the ends behind the Hegelian phenomenology. Since they are the most comprehensive expressions of intent which any of the six phenomenologists antecedent to Husserl proposes, they encompass the projects of each of the other five phenomenologists. Nevertheless, Hegel's phenomenology does not have a completely comprehensive ultimate end because Hegel never makes it clear whether phenomenology (as the foundation science) has ultimate practical implications or not. Unlike Robison, he does not specifically describe the uses to which phenomenology may be put. The result of this omission is that the Hegelian philosophy can be taken either as a program for the pure contemplation of history or as a program for the violent "encouragement" of history.

5. The Hegelian Phenomenological Technique

The Hegelian phenomenological technique is at many points obscured by a ponderous vocabulary and unorthodox logic. Nevertheless, it is possible to discern the general outlines of a phenomenological technique whose purpose is the self-critical examination of subjecthood and objecthood as they are constituted by consciousness' evolution.

This purpose is accomplished in four methodological steps. First, one steeps oneself in the perceptual and conscious experience of the object's concrete qualities. Second, one reduces the content of these experiences into a series of fixed ideas. Third, one composes a series of complex, precise and subtle descriptions of these ideas. These descriptions should be so comprehensive that they express the inner structure of the experience as the product of the subjecthood of the experiencing subject and the objecthood of the experienced object. Fourth, one does not stop with the third step but investigates the evolution of the object in relation to consciousness. This means one examines the life, or inner necessity, of the object by reactivating the object's sedimented meanings which are expressive of the path consciousness has followed in its historical constitution of the object. This last step is accomplished by a reduction (or deconstruction) of the experience of the object to appearance, the instrument for this deconstruction being the Hegelian dialectic.

The Hegelian dialectic is peculiarly ambiguous. On one hand it is an instrument for the deconstruction and, then, reconstruction of conscious evolution. On the other hand, it is the structural principle *behind* conscious evolution. This peculiar bivalence is what, in the Hegelian scheme of things, makes the dialectic reliable. It is a logical heuristic which, at the same time, participates in the very principle of development which it is set to describe.

The Hegelian dialectic consists of three sequential moments: (a) the differentiation of the ego from object-constituting consciousness; (b) the differentiation of consciousness into three contents: (i) the conceptualized object, (ii) the object intended as transcendental to consciousness and (iii) a judgment of the correspondence between i and ii; and (c) the redoubling of consciousness which results in a new object and new concept when the judgment of identity is frustrated. When this last step is accomplished, then a modification of both the apparently transcendental (but really immanent) object and immanent concept occurs. This last moment is what Hegel calls the dialectic of negativity. This dialectic is the motive force behind the evolution of consciousness, for all new ideas emerge from the contradiction of old ideas and old realities and their sublation in new concepts and new intended realities. The formal structures of this dialectic may also be used as an instrument to deconstruct contemporary concepts and transform the sublated meanings which inhere in them back into the original theses and antitheses which produce the contemporary idea. The morphogenetic process of cultural development may, therefore, be construed as an evolution constituted and driven by the three moments of the Hegelian dialectic. Access to past meanings or stages of consciousness is obtained when one unravels the "tangled skein" of meanings by means of these moments.

CHAPTER V

HAMILTON: THE ROLE OF PHENOMENOLOGY IN PHILOSOPHICAL PSYCHOLOGY

1. The Hamiltonian Phenomenology in Context

Sir William Hamilton's *Lectures on Metaphysics* is the second English philosophical site in which the word 'phenomenology' is employed and in which a developed interpretation of this word's meaning emerges.[1] The significance of this emergence is proportional to the originality with which Hamilton charges the word. A measure of this originality can be obtained by comparing his phenomenology with that of Robison. However, it is barely believable that the former emerged in an intellectual environment continuous with that of Robison; in many respects, Hamilton's phenomenology is the polar opposite of Robison's because it differs from the Robisonian phenomenology according to ancestry, function, style, and intent.

1.1. The Ancestry of Hamiltonian Phenomenology

In comparison to the distinct origins of Robison's philosophy, the philosophical ancestry of Hamilton's metaphysics is tangled. It is unclear which philosophies are to be counted as influences upon Hamilton's system and which are not. Only one influence stands out with any resolvability, and that is Kantian transcendentalism. But one is able to establish a connection between Kant and Hamilton only by ignoring the superficial resemblances between Hamilton's metaphysics and other philosophies and by concentrating upon the manner in which the architectonic of Hamilton's exposition mimics concepts and structures typical of Kantianism. Except for Kant, Hamilton's other ancestors are obscured. Largely, this is because of a stylistic quirk which mars almost every lecture: Hamilton's excessive indulgence in intolerably lengthy quotations.[2]

---

[1] Sir William Hamilton, *Lectures on Metaphysics and Logic*, 2nd ed., ed. Rev. H.L. Mansel and John Veitch, Vol. 1 (Edinburgh: William Blackwood, 1851).

[2] The penchant for citations lends Hamilton's work an eclectic character which is, perhaps, undeserved. When his work is taken at face value, however, the same judgment may be pronounced upon it which may be fairly pronounced upon any eclectic system: it is a thematic contradiction because it operates as a circumstantial arrangement of essentially unrelated themes. Hamilton's use of widely ranging quotations, without regard for their larger context, forces the conclusion that his thought cannot be truly systemic because no system can reconcile the apposite themes standing behind so many thematically different sources. On the other hand, one might think that Hamilton's use of citations could provide the inroad needed to discover his philosophical ancestry. Is there a better way to uncover the intellectual influences upon

Hamilton's disposition to quote widely differing philosophers in order to bolster his arguments also undercuts the possibility of establishing either a homological or a causal proof of his philosophical ancestors. Evidence that Hamilton has borrowed terminology, has read important texts and has been instructed by the great teachers of philosophy abounds in the *Lectures on Metaphysics*. After the search for homologies and causal *nexûs* is completed, only Kantian transcendentalism retains a univocal presence. No other philosophical influences can be established because Hamilton evidences little regard for context

There is yet another way in which Hamilton's passion for citations contributes to the dubitability of his arguments. By citing past savants, whose apparent agreement with him lends his philosophy respectability by association, Hamilton bares himself to the criticism that his lectures are a mere *argumentum ad verecundiam*: they convince only because they are based upon the assertions of philosophers venerable, famous and dead. Hamilton seems to ask the reader to accept his conclusions not on their own merits but because they agree with the discoveries of authorities. In this, he resembles the biblical positivist who employs the proof-text hermeneutic.[3]

Despite all that has been said about Hamilton violating context, one must admit that the passages he does employ are used in such a way that little actual harm is done to the grand systems of which they are parts. If one had the time and the energy to examine the original context of every quotation, one would find them in superficial agreement with the points Hamilton is intent upon making. To criticize Hamilton's hermeneutic is not to deny this; it is to observe that, though their intentions may

---

a thinker than to cite the opinion of those whom he respects? A careful study of the *Lectures on Metaphysics* makes the plausibility of the point behind this rhetorical question dubitable because Hamilton demonstrates little hermeneutical sensitivity. One can not be sure that he faithfully represents the opinions of those he quotes. He plays so fast and loose with passages from famous philosophers that it is impossible--upon reading of the Lectures alone--to discover his genuine antecedents.

What would one need to do, then, to demonstrate a philosophical influence upon Hamilton? One or two things would have to be established. Either it would be necessary to establish structural homologies between Hamilton's philosophy and its antecedents or it would be necessary to establish a clear causal connection. The discovery of structural homologies would count as a weaker proof of lineage because without a palpable link between Hamilton and his ancestors--that is without evidence that he had read certain books, had been taught by certain teachers, or had inherited an old terminology--the homological proof of inheritance might rest upon coincidental resemblances. The homological proof, like the Darwinian theory of evolution, really only establishes that similar conditions give rise to similar adaptations. From this alone one can no more infer that Hamilton is the direct descendent of Kant than one could prove that the porpoise is the direct descendent of the shark. A further *genetic* principle is demanded. One must be able to establish an unbroken *thematic* continuity between philosophical antecedents and consequents by way of intentions and artifacts, individuals or schools.

[3]Like the biblical positivist, Hamilton places confidence in an argument according to the authority supporting it, and, like the biblical positivist, Hamilton is vulnerable to two criticisms. First, there is no reason, aside from compelling logic, to accept an opinion simply because there is the halo of authority about it. Second, even if one grants that a text is to be accepted because of the stature of its author, the application of the proof-text method can endanger the meaning of the text if it causes the text to be isolated from its context. The proof-text method has plausibility only if the cited document is treated as a contextual whole having authority; it must be united as a homogeneous thematic field with a relatively univocal meaning. Divine revelation and sublime philosophical insights are alike in this: both have force insofar as their integral meaning is respected; neither may be pragmatically divided into convenient rhetorical units. If texts are to be venerated, or simply appreciated, they must be interpreted honestly according to the singular dictates of the intentionality behind them, not according to their reputations alone. These are the conditions for discovering the claims texts make upon one.

superficially agree, the essential themes of Hamilton and his preceptors are at odds with one another. Hamilton's disregard of context is dangerous only when it leads to the complete identification of his purpose and the themes behind the passages he quotes.

1.2. The Function of Hamiltonian Phenomenology

Returning--this time more sympathetically--to consider Hamilton's arguments from authority, it is possible to moderate the earlier criticisms by observing that this argumentative form is, in part, dictated by the function of the *Lectures*. Hamilton composed them first during the Edinburgh term 1836-1856.[4] As a first course in philosophy, they served to wet the feet of freshmen in the living waters of the Western intellectual tradition. The quotations Hamilton selected to this end were chosen with three rhetorically artful effects in mind: first, to impress upon youth the conservatism of the philosophical enterprise; second, to prove the unsuppressibility of ultimate philosophical questions; third, to disclose the philosophical discoveries which endured the passage of time. In attempting to teach these lessons, Hamilton hoped to establish the continuity of his own principles with the conservatism, unsuppressibility and endurance of Western values. He hoped that quotations from "the Greats" might serve especially well to enhance the regard of freshmen.

Whether or not Hamilton convincingly demonstrated his continuity with the Western intellectual tradition, one cannot fail to observe that his attempt to teach freshmen provides one of the chief points of contrast between the function of the *Lectures* and the function of Robison's encyclopedia article. Hamilton wrote for students; Robison wrote for the wide audience of readers of the *Encyclopaedia Britannica*.

1.3. The Style of Hamiltonian Phenomenology

Function is not the only point of contrast between these authors, however. Style is also relevant. Though the works of Hamilton and Robison were conditioned by historical circumstance and considerations of space, the characteristics of these limitations are different for each work. Robison was forced to write succinctly both because spatial limitations were imposed upon encyclopedia contributors and because the ideal of succinctness was a part of the Encyclopedicists' axiological outfitting. In contrast, no similar spacial limitation was imposed upon Hamilton's work. It was to his advantage to lend leisurely expression to philosophical arguments--leisurely expression replete with many quotations--because he believed this technique well suited for the teaching of college students.

1.4. The Intention of Hamiltonian Phenomenology

Historical milieu also provided a point of contrast between the works of Robison and Hamilton. Although both authors matured in intellectual environments continuous with one another, the historical vicissitudes of each milieu were quite different. When Robison wrote, Kant had made a negligible impact upon English philosophy. The Continental philosophers of the Enlightenment were, of course, well known--Robison

---

[4]Hamilton 61-62.

demonstrates an appreciation of them--but Robison's staples were Aristotle, Bacon and Hume. Philosophy, for Robison, was paradigmatically empiricistic and nature-directed. He showed no awareness of the "transcendental turn" which critical philosophy on the Continent had taken. By the time Hamilton wrote the *Lectures*, however, the intellectual climate had changed. The significance of Kantianism had come to be appreciated, if not understood, quite well, and Hamilton's philosophy clearly reflects the English discovery of Kant. Nevertheless, like most Englishmen, Hamilton was unable to cut his moorings to the indigenous philosophical tradition. Although *a prioristic*, Hamilton's philosophy has a noticeable empiricistic bent, as well.

The historical vicissitudes which conditioned the intellectual climates in which Robison and Hamilton wrote also had a very direct influence upon each author's concept of phenomenology's object or end. In Robison's thinking--guided as it is by the empiricist tradition--phenomenology is object-directed. Phenomenology, the science of appearances, is directed to the description of things in the external world; it is not directed to the description of internal realities or experiences nor to the description of the constitution of knowledge. For these reasons, Robison's philosophy mimics the empiricist method in all its naive disinterest in the foundations of experience. If Robison's phenomenology may be termed "critical," it may be termed "critical" only in that it is directed towards exploding the *idols* which interfere with our understanding of reality; it is *not* critical in that it neglects to search for the constitutive foundations upon *a priori* grounds.[5] Rather, reality--out there--is presupposed as a knowable thing-in-itself.

Robison believes in the fundamental trustworthiness of knowledge as demonstrated in the mind's grasp of external realities. His philosophical criticism is directed toward making this trustworthiness constant and better. Philosophy is not to involve critical self-reflexivity as defined by the transcendental idealists. Philosophy is to be critical only insofar as it is analytically to minimize false interpretations of the externally objective world of nature.

In contrast, Hamilton's philosophy--instructed as it is by Kantian transcendentalism--demonstrates an awareness that for phenomenology to be deep it must critically investigate the structures of consciousness. Hamilton begins with consciousness because consciousness is the precondition for any knowledge whatsoever. For phenomenology to succeed, it must begin with an analysis of the root of experience of the world; it must begin with unbiased description of consciousness in the act of constituting reality. Hamilton, unlike Robison, does not assume that reality is a knowable thing-in-itself. Only the raw data of experience, the structures of consciousness and consciousness' constitution of the world exist.

---

[5]To be critical, a philosophy must question the conditions for the possibility of knowledge; it cannot assume that these conditions are given to consciousness self-evidently. Robison's phenomenology is not critical in the fullest sense of the word, because he does not subject the part-whole relationship to analysis. Had he done so he might well have discovered that it is not an *a posteriori* idea derived from experience but a logical category which antedates experience and makes experience possible.

2. Hamiltonian Phenomenology

Hamilton's discussion of philosophy demonstrates four initial intentions. First, Hamilton is intent upon explaining what philosophy is. Second, he is intent upon explaining under what conditions philosophy is possible. Third, he is concerned with what philosophical methods are. Fourth, he is concerned with how philosophy is ordered. Only after Hamilton has satisfied each of these concerns does he engage in an exposition of phenomenology. Since Hamilton's notion of phenomenology depends upon his notion of philosophy, the following exposition will be guided by this sequence of substantial dependence.

2.1. What Philosophy Is for Hamilton

Philosophy, for Hamilton, is *the* preeminent science. It is that kind of knowledge which has as its aim the elucidation of what knowledge is and what makes it possible.[6] Inasmuch as philosophy investigates these themes, it is forced upon two different descriptive trajectories. On one hand, it is committed to describing knowledge and the objects of knowledge. On the other hand, it is committed to establishing the conditions under which knowledge is possible and--once this is established--under what conditions knowledge is facilitated.

Hamilton's interpretation of philosophy as knowledge of what knowledge is heralds the appearance of a new philosophical discovery upon the English intellectual scene. It makes axiomatic a regulative principle which had previously been the exclusive property of the German idealists: the principle that philosophical investigation presupposes the recognition of consciousness' self-reflexivity. Though Hamilton never uses the term 'self-reflexivity of consciousness,' its meaning is implicit in his assertion that the validity of knowledge must be established from within knowledge. It is also implicit within his conception of mind as that which constructively mediates all experience including its own workings.[7]

2.2. The Conditions for the Possibility of Philosophy according to Hamilton

The approval of the principle that knowledge must be self-reflexive leads Hamilton to a specific methodological viewpoint: inasmuch as a single transducer, the mind, mediates all knowledge, a single method, philosophy, is sufficient to establish the conditions of this mediation. If the mind mediates all experience--including the experience internal to consciousness--then the mediation to which the mind subjects the objective, natural world is no different, in principle, from the mediation to which the mind subjects the world of consciousness. Consciousness, in respect to the mind's mediation, has no special privilege; it is not to be understood as a different phenomenon because it is on the "inner side" of experience. In respect to objective knowledge, there

---

[6]Hamilton 61-62.

[7]Hamilton 192-193.

78

is no "inside." Whatever the mind takes as object--even itself--must be constituted typically in the same manner as experiences which come from the "outside" world. 'Outside' and 'inside' have meaning only in reference to the control the mind has over the phenomena it observes. "Outside" are all the phenomena which remain, in some sense, unalterable by willful modifications of consciousness. "Inside" are the phenomena more susceptible to conscious, willful modifications. A single philosophical method applies to both varieties of phenomena.

A particular interpretation of the act of understanding may be associated with this view of philosophical objectivity. Hamilton rejects every interpretation of knowledge processes in which the mind is construed as passive. He rejects the thesis--a thesis which gets attention in the writings of Aristotle and Locke--that the mind is a *tabula rasa*. He rejects the view of consciousness which compares mind to a wet clay tablet passively accepting the impressions of objects acting as styli. Rather, the mind seizes upon amorphous phenomenal experience and constructively shapes it into forms which can be translated into predictive generalizations. Natural phenomena and mental phenomena, alike, undergo this constitution. Thus, in direct contrast to the realist or empiricist epistemology, in which objects inform consciousness, Hamilton proposes the idealistic thesis that active consciousness imposes its categories upon passive phenomena.[8]

2.2.1. The three categories of knowledge

The activity of consciousness shapes raw experience into three, qualitatively different kinds of knowledge: cognitive knowledge, aesthetic knowledge and conative knowledge.[9] Corresponding to each variety of knowledge is an object domain. Cognitive knowledge has as its object the *Intelligible*, whatever by virtue of its formal properties may be turned into descriptions and predictions about spatio-temporal experience. Aesthetic knowledge has as its object the *Beautiful*, whatever by virtue of its material properties and formal construction may be transformed into descriptions and predictions about what is aesthetically pleasing. Conative knowledge has as its object the *Ought*, whatever by virtue of its material properties and formal construction may be transformed into descriptions and predictions about will and obligation.

The first of these varieties of knowledge presupposes a reflexive definition. To use the phrase 'cognitive knowledge' is not to imply a parity of composition between it and either aesthetic or conative knowledge. Cognitive knowledge, as logic, takes as its components the formal principles of reasoning and arranges them according to formal constructions which make use of the same principles. Only when cognitive knowledge is derived from spatio-temporal events does it possess some parity with the other two varieties of knowledge, for then the phenomenal appearances of these events become the material components of experience. Unlike either aesthetic or conative knowledge, cognitive knowledge may have an object domain and constructive method which

---

[8]Hamilton 140-141.

[9]Hamilton 183-184.

originate in the same formal principles. Only cognitive knowledge may entail a retortion upon itself.

Each domain of knowledge further represents a distinct, categorical *a priori*. Cognitive knowledge is founded upon *a priori* relations which are formal and abstractly quite pure. The formal relations behind logic, geometry, arithmetic and algebra belong to this category, exclusively. Aesthetic and conative knowledge also have aspects which are subject to such formal interpretation, and, thus, it is possible to provide definitions of beauty, obligation, etc., which make good logical sense. The experiences upon which these definitions are founded, however, are neither logically reducible nor purely cognitive. One cannot give a purely cognitive explanation of why beauty is what it is or why the good is what it is. Each is given with an *a priori* validity which is not reducible to its formal properties.

Relative to the other two varieties of knowledge, cognitive knowledge is independent. It can exist in a purified state having virtually no aesthetic or conative components. Thus, abstractive descriptions of spatial objects do not possess an aesthetic or conative content, though the prescriptions for arriving at such descriptions might contain such contents. The definition of a line as "the shortest distance between two points" is capable of purely formal representations having no reference to either aesthetic or conative principles. However, if one were to say "'the shortest distance between two points' is a good definition of a line," then an aesthetic principle would be entailed. Inasmuch as aesthetic and conative descriptions must be expressed in propositional form, they must of necessity possess a cognitive aspect. The converse is not true for cognitive knowledge, however. Cognitive knowledge is thus superordinated with respect to aesthetic and conative knowledge.

If there are inexplicable and irreducible experiences which found each domain of knowledge, as well as axioms which follow from these experiences, then it is impossible to seek reasons for their being what they are. To speculate as to why these experiences occur or why their derivative axioms have pragmatic value is to overstep the boundaries of the reflexive investigation of knowledge. To look beyond what consciousness mediates is to do metaphysics, and Hamilton will allow no metaphysics until legitimate procedures are discovered which will enable it to be rationally founded.

In the beginning lectures, Hamilton recoils from answering the metaphysical questions of why we know, why there is beauty and why there is obligation to consider the conditions under which one may know something. He also defers an investigation into the Beautiful and the Ought in preference to an investigation into the conditions of intelligibility. He is concerned with what it means to know something philosophically. The Ought and the Beautiful are entailed by this investigation only as they function as the regulative components of a criteriology of knowledge. Hamilton avoids considering them according to the ultimate aims they claim for themselves.

Mediation and constitution also contribute to an understanding of knowledge but only as far as knowledge is the product of psychological mechanisms which are responsible for the categories of experience. The mechanisms by which mediation and constitution are explained do not, however, exhaust the meaning of knowledge. They limitedly present knowledge as the natural product of psychological processes. Mind, to bowdlerize Marx, secretes concepts the way the liver secretes bile. But the

80

mechanistic side of knowledge's constitution has value only in explaining the automatic, passive character of mediation and constitution. What is further required is consideration of the personal element paradigmatic of consciousness. What one does when one knows as well as what knowledge is from the subjective perspective of the knower must be elucidated. For Hamilton, knowledge under the direction of the ego is science, and science is the active discovery of causal relations.

2.2.2. Knowledge and causation

Hamilton accepts as an indisputable, universal condition of knowledge that man reasons causally. By human constitution "we are necessitated, to regard each phaenomenon as only partially known, until we discover the causes on which it depends for its existence."[10] Since philosophy is the reflexive and ultimately critical science, it must begin with the foundation-cause of experience. It must investigate "the universal and principle concurrent cause in every act of knowledge."[11] Science or philosophy must take mind as the first cause by applying the same method as it would in interpretating any phenomenon as a process of contiguous causes and effects.

Notice the subtlety here. Hamilton argues that for the mind to attain scientific knowledge of itself, it can only do so by reasoning from cause to effect. Yet, at the foundation of this method is the very principle by which the mind transcends the merely phenomenal, for if there are necessities which characterize the mind's behavior, then these necessities must be called in to explain how we know. As the mind and its behavior are the necessary preconditions of causal reasoning, they possess a form of a priori validity with respect to the possibility of knowledge; it is phenomenology's purpose to unveil these necessary mental structures. Before phenomenology may be appreciated, however, one must understand what Hamilton means by 'cause' and 'effect.'

Hamilton's interpretation of the terms 'cause' and 'effect' is peculiar. Causes are known only through their effects; they are related to their effects as coefficients because the mind constructs an equivalence between them by beginning with the effect and then reasoning about the collocation of causes which might have produced it. All wondering about the causes of current or past experience takes this form. Causal reasoning always begins with effects.[12]

If one wonders about eventualities, this wondering is rational only if one has an understanding about the possible causal connections between present events and events in the future. The origin of the capacity to connect events causally is innate; it is not learned. Though the capacity to connect cause to effect may be innate, the experiences which give rise to such connections are not. We learn to establish causal

---

[10]Hamilton 57.

[11]Hamilton 62.

[12]Hamilton 60, 97. In challenge to this notion of causation, it might be asked, "What if one begins with an action in the present and wonders about its future effects?" "Does one not, then, begin with a cause?" Hamilton provides no explicit answer to these questions, but (based upon his skeletal discussion) it may be possible to construct a reply. This reply will also serve as an elaboration of the Hamiltonian theory of causation.

generalizations, from which we predict the future, based upon individual experiences in the present. To understand how we wonder about the future, we must begin with causal experience in the present.

A cause is defined as that which is responsible for an effect. But what is an effect? According to Hamilton, everything which appears in the world--except God--is an effect. Everything which has resulted from a something else is the effect of something else. However, if everything is an effect, and if everything must have a cause, then some effects must have a dual nature. Some effects must be causes with respect to future effects. 'Cause' and 'effect' are, thus, relative terms indicating a peculiar asymmetry. Though one may experience effects which, in turn, are not causes--these are the ineffectual causes--we never experience effects which do not have causes. To understand something is to understand what has gone before it. Logically, causes represent the necessary preconditions of effects, but effects are merely the sufficient results of causes. Effects need not exist.

Wonder about causal experience always begins with present events or effects. Even if one looks to the future for the effects of the palpable experience of the present, one possesses the possibility of establishing a connection between present and future only if one has accumulated a store of the possible connections between causes and effects. Only after one has experiential proof of the relation between an effect and a horizon of possible previous causes can one selectively eliminate the non-efficacious factors. This selection is always initiated in present experience to satisfy the desire to control this experience. Even experimentation begins with a noticed regularity between a field of effects and a field of causes, a regularity which is investigated because of the interest in controlling or reproducing certain effects. When one wonders about the future effect of present actions, one wonders rationally only inasmuch as it is possible to construct an analogy between the *nexûs* of past causes and effects and the *nexûs* of present events and their future possible effects. Granting, then, that the capacity to connect cause and effect is an innate precondition of experience, and further granting that one is born into this world *in media res*, one must necessarily begin experience with effects and reason from effects to causes. 'Cause' has no meaning without a prior interest in effects.

It is possible to attempt another defense of Hamilton's thesis, this time by arguing from the agent's attention to the causal terms. It is a universal of all experience, that the immediacy of experience is largely responsible for experience's significance. When one wonders about events in the present, one often measures the significance of these events by the interest one has in their causes. Significant events are often those we wish most to control. The best way to do this is to understand what causes them.

The locus of significance for a cause-cum-effect is in the effect. When we wonder about an event in the present--an event which has significance--we reflect upon what *caused* it. When one wonders about the results of present actions, again the focus of significance is directed toward the future in that one's concern is directed to what the future effects of this action will be. The significance of causation is always in the effect; the cause, however, explains why the effect occurs. The effect is the fruit of the cause's potency; it is the significant thing to be explained so that it can be reproduced or avoided. Worry about the future is directed toward the significance of our actions as embodied in their effects. Worry about the present is directed to immediate circumstances. In either case, the hunt for causes is spurred on by the significance of the effects.

The process of causal reasoning, the reasoning from effect to cause, can continue indefinitely or until one arrives at something which one cannot conceive of as an effect. This reasoning results in a progressive simplification both in the number of the diachronic causes preceding the intended effect as well as in the number of synchronic causes during each temporal stretch. The universe, thus, demonstrates a determinate causal character. It has the structure of a convergent causal tree. This convergence is significant because it provides an analogy which, when psychologically interpreted, discloses the unity of human consciousness. It provides an illustration that the constitution of reality has a single causal origin and that this origin is an analogue to consciousness. Metaphysically interpreted, this causal structure reveals the world's unitary source, God. It functions as an illustration that since the mind discovers causal orders which are independent of its own constitution, and since these orders ultimately originate in an uncaused cause, the world exists contingently dependent upon God.[13]

2.3. The Hamiltonian Philosophical Method

Hamilton believes that causal reasoning ought to follow a scientific method. The question of how to discover this method haunts the earlier portions of the *Lectures on Metaphysics*. Like Bacon and Descartes, Hamilton makes the discovery of this method the precondition of this philosophy. The method which he finally approves has the following salient principles:

> . . . to observe with care, --that is to analyze; to reject every element as hypothetical, which this analysis does not spontaneously afford; to call in experiment in aid of observation; and to attempt no synthesis or generalization until the relative analysis has been completely accomplished.[14]

This method is thorough-goingly phenomenological. It is to begin with observation, rejecting everything which is not self-evidently a part of the experience of the phenomenon. Hypothetical residues are to be held in suspension until experiments and causal inferences allow one to postulate their existence. Finally, the end of the scientific method is achieved when, on the basis of description, analysis, hypothesis and experiment, an explanatory synthesis is accomplished.

Three of Hamilton's terms require elucidation. By 'analysis' he means the mental "decomposition" of phenomena. Analysis proceeds by taking any object whatsoever and descriptively breaking it down into self-evident parts. It includes no speculation as to the underlying connection not given in the immediate experience of the object. At this stage of analysis, no explanation is attempted. Only very accurate description is sought.[15]

---

[13]Hamilton 60,97.

[14]Hamilton 108.

[15]Hamilton 97-98.

By 'hypothesis' Hamilton intends a proposal not yet founded upon reasonable postulates. Hypotheses have as their end the fulfillment of mind's desire to reduce facts to coherency, simplicity and comprehensibility. The two conditions under which a hypothesis is allowable are: first, there must be an actually existent object to be explained; second, it must be the case that a hypothetical leap is demanded, or it must be the case that the object cannot be explained except by a postulate. Hamilton further distinguishes an excellent hypothesis from a specious hypothesis by the following: first, it must involve nothing contradictory; second, its probability must be proportional to its explanatory capacity; third, its probability must be proportional to its independence from further hypotheses.[16]

Finally, by 'synthesis' Hamilton means creative reconstitution transcending the mere mechanical assembly of parts. This reconstitution is not the mere reassembly of the parts distinguished by analysis. That would get science no further than phenomena as they are immediately given. Rather, this reconstitution requires the incorporation of hypotheses, and it results in the production of general laws.

To accomplish a synthesis one must "extract the one out of the many."[17] This means one must look to mutable and absolutely individual phenomena with the intention of observing, comparing and isolating common qualities. Once these qualities are discovered they are to be related to their causal milieu so that a general law may be inferred. As a mere proposal without experimental verification, such inferences are merely hypotheses. When, however, hypotheses are applied to concrete natural conditions--usually under the protocol of the experimental method--their predictive value is either tentatively confirmed or positively disproven. Whatever the outcome of crucial experiments, the intention of all synthetic reasoning is to move from limited antecedent conditions to unlimited consequent generalizations. Synthesis is creative. It discovers more than is contained in its premises. One might say, to paraphrase Samuel Butler, that synthesis is the art of drawing sufficient conclusions from insufficient premises.[18]

Hamilton's notion of synthesis betrays a Kantian influence in that it allows that the uniformity of nature is dependent upon the tendency of mind to connect cause and effect. This tendency is recognized as an a priori capacity of mind. Unlike Kant, however, Hamilton seems to believe that there is an order of causation existing independently of human consciousness. His remarks that God's existence is implied by the natural causal order can be interpreted in no other fashion. Hamilton believes in discernible natural laws apart from the constitution of consciousness.

In Hamilton's understanding, analysis, hypothesis and synthesis are related as follows. Analysis is the descriptive prerequisite to hypothesis and synthesis. Hypothesis is the tentative assertion of a generalization, and synthesis is the universal generalization of a hypothesis established by scientific experimentation. Operating together these

---

[16]Hamilton 168-172.

[17]Hamilton 101.

[18]Hamilton 98-103.

methodological components allow us to abstract systems from apparently random phenomena.

The legitimacy of science is not exhausted by the protocol of method. Hamilton thinks that there are virtues and tendencies which enhance the scientist's or philosopher's ability to apply the synthetic method. The natural tendencies which lead man to seek knowledge may be considered the behavioral preconditions for the emergence and evolution of the synthetic method itself. Thus, Hamilton reduces the desire which gives rise to science to three behavioral surds: (1) the *necessity* to connect causes and effects (already mentioned above), (2) the *necessity* of carrying knowledge to some form of unity, and (3) wonder and curiosity.[19] These desires must be accepted as natural and irreducible. Apart from a scientific knowledge of what science is, man cannot hope to discover *why* he connects causes, *why* he wishes to bring thought to unity, or *why* he wonders or is curious. Hamilton believes that the tendencies which give rise to science are innate. Behaviorally, they are inexplicable.

Though the drives which compel man to seek knowledge are inexplicable, the virtues which promote science are not. The beneficence of the scientific virtues becomes quite evident as soon as one begins to investigate *how* these virtues contribute to the success of the scientific method.

The virtue which Hamilton judges to be of paramount importance to the success of science is fairness to the data at hand or the absence of prejudice.[20] By 'absence of prejudice' Hamilton means the positive suspension of any belief which might interfere with the presentation of data to the observer. To be fair to data the scientist must suspend his adhesion to those previous opinions, customs or beliefs which might predetermine the interpretation he places upon his observations. Only conclusions which are the products of sustained self-examination and strict deduction are to be retained.

The virtue of fairness possesses two aspects: a negative aspect representing the doubt a philosopher ought to entertain regarding his past opinions and prejudices and a positive aspect representing the positive act of unbiased observation. To explain the negative aspect of fairness, Hamilton quotes Descartes with approval.

> To philosophize . . . seriously, and to good effect, it is necessary for a man to renounce all prejudices; in other words to apply the greatest care to doubt all of his previous opinions, so long as these have not been subjected to a new examination, and have been recognized as true.[21]

Philosophy is, thus, among other things, the "art of doubting well," but without doubt's positive resolution in truth "[d]oubt as a permanent state would be intellectual death."[22] For Hamilton, fairness requires that the savant begin in critical doubt but end

---

[19]Hamilton 66.

[20]Hamilton 81.

[21]Hamilton 90.

[22]Hamilton 90.

in positive certainty. In Hamilton's philosophy, doubt does not become the sole methodological focus as it does in scepticism. Doubt is a means to an end; it is not an end in itself.

Once one has turned the ray of doubt upon the preconceptions one naturally brings to the data on hand, one can then engage the positive aspect of fairness: the act of unbiased observation. The philosopher, in observing the world, must describe its phenomena exactly as they manifest themselves to his consciousness. But the mind to which these appearances are given must not be usually predisposed. Rather, it must be a consciousness pliant to raw impressions, a consciousness which does not interrupt or impede the pure experience of the object. Consciousness must, still, be under the control of the ego but it must be nearly passive. Only then can the philosopher experience the world as it gives itself to lucid consciousness. Then it is possible to describe the world as it actually is or, in other words, as it gives itself to consciousness' unpredisposed constitution of reality.

Along with fairness, two other virtues are of value to the philosopher. The first is intellectual industry or the elimination of sloth. The second is intellectual humility or the elimination of pride.

Sloth Hamilton sees as, perhaps, the most dangerous impediment to philosophy done well. It is a danger not only because sloth is a great barrier to a philosopher's initiating the search for truth but also because it is the chief vice which keeps philosophers committed to their unexamined assumptions. Philosophers who are very industrious--very industrious, that is, as measured by their written output--are often the laziest thinkers. This is tragic because the philosopher, of all people, ought to exemplify intellectual industry. It may well be that the greater part of humanity will "spare themselves the trouble of a long laborious inquiry." or will always "fancy that a superficial examination is enough."[23] Be that as it may, the philosopher ought to behave differently. He is expected to exercise a critical industry unrivalled by the practitioners of the other sciences. The philosopher must live the examined life rigorously.

Finally, Hamilton considers pride's interference with the achievement of philosophical ends a danger because it is the spirit of pride to prefer fame to truth. In fact, it may be that essentially the same motives are operative in the demagogue's desire to captivate an audience as are operative in an intellectual's desire to appeal to a segment of the reading public. There is no better example of an intellectual puffed-up with pride than that of the Greek sophists, who would facilely adjust their arguments--not to mention their fees--to suit whatever audience they were addressing.

Pride is manifest not only in serving philosophical fashion. It frequently manifests itself as a desire to do the impossible or to investigate the impossibly obscure. In these cases it is usually the intention of the scholar to gain fame by needlessly breaking new intellectual ground or by so narrowing an intellectual topic as to make him the only scholar understanding the topic or its significance. Hamilton describes this variety of philosopher as "disdaining what can be easily accomplished" and as applying themselves

---

[23]Hamilton 94.

"to the obscure and the recondite."[24] The result is that the "vulgar and easy foundation on which the rare and arduous is built" cannot sustain the significance these scholars attach to it.[25] Their desires to become famous are frustrated. No good scholarship comes of this pride but merely "a farrago of confused and ill-assorted notions."[26] Hamilton believed that a philosopher's chief aim ought to be to address himself humbly, energetically and fairly to ultimate questions in their broadest significance.

2.4. Hamilton's Architectonic of Philosophy

Once Hamilton has established what philosophy is, under what conditions it is possible and what its methods are, it is a simple matter for him to sketch the sequence of sciences which characterizes the various subdivisions of philosophy. The division he intends can be schematically represented as in Chart 4.

According to Hamilton, philosophy can be divided into three major disciplines: phenomenology, which is the descriptive science of cognitions, feelings and conations; nomology, which is the science which demonstrates the law-like behavior of cognitions, feelings and conations; and ontology, which is the science of inductions about God's being and the soul's immortality. Corresponding to each of these branches is a methodological step or combination of steps which constitute each discipline's protocol. Thus, phenomenology is essentially informed by an analytical method, a method directed to the description of consciousness but it is a method free of preconditions and explanations. Nomology, on the other hand, is a more perfect science because its method transcends mere analytical description and employs both hypothesis and synthesis to achieve the certainly of synthetic *a priori* knowledge. Finally, ontology makes use of both analysis and hypothesis, but it is incapable of effecting the synthesis which would make it a complete science. Ontology, inasmuch as it is concerned only with good possibilities, can never attain the deductive certainty of nomology.[27]

Corresponding to the major subdivisions of philosophy is a temporal order indicating the dependency of one science upon another. Since, necessarily, all science must begin with a good acquaintance with the objects of study and, furthermore, since Hamilton believes that the foundation of the object-subject relation is to be found in consciousness, the phenomenological description of things given immediately to consciousness is the primary science. Phenomenology is the prerequisite to nomology and ontology because both are incapable of applying their unique methods without having a dependable set of data to work upon. Neither can function without the certainty that unique object domains exist and have clearly defined characteristics. Only if these conditions are fulfilled can hypotheses, then, be proposed and resolved in syntheses.

---

[24]Hamilton 94-95.

[25]Hamilton 95.

[26]Hamilton 95.

[27]Hamilton 121-122.

CHART 4

The Divisions of Hamiltonian Philosophy

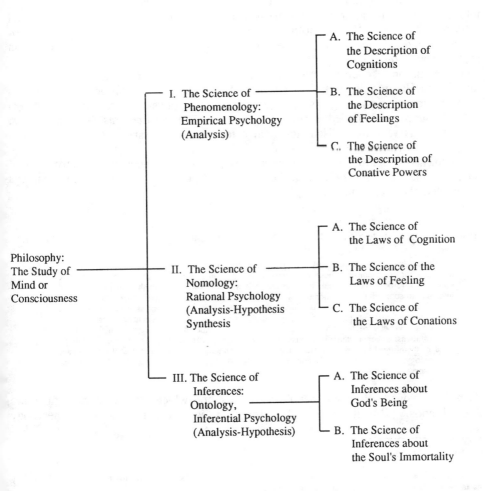

Philosophy:
The Study of
Mind or
Consciousness

I. The Science of
Phenomenology:
Empirical Psychology
(Analysis)

   A. The Science of
the Description of
Cognitions

   B. The Science of
the Description
of Feelings

   C. The Science of
the Description of
Conative Powers

II. The Science of
Nomology:
Rational Psychology
(Analysis-Hypothesis
Synthesis

   A. The Science of
the Laws of Cognition

   B. The Science of the
Laws of Feeling

   C. The Science of
the Laws of Conations

III. The Science of
Inferences:
Ontology,
Inferential Psychology
(Analysis-Hypothesis)

   A. The Science of
Inferences about
God's Being

   B. The Science of
Inferences about
the Soul's Immortality

88

Ontology is the last science in the order of dependency because it depends upon both ontology and nomology for its data. It is a "fringe" science. It is directly concerned with neither the immediacy of perception--as is phenomenology--nor with the laws which may be constructed upon the basis of such description--as is nomology. Its immediate concern is to provide possible explanations for the broadest generalizations about reality, explanations which cannot be derived from direct experience or strict deduction. Thus, it depends upon phenomenology and nomology to carry it to that margin where neither phenomenology nor nomology can function. It depends upon phenomenology and nomology for an explanation of what the world is like, but it alone attempts to explain why the world is what it is. Ontology, even when done well, is the most tentative of the sciences, and this uncertainty serves especially to underscore its dependency upon description and deduction.[28]

Once Hamilton's schema for the sciences is clearly displayed, one begins to sense that the title of Hamilton's work, '*Lectures on Metaphysics*,' is inappropriate. According to his own admission, ontology is the equivalent of metaphysics since ontology studies the narrow margin of knowledge *beyond* nomology.[29] In the *Lectures on Metaphysics*, however, there is very little discussion related to ontological issues. Hamilton devotes most of his energy, and most of the text's space, to a discussion of the phenomenology and nomology of cognitions. Hamilton's work might have been more aptly entitled '*Lectures on the Phenomenology and Nomology of Cognition*.' Metaphysical concerns are mentioned there only in passing.[30]

2.4.1. Hamiltonian Phenomenology

Hamilton clearly describes the utility of phenomenology in the following passage:

> In the first branch [of philosophy], the Phaenomenology of mind, philosophy is properly limited to facts afforded in consciousness, considered exclusively in themselves. But these facts may be such as not to be objects of knowledge in themselves, but likewise to furnish us with grounds of inference to something out of themselves. As effects, and effects of a certain character, they may enable us to infer the analogous character of their unknown causes; as phaenomena, and phaenomena of peculiar qualities, they may warrant us in drawing many conclusions regarding the distinctive character of that unknown principle, of that unknown substance, of which they are manifestations, although, therefore, existence be only revealed to us in phaenomena, and though we can, therefore, have only a relative knowledge of either mind or of matter; still by inference and analogy, we may legitimately attempt to rise above the mere appearances which experience and observation afford.[31]

Hamilton understands phenomenology as a method which leads to nomological and ontological ends. But its own end, description, is fulfilled when phenomenology

---

[28]Hamilton 124-125.

[29]Hamilton conceives of ontology as being hypothetical in nature. As such it is related to the real world in very tenuous fashion; it has none of the certainty of nomology.

[30]Hamilton viii.

[31]Hamilton 124-125.

achieves the descriptive project initiated in some field of knowledge. If a physicist asks what series of appearances constitutes what is meant by an atom, then phenomenology fulfills its task by providing a description. Notice, however, that phenomenology has to do with these appearances only. It does nothing to prove physical laws or regularities, save provide the descriptions upon which they are based. Phenomenology is concerned with rigorous, analytical description, but this description may be used for other purposes by other sciences. For this reason Hamilton agrees with Robison in calling phenomenology "history."[32]

Historical knowledge must be differentiated from predictive or nomological knowledge because it has no pretense to universality. History "is properly only the narration of a consecutive series of phaenomena in time, or the description of a co-existent series of phaenomena in space."[33] It is the most purely descriptive variety of knowledge because "it is given us by experience or observation, and not obtained as the result of inference or reasoning."[34] One can see that Hamilton's notion of history is quite different than that which prevails today. Few historians today would hesitate to claim that their discipline is nomological: for it not to be would make it trivial by modern scientific standards. But for Hamilton or Robison, the high order of complexity which typifies the phenomena of history seems to preclude the possibility that history can be nomological. History is a science only in that it entails very precise analysis.

Because phenomenology is equated with history, its *modus operandi* must be identical with that of history. The phenomenology of mind, the foundation science of philosophy, thus studies those serialities which constitute consciousness. However, in this assertion of phenomenology's purpose a dilemma lies hidden, a dilemma based upon the nature of the object to be studied. The mind's opacity to its own self-reflexivity makes it impossible for a complete phenomenological description of consciousness ever to be carried out. If phenomenology is to describe phenomena as they give themselves immediately to experience, then it will not be able to describe notions such as seriality, regularity, temporality, etc., because these notions cannot be reduced to phenomena alone. They are the synthetic *a priori* products of phenomena and the categories which constitute reality. They cannot be reduced to experience because they represent something beyond experience which gives experience its structure.

The dilemma may be further intensified. How can phenomenological description be given for absolutely unique events, if phenomenological description is expressed in common language and employs generalizations and constructions which are the productions of consciousness? In simpler terms the dilemma is this: phenomenology demands that description utterly reduce conscious behavior to a field of unique experiences, but in doing this, the mind must employ the very laws which it attempts to reduce. Hamilton, though not expressing the dilemma in this form, demonstrates an

---

[32]See Chapter III.

[33]Hamilton 53-54.

[34]Hamilton 54.

awareness of the difficulty. He understands that because the mind's reflexivity is not absolute--it cannot, for example, think about itself while thinking about itself--the nomological forms must merely be accepted. In that these structures define the conditions under which experience and knowledge are possible, even phenomenology contains a nomology of sorts.

In granting that the forms of consciousness must interfere with the phenomenological project, Hamilton recognizes that a number of difficulties attend the description of consciousness. The first, that of the incompleteness of consciousness' self-reflexivity, he describes with reference to a specific sort of conscious alteration.

> . . . [T]he mental energy, instead of being concentrated, is divided, and divided into two divergent directions The state of mind observed, and the act of mind observing, are mutually in an inverse ratio; each tends to annihilate the other. If the state to be observed is intense, all reflex observation is rendered impossible, the mind cannot view as spectator; it is wholly occupied as an agent or patient. On the other hand, exactly in proportion as the mind concentrates its force in the act of reflexive observation, in the same proportion must the direct phaenomenon lose in vivacity, and consequently in the precision and individuality of its character.[35]

Three additional, equally significant, barriers arise from the mind's structure. As it is in the nature of mind to be a complex tangle of conscious acts and perceptions, the reflective consciousness finds it difficult to "weed out" the merely accidental phenomena of consciousness from conscious structures which are necessary. It is difficult to separate the merely habitual conscious acts from those which function as universal, *a priori* constants of all human experience.[36]

Furthermore, even if one has successfully identified the necessary structures of consciousness, it is impossible to understand their workings except serially or through the abstractive representation of them against an imaginary spatio-temporal field. To construct a model of the mind's behavior, it is impossible not to rely upon the very constitutive categories which the mind uses to construct the abstract notions of homogenous time and space. Yet, to describe the mind's workings as if they were *contained* within these categories, instead of being the events responsible for the production of them, is to undercut the pure description of mental phenomena which phenomenological reflexivity has as its ideal. Only for the materialist are there actual mental times and spaces.[37]

Finally, there is an additional and, indeed, insurmountable barrier which stands in the way of phenomenology's *perfect* achievement. It is memory.

Since it is the ideal of phenomenology to provide unmediated description of the most minute aspects of consciousness, it must begin with immediate experience. Immediate experience must provide the experiential atoms which phenomenology will descriptively distinguish and which nomology will turn into theories, laws, and models.

---

[35]Hamilton 375-376.

[36]Hamilton 379.

[37]Hamilton 377-379.

Unfortunately, we have access to these atoms only through our memories of them. Conscious experience is necessarily remembered experience. Since it is impossible to describe without remembering, it is impossible to give a phenomenological description of an object and to still retain that object's immediacy. No matter how brief the duration between experience and description, in that there is a duration, memory is called into play and phenomenology is experientially once removed.[38]

2.4.2. Nomology

Though these difficulties complicate phenomenology's task, Hamilton does not believe that they are fatal to it. Paradoxically, it is through the opacities of consciousness that phenomenological reflexivity discovers the instrument for producing descriptions of the mind's nomology. It is through the frustration of an idealized method that a practical method is engendered. Posed as problems for solution, the above difficulties result in the phenomenological searching-out of phenomenology's limits. Their solution also results in the discovery of the *a priori* structures of consciousness.

Returning to the last quotation, notice how the mind's nomology is revealed by the impotence of the phenomenological method. Hamilton argues that the attempt to describe certain sorts of mental states results in an alteration of those states. By intensely attending to an emotional state, that state vanishes. Similarly, that same emotional state may increase in intensity in proportion as it is left unattended. In his attempt to describe an emotional state, Hamilton achieves quite another end. He succeeds in discovering a relationship between attention and emotional intensity. Furthermore, he discovers that its mode of establishment proceeds directly from the limitations of the phenomenological method.

Because consciousness and phenomenology--which is essentially related to consciousness--are not perfectly reflexive, the nomologies of mind are observable. The inability of mind to turn itself inside-out, as it were, reveals an unbridgeable differentiation between thought as an act and thought as an artifact. Were it not for such an internal ordering, consciousness would be like the mythical worm Ouroboros, eternally swallowing its own tail, or like the Aristotelian god, who is thought thinking itself. There would be no point from which one could distinguish act from actor, contemplation from contemplator or thoughtful activity from passive content. The phenomenologist would be hopelessly lost in the endless contemplation of his own thought. The opaque, irreducible structures of consciousness, thus, function as the very conditions under which a description of mind's nomology can be provided.

In observing the alterations which the phenomenological method includes in the cognitive processes, Hamilton discovers four particularly important mental structures. The first is the subject-object dichotomy; the second is extension and retraction of attention; the third is memory; the fourth is unconscious latency.[39]

---

[38]Hamilton 379.

[39]Hamilton 195, 218-220, 233, 238, 339.

Hamilton argues that the subject-object distinction is an unavoidable precondition of consciousness not only because it is a product of the infant's first experiences of the world but also because it is the primordial source of every other dichotomy humans experience. The root of this dichotomy is the genetically primitive distinction between actor-acted upon, controller-controlled or perceiver-perceived which the young child spontaneously makes. It is evident to the infant that there is a difference between the sphere of his efficacy, which is under the control of his will, and the sphere of his impotency, which is beyond his control.[40] The former is related to his body and mind as well as the acts he can perform by using them. Later, he will define this sphere by including the possible instrumentalities which he may efficaciously employ to achieve his desires. The latter sphere consists of all things beyond the infant's control, all things which stand as an impediment to the fulfillment of his desires. The child quickly distinguishes between the control he exercises over his bodily functions--a control he has over the surrounding environment--a control which, in his early years, is quite slight. Later as he grows more intellectually sophisticated, he may recognize that this dichotomy can be extended to the processes of consciousness themselves.

In its most primitive extension to consciousness, the dichotomy is identified with the simple distinction between subject and object. The subject is associated with the cognitive complexes under the control of the ego or will, and the object is associated with anything standing over and against the subject and having its own weight and opacity. What chiefly served to define the object is its resistance to manipulation. Even when instrumentalities are effective in shaping an object into a desired form, the subject is aware of the object's resistant rigidity. The care that must be taken not to destroy the object's integrity is a demonstration of its otherness from the subject. Independent integrity and resistance to manipulation are how consciousness defines objectivity.

From one's early experience of the world and the distinction one naturally makes between oneself and psychic or somatic resistances, it becomes possible to generalize the properties one encounters into metaphysical distinctions. It becomes possible to describe the difference between subject and object in terms of activity and passivity or action and passion.

The distinction between activity and passivity is not, however, simply isomorphic to the distinction between the subject and its object. The relation between subject and object, though giving rise to the distinction between action and passion, is actually a complex bundle of active and passive influences. Both the subject and object have aspects which, relative to one another, are active and others which, relative to one another, are passive.

> Activity and passivity are not, therefore, in the manifestations of mind, distinct and independent phaenomena. . . . They are always conjoined. There is no operation of mind which is purely active; no affection which is purely passive. In every mental modification, action and passion

---

[40]Hamilton 225-256.

are the two necessary elements or factors of which it is composed. But though both are always present, each is not, however, always present in equal quantity.[41]

It is the activity of mind which characterizes its ability to arrange knowledge into orderly tableau, to ignore insignificant details and to attend to what it deems important. Likewise, it is the passivity of objects which enables them to be manipulated either physically or mentally. On the other hand, it is the activity of objects which prevents them from being bent either conceptually or mentally into any form the mind may wish. It is their activity which insures their integrity. It is the mind's passivity which, in the face of a resistant object in the face of a persistent perception or concept, prevents consciousnesss from shaping experience exactly as it wishes. Consciousness is a dialectical struggle between the subjectivity of mind and the objectivity of experience. But subjectivity and objectivity are more complexly defined by the passivities each possesses, as well. Consciousness as subjectivity is, thus, an aggregate of activities and passivities under the control of the ego but stimulated by the mind's encounter with experience.

From the pole of the subject, the subject-object relation is active when turned reflexively upon itself. From the object pole, however, the relation is passive. This means that the activity of consciousness completely undercuts its own structure in that, by reflexively turning upon itself, it makes part of itself a passive object standing opaquely against its own active interest. Consciousness can know anything only as an object. When it investigates itself as an object, the interest it takes in itself takes precedence over the act of interest which is taken as an object. Mind's unitary nature prevents it from maintaining more than one level of objectivity at any one time. To be able to know what it means to know while in the act of knowing would mean to know without an object. But this is impossible. The subject-object dichotomy cannot be bridged by conscious reflection because it is fundamental to consciousness. When the conscious mind reflexively attends to its own operations it may either construct a static icon of its own operations or it can attempt to grasp itself in action. If it takes the latter course, then it discovers not what it actively is but what it is like when engaged in retortion upon itself. Subjectivity is not transparent to subjectivity. The closest consciousness comes to knowing itself lucidly in its own activity is either by means of a constructed object or by means of the behavioral modifications it undergoes in retracting from itself. Either variety of retortion can disclose the stable structures of consciousness.

Another important mental structure is disclosed by the investigation into the subject-object dichotomy. This is the ability either to concentrate or dissipate attention.

Given any experiential field, there are certain portions of that field which stand out as being more or less malleable to the instrumentalities of consciousness. We have experience of the world as more or less likely to be understood, more or less able to be held in attentive grasp, more or less interesting. Those which can be focused upon as objects of intense concentration we sense as being more significant, more active, than

---

[41]Hamilton 310.

94

those which awaken no attention at all. The passive components of our experiential field are, likewise, considered insignificant because they have little effect upon consciousness. Active components of experience are judged more significant than the passive components because they provide objects which can be better clarified and brought into conscious resolution.

Some of the ability to focus upon an object in the experiential field is independent of that object's efficacy. Consciousness, itself, possesses an active capacity which enables it--with some difficulty--to focus upon experientially insignificant events and to bring these into experiential prominence. Similarly, it is a capability of the active aspect of consciousness to be able to diminish the significance of events, though they stand out as naturally quite prominent. With its active power to shape experience, the mind finds it possible to constitute its own reality. It can control experience's significance by homogenizing the prominence of events in the experiential field or by making events heterogeneous by increasing the prominence of some events and diminishing the prominence of others.[42]

In everyday experience, the activity of objects in the experiential field is a good guide to their significance, but to the philosopher or scientist these same events may be insignificant. Scientific concern with consciousness brings objects of little significance to the common man, into high resolution. The common man believes he can live his life well without giving these objects a moment's concern; for practical purposes they are irrelevant. Phenomenologists find it urgent to study these objects, however, because they believe that such study will reveal subtle conscious processes. Because of the weakness of these objects' prominence as compared against the foreground of efficacious objects of everyday experience, the phenomenologist is, at first, quite graceless at attending to mental phenomena. He often finds the most direct path to phenomenological observation barred.

Many of the objects which attract the attention of the phenomenologist are susceptible to the subtlest alterations of intentionality. If we concentrate intensely upon an emotion as it is experienced, then we alter the experience of that emotion and make its peculiar intentionality vanish. The conditions under which the ego can control the focusing of attention, or its dissipation, thus determine the conditions under which phenomenological description can be effective. There is, however, a class of phenomena which poses many difficulties for phenomenology because the intentionality associated with it makes effective phenomenological description practically impossible.

When one perceives a flower so that one's attention is riveted to it, the result is an experience having aesthetic and intellectual components all of which are directed toward or resultant from an intended object. Attending to a flower one experiences the object to which one is directed. When, however, in the act of attending to a flower one decides to shift the ray of attention away from the flower and to the observation of the act of attending to a flower, then the original experience vanishes. Attention, as an act,

---

[42]Hamilton 238.

must retain a thematic unity though it may take multiple objects.[43] One may attend to a flower bed, for example, but one cannot multiply the levels of attention about that experience of a flower bed at will. The motif of an act of attention invariably interferes with the experience of an object attended to, if that object is an act of attention. Though attention may function negatively to reveal those situations under which it cannot take an object without interfering with a conscious intention, its value in reflexively disclosing its own nature is limited. When an object has no integrity of its own, or when that integrity must be sustained by a constant act of attention, then that object will not be immediately susceptible to analysis. We may grant that attention has a valuable function in that it can reveal the constitution of many forms of experience, but it has its limits. Attention finds it difficult to examine its own intentionality.

The difficulty would be irresolvable if it were not for a third structure of consciousness which allows the frozen suspension of experience. If it were not for memory, Hamilton argues, science and, indeed, phenomenology would be impossible. There would be no means for observing intentional relations without causing those relations to be altered. Memory saves the phenomenological enterprise by making the observation of the active relations of consciousness possible; it allows the conversion of these dynamic processes into static objects. These objects are then easily related to the subjectivity of consciousness. It is memory's unique character in bringing about the production of experiential icons which qualifies it as an independent structure of consciousness.

Memory is a form of mediate knowledge. It cannot be considered immediate knowledge because it consists of the residues of past experience. In an act of memory one brings to prominence "a present state of mind which we are conscious of not as absolute, but as relative to and representing, another state of mind, and accompanied with the belief that the state of mind, as now represented, has actually been."[44] In an act of memory, all one immediately knows is the representation before one. The correspondence between a memory and past experience seems like a tenuous connection upon which to base knowledge, there are methods for testing and insuring the accuracy of memory.

The most obvious test of memory is direct observation. If one doubts that something *was*, insofar as that thing may still be, one can check one's memory of the thing or event against the thing or event itself. One can compare icon with model. This is the comparative test of memory. If, however, the memory is of something which has, subsequently, passed out of existence or out of reach, then one has recourse to another test. This is the test of memory by consistency. It proceeds by the comparison of a particular memory against the whole field of present and remembered experience. If all experience is consistent with one's memory of that particular experience, then that memory is probably accurate.

---

[43]Hamilton 243-244.

[44]Hamilton 218.

The above represents the tests of memory. There is a method by which the certainty of memory may be enhanced while it is being formed. One can preclude--or, at very least, diminish--the possibility that one's memory will be in error by applying a method which is part of phenomenology. This is the method of focused observation. By excluding irrelevant experiences from the field of conscious attention, one can increase the likelihood that the memories of the objects of attention will be firmly entrenched. By concentrating upon one's experience one can intensify one's memory of it. One improves a faulty memory by focusing one's undivided attention upon significant experiences.

There is one further difficulty with memory: as an artifact, a memory is determined by both the conscious and unconscious states which contributed to the field of experience at the time the memory was formed. Memories are, thus, limited to the set of conscious modifications experienced at the time the original perception took place. Thus, for phenomenology to succeed, a study of attention and attentive states would have to include a taxonomy of all conditions which alter the perception of phenomena. It would be necessary to match each memory with the attentional modifications consciousness was undergoing at the time the memory was formed. From this one could develop sequences of conscious alterations which might be quite valuable as catalogues of the conscious instrumentalities available for phenomenological observation. One would also discover the alterations worked upon phenomena by conscious states.

The importance of memory to the phenomenology of mind is evident when one considers the difficulties involved in the attentive observation of the intentional acts of consciousness. It is by means of memory that intentional processes may be preserved and later produced for examination. It is by memory that the dissipation of an intense attentive state may be circumvented. This state can be transformed into an object, an artifact which can be examined at leisure, and reproduced again and again for inspection.

The final structure of consciousness which is revealed by Hamilton's phenomenological investigations is that of latency. By the latent structures of consciousness Hamilton means structures which manifest themselves as not under the direct control of volition but as contributory constituents of the higher mental processes. Hamilton has three classes of phenomena in mind. First, there are acts which, though not manifesting themselves at every moment of conscious life, do regularly manifest themselves as recurrent behavioral tendencies. These might be called habits. Second, there are phenomena which, though not regularly existing on the surface of consciousness, spring into existence when relations are perceived or things are remembered. These may be called associations. Third, there are phenomena which manifest themselves as feelings or attitudes in conscious life but which have their origins beyond its scope. This faculty might be called the unconscious.[45]

What Hamilton has to say about each of these faculties is trivial in comparison to the treatment they have received subsequently by Freud and others. What is significant about his discussion is the role he assigns to them. Hamilton rightly recognizes in them the origin of the behavioral surds which cannot be discovered in the rational structures

---

[45]Hamilton 339.

of consciousness. In latency we have the origin of the creative genius of man, the genius which allows the association of unlike ideas to produce something new. Latency also serves to explain the compulsiveness with which men reject new ideas or spend their lives attempting to discover new ones. Finally, latency covers all those desires which have no reference to rational processes of thought but which are often the motive forces behind human culture.

3. The Objects of Hamiltonian Phenomenology

Hamilton divides phenomena into three varieties: cognition, feelings, and conations; these varieties exhaust human experience of the world. Cognitions are those phenomena which by virtue of their formal properties are productive of descriptions or predictions about spatio-temporal experience. Feelings are those phenomena whose formal and material properties are such that they are aesthetically effective. Conations are those phenomena whose material properties and formal construction are such that they are productive of descriptions about morality and ethics. Each variety of phenomena has a corresponding categorical *a priori*. Thus, one cannot hope to explain the formal principles that found either cognitions, aesthesis or conation; they are merely given and can only be worked out according to a logic which is derivative from their *a priori* natures. In postulating the division of phenomena in this fashion, Hamilton divides the forms of knowledge into three parts whose only common methods are logic, analysis, synthesis, and hypothesis. There is no question of phenomena belonging to the cognitive realm being subject to aesthetic or conative analysis, although he does allow the possibility that both aesthetic and conative objects can be subjected to cognitive analyses. This last methodological asymmetry is allowed because cognitive phenomena do not have parity with aesthetic or conative phenomena. Cognitive phenomena are devoid of aesthetic or conative components but the converse is not true. Both aesthetic phenomena and conative phenomena have cognitive components, or they would be utterly unintelligible.

Believing consciousness to be constitutive of all experience, Hamilton describes the three varieties of phenomena as though they are explicable through the concepts of psychology. He does not subject them to a pure philosophical analysis by way of the *a priori* conditions of knowledge in the Kantian fashion. Nevertheless, what emerges are conclusions which closely resemble those of Kant, though in Hamilton's case they are tied to the mechanics of mind and not to the structures of a purely philosophical analysis of consciousness. Because mind mediates whatever lies behind experience, its relations to phenomena, and particularly its operations which construct phenomena, play as active a role in determining what a phenomenon is as does the material content which is given in the phenomenon. Phenomena, for Hamilton, are as much vehicles for disclosing the inner workings of the mind as they are embodiments of cognitive, aesthetic and conative experiences. The psychologistic analysis of phenomena, thus, has value in that it discloses the contributions mind makes to experience. But psychological analysis cannot be encouraged at the expense of epistemological analysis, nor can it be substituted for it.

Epistemological analysis--analysis which is concerned with phenomena as the embodiments of cognitive, aesthetic and conative experiences--is of particular significance to sciences other than psychology because such analysis results in purified phenomena, phenomena which by being reduced to their *a priori* and formal components can be employed to refound the sciences on more certain bases. However, the psychologistic study of mind's constitution of its objects must be annexed to this epistemological analysis because it is one of the means by which an epistemological analysis is made possible. To be able to understand consciousness' operation in the constitution of phenomena is to be able to control it because knowledge of the mind's constitutive contributions comes only through actual attentional modifications. To exercise such control is the only means available for the disclosure of an uninterpreted phenomenon. Only through the coordinated application of epistemological and psychological analyses can nomology and ontology be developed without the interference of sedimented concepts, habitual thought and habitual moral and aesthetic responses.

Hamilton's understanding of phenomena has much to recommend it, particularly in its anticipation of a number of features of Husserlian phenomenology such as the constructive role consciousness plays in the experience of objects as well as the necessity of returning to the phenomenal giveness of things in order to refound the sciences upon uninterpreted appearance. However, Hamilton's phenomenology is defective in that he couches his positive anticipations of Husserl's phenomenology in a language--which like the neurophysiological terminology of Lambert--refers to a tacit model of psychology. In Hamilton's case, it is a model of psychology which is not particularly materialistic but, nevertheless, replete with equations between "mental energies" (and other kindred terms) and intentional acts. Like Lambert's phenomenology, the phenomenology of Hamilton can be subjected to criticism for not avoiding theoretical contamination. By being chained to an explanatory model which is empirical, and likely to become outdated, Hamilton's phenomenology is, thus, a matter of the language in which it is couched and not a matter of the fundamental accuracy of its phenomenological descriptions. Likewise, the phenomena disclosed by it are likely to be interpreted only in the language of the psychological model with which it is associated. As soon as the model dies, the technical vocabulary dies. Along with the technical vocabulary, all phenomenological descriptions which appear to depend upon the outdated model (and its associated discourse) die also. From this, it may be concluded that a goal of phenomenological theory should be the development of a descriptive language which is not theory-laden nor susceptible to invalidation by the vicissitudes of scientific development. It is this language which should found theory and not *vice versa*.

4. The End of the Hamiltonian Phenomenology

In contrast to the ultimate and proximate ends of the Hegelian phenomenology, the ends of the Hamiltonian phenomenology are less distinct and more diffuse. Like Hegel and Robison, Hamilton intends to create a science which will result in descriptions which are fundamentally reliable so that the explanatory sciences will not be burdened with presuppositions. Therefore, the ultimate end of the Hamiltonian phenomenology is most accurately described as the creation of a system of rigorous nomological and ontological descriptions. On the way to this ultimate end, Hamilton--in keeping with the significance he accords the constitutive role of consciousness--interposes, as the proximate end of his phenomenology, the development of rigorous and analytical descriptions of observations which have been controlled to eliminate importations not given in the pure experience of the phenomena. The objects of these descriptions can either be mental or physical phenomena occurring consecutively or concurrently in space and time, but they must be described without reference to theoretical constructs. From these neutral observational descriptions, nomology and ontology can build their explanations.

5. The Hamiltonian Phenomenological Technique

In purpose, there is little difference between the Hamiltonian and Robisonian phenomenological techniques. Like Robison, Hamilton describes his phenomenology as having much the same end as history. Like history, phenomenology is to be a narration of consecutive events in time, concomitant events in space or both. But, as such, it is always to be the result of observation and not inference. Hamiltonian phenomenology has as its purpose the observation and analysis of phenomena. It is ordered to exclude anything which is hypothetical or not produced by careful analysis. But in addition to an essentially Robisonian program of analytical description, Hamilton also allows the introduction of simple experiments of consciousness designed to induce variations in the appearances in order to separate adventitious from essential phenomenal properties. In this respect, the Hamiltonian technique bears a resemblance to those of Lambert and Husserl; conversely, the Lambertian and Husserlian methods of perspectival variation may be considered thought experiments.

Those steps which he associates with the scientific operations he calls 'analysis' are those Hamilton most properly considers phenomenology. What Hamilton intends by analysis is the conscious decomposition of phenomena (objects) into apodictic parts which are free from hypothetical importations. The resultant narratives are to recognize and describe only the analyzed parts of the decomposed objects without reference to the original tissue of inference or belief which holds these parts together in meaningful wholes. Since Hamilton recognizes consciousness as fundamentally constitutive of the object, his explanation of analysis is worked out within the context of psychology (or philosophy of mind), the science he believes founds the other inductive sciences.

Hamilton provides no clearly conceived procedures by which a philosopher can begin phenomenological analyses. Rather, his description of phenomenological analysis does little more than point out the conscious operation to be used instrumentally to accomplish phenomenological analyses. This operation is reflexive attention.

Analysis of phenomena--that is the separation of the objective constituents from the conscious contributions to appearance--is accomplished by the mind's attending to its self-reflexivity. But this attention is at every point frustrated by the fact that attention introduces an additional condition into that medium which it wishes to study. To attend to the act of loving, while trying to keep that conscious act focused on its object, is impossible. Consciousness cannot be perfectly polythematic when reflection is engaged; consciousness cannot transparently understand itself while engaged in another object-oriented act. Hamilton's solution to this dilemma is to make the object of attention the very alteration in the object oriented-act which is induced by attention. This means that attention becomes an instrument for studying the conscious construction of the world by inducing regular changes in it and then watching the invariant residue (or object content) which remains when the object constituting act is disengaged. If one wishes to study a loved object for example, one attempts to attend to the relation between the object of love and the subject of love. What happens is that the relation immediately dissolves as soon as it is examined. What is left is a disengaged object (the beloved) at one pole and a disengaged subject at the other. This disengagement then allows the consideration of the object without reference to that relation of love which is superadded to the primordial experience of the object. The relation of love is put out of play and unbiased judgments about the ugliness, height, and weight of the object may be made. In the same way, all relations between object and subject, which are not the primordial constituents of the object, may be attended to and thus put out of play. Any relation which is not an essential property of the object may be thus disengaged and demonstrated to be a contribution of consciousness. Phenomenological analysis, interpreted as the focusing of the ray of attention, is a destructive technique but a very effective one for separating conscious loadings of an object from its primordial giveness. Even so, its range of applications are limited insofar as some acts of consciousness merely evaporate when made the objects of reflexive attention.

CHAPTER VI

WHEWELL: THE ROLE OF PHENOMENOLOGY IN THE INDUCTIVE SCIENCES

1. The Whewellian Phenomenology in Context

After Hamilton, William Whewell was the next English philosopher to think innovatively about phenomenology and its relevance to scientific method. Unlike Hamilton, Whewell had the rare distinction of being both a practicing scientist and a ruminating philosopher. But Whewell was a rarity in another sense. He was a thinker who might--for lack of a more suggestive metaphor--be called an intellectual amphibian because he was equally at home in a wide variety of intellectual environments. In *Modes of Thought*, Alfred North Whitehead quotes a rhyme which he claims is consonant with the legend at Trinity College about Whewell. The verse goes:

> I am Master of this College:
> And what I know not,
> Is not knowledge.[1]

And Sydney Smith, as if to gloss this poem, succinctly says of Whewell: "Science was his forte and omniscience his foible."[2] Among his many accomplishments, Whewell was an active member of the Royal Society, the British Association for the Advancement of Science and the Geological Society. He held chairs in mineralogy and moral philosophy at Cambridge, was a Master of Trinity College, Cambridge, and an ordained Deacon in the Church of England. He was selected as one of eight contributors to the Bridgewater Theses--he wrote a work on *Astronomy and General Physics Considered with Reference to Natural Theology*--and made original contributions to fields as diverse as crystallography, physical dynamics, physical statics, engineering, economics, scientific nomenclature, hydrostatics, mineralogy, meteorology, the history of ecclesiastical architecture, moral philosophy, theology and, of course, the history and philosophy of

---

[1]Alfred North Whitehead, *Modes of Thought* (New York: The Free Press, 1966) 43.

[2]William Whewell, *The Philosophy of the Inductive Sciences Founded upon Their History*, 2 vols. (New York: Johnson Reprint Corp., 1967) 1: xiv.

science.[3] Insofar as these experiences broadened and shaped Whewell's understanding of the inductive sciences, they also influenced his understanding of phenomenology's role in these sciences.

Although Whewell employed the term 'phenomenology' in his *History of the Inductive Sciences* (1837), his mature understanding of the concept and its relation to scientific epistemology is best expressed in his later, great work *Philosophy of the Inductive Sciences*.   This work appeared in 1840--a mere three years after the voluminous earlier work--and was designed to serve as a moral, or postscript, to its predecessor.[4] Because the *Philosophy of the Inductive Sciences* represents Whewell's attempt to distill what is efficacious in scientific method as well as to explain what this distillation means for epistemology in general, it is the best work to examine in order to gain an appreciation of the Whewellian phenomenology. For this reason, the *Philosophy of the Inductive Sciences* will be the single textual field which will be mined with the intent of uncovering the nuggets of meaning Whewell attached to the word 'phenomenology.'

The *Philosophy of the Inductive Sciences* is an unusual work both in structure and execution. Superficially, it resembles Bacon's *New Organon* and it contains internal evidence which indicates that Whewell intended to write it, *mutatis mutandis*, as the nineteenth century version of Bacon's classic. Whewell's use of literary forms such as aphorisms remind one of Bacon's earlier work. But aside from cosmetic resemblances, essentially--and particularly as regards its epistemology--the *Philosophy of the Inductive Sciences* is not in the mainstream of British empiricism. Nowhere in it does Whewell really take a cue from Bacon. Instead, as with Hamilton, the source of Whewell's inspiration is Kantian epistemology. But unlike Hamilton, Whewell has no intention of either transposing Kant's thought into English or of parroting Kantian philosophical arguments. Rather, Whewell intends, by returning to the root evidence for the transcendental method, to demonstrate that the Kantian epistemology everywhere permeates the common practice of the natural sciences. However, in his attempt to demonstrate the omnipresence of Kantian principles, Whewell's honesty about scientific practice makes him come to conclusions which, if not antithetical to Kantianism, are certainly not Kantian orthodoxy. It is this portion of the *Philosophy of the Inductive Sciences* which demonstrates Whewell's proclivity to trust in observation above all else. It is this portion which is phenomenological in that it is a description of the way science is actually practiced. From these descriptions and from the deductions which are implied by them, Whewell's most important discoveries issue.

---

[3]Whewell 1: ix-xix.

[4]Whewell 1: xxi.

2. Whewellian Phenomenology

Unlike earlier interpretations, Whewell's understanding of phenomenology is equivocal. On one hand, he makes phenomenology a concrete part of the palaetiological sciences. In this capacity, phenomenology is a unique method given over to a unique domain of objects. Palaetiological phenomenology is historical, atheoretical and quite primitive. On the other hand, looming behind Whewell's discussion of the other sciences is a notion of transdisciplinary phenomenology which represents a generalizable method applicable to any discipline. Like the phenomenology contained in Hamilton's *Lectures*, this variety of phenomenology is essential to the development of all sciences; it is a method which, because it is enlivened by theory, leads to new discoveries. At face value, these two meanings of 'phenomenology' seem quite different but, as different as these meanings seem, they are not unbridgeable. They intersect under another interpretation.

Though Whewell's understanding of palaetiological phenomenology seems at odds with his understanding of transdisciplinary phenomenology, the former is merely an instantiation of the latter at an earlier evolutionary stage. Palaetiological phenomenology is that method which provides the possibility of a scientific history based upon precise observation. But the development of phenomenology, in all its forms, is linked to refinement of inductive techniques.

Though an old and venerable discipline, history's appreciation of inductive methods is quite young. History has not yet developed the inductive tools necessary to perfect its phenomenology. Thus, palaetiological phenomenology is stunted. In contrast, those sciences which are younger by virtue of years, but which have better formal methods, possess phenomenologies which have far outpaced the primitive techniques of palaetiological phenomenology. The formally rigorous methods of natural science have accelerated the evolution of the phenomenological techniques. Nevertheless, both palaetiological phenomenology and transdisciplinary phenomenology share a common meaning. They both represent the same method of observation at two different stages of development and levels of generality. Palaetiological phenomenology is a parochial throwback, a science tied to the primitive inductive methods of the historical sciences. In contrast, transdisciplinary phenomenology is a progressive technique, a science perfectly adapted to the formal methods of the natural sciences. However, the complete significance of the ambiguity in Whewell's understanding of phenomenology, and the significance of its resolution, can be appreciated only after the philosophy which underlies the inductive sciences is understood.

Whewell expresses as the general intention behind the *Philosophy of the Inductive Sciences* the goal of understanding "the essence and conditions of all real knowledge" and of explaining "the best methods for the discovery of new truths."[5] This is not best accomplished speculatively but through a study of those disciplines which have proven themselves by yielding indubitable and enduring methods and truths. In other words,

---

[5]Whewell 1: 1.

104

the best method for getting at the cognitive and experiential conditions which underlie sure knowledge is to make a study of those disciplines whose methods work.

2.1. The Whewellian Notion of Science

The class of disciplines which have effective methods for arriving at truth are termed "sciences." They are those disciplines to which both history and the learned testify as having cumulative evolutions marked by the discovery of universal laws. Of the sciences, Whewell makes a distinction between two groups. The material or experiential sciences are those disciplines designed to produce an understanding of the material world "by collecting general truths from particular observed facts."[6] This method is called "induction." But the material sciences and their inductive methods do not have claim to the only admissible scientific procedures. There is another class of sciences which appropriates an entirely different domain of objects as well as different rational technique. This is the class of the pure or formal sciences.[7]

The pure sciences do not engage in the collection of inductions derived from experiences of the world nor in the inductive abstraction of general laws from individual inductions. Rather, the formal sciences are directed to trace the laws consequent from the *a priori* ideas indigenous to consciousness. They are oriented to reveal the most extensive possible system of logical relations and abstractions which follow from these ideas. The method by which they achieve their object is reductive and consists of reasoning not from particular to general but from *a priori* ideas to the consequences which follow necessarily from them. The formal sciences are the most rigorous of all sciences because they produce ineluctable derivations from indubitable axioms. But they are as sterile as they are rigorous. They can say nothing of the world of experience, unless observations about the world are introduced into them. But this is possible only through induction. Induction is, therefore, seen by Whewell to be the most fruitful of the scientific methods because it makes sense of phenomena and material beings and not only of ideas. It is induction which is the primary object of study in the *Philosophy of the Inductive Sciences*. Deduction is considered only as a method which is employed to strengthen the discoveries of induction.[8]

Having delineated his object of study, Whewell must consider how best to describe the methods of the inductive sciences. To write a philosophy of them, he must have a rigorous means for describing them. Whewell is, thus, in the peculiar position of requiring a scientific method for the investigation of scientific method. The protocol at which Whewell arrives is descriptive in the same sense as the phenomenologies upon which the inductive sciences depend. The key to the

---

[6]Whewell 1: 2-3.

[7]Whewell 1: 2-3.

[8]Whewell 2: 92-93.

phenomenological study of induction is the ability to provide a fortuitous decomposition of inductive method into its constituent elements.[9]

Behind his treatment of scientific method, Whewell harbors two assumptions which shape all his thinking. First, he believes the themes which found the inductive sciences are *a priori* laws of consciousness; these laws describe structures which exist *in potentia* prior to scientific experience of the world. Second, he believes that, though the necessary ground of science, these *a priori* laws are discovered and elucidated gradually by means of a dialectic with experience. The discovery of the *a priori* structures of scientific consciousness depends upon man's conscious struggle to understand nature. Ideas become clear, distinct and indubitable only as the techniques man employs to study the external world are perfected. As these techniques improve, the empirical world reflects a clearer image of embryonic ideas already in consciousness. The investigation of empirical reality is a process of self-discovery: by means of his *a priori* ideas about reality, man is able to construct tools and rationales by which to study nature and, in the process, to clarify the very ideas which made these tools and rationales first possible.

2.2. The Whewellian Syzygies

Whewell distinguishes two different classes of ideas which contribute to the scientific discovery of the world. The first class consists of paired antitheses or opposites which express the parameters of human thought. These paired opposites are aspects of a greater underlying antithesis fundamental to human existence; they are particularizations of that experience we all have of the duality of existence. The second class consists of the single, unopposed motifs which make the various branches of the sciences possible. Some of these ideas are also recognized as fundamental to our everyday experience of the world, though it is in their scientifically refined forms that their importance in the constitution of experience is most clearly seen.

Eight antitheses or syzygies constitute the class representing experience's fundamental dualism. These aspectual pairs define the ideational limits placed upon the conceivability and protocol of the different sciences, but they have no direct bearing upon the objects that these sciences study. These antitheses do not add positive content or direction to any particular science but, instead, represent the conditions which found the possibility of all scientific knowledge. These pairs are better termed 'syzygies' than 'antitheses'--even though Whewell never uses the former term--because they are interdependent; their contents are yoked and inseparable.[10] When one thinks of one term of these pairs--the other term appears consciously contrasted with it. One can have

---

[9]Whewell 1: 12.

[10]Whewell 1: 44-45.

knowledge of one term of a syzygy only because one also has knowledge of its antithetical mate.[11]

2.2.1. Thoughts and things

The first syzygy, Whewell considers, is the antithesis between thought and things. Whewell holds this dichotomy to be the "simplest and most idiomatic" because it is immediately given to even the most unreflective individuals.[12] It is based upon the experience of thoughts being the thinker's property, subject to his purely private manipulations and engendered at will. In contrast, other things seem to exist in their own right detached from personalities and outside of consciousness. These things can be heard, tested and touched but they always stand apart from consciousness because they are never completely in its control and never completely reduced by it. In relation to thoughts, consciousness is active; it shapes and controls them. In relation to things, however, consciousness--at least initially--is passive; things have a substantiality all their own; they act upon experiencing subjects and their senses.

2.2.2. Necessary and empirical truths

The second syzygy, the antithesis of necessary and experiential truths, depends upon the polarization of thoughts and things. Necessary truths find their origin in the necessary structure of thoughts, but contingent or experiential truths derive from the passive observation of the external world, the world of things.[13]

Whewell interprets the difference between necessary and contingent truths in the conventional Kantian fashion. Necessary truths are those which, because they are endemic to consciousness and its capabilities, cannot be thought of as being other than they are. That $12 + 15 = 27$, that all angles of a Euclidean triangle are equal to $180°$, or that knowledge cannot be imagined as other than governed by the Whewellian syzygies are all examples of necessary truths, truths which are self-evident. In contrast, that the earth is the third planet from the sun, that the Germans have lost two world wars, that Henry Ford invented the Model T, all of these are truths only as it so happens; things might have occurred differently had the circumstances been different. This latter kind of truth is termed 'a truth of experience' or 'a truth of contingency'

---

[11]Whewell 1: 29. The investigation of opposing ideational parameters Whewell says he learned from modern German philosophers. Whewell, thus, possibly corroborates his dependence upon Kant, Fichte, Schelling or Hegel. But in contrast to typically posed philosophical antitheses, Whewell's syzygies are categorically inconsistent. Though they are supposed to be rooted in a single, underlying duality, they consist of epistemological, ontological, methodological and criteriological pairs grouped together in no order which expresses these pairs' dependence upon one another. A further problem with Whewell's discussion of the syzygies is that it has little apparent relevance to the project of the *Philosophy of the Inductive Sciences*, except to demonstrate the indispensability of particular mental structures to experience. Unfortunately, Whewell does not concern himself with how these syzygies can be used as tools for the study of consciousness. But simply because Whewell does not discuss the significance of the syzygies to the natural sciences (and to the phenomenological study of consciousness in general) does not mean that such a connection does not exist or that such a connection is irrelevant.

[12]Whewell 1: 17.

[13]Whewell 1: 9, 58-59.

because acquaintance with the way things have been, but *not necessarily had to have been*, allows assent to their truth. No self-evident necessity is binding here. History is apprehended as a chain of unique events. Although it may be possible to provide good reasons why some events occur, experiential knowledge always contains a synthetic component which transcends the facts taken alone, and lone facts are, of course, always otherwise imaginable.[14]

Necessary and contingent truths hold particular significance for the study of the inductive sciences because these truths constitute the forms of reasoning which the inductive sciences employ. Necessary truths obtain from a syllogism or a chain of syllogisms which are premised upon more fundamental necessary truths. Experiential truths possess no similar certainty. They are derived from experiences of a number of occasions sufficient to justify the supposition that a general law holds between these occasions. A notion is then constructed under which experiences are grouped as a demonstration of this notion's support. The process for syllogistically arriving at necessary truths Whewell terms "deduction," and the process of reasoning to arrive at truths by multiplying experiences without referring to syllogisms or necessary truths Whewell terms "induction."

2.2.3. Induction and deduction

Induction and deduction are the third Whewellian syzygy. Like the other syzygies, deduction and induction represent complementary constituents of thought which, no matter how interdependent, oppose one another. In deduction, reasoning proceeds "from general truths to particular applications of them."[15] In induction, this order is reversed. Induction proceeds "from particular observations to a general truth which includes them."[16] Whewell describes deductive reasoning as occurring in a downward direction since universal propositions are imaginatively represented as standing above particulars. Induction, in contrast, is the movement of reason upwards. Necessary truths are discovered much in the same way as the sums of arithmetic problems: once one understands the meaning and necessity of arithmetic relations and operations, the solutions of particular problems follow with an easy compulsion. Induction, in contrast, is more like the guess one makes at a child's riddle: one collects all the disjoint clues under an explanation which unites them all.[17] Deductive conclusions are more certain than inductive conclusions, but deduction is more sterile and uninteresting. Induction carries more interest with it because it lacks the certainty of deduction and because it is directed toward a world of things. Induction carries with it our interest and curiosity about why things are the way they are, a curiosity which is intensified when evidence is sketchy. Induction produces new knowledge which is new in the most interesting

---

[14]Whewell 1: 19.

[15]Whewell 1: 22-23.

[16]Whewell 1: 22-23.

[17]Whewell 1: 23.

sense because inductive knowledge cannot be reduced to elements or premises already given in its data; a heuristic must be imported from beyond empirical experience. Deduction is closed upon itself; it is unable to reveal anything which is not already contained in its premises.

The ability of induction to carry one beyond premises and bare phenomena points to the peculiar intentionality characteristic of the mental processes engaged by inductive thinking. In deduction, the reasoning from axioms or general principles can be accomplished quite mechanically, yielding valid deductions even when premises are false. One merely memorizes the common deductive forms--as the Medieval theologians did--and if one can cast ideas in the proper propositional form, one can deduce flawlessly. But induction is a different matter. Induction includes a synthesizing act of consciousness which cannot be reduced to an infallible procedure. What induction requires is that the scientist makes an inductive leap which transcends the particular facts given as the data for the inductive judgment. The scientist must bring together in a synthetic act of consciousness a new arrangement or articulation of the facts which is not given in the experience of the facts alone. The scientist must impose, from beyond the field of facts, a new principle of intelligibility--*a principle of connexion* as Whewell calls it--which lends to those facts an explanation which illuminates and explains them. The result of induction is that facts are seen in the light of a theory, a light brilliant enough to make the facts fuse with it to become indistinguishable from it.[18]

2.2.4. Theory and fact

The next syzygy--that of theory and fact--stands in close relation to the inductive pole of the syzygy of the techniques of reasoning. As Whewell puts it, "A Theory is an Inductive Proposition, and the Facts are the particular observations from which . . . such Propositions are inferred by Induction."[19] More properly, the antithesis between theories and facts may be construed as an analogy between thoughts and things because a theory stands in relation to its component facts as a thought stands to the things which it intends, "for a Theory (that is, a true Theory) may be described as a Thought which is contemplated distinct from Things and seen to agree with them; while a Fact is a combination of our Thoughts with Things in so complete agreement that we do not regard them as separate."[20] A theory is precisely this: an inductive proposition (or set of propositions) explaining a mass of facts and containing more in its explanation than can be discovered in the facts alone. A theory, like an induction, adds something which is not given in the facts but which, nevertheless, proves indispensable for seeing those facts in intelligible configuration. So convincing may a theory become that the facts--as separable data--may disappear altogether and become so blended with the theory's hypothetical content that only a new fact, a welded conglomerate of old facts and new

---

[18]Whewell 2: 55.

[19]Whewell 1: 23-24.

[20]Whewell 1: 24.

hypotheses, remains. Whewell believes this fusion of theory and fact to be the common matter of everyday experience. Ultimately, theory and facts are relative terms. Thus, experience of reality is ubiquitously theory-laden.

> . . . the distinction between Theory . . . and Fact is this: that in Theory the Ideas are conceived as distinct from the Facts: in Facts, though Ideas may be involved, they are not, in our apprehension, separated from the sensations. In a Fact, the Ideas are applied so readily and so familiarly, and incorporated with the sensation so entirely, that we do not see *them*, we see through *them*. . . . And thus, a true Theory is a Fact; a Fact is a familiar Theory. That which is a Fact under one aspect is a Theory under another. The most recondite Theories when firmly established are Facts: the simplest Facts involve something of the nature of Theory.[21]

The indistinguishability of fact and theory calls for an explanation of how this indistinguishability is possible and how the confusion of fact and theory can be avoided. The possibility of confounding fact and theory, as well as the possibility for avoiding such confusion, is explained by the fifth syzygy, the antithesis of ideas and sensations.

2.2.5. Ideas and sensations

The syzygy of ideas and sensations is ontologically prior to the syzygy of theory and fact because the former is a reflex of consciousness, but the latter presupposes the existence of the former plus conscious acts such as manipulation, reflection and deliberation. No one thinks without the automatic emergence of both ideas and sensations. Ideas stand in relation to sensations as that which provides structure stands in relation to that which accepts structure. Ideas, unlike sensations, do not originate from a source external to consciousness but exist as potential configurations of sensations awaiting the appropriate sensations to fulfill them. This is not to say, however, that ideas are passive with respect to sensations. Sensations are impossible without ideas just as ideas are impossible without sensations. Sensations have no predisposed forms which when acted upon are molded into ideas. Only ideas can give form to sensations. But there is no real priority in ideas except as potentials waiting to embody sensorial content. Genetically, therefore, neither interpreted ideas nor interpreted sensations possess a priority of emergence.[22]

---

[21]Whewell 1:40. The suggestion that one "sees *through*" familiar theories, as if these theories were instruments like the tube and optics of a telescope, is quite telling. Even more telling is Whewell's assertion that in facts ideas and sensations cannot be disengaged. In true theories, as in facts, ideas (the Principles of construction) and sensations (the formless content of ideas) are melded together. Theories become facts if their ideational constituents become indistinguishable from their constituent sensations. Theories remain theoretical only as this remains impossible. Thus, Whewell believes that ⌐ sublated theoretic intentionality permeates conscious experience of the world. The world cannot be interpreted without the imposition of inherited, collective human representations. Social and scientific realities are the products of presupposed theories, theories so intuitively part of everyday perceptions that their theoretical content goes unrecognized. Whewell does not believe that the theory-ladenness of reality relativizes experience, however. Indeed, it is Whewell's purpose to demonstrate the legitimate method by which those judgments about experience which have not been arrived at scientifically can be tested.

[22]Whewell 1: 42-44. None of this is to say that ideas and sensations are not contrastable. We do have ideas--very abstract ideas--which are relatively devoid of sensorial content. And we can ideally intuit what a non-sensorial idea might be like. We can not, however, *visualize* such an idea. The word 'visualize' is dependent for its meaning upon certain acts of consciousness which allow us to give sensorial content to abstractions. Conversely, though we can focus

2.2.6. Reflexion and sensation

Whewell's discussion of the sixth syzygy, that of reflexion and sensation, is a reiteration of much he discussed concerning the fifth syzygy. Again, he stresses the inseparability of each pole but adds little new information to his discussion of ideas and sensations. He does lay emphasis upon the processional and volitional aspects of reflexion in order to contrast them with the automatic, passive aspects of sensation. Reflexion is the mental act by which already formed sensations are ordered, compared and used. As is the case with the syzygy of ideas and sensations, the syzygy of reflexion and sensation is integral. Even though sensation seems detachable from reflexion by virtue of its apparent temporal priority, Whewell observes that even the most primitive sensation is a potential for conditioning by conscious reflexion. Without the interaction between sensation and reflexion, the confusion between fact and theory would never obtain. The conscious acts which are responsible for reflexion also bear the responsibility for the confusion by which theories are transformed into facts and ideas into sensations.

2.2.7. Subject and object

Consciousness of the volitional component of sensation gives rise to the seventh syzygy, that of subject and object. In perceptual experience, the individual is aware that he has little conscious control over the mechanisms which convey the external world. He can, of course, stop up his ears or shut his eyes, but in doing either he is aware that he is merely constructing barriers to prevent the outside world from impinging upon his senses. From such experience, the mind misconstrues itself as passive rather than active. Its operations are imagined to be mere reflexes of external objects. However delusive this initial experience may be, it serves the useful function of revealing the distinction between the self and a world never completely in control; it reveals the distinction between what one is and that which is distinguishable from one.[23] Though Whewell admits that the distinction between subject and object is a legitimate one, and that perception is trustworthy insofar as it brings cognizance of this distinction, he does not believe that the naive interpretation of perception as a passive act represents a reliable relation between the human subject and his field of objects. From the emphasis accorded the constructive role of consciousness, it follows that Whewell's understanding of perception is one that gives consciousness a more active role in perceptual constitution than it has in the epistemology of the empiricists. Nevertheless, Whewell does admit that perceptions convey knowledge of things existing beyond man's private mental life. Because we can form intuitive, non-sensory approximations of ideas, we can distinguish a polarity between the components which we add to experience and the

---

our attention upon a patch of red and, yet, ignore the significance of that patch to the rest of the sensorial field, we cannot undercut the reality of the visual field itself; we cannot sense red without simultaneously constituting the spatial characteristics which are ground for the perception of any color and which, according to Whewell, are ideationally constructed in a manner analogous to ideas in the control of the volition.

[23]Whewell 1: 26.

components of experience which come from beyond the closed workings of consciousness. The world can be imaginatively partitioned into two poles: one which is identified with conscious subjects and one which is identified with their objects.

> According to the technical language of old writers, a thing and its qualities are described as *subject* and *attributes*; and thus a man's faculties and acts are attributes of which he is the *subject*. The mind is the *subject* in which ideas inhere. Moreover, the man's faculties and acts are employed upon external objects; and from objects all his sensations arise. Hence the part of a man's knowledge which belongs to his own mind, is *subjective*: that which flows in upon him from the world external to him, is *objective*. And as in man's contemplation of nature, there is always some act of thought which depends upon himself, and some matter of thought which is independent of him, there is, in every part of his knowledge, a subjective and an objective element. The combination of the two elements, the subjective or ideal, and the objective or observed, is necessary in order to give us any insight into the laws of nature.[24]

Like Hamilton, Whewell identifies the subject-object distinction with those components of experience the individual can or cannot control. But Whewell goes further. He pointedly identifies the mind's subjectivity with ideation and the world's objectivity with the content of ideas and sensations. He equates subjectivity with the formal principles upon which reality is constructed, but he equates objectivity with the material principles. This equation brings him to the final syzygy of matter and form. Because it is so abstract, this syzygy encompasses all others.

2.2.8. Matter and form

The syzygy of matter and form suggests itself in every different variety of experience. When the artisan works in some medium, the medium which he shapes, blends or structures is passive relative to his actions. Through his activity, an artifact is brought into being. This is not to say, however, that the medium does not possess an original form or structure. Indeed, it does. Every medium has a consistency, shape or color which--all things being equal--is regular and predictable. Passivity, simply because it is one pole of a syzygystic relation, is never absolute. All objects, no matter how passive with respect to some acts, possess an ontic density, a formal or actual inertia, which makes them what they are. Inasmuch as an object is passive in respect to some act which may be taken to change that object, that object is the material which is formed by an act. Form is defined as that which acts upon matter to bring it to some determination. Since matter and its passivity cannot exist without some form and activity and since form cannot exist without material upon which to act, 'form' and 'matter' serve well to designate the fundamental distinctions which are the constants of all being.[25]

The syzygy of matter and form is particularly significant in that it illuminates the nature of the inductive sciences. The ideas of space, time and number are the forms which mold sensation and which are abstractively detachable from experience's

---

[24]Whewell 1: 30.

[25]Whewell 1: 33-34.

perceptual content. The sciences of space, time and number effect a homogenization of their respective objects which enables these objects to be represented in terms of the abstract relations of formal logic and mathematics. Complementarily, there are other sciences which are not as abstractly relational but depend, instead, upon the *material* aspects of the beings studied. These are the sciences which are directed to the study of beings, insofar as these beings manifest behavior which is not completely reducible to logical and mathematical formulae. Whewell terms the former sciences *formal sciences* and the latter *material sciences*.

As a material science becomes more mathematically rigorous, it gradually becomes more formal, though it is quite possible that there may exist sciences which will forever be incapable of rigorous formal expression. Mathematics and physics are the most rigorous examples of the formal sciences. In contrast, those sciences which are directed to the empirical study of qualitative characteristics--sciences such as biology, history or astronomy--are not as formally pure as mathematics. Nevertheless, neither is mathematics perfectly formal nor is a narrative history perfectly material. Perfect formality and perfect materiality in the sciences represent ideal poles which are never actually achieved. With respect to each ideal pole, sciences may be ranked as relatively more material or relatively more formal. With each relative ranking, Whewell associates governing motifs or ideas which characterize the corresponding sciences' interests and methodologies.

2.3. Governing Motifs and the Subject Matter of the Inductive Sciences

According to Whewell, the ideas which govern the individual sciences must not be confused with the more primordial distinctions we have termed 'syzygies.' Although it is possible to apply the term 'idea' to either syzygies or governing motifs, these two varieties of ideas must not be conflated. As examples of the general term 'idea,' however, syzygy and governing motifs share properties. They are alike in that they are elements, "supplied by the mind itself, which must be combined with sensation in order to produce knowledge."[26] They are not objects of thought *per se*, but Whewell defines them as the laws (or necessary structures) which make thought possible by giving "to our Notions whatever they contain of truth."[27]

2.3.1. Distinguishing features of syzygies and motifs

The necessity which syzygies and governing motifs share lends them four salient properties indispensable to rigorous knowledge. First, one can intuitively see that both represent ideas which, given the appropriate perceptual conditions, must be true. Second, both structure states-of-affairs which (when described propositionally) yield axioms which insure trustworthy and unavoidable deductions. Third, both represent ideas which, when grasped, cannot distinctly be conceived otherwise. Fourth, both

---

[26]Whewell 1: 29.

[27]Whewell 1: 29.

represent ideas or truths with universal application: there can be no exceptions to the class of beings which they *correctly* designate.[28]

Whewell provides the following succinct description of the nature shared by syzygies and the governing motifs of the sciences:

> These Ideas entirely shape and circumscribe our knowledge; they regulate the active operations of our minds, without which our passive sensations do not become knowledge. They govern these operations, according to rules which are not only fixed and permanent, but which may be expressed in plain and definite terms; and these rules, when thus expressed, may be made the demonstrations by which the necessary relations imparted to our knowledge by our Ideas may be traced to their consequences in most ramifications of scientific truth.[29]

Even though syzygies and governing motifs are alike in that they are ideas, they are quite different in the characteristic meanings which distinguish them as kinds of ideas. Syzygies are more fundamental than governing motifs because syzygies are the most general distinctions which found the possibility of consciousness, but governing motifs are independent ideas which characterize the various domains of conscious investigation. Syzygies' primacy in the architectonic of knowledge is best understood when one grasps that *syzygies are ideas which convey the difference between ideas and the content upon which ideas act.*

Though syzygies represent the general conditions which define the possibility of knowledge, governing motifs represent the conditions under which scientific knowledge is individuated by discipline. Governing motifs are the unpaired ideas which structure the investigative intentionality behind the particular sciences as these sciences are actually practiced. They are the necessary products of consciousness as it comes into contact *with*, and takes a thematic interest in, the real world. Both syzygies and governing motifs arise simultaneously, yet governing motifs stand to syzygies in a relationship of logical dependence. Syzygies are the necessary conditions for the emergence of governing motifs, and the governing motifs are sufficient occasions showing the primacy of the syzygies.

Governing motifs, as they exist in the mind, can never adequately engender a scientific discipline before some act of interpretation takes place. This is because governing motifs exist in the mind in potentially rich but indistinct forms. The global content of a governing motif cannot be reduced to an exhaustive definition; every motif possesses an undepletably rich meaning. Nevertheless, in that it is possible to express concrete aspects of each governing motif, it is possible to employ it as a guiding theme for the inductive sciences. "The Idea itself cannot be fixed in words; but these various lines of truth proceeding from it suggest sufficiently to a fitly-prepared mind, the place where the Idea resides, its nature, and its efficacy."[30] Therefore, it is possible to fix

---

[28]Whewell 1: 66.

[29]Whewell 1: 73.

[30]Whewell 1: 73.

aspects of a governing motif in words by means of a concept which singles out some of the motif's necessary and universal relations to a particular scientific task.

Concepts are always framed with reference to particular circumstances and thus possess a specificity atypical of the ideas from which they emerge. The care with which conceptions are nursed into existence is special. "The Conceptions must be . . . carefully *unfolded*, so as to bring into clear view the elements of truth with which they are marked from their ideal origin."[31] Nevertheless, it is the conception's reference to empirical experience which serves to distinguish it from its parent idea. Governing motifs indicate the general conditions under which a discipline is possible, whereas concepts indicate objects which can be studied. The indistinctness of a governing motif is a result of its being potential and ideal; the specificity of a concept based upon a governing motif derives from that concept's being.

2.3.2. Axioms, definitions and propositions

The concepts which, under a particular governing motif, constitute a science can be expressed propositionally by means of axioms and definitions. Taken individually, neither may be sufficient to capture a concept. Taken in conjunction, however, axioms and definitions augment one another. Together they are fully capable of representing a concept, providing they are adequate within themselves.

Whewell calls axioms "enunciations of the necessary and evident conditions imposed upon our knowledge . . . by the governing motifs which they involve."[32] Axioms are the propositional expression of universal relations abstracted from the science's governing motifs. Their test of validity is that their truth and their obviousness is given indubitably in the comprehension of their meaning. For each science, axioms are the self-evident first principles from which deductions follow.

Definitions, on the other hand, do not possess the same kind of validity as do axioms. Definitions rely upon empirical experience to flesh in their content and guarantee their necessity. Experience under the constraints imposed by scientific protocol, results in definitions "determined by a necessity no less rigorous than the Axioms themselves."[33] Though definitions may result from scientific observations, deductions and inductions which are compelling, the necessity of definitions does not resemble that of axioms. Unlike axioms, the necessity of definitions cannot be established upon the definitions' meanings alone. The search for a definition's necessity must lead outward beyond that definition's meaning to the scientific operations which establish its connotation. It is in the scientific protocol responsible for the definition's emergence that the necessity of the definition lies.

If axioms can be adduced to found a science, these are always to be preferred to definitions. Definitions cannot assume the function of axioms because definitions

---

[31]Whewell 2: 5.

[32]Whewell 1: 67.

[33]Whewell 1: 72.

are based upon specific observations. An axiom, if well formed, explains the conditions for these observations as a class. Axioms, thus, have greater explanatory value. If precisely formed, they can provide an explanation for a whole class of empirical observations. Nevertheless, an exclusive choice between axioms and definitions is rare. Both add slightly different interpretations to the governing motif which they express. Through axioms we have an insight into the *a priori* aspects of the governing motifs. Through definitions we have an insight into their contingency, into the manner in which governing motifs may be entangled in empirical experience.

Although both axioms and definitions are propositions--as the term 'proposition' is commonly meant--Whewell identifies a third class of statement forms which he refers to as 'propositions' in a peculiar sense of the word. Propositions, in this narrow sense, are statements of fact not having a binding necessity of any kind. These propositions are statements established upon purely empirical evidences, evidences which yield no immediate proof of any underlying irresistibility. These propositions may become axioms or definitions providing the necessity contained in them is drawn out. As logical necessity, clarity and distinctness are brought to the fore, propositions become definitions. This is the portion of a scientific theory which is propositional in the narrow Whewellian sense.

2.3.3. Governing motifs and the order of the sciences

Whatever the propositional form of a concept, concepts are differentiated by content according to the governing motifs which they aspectually grasp. Whewell distinguishes concepts by describing the positions their governing motifs occupy relative to one another. This description is a prerequisite to Whewell's larger purpose because he believes that no general method of scientific discovery can be discerned before the governing motifs of each inductive science are understood in relation to the domain which each demarcates. Like other practitioners of quite different phenomenological methods, Whewell finds it essential to draw his conclusions about the general nature of science from the individual sciences as they are practiced.

The sequence in which Whewell lists the inductive sciences reflects their order of dependency and the simplicity of their respective governing motifs. At the head of this sequence, Whewell places arithmetic, the science which is the most abstract and formal. At the end of the sequence, Whewell places palaetiology, the science which is the most concrete and material.

Arithmetic takes number as its governing motif, a motif singular among others for its simplicity, abstractness and logical rigor. Geometry builds upon number by adding a notion of space which is homogenous and arithmetically representable. Astronomy adds to space and number a third motif, time, but it interprets all three motifs under a material aspect, stellar history, to explain the behavior of empirically existing celestial bodies. To the materialized motifs of space, time and number, the mechanical sciences add two, materially interpreted, motifs: dynamic and material causation. To these, the secondary mechanical sciences--or as Whewell calls them, the mechanico-chemical and purely chemical sciences--add polarity, chemical affinity, substance and symmetry.

Following the mechanico-chemical sciences, an apparent discontinuity occurs in the borrowing of governing motifs. On the opposite side of the thematic rift, Whewell arranges the following sciences. First, he lists the so-called classificatory sciences, Mineralogy, Botany and Zoology--sciences all dependent upon the analogical interpretation of the motifs of resemblance and natural affinity. After these, he lists the sciences which have assimilation, irritability and teleological causation as additional motifs. These are the physiological sciences. Finally, Whewell lists those sciences of living beings which are the most complex but which depend upon the physiological and classificatory sciences. This class consists of the palaetiological sciences or the sciences of history which take historical causation as their unique governing motif. Although Whewell bases his generalization of the inductive method on an investigation of the meaning and governing motifs of all of the inductive sciences, a discussion of all of these sciences is beyond the scope of this chapter. Instead the focus, here, shall be on the transcategorical motifs which, though associated with methods on both sides of the thematic rift, are especially characteristic of phenomenology.

2.3.4. Phenomenology and the motif of classification

Of all possible transcategorical motifs, classification and causation recommend themselves as most significant because they govern two indispensable moments of scientific method. Classification--as a method named after its motif--is a subset of all descriptive techniques, descriptive techniques Whewell classes under the general heading 'phenomenology.' It is phenomenology's general purpose to yield unbiased descriptions of objects singled out for explanation. The general purpose of phenomenology-proper is concerned with description alone. Into it no principle of order need necessarily be introduced. Phenomenology, in this narrow sense, describes without prescription; the orderly arrangement of descriptions is alien to it. In contrast, taxonomy, the other subsidiary purpose of phenomenology, is directed to bring the descriptions of phenomenology-proper into a systematic, tabular order. Taxonomy provides the superstructure which gives the disorganized mass of phenomenological description a shape and an intelligibility.

Whewell believes phenomenology-minus-classification to be essential to the development of every inductive science, for without precise description further methodological refinements are pointless. Whewell is not convinced, however, of the indispensability of taxonomy to every science. He is hard-pressed to recount any contribution taxonomy was responsible for in the formation of 19th century physics and is only dimly aware of the contribution it was beginning to make in 19th century chemistry.[34] As for the transcategorical theme of causation, Whewell does not hesitate to claim that it governs all science. Unlike classification, causation's immediate relevance to all varieties of science is immediately apparent.

---

[34]From the present historical vantage point, this inability to see the importance of classification for the hard sciences is quaint. With the periodic theory of the elements and the advent of subatomic particle theory, the necessity of elaborate taxonomies for physics and chemistry has been proven. Today, the success of the natural sciences has left little doubt that taxonomy must be taken as an inalienable extension of the phenomenological method.

Whewell initiates his discussion of the significance of classification and causation by arguing that the palaetiological sciences--the sciences responsible for investigating the historical causes of phenomena--would be impossible should these themes be abandoned. All attempts to explain historical phenomena require that one (1) disregard preconceptions, (2) accurately describe the phenomena at hand, (3) classify phenomena on the basis of likenesses and differences and, then, (4) seek explanations which elucidate the emergence of these phenomena from the causal field in which they nest.[35] Explanations in the palaetiological sciences presuppose that taxonomy has been carried out properly. The way to the correct execution of the taxonomic method is through a correct understanding of its intentionality, objects and protocol.

Intentionally, taxonomy is directed to the arrangement of ordered patterns from the chaotic multiplicity of phenomenological descriptions. The objects of taxonomy are the likenesses which we find in experienced phenomena. Taxonomy's purpose is to seek the limits to the similarity of objects as well as the universal rules by which a class name may be employed to designate experiences of phenomena.[36]

In the achievement of these ends, the taxonomist never assumes the role of passive observer because there are no uninterpreted phenomena. Nevertheless, classification does possess a relatively passive component. All attempts to trace the history and origin of entities require that one attend to the laws that these entities actually embody. But these laws would never be discovered without the active involvement of man's synthetic faculty in the comparison and grouping of likenesses and differences. Still, classification should, in no sense, be arbitrary. It should not result from purely capricious acts of comparison and reflection. A taxonomy must have the enunciation of scientific truths as its end and can only be accomplished if the intentionality behind the taxonomic selection is directed toward those resemblances which make science possible, toward those resemblances which are typical and invariant.

Inasmuch as the mind orders its sensory impressions by means of mental acts, the structure and relations between these acts--and not only their content--contribute to the likenesses which the mind perceives in the phenomena. Thus, what makes a taxonomy scientific has to do with the constituent mental acts that it involves--that is, its rationale of selection--as well as the phenomenal content upon which these mental acts work. Together, both aspects cooperate in the production of a notion of likeness. But variant understandings of likeness are possible. A better notion of likeness differs from an inferior notion of likeness in that the former yields a taxonomy more likely to lead to dependable predictions and generalizations about a class of phenomena.

Traditionally, the structure of any taxonomy has been said to be describable through the use of five words. These terms were first explained by Porphyry in his introduction to *The Categories* of Aristotle, *On the Five Words*, and Whewell unhesitatingly adopts them as the starting point of his own discussion of taxonomy. The first two of these words, 'genus' and 'species,' designate classes which are defined

---

[35]Whewell 1: 642-643.

[36]Whewell 1: 367-368, 471-473.

in relation to one another. A species stands to a genus as one of the genus' sub-classes, and a genus stands to a further super-genus as one of that super-genus' subclasses. A genus always consists of a class of distinguishable species. The genus is a super-class including all species having a set of shared properties. The species, therefore, are distinguished from one another by the addition of traits not represented in the genus but which are present in each species uniquely and exclusively. The unique traits which serve to distinguish one species from another are termed that species' difference or the specific difference of the species. The lowest species, however, is defined as the class in which there are no further subclasses but only individuals distinguishable from one another by characteristics which are not sufficient to constitute a further sub-species.

'Difference' is the third term of classical taxonomy. It is that which is intentionally excluded when a number of coordinate species are brought together under a genus. The fourth word, 'property,' designates any trait which is a universal concomitant of any class of entities. Differences, insofar as they characterize one species as differentiable from another, are properties just as are the traits which compose the classifications of related and proximate species.

A fifth word, 'accident,' is used by Porphyry and Whewell to designate any trait which may be present or absent in an entity without making that entity taxonomically placeable. Accidents do nothing to define entities as members of further sub-species because accidents can be indiscriminately present in or indiscriminately absent from an entity belonging to any class without alteration of that entity's nature.[37]

Taxonomies are distinguished according to whether their architectonics of species and genera are based upon essential relations or according to whether their architectonics are arbitrary or based upon a principle of ordering which does not capture the essential type under consideration. If genera are defined according to whether the species are associated in virtue of either natural affinity, general resemblance, or real propinquity, then the taxonomy will be an essential one. If, however, classifications are formed according to either general resemblances, accidental properties or definitionally irrelevant properties, then the taxonomy is merely an imaginative construct. In the case of either taxonomy, two different intellectual acts are employed. The naive recognition of features without expression of an underlying, general system is called *diagnosis*; the systematic arrangement of resemblances which founds the diagnosed traits is called *diataxis*.[38]

---

[37]Whewell 1: 477-479. Actually, Whewell is more rash in his description of accidents. He maintains that they are a class of traits which may be present in or absent from a *subject* without destroying that subject. Certainly, this is mistaken. An accidental separation of a man's head from his shoulders *is* sufficient to bring about his destruction. But that same accident is not sufficient to destroy the nature of man in general. An accident, in the Aristotelian sense, can be responsible for the destruction of its subject. However, to the order of essences, an accident can add or subtract nothing. Nevertheless, from the Aristotelian viewpoint, it is the accidental existence of individual subjects which makes the existence of essences possible, since no subject, except God, need necessarily exist. Whewell's confusion over the efficacy of accidental traits cannot entirely be blamed upon Porphyry. Rather, it is probably as much the product of Whewell's Platonization of of Kant. In Platonic thought, the Aristotelian interpretation of the relation between individual and essential existence is inverted: the individual exists because his essence exists as the emanation of a pre-existent, supersensible, form.

[38]Whewell 1: 510.

The traits associated with a particular diagnosis become the means by which an object is placed in a particular taxonomy once one has completed a consistent diataxis. However, neither diataxis nor diagnosis can be accomplished before one adopts a classificatory theme. In artificial or inessential taxonomies, the differences between the taxonomic theme and the acts of diataxis and diagnosis are blurred. Often, naive diagnostic features provide the rationale by which the order is constructed. In this case, the taxonomic theme is the *a posteriori* relations between accidental traits. The resultant taxonomy is founded upon the mere association of phenomenal regularities with the result that both diataxis and diagnosis follow the same formal rules. In such accidental taxonomies, diagnostic traits are not understood as signifying a more profound, underlying order; rather, the only order which is grasped is the one revealed by the similarity of accidental appearances. Empty formal regularities become the principles of organization behind both sets of mental acts.[39]

In those taxonomies which are constructed to display natural (or essential) principles of order, an idea of likeness is adopted which captures the immutability of the type of the entities studied. Behind these taxonomies is the assumption that entities, insofar as they constitute rigid species, contain within themselves a nature which is intelligibly representable. The notion of likeness which this variety of taxonomy employs is not based upon a simple comparison of traits but, instead, depends upon what makes entities truly what they are. This implies that for one to construct an essential taxonomy, one must rigorously study the entities before one can come to conclusions about any system of resemblances. One must study not only the simple appearances of entities but also the organic functions which serve to distinguish one class of beings from another.

Essential taxonomies presuppose an intentionality which seeks the essential functions of an entity *through* that entity's appearances without confusing those appearances with the entity's structure and function. Once one has reasoned from appearances to a plausible account of an entity's function, then one can proceed to construct a generalizable notion of likeness by which one can classify that entity. The relation between diataxis and diagnosis in an essential taxonomy is dialectical. One begins with an imprecise diagnosis of appearances in order to propose a tentative diataxis. Diataxis is then employed to test the predictive value of the original diagnosis. As predictions are contradicted by observations, illegitimate diataxic principles are rejected. As diataxic principles lead to correct predictions of never-before observed appearances, diataxic principles are corroborated. As diagnoses which have no bearing upon the predictive value of diataxes are identified and separated from those diagnoses which support diataxes, the inessential diagnoses are discarded. In this manner, essential taxonomies are perfected: system and observation dialectically condition one another until a taxonomy is produced by which an entity's essence may be diagnosed and placed within a field of diataxic relations. Nevertheless, the diagnoses and diataxes characteristic of essential taxonomies are neither formally identical nor do they, in every case, necessarily depend upon one another. Though a large class of diagnostic principles

---

[39]Whewell 1: 511.

may be mapped isomorphically onto a corresponding class of diataxic principles, each has a proper domain in which it operates with relative autonomy in order to correct the other. Diagnoses depend upon the principles of good observation; any principle of ordering which they autonomously possess is founded upon pure appearance. Diataxes, in contrast, depend upon the principles of logic and organization; they are thematically directed toward revealing regularities which are global but which may exist *behind* appearances which stand to these regularities as flags signifying their presence.

Essential taxonomies do not come into existence as fully developed systems but originate from tentative, artificial arrangements. At the beginning of a science, there is no self-evident idea as to which structures are to govern the distinction between natural classes. No one has any notion about which themes must be employed to construct ideal types which will correctly found genera and species. By default, appearances become the principles of classification. Artificial systems begin with the simplest method of classification: they classify marks and appearances which roughly indicate differences between identifiable natural groups. Once these marks have been catalogued, and their correspondences and differences systematized, the derived rules of classification are applied without any consideration given to the relations between the characteristics and the real function of the beings classified. Artificial taxonomies contain elaborate classificatory schemas which often serve well to distinguish one class of beings from another, but these schemas do little *to explain* crucial affinities between class traits and functions.[40] Artificial taxonomies fail to explain essential functions because they do not recognize a hierarchy of the relative importance of entitive characteristics which is based upon anything other than appearances. Appearance is the sole arbiter of class differences. Taxonomic distinctions are based upon differences within a homogeneous field and are not referred to any criteria beyond this field.

Whewell describes the limitations of the artificial system of classification as follows:

> It is easy to see that some organs are more essential than others to the existence of an organized being; the organs of nutrition, for example, more essential than that of locomotion. But at the same time it is clear than any *arbitrary* assumption of a certain scale of relative values of different kinds of characters will lead only to an Artificial System. . . . It is clear that this relation of importance of organs and function must be collected by the study of organized beings; and cannot be determined *a priori*, without depriving us of all right to expect a general accordance between our system and the arrangement of nature.[41]

Because they are so concerned with function, essential taxonomies are *a posteriori* and experience-based. Constant observation of the beings to be classified guarantees that an essential taxonomy will correctly represent crucial differences between natural classes. It is the appeal to the experienced behavior of beings which, in addition to function, is the regulative principle of essential classification.

---

[40]Whewell 1: 496-498, 536.

[41]Whewell 1: 536.

Whewell distinguishes four kinds of essential taxonomies which have been deeply experience-based. The first three of these were given extensive treatment by the French taxonomist Decandolle. The last is Whewell's contribution to taxonomy. They are: (1) taxonomies founded upon blind trial, (2) taxonomies founded upon general comparison, (3) taxonomies founded upon the gradation of groups and, finally, (4) taxonomies founded upon natural affinity. The last kind of taxonomy Whewell calls that founded upon the method of type.[42]

The taxonomic method of Linnaeus best represents the taxonomies based upon blind trial. In Linnaeus' system, all *a priori* rules were rejected and only the rules of simple resemblance were allowed. He neither considered symmetry nor principles of spatial structure relevant to natural classification as governing principles nor would he admit function as a legitimate theme either. All general affinities had to be based upon a blind trial of resemblances without any preconceived notion of what ought to be a principle of classification. In a sense, Linnaeus' method was the most purely phenomenological of all taxonomies. Exactly for this reason, it was a taxonomy without direction because it homogenized the marks of classification by assigning no class a superior or inferior weight. All resemblances were of the same significance. Though it sought the essence of a natural class, it contained no principle for deciding which were significant and which were insignificant features.

In contrast, taxonomies of general comparison are based upon coincidences between traits which must exist in every entity of a particular class. Unlike the practitioners of the method of blind trial, its practitioners do not randomly select and compare appearances in order to build classes of resemblances. Rather, the proponents of this method take a holistic approach. They believe that a taxonomy is complete only after every conceivable trait and all possible relations of resemblance have been enumerated. Only after this is accomplished is a system of cross-classification by character and likeness complete. Whewell, and Decandolle before him, detected the flaw in this method and described it as follows: "it supposes we know, not only all the organs of . . . (beings), but all the points of view in which it is possible to consider them."[43] This method is wholly fatuous and "altogether vicious; for it supposes that all these points of view, and all the resulting artificial systems are of equal importance."[44] Like the method of Linnaeus, taxonomies of general comparison fail because of a lack of clear direction. They possess no motif to guide their criteria of selection and comparison. Moreover, to compensate for this deficiency, their practitioners substitute an impossible task: they seek descriptively to exhaust all adumbrations of natural beings. But this is not all. Practitioners of the comparative method even further compound this method's absurdity by demanding that this impossibly monumental descriptive task be completed *before* a taxonomy can be attempted. Without a motif to

---

[42]Whewell 1: 494.

[43]Whewell 1: 499-500.

[44]Whewell 1: 499-500.

limit the appearances which are to count in comparison, the practitioners of the comparative method must attend to all appearances. But simply because this is an infinite task, by the comparative method's own principles no taxonomy can ever result.

It is the third variety of taxonomy which approaches nearest to what Whewell considers reasonable classification, but even it possesses defects. A taxonomy based upon the gradation of groups, like the two previous methods, does not presuppose *a priori* truths but is directed to the empirical comparison of entities. Unlike the practitioners of the previous methods, however, the practitioners of the method of the gradation of groups do seek a hierarchy of structural features. They seek functions and traits which may be classed as more or less essential to their subjects. In this, they return to the ideal of taxonomy put forth by Aristotle and Porphyry. Unfortunately, this method is weak in that its practitioners can come to little consensus about under what themes such hierarchies ought to be ordered. The method of gradation, in itself, contains no positive prescriptions as to which criteriological principles should count in directing its diataxis. Without such prescriptions, no universally applicable taxonomic method can ever be perfected.

Whewell does offer a remedy to the defects of this method. Based upon the supposition that each science must possess a motif (an *a priori* idea which makes it possible) Whewell argues that taxonomy too must be founded on a motif which will give it consistent direction. All of the preceding taxonomic methods are misconceived and misdirected in that their methods are too general. What is needed is a method founded upon a clear and distinct idea of what it is that taxonomy is supposed to order, a clear and distinct idea of significant structural principles. Thus, taxonomy must be grounded in a principle which is necessary, completely lucid, and intuitively self-evident. It must be the fulfillment of an intention directed to the discovery of essential features. But, also, it must be a principle which does not impose any preconceptions upon specific data except to provide a plausible method by which the data can be interpreted. The governing motif which Whewell associates with the scientific grounding of taxonomy is natural affinity.

Natural affinity alone supplies us with the correct trans-categorical motif for diataxis and diagnosis because it alone is constituted by two distinguishable principles essential to the meaning of taxonomy. The methods of blind trial, comparison and the gradation of groups all fail because they do not contain criteria for delineating domains of significant natural features. In contrast, taxonomy by natural affinity possesses two principles which can found a viable criteria for diataxis. First, the principle of natural affinity presumes that causes acting to effect a change in one part of a being--particularly as these causes alter the essential function of that being--transitively affect the beings's other parts. Second, natural affinity presumes that natural taxonomic groups ought to be based upon the affinity between their members as well as upon the affinity between the causes under the influence of which their members evolve.[45]

Two elemental ideas of affinity may be disentangled from these presumptions: an affinity which holds between an individual environment and the function of an

---

[45]Whewell 1: 357.

individual entity and a more general affinity which holds between classes of entities and classes of environments, an affinity indicative of a constant relation between form and environment, regardless of place and historical period. The first idea of affinity is primordial; upon it the class notions of taxonomy are constructed. The second idea of affinity is derivative; it presupposes that individual relations have been established. The first idea requires the particularistic intentionality associated with the lowest level of causal reasoning: from these individual conditions arises this individual being. The second idea requires the intentionality of generalization associated with the higher level of causal reasoning: these general conditions always give rise to a being of a such and such a type. From both kinds of causal reasoning a viable form of diataxis emerges. Taxonomic groups are rightly formed when individual and class traits are used to judge the natural groups into which entities fall.

Once the taxonomist of natural affinities begins to assemble a rudimentary notion of a natural group, he looks to the representative ensemble of beings with the intention of determining its centroid, the ideal construct or real entity which typifies its class "according to total resemblances."[46] The central type is that entity--either real or imagined--which all other members of the same class resemble more than any other entity. Around this central and defining type, all other members of the same class are extended at different distances in *affinite* space. The central type thus, may, be likened to a nucleus. As entities resemble it, they cluster close to it. As entities differ from it, they occupy affinite positions distant from it.

> In such an arrangement (a taxonomy of natural affinity), it may readily be conceived that though the nucleus of each group may cohere firmly together, the outskirts of contiguous groups may approach, and may even intermingle, so that some species may doubtfully adhere to one group or another. Yet this uncertainty does not at all affect the truths which we find ourselves enabled to assent with regard to the general mass of each group. And thus we are taught that there may be very important differences between two groups of objects, although we are unable to tell where the one group ends and where the other begins; and that there may be propositions of indisputable truth in which it is impossible to give unexceptionable definitions of the terms employed.[47]

A natural class, though liminally quite fuzzy, becomes more specifically determined as one discursively approaches its centroid. A class based upon a natural affinity is defined by its nuclear type according to "what it eminently includes" and "not by what it strictly excludes."[48] The same principle operates at every level of taxonomic generality. A typical entity representative of a species occupies that species' nuclear point. As members of that species have characteristics which deviate from the characteristics of that species' nucleus, they form a dispersion pattern extended in affinite space. The same is true of species and genera and so on for any relative classes, whatsoever.

---

[46]Whewell 2: 371.

[47]Whewell 2: 371.

[48]Whewell 1: 494.

> A type is an example of any class, for instance, a species of a genus, which is considered as eminently possessing the characters of the class. All the species which have a greater affinity with this Type-species than with any others form the genus, and are ranged about it, deviating from it in different directions and different degrees. Thus a genus may consist of several species which approach very near the type, and of which the claim to a place with it is obvious; while there may be other species which straggle further from this central knot and which yet are clearly more connected with it than any other.[49]

In that an entity possesses the leading functional attributes of the type which defines its species, it is classed within its species; in that a species possesses a class of leading functional attributes like those of the type which defines some genus, it is classed within that genus. As the affinity between functional attributes in the ideal type and functional attributes in its relatives increases, the relatives are defined as nuclear.

The utility of natural affinity as the governing idea of taxonomy is indubitable because it is the only conceivable principle by which natural entities can be ordered according to essence. But, although the introduction of natural affinity does much to set taxonomy in order, one finds it difficult to see how it represents an irreducible motif. Its meaning harbors an ambiguity. There are at lease three primordial governing motifs which conceal themselves in the idea of affinity. Thus, the notion of affinity is a hybrid, a synthesis. Without the elemental ideas of causation, identity and organization, it is difficult to see how Whewell's claim that affinity is an *a priori* condition of taxonomy is plausible. Natural affinity depends upon each of these motifs essentially. From them it receives its compelling necessity.

The motif of organization gives taxonomy its unique character as a scientific method. But organization may be further subdivided into two more fundamental motifs: mechanistic organization and teleological organization. The former can be reduced to the motifs of physics. The latter can be distinguished from the former as having an additional irreducible content, the motif of teleology. It is teleology which accounts for the difference between living and inert organizations. As a transcategorical, however, natural affinity is abstractable from the distinction between the two motifs of organization contained within it. Teleology serves only to distinguish biological instantiations of diataxis from instantiations in the physical or mathematical sciences. The ambiguous idea of organization is sufficient to cover both kinds of beings to which the taxonomy applies.

We may relate natural affinity (classification) to the scientific method as follows. Science, in that it takes description as its first task, must take natural affinity as its first guiding idea and taxonomy as its initial path-finding method. However, in the scheme of ideals expressive of the possibility of knowledge, affinity is composite and epistemologically secondary. Epistemologically, causation and identity precede natural affinity. Without identity and causation, natural affinity would be impossible, just as taxonomy would be impossible without the complementary methods of formal reasoning and etiology. This is not to contradict what was said above. The practical and epistemological orders *are not identical*. Nevertheless, in the experience which precedes

---

[49]Whewell 1: 494.

classification, causal reasoning and formal reasoning, the motifs which characterize the various methods exist *in potentia* and can be revealed in any order the researcher may choose. But the researcher's *arbitrary* choice of one of these motifs (and arbitrary exclusion of the others) is not *as expedient* as the protocol which Whewell outlines.

Though natural affinity, identity and causation dialectically condition each other's definition, the methods of description and taxonomy should precede etiology because description and classification presuppose less theoretical baggage. Because description and classification import the fewest theoretical constructs--fewest, that is, in comparison to etiology and hypothetical thinking--they serve as the most unbiased paths to subsequent methods. This does not alter the fact that the motifs which the later methodological steps presuppose are more primordial than natural affinity. Description and taxonomy lend phenomena a tentative order and structure which are subject to the manipulations of etiology and theory. Only when the structural features which taxonomy describes are explained by etiology or one of the subsequent methodological steps do the primordial governing motifs gain clarity and distinctness. Natural affinity, therefore, is often unclearly expressed in the first stages of a taxonomy's construction. However, as the researcher employs subsequent explanatory methods, the primordial motifs buried in the experiences of natural affinity emerge and the primordial classificatory principles are further clarified. This is the dialectic which occurs in the practical application of governing motifs.

2.3.5. Etiology and the motif of causation

Even though Whewell attributes much significance to the phenomenological procedures of description and classification, phenomenology would be pointless without etiology. Before a systemic etiology may be carved out, the phenomena to be investigated must be set in an intelligible order, an order based upon the natural affinity between individuals.[50] But the order which characterizes a taxonomy can never be a substitute for the explanatory power etiology brings with it. Even if a taxonomy provides a reasonable system of classes which are observationally indubitable and quite necessary, not until reasons are provided as to *why* the classification works and *why* the entities so ordered are essentially capable of such classification can the taxonomy be considered scientific. Etiology is a necessary intermediate step between the elementary step of description and the consummate step of theoretization. The attempt to construct a theory by moving straight from phenomena to theory has always ended in failure.[51]

The investigation of causes belongs to science as one of its essential features. To explain a phenomenon is to be able to predict its behavior as well as to be able to explain under what conditions it arises. Without being able to do either of these things the researcher can not claim to have scientific knowledge of the objects he studies. Yet, Whewell realizes that the necessity of etiology undercuts science's dependence upon phenomenology. Because etiology by its nature must be synthetic, it must add to

---

[50]Whewell 2: 103.

[51]Whewell 2: 103.

observed phenomena principles of explanation which are not evidently contained within the phenomena.

In the experience of a phenomenon or a field of phenomena, we experience nothing by which the succession of appearances may be corrected. We see no causes which, though distinguishable from the appearances we experience, connect these appearances together. "We see that one occurrence follows another, but we can never see anything which shows that one occurrence *must* follow another . . . ."[52] No sensation or perception can reveal this connection; no guarantee that certain conditions give rise to certain phenomena can ever be based upon observation alone. In order to postulate a law which practically holds for the behavior of phenomena, we must introduce an idea which transcends the bare perception of phenomena; we must introduce the idea of connection.

Whewell is sensitive to the positivist's charge that the introduction of hypothetical causal principles violates the integrity of phenomenological description and the taxonomies based upon it. Though writing before Comte, Schlick, and Carnap, Whewell is familiar with the assertion that science must adhere solely to perceptions and sensations, that a rigorous science is one which imports no metaphysical constructs from beyond experience but takes uninterpreted experience as its object. But Whewell rejects the premises of the positivists because he does not believe that uninterpreted experience is possible. For him the question is not "How shall science get back to pure experience?" but "How shall science minimize the unnecessary theoretical terms which it imports into science?" Whewell believes that the importation of causal terms into science is unavoidable and, indeed, is to be welcomed. It is impossible for men to study laws of phenomena without speculating about the causes which produced them.

> Men cannot contemplate the phenomena without clothing them in terms of some hypothesis, and will not be schooled to suppress the questionings which at every moment rise up within them concerning the causes of the phenomena.[53]

The causation of the positivists is a barren refuge. Though it prevents the proposal of new hypotheses, it tacitly reinforces the acceptance of old interpretations of phenomena without seeking their criticism. It is only though the dialectic of description, explanation, experiment, and interpretation that science progresses. An essential part of this progress is the proposal of causal principles. Science cannot proceed without it.

But how does Whewell construe the notion of cause? Why can it be classed as one of the transcategoricals which function as governing motifs to make the sciences possible?

Like the idea of natural affinity, causation represents an *a priori* condition of knowledge which transcends experience. "By Cause we mean some quality, power or

---

[52]Whewell 1: 167-169.

[53]Whewell 2: 103.

efficacy, by which a state of things produces a succeeding state."[54] Because empirical knowledge would be inconceivable without causation, and because we are well convinced of the truth and power of such knowledge, we must admit causation as a governing motif. Without it, even simple day-to-day experience could not be imagined. Thus, we are not to test the transcategoricals by criteria which are not proportioned to their true nature. Simply because scientific knowledge is a fusion of empirical experience, phenomenological description, and *a priori* ideas, we cannot hope to test scientific knowledge with criteria that have relevance to only one of science's parts.

If the value of the motif of causation is indubitable for all the sciences, this does not necessarily mean that the same kind of causation has the same value for every science. Like the motif of natural affinity, causation may be instantiated according to the different demands the individual sciences place upon it. Just as each science must have a fundamental idea or governing motif to distinguish its subject matter from the subject matter of other sciences, each science must also claim a unique interpretation of causation, an interpretation which, though agreeing generally with the transcategorical idea of causation, will possess a content unique to its parent science. Thus, a general order of foundedness holds between the motifs phenomenology reveals and the respective etiologies which accrue from these motifs. Though the transcategoricals 'cause' and 'natural affinity' are ideals which depend upon one another to found the very possibility of science, the instantiations of cause are dependent upon the revealed motifs which guide the particular sciences. The varieties of natural affinity which are responsible for the essential features of distinguishable ontologies also shape the kinds of causation which are attributed to these varieties.

In creating an etiology for a discipline, the researcher must not bend taxonomic relations to fit a preconception as to how these relations ought to be explained. Rather, he must adapt the general principle of causation to the new motifs which have been discovered diataxically. The etiologist must assume that any class of beings which warrants a unique governing motif also warrants a unique causal principle by which its class affinities may be explained.[55]

---

[54]Whewell 1: 166. The operative words here are 'power or efficacy.' Whewell believes that the characterizing mark of the idea of causation is its efficacy. A cause must necessarily produce an effect. In agreement with Hume, Whewell admits that the experience of phenomena is the experience of the constant conjunction between events but that nothing in *empirical* experience gives us grounds to infer a necessary connection; nothing in empirical experience allows us to conclude that any inference from a causal connection is more than probable. Though accepting Hume's sceptical conclusions, Whewell adopts the Kantian tactic. Granted, if we can find no phenomenal evidence for causal connection, then causal connection (as an *empirical* principle) is unfounded. But who can, with any authority, maintain that empirical experience must be the sole arbiter of scientific principles? All scientific practice militates against the Humean position. The progress of sciences has occurred because of the introduction of causal terms. It has resulted because of a principle which is not itself empirical. Thus, Whewell turns the Humean argument on its head. Just because we can derive assertions involving the idea of cause "which are rigorously necessary and universal"--as tested by experiment--and just because experience cannot in itself demonstrate anything more than it contains in itself, the principle of causation must be accepted as a legitimate importation of those ideas beyond empirical experience which found the possibility of knowledge.

[55]Whewell 2: 97-100.

As we ascend the hierarchy of the sciences, we find different causal notions attached to each discipline. In physics we find causes related to mechanical force, in chemistry causes related to chemical affinity, and in biology causes related to the animal soul, perception, and will. As we ascend to the human sciences, we find causal notions related to teleology--that is to design and purpose--as well as causal notions associated with the idea of personality. Beyond the human sciences and as their annex, we find associated causes related to the origin and ultimate purpose of the universe.[56]

As in the case with natural affinity, we find two major generic divisions for classifying different kinds of causes. On one hand, we have causes which explain the mechanistic behavior of nature. Among these are the "hard" sciences, the sciences Whewell considers exemplarily inductive. On the other hand, we have causes which explain volition, design and purpose, all of which characterize conscious beings, beings having unique histories. By an interesting lapse in reasoning, Whewell also classes sciences such as geology and evolutionary zoology together with the human sciences. He feels justified in doing this based upon the analogy he develops between the unique history of the geological and zoological phenomena and the unique history of man's cultural evolution. To the union of both varieties of history, Whewell gives the title palaetiology, the scientific study of unique past phenomena through the traces they leave in the present.[57]

In an equivocal sense, the natural sciences Whewell terms 'palaetiological' are historical. In that they do represent a unique sequence of events they must be based upon phenomenal traces which have survived until the present. In this, they are like human sciences. But unlike the human sciences, they do not have as their object plans, designs and volitionally controlled acts which bring them into being. The correct place for speculations about supernatural volitions and agency is not in any particular mechanistic science, unless a specific example of such intervention may be produced. The correct place for such speculation is either the human sciences or cosmology which is a hybrid annex of both the natural and human sciences.[58]

---

[56]Whewell 2: 435.

[57]Whewell 1: 638. Though Whewell distinguishes the palaetiological sciences from the mechanical sciences, the distinction he makes is unconvincing both because he is unable to prescribe any unique motif for this class of sciences--except for a provisional motif he terms "history"--and because he is unable to associate any unique species of causation with this motif--except for a form of causation he terms "historical." Whewell's real motive in classing these sciences together has more to do with Whewell's theological presuppositions than it has to do with a real analogy existing between natural and human history. Because Whewell believes the hand of Providence shapes both natural and human history according to the designs of the Divine will, he allows that much of the novelty in geological and biological evolution may be the product of divine intervention. However, subsequent scientific theory prohibits such an intrusion of theological principles into scientific interpretation. Divine intervention is not *necessarily* required to explain either the emergence of animal life or cataclysmic geological events. According to 19th century scientific theory, the chemical and climatic processes which occurred during past epochs are part of a closed causal net. The universe is regarded as a closed system, and the explanations for its evolution are sought in the purely mechanical behavior of that system. Nothing like a will or design *need* be introduced.

[58]Whewell 1: 620-623, 658. The causes which distinguish the human sciences from the mechanical sciences are essentially linked to the motifs of volition and teleology. The behavior of individual people distinguishes itself from that of atoms by its complex heterogeneity, and by the fact that human volition violates the understanding of the universe as a closed causal net. In the affairs of humans, that conscious attempt to achieve an end introduces a new causal element

2.3.6. Theory and the motifs of conciliance, colligation and simplicity

Besides phenomenology and etiology, one additional component is required to complete science as an inductive method. The required component is theory. Theory differs from phenomenology and etiology in that its methodology is much more difficult to describe and control. Theory distinguishes itself in this respect because it possesses unique governing motifs. It is the end of theory to employ phenomenologically and etiologically defined facts to construct hypotheses which unite these facts into global, explanatory systems. Theory leads to the systematization of as many different observations and inductions as a single hypothesis can bear. In that theory leads inductively to hypotheses, it differs little from etiology; it signifies merely another part of inductive method. But theory is inductive in a more far-reaching sense than etiology. Etiology is limited to the investigation of a wide variety of causal phenomena under pre-scribed governing motifs. Theory transcends the boundaries between different phenomena and different causal styles.

Etiology begins with a study of concrete phenomena and observed phenomenal regularities and finishes with the construction of abstract causal laws which hold for discrete ontologies. In etiology, any causal hypothesis has its origin in appearances which have been described by phenomenologist and catalogued by taxonomists. Etiology introduces no new phenomenal data or theoretical constructs to explain its objects; it produces law-like explanations from bare appearances, nominalistically. In etiology, appearances alone dictate causal hypotheses. When these hypotheses are tested, then causal laws are established.

Theory, like etiology, results in abstractive generalizations about ontologies, but it does so by virtue of an inductive method uncharacteristic of etiology. Whewell calls

---

which cannot always be explained by reference to its causal antecedents. Whewell believes that this sort of causal reasoning can be extended to encompass the universe as a whole. Because scientists are hard pressed to explain what precedes that finite chain of natural causes we term 'the universe,' and because they must admit that whatever did precede it had to be a principle of order, scientists, if they are to be consistent, must postulate the existence of a qualitatively different first cause. To deny the first cause's existence is to violate the general axiom of causality which stipulates that every effect must have a cause. A causeless chain of causes and effects is singularly unintelligible. The scientist must therefore pose what Whewell believes is an ultimate question, a question having both moral and cosmological implications. He must ask himself "Why did the universe come into being?" The act of postulating both a first cause as well as a teleological cause Whewell terms the "spontaneous recognition of the relation of means to end." This postulate and this postulate alone he believes to be "the assumption which makes organic arrangements intelligible." As a fundamental idea, the final cause is "not generated but unfolded: not extracted from the external world, but evolved from the world within." In that man is familiar both with his own nature as creator as well as with the necessity entailed by the idea of causation, he is able to contemplate God's purpose as it is manifested in the world. The scientist can rethink God's intentions when he considers the world under the motifs of first and final causation.

Analogously, the notion of teleological causation may also be employed to explain interruption in the natural causal order. When a scientist has exhausted every plausible natural explanation of such interruptions, when he has exhausted explanations based upon the strictest mechanistic principles, then he must either posit a supernatural intervention "or declare" himself "altogether unable to form the series into a connected chain." The teleology of human behavior thus becomes a dim analogue of God's amendment of physical law. Because events which seem to have no natural causes violate the axiom of causality, they must either be referred to a supernatural agent, or they must have their investigation postponed until the natural phenomena with which they are associated become better understood. By the principle of teleological causation, Whewell's philosophy makes way for the possibility, if not the eventuality, of a science of the miraculous.

this inductive procedure "successive generalization." Successive generalization, however, differs from causal generalization in that it provides global explanations for very different causal realms.[59]

In a sense, theory works in an opposite direction from etiology. Theory leads to expansive generalizations about different classes of beings. Etiology stops at the construction of causal orders which correspond to these ontological classes. Theory relates and simplifies. Etiology distinguishes, compounds, and systematizes. Theory is more creatively synthetic; it proposes theoretical constructs, which have not been observed but which are posited as the missing links in the fabric of nature. Etiology directs us to see the world as compartmental, as particulate, as divided into independent causal realms each resembling one another enough to share general features but arising from generically different phenomenon. Theory leads us to discover noumenal relations between phenomena, relations whose evidence is mediated by the interpretations of the causal relations holding between appearances. Etiology derives from what can be seen. Theory is removed from the visible and builds on etiology. Etiology is unable to take us further than causal regularities. Theory proposes the *Weltbild* which makes those causal regularities explicable.

Although it is easy enough to list the differences between theory and etiology, to specify how theory ought to be practiced is quite another matter. This is because the means a scientist employs to arrive at a good theory are not always susceptible to reduction into simple rules. Theoretic means are often quite intuitive, and being intuitive they are often quite intangible. Of the two most important prerequisites for construction of a viable theory, Whewell recognizes the invention of a good hypothesis (or "gathering conception") as the most intuitive.

The invention of a theory requires that the researcher possess an appropriate set of intellectual abilities or predispositions as well as a set of governing motifs. Chief among the abilities required for the invention of hypotheses are the abilities to visualize many possibilities and to make many reasonable guesses until a happy guess occurs.[60] But as important as these abilities are, the ability to succeed in the inductive sciences is directly related to the ability to rehearse hypothetical possibilities in rapid succession and according to many different possible serialities. The scientist must be able to perform feats of imaginative variation and hypothesization rapidly, first taking his object through their many possible changes and then proposing a hypothesis which relates these changes to the causal field surrounding the objects. Or the scientist may choose an alternate route. He may assume the hypothesis as a given and then imagine the consequences of its being true. He may guess whether the future behavior of objects will follow the hypothetical pattern predicted by the past and present behavior of objects. When done with "boldness and license," such mental gymnastics engender scores of theories, some of which are useful. It is the ability to produce rapid

---

[59]Whewell 1: 663-664.

[60]Whewell 2: 41.

imaginative variations and proposals which is the trait most typical of scientific genius and which is quite alien to lesser intellects.[61]

But besides the talent which marks scientists as a breed apart, an additional predisposition is the *sine qua non* of theorization. It is a predisposition which is in greater supply by virtue of being a necessary condition of man's intellectual life, though it is hardly less important just for this reason. The additional predisposition which is fundamental to theory is the restless desire to introduce order into a field of facts.

The will to order is a fundament of theoretical protocol for two reasons. First, because the ability and the desire to see order are parts of consciousness' exigencies, theory is a primary mode of knowledge. Neither the syzygies nor the governing motifs can be separated from the idea of order. Knowledge in general, and particularly knowledge as Whewell defines it, includes the necessary imposition of objective or subjective theories upon reality. Knowledge without order is meaningless. Second, because the relations between theory and fact is such that facts cannot be read except through some theory, the will to order becomes synonymous with an existential hermeneutic. To live is to impose order on the world. Theory is the only window the scientist has upon reality because theory alone provides the possibility that facts may be distinguished from theory, and theory alone insures that the facts will be given a unifying interpretation. Nevertheless, a *good* theory is one which dissolves itself into the self-evidence of its constituent facts. A good theory is one which, in adding significant interpretation to the facts, seems so natural, so obvious, that it is impossible to explain where theory begins and where the facts leave off. A good theory is one which, though it orders the facts, is not invasive. Theory *is* the will to order in its most creative and revealing embodiment.[62]

Aside from the abilities and predispositions which contribute to theory formation, three transcendental governing motifs provide the objective criteria by which a good theory can be distinguished from a bad theory. They are: (1) The idea of conciliance, (2) The idea of colligation and (3) The idea of simplicity. A good theory is one which conciliates, colligates, and simplifies data, facts, hypotheses, or theories on hand.[63] These motifs also represent ends which the scientist should strive to achieve. As criteria for a good theory, the ideas of conciliance, colligation, and simplicity are ideal ends. They govern the teleological intentionality of scientific investigation.

A theory results in the conciliation of data when it provides an explanation which relieves any apparent contradictions and makes the data complement one another. An example drawn from paleontology illustrates this motif. Suppose some paleontologist discovers that a direct proportion exists between the age of a fossil and its depth in geological strata. Upon this relation, it is possible to date different fossils relative to one another so that a fossil found at a lower strata is dated older than a fossil found at

---

[61]Whewell 2: 41.

[62]Whewell 2: 54-55.

[63]Whewell 2: 36-73.

a higher stratum. Now, suppose that fossils which are always found in lower strata and which have never known to be found outside of their strata are, one day, found in higher strata. And further suppose that the paleontologist knows, by some other means, that these fossils are the remains of animals which were long extinct before the higher strata were formed. How can one account for the apparent contradiction between the facts? One might either admit the irresolvability of the contradiction and ignore the fossil evidence, or reject the hypothesis that fossils can be dated by their placement in strata. However, by inventing a hypothesis which conciliates both facts, their contradiction may be resolved without having to reject either. If one introduces the hypothesis that sometimes the dynamic movement of the earth causes strata to buckle, thus driving their contents into higher or lower geological strata, then both facts may be made amenable to one another. The hypothesis of the movement of the earth's crust accounts for apparent contradictions in two different factual orders. The distinguishing mark of the conciliation of facts or hypotheses is that the hypothesis posed to make the conciliation must let the facts stand relatively untouched. They should be distinguishable but have a new interpretation which makes them complement one another. Also, the conciliatory hypothesis should have explanatory value outside of the paradox it resolves.

The colligation of facts may be instructively contrasted with the conciliance of facts. It is the property of colligation to fuse and relate propositions, explanations, or hypotheses so closely that they may be considered identical. A hypothesis which colligates brings about a reinterpretation of the propositions upon which it operates. Once colligated, these propositions are indistinguishable, indistinguishable--that is--when taken under the meaning of the hypothesis which binds them together. For example, today physicists find themselves faced with a seemingly irresolvable duality in their interpretation of the physical phenomenon of light. Under certain conditions, light seems to behave as if it were particulate; under other conditions, light behaves as if it consisted of waves of energy moving through space. At the moment, neither interpretation is reconcilable with the other. The predicament is complicated by the fact that both the corpuscular and wave explanations refer to the same phenomena. Though we have no idea what sort of hypothesis would resolve the contradiction between these models, we do have a very good notion of what this resolution would produce. The resolution of the particle-wave duality would result in a colligation of concepts. No longer would we have either an exclusive wave or exclusive particle theory of light. We would have a theory which explained the salient features of each by transcending both. The colligation of behavioral characteristics which would result would be isomorphic to features of each model but it would differ in that it would contain additional observational and theoretical content distinguishing it from either. This additional content would be so compelling and of such indubitability, that it would be impossible to read the earlier evidence of the corpuscular or wave theory of light and find either convincing. A theory which colligates propositions irrevocably changes their meaning. It so improves upon them that their earlier persuasiveness can hardly be imagined. A theory which colligates propositions produces explanations for the phenomena originally explained by the defective theories as well as incontrovertible evidence why the earlier theories were false.

Simplicity is the third motif governing theorization, and as a governing motif it is quite distinct from either the ideas of conciliance or colligation. It is the property of good theorization to drive a theory's constituent propositions together to form a simply unity. A good theory is thus distinguished from a bad theory in that the good theory explains the same phenomena but with the need for fewer theoretical constructs. Although the idea of simplicity is closely related to the idea of colligation--in the sense that both tend toward a single explanation for the complex states of affairs--a subtle difference may be perceived. Whereas colligation results in the unification of propositions without necessarily demanding an attendant reduction in theoretical terms, simplicity tends towards both the unification of propositions *and* the reduction in the number of terms used to describe a given phenomenon.

Simplicity is the intention behind Ockham's razor. It drives the theorist to eliminate any propositions which do not have explanatory value. Furthermore, it is simplicity which represents the reductive tendency of theory. Simplicity drives the theorist to search for a single entity or law which, though conditioned by different circumstances, may serve to explain different ontic realms. The reduction of biological or chemical laws to physical laws exemplifies the theoretical process of simplification. Even if a scientist possesses the talent for visualizing possibilities, even if he possesses the will to order and the pliability to let himself be guided by the ideas of conciliance, colligation and simplicity, even then his fulfillment of these conditions may not produce a good theory. The final condition which must be placed upon theorization is that, not only must it explain, it *must predict*. It must divine even those events which have never before occurred.

> The hypotheses which we accept ought to explain phenomena which we have observed. But they ought to do more than this: our hypotheses ought to foretell phenomena which have not yet been observed. . . . That these cases belong to past or future times, that they have or have not already occurred, makes no difference in the applicability of the rule to them. Because the rule prevails, it includes all cases; and will determine them all, if we can only calculate its real consequences. Hence, it will predict the results of new combinations, as well as explain the appearances which have occurred in old ones.[64]

It is one of the functions of experiment to test the ability of hypotheses to predict the behavior of phenomena. Not only does the scientist use experiments to compound uniform observations of phenomena in order to make his hypothesis more precise, he uses experiment to construct new sets of conditions designed to test the general predictability of his hypothesis. The dialectic of proposal and experiment is the practical annealing which produces good theories.

Because good theories result from the dialectic of proposal and experimentation, Whewell understands the ability to predict never-before experienced phenomena as a proof that induction provides *actual* insights into physical reality. Thus, theory is the exemplar of induction because theory represents an expansive guess at the real structures of reality. When, tested by experiment, the guess proves accurate, the scientist can take this as evidence that he can decipher the secret language in which natural law is written.

---

[64]Whewell 2: 62.

134

> To trace order and law in that which has been observed, may be considered as interpreting what nature has written down for us, and will commonly prove that we understand her alphabet. But to predict what has not been observed, is to attempt ourselves to use the legislative phrases of nature; and when she responds plainly and precisely to that which we thus utter, we cannot but suppose that we have in a great measure made ourselves masters of the meaning and structure of her language.[65]

Here, Whewell seems to deny his Kantian roots and to argue that the methods of inductive science lead not to a subjective transcendentalism but to a variety of Platonic realism. In a curious reversal of the Kantian epistemology, Whewell maintains that the ability to predict the future is evidence that the categories written on our minds recapitulate categories implicit in nature.[66] Whewell believes that we have not acquired this ability naturally. It is not a product of chance. Its presence in man is evidence of something man shares with God. Thus, to theorize well is, in a sense, to read God's mind because the syzygies and governing motifs which structure our consciousness possess real correlates which have served as the models upon which God has constructed nature. Theory is the nearest man comes to sharing a thought with God.

Having disposed of the general methodologies and conditions of the inductive sciences, Whewell finally addresses the practical steps which result in the concrete application of the general scientific methodologies. Whewell's last task in the *Philosophy of the Inductive Sciences* is to explain how scientists *practically* succeed in making scientific discoveries.

The relatively primitive level of the development of scientific practice limits Whewell's ability to accomplish this task. The concreteness of Whewell's practical prescriptions follows the precision and development of the general methodologies of his time. As the general methodology is precisely conceived, Whewell's practical applications are specific and well developed. As the general methodology is vague or intuitive, Whewell's practical applications are loose and general.

Three major steps and seven constituent substeps comprise the means for the enactment of inductive science. The first major step, the explication of ideal conceptions, consists of two substeps: (1) education and (2) discussion. The second major step, the decompositions and observation of complex facts, consists of two further substeps, as well: (1) the decompositions of facts and (2) the measurement of phenomena. Finally, the third major step, the colligation of elementary facts by means of conceptions, consists of three substeps: (1) the inductions of laws of phenomena (2) the induction of causes and (3) the application of discoveries.[67]

These steps and substeps may be related to the previously discussed general methodologies according to the following scheme. The explication of ideal conceptions (with its steps of education and discussion) corresponds to no general methodology but,

---

[65]Whewell 2: 64.

[66]Whewell 1: 37.

[67]Whewell 2: 335.

instead, represents the preliminaries requisite to begin scientific investigation. The decomposition and observation of facts and measurement of phenomena, constitute what Whewell understands as phenomenology in the strictest sense. Finally, the colligation of elementary facts by means of conceptions represents no single general methodology but is rather trisected according to its constituent steps in such a way as to be correlative with taxonomy, etiology and theory. Thus, the induction of laws of phenomena represents what Whewell understands as taxonomy or phenomenology in the broad sense; the induction of causes represents etiology; the application of discoveries represents theory. The general methodologies and practical steps of inductive science may graphically be represented as in Chart 5.

3. The Objects of Whewellian Phenomenology

The Whewellian notion of phenomena, in some respects, corrects and enlarges the Hamiltonian notion of phenomena. Like Hamilton, Whewell believes phenomena to be intelligible upon the basis of *a priori* principles which serve to order phenomena so that they become thematically distinct objects of science. The themes which compartmentalize the total field of phenomena are the themes which the individual sciences adopt as their subject matter. However, Whewell--natural scientist that he is--also appreciates the role the empirical, *a posteriori* aspects of phenomena play in defining the sciences. These aspects give meaning to the phrase 'inductive science,' for without them there could be no phenomena belonging to the fields of investigation characterized by historical or physical change. Together, the *a priori* and *a posteriori* sides of phenomena co-found the possibility of the inductive sciences.

For Whewell, a careful phenomenological analysis of the empirical sciences discloses a set of syzygies (or transcendental ideas). These syzygies are fundamental, *a priori* distinctions which exist as part of consciousness' structure and have the form of yoked, interdependent concepts. When confronted with individual or complex sensations, these syzygies order the sensorial content in such a way as to make it the object of knowledge. Syzygies are the fundamental conceptual distinctions which are transcendental; they are the principles which order any material content of thought whether that content is the purview of a particular science or not. Thus, syzygies stand to the governing motifs of the sciences as their transcendental foundation. Like the syzygies, the governing motifs (a) are intuitively evident, (b) result in universal truths and (c) cannot be conceived otherwise. But the governing motifs of the sciences differ from the syzygies in that (1) their application is limited to a particular material content and (2) they are unpaired ideas. These motifs are the formal and constitutive principles of the phenomena (facts) studied by the sciences. But phenomena cannot be absolutely reduced to the principle of order supplied by consciousness and an external material principle. Were Whewell not clear in maintaining that phenomena are classifiable according to distinct material characteristics (and are, thus, not completely malleable to the ordering powers of consciousness), there would be no necessity in postulating an external principle constitutive of experience. Had he failed to recognize a principle of

136

CHART 5

The Structure and Method
of the Inductive Sciences
According to Whewell

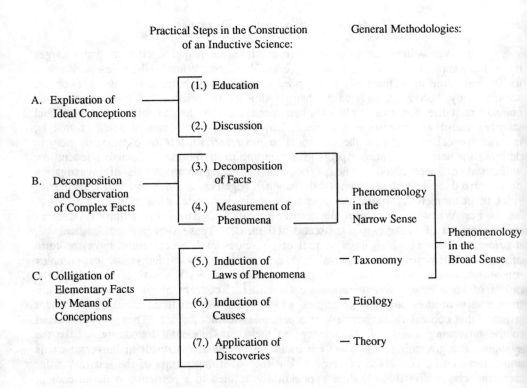

Practical Steps in the Construction
of an Inductive Science:

General Methodologies:

A. Explication of
   Ideal Conceptions

    (1.) Education

    (2.) Discussion

B. Decomposition
   and Observation
   of Complex Facts

    (3.) Decomposition
   of Facts

    (4.) Measurement of
   Phenomena

Phenomenology
in the
Narrow Sense

Phenomenology
in the
Broad Sense

C. Colligation of
   Elementary Facts
   by Means of
   Conceptions

    (5.) Induction of
   Laws of Phenomena — Taxonomy

    (6.) Induction of
   Causes — Etiology

    (7.) Application of
   Discoveries — Theory

of order in the phenomena themselves, then his system would have been little more than a variation on the Hegelian idealism, all change having been interpreted as nothing more than the necessary sporting of mind. But since Whewell presumes phenomena to have an indigenous principle of order antecedent to conceptualization, a principle which, to be sure, brings the governing motifs from potency to act, he postulates an external world characterized by *a posteriori* truths and known through the instruments of the sciences. The conceptualization of phenomena is, therefore, the complex product of *a priori* ideas in consciousness and *a posteriori* material principles which exist in the phenomena.

Phenomena, conceptualized singly or in configurations and given propositional expression which captures their character, are termed 'facts.' Empirical science operates upon the phenomena, and derivatively upon the facts, in order to improve a theory in the context of which the phenomena are interpreted. However, along with the alteration in the theory in which the facts reside, the interpretation of facts is altered, too. Whewell does not believe it is possible to have a fact without an interpretation because all facts are interpreted within theoretical contexts. For Whewell facts are theory-laden. Whether the phenomena which are the objects of facts are theory-laden is a moot point because the only ends for which they are described are the support or refutation of a theory. Thus, though theme-neutral observations of phenomena may be possible without the governing motifs of the sciences to provide a theoretical program for observation, phenomenological description is aimless. Because phenomenological description is not an end in itself but a means to furthering the projects of the sciences, the only value it has in Whewell's system is as an instrument. The individual sciences contribute the themes which give observation its practical worth. Without this direction, the attentional modifications which observation undergoes would, in all probability, be useless.

Although informed by a deep knowledge of the operations of the inductive sciences, Whewell's analysis of phenomena is limited because it is primarily concerned with the analysis of physical phenomena. Historical or social phenomena receive treatment, too, but it is minimal. Therefore, when Whewell describes the techniques of observation which have applicability in the inductive sciences, he tacitly assumes a model of observations based upon the inductive sciences. The problem with his basing a general formulation of scientific observation upon the physical sciences is not that this formulation forces those in the human sciences to adopt the experimental methods and rigor of the physical sciences--for, insofar as this is possible, it is a result devoutly to be wished--but, rather, by taking physical observation as a model, he ignores the peculiarities of observation related to the phenomena of human behavior. Whewell apparently forgets that, because of at least one circumstance, phenomenologists of human behavior are in a much better position to discover the psychology of human beings than physicists are able to discover the physical workings of atoms: phenomenologists of *human nature* share this nature with their object in a more directly accessible fashion than physicists do with atoms. By reflection on their own psychology, motivations, values, and so on, humanistic phenomenologists can know their objects of study from their "insides" as well as their "outsides."[68]

Although Whewell recognizes that the human sciences have qualitatively different governing motifs from the physical sciences, he does not prescribe a method of observation suited to these motifs. He assumes that the observational method of the physical sciences is adequate for the developing social sciences. Though he might demonstrate how the motif of teleology--the motif which ranges across all the human sciences--requires a new observational method, he never does this. This is the chief defect in Whewell's analysis of phenomena; he assumes no generic difference between the objects of the physical and social sciences.

4. The Ends of the Whewellian Phenomenology

Any discussion of the ends of the Whewellian phenomenology is complicated by the fact that Whewell's work *The Philosophy of the Inductive Sciences* may be taken as a transcendental exemplar of the phenomenologies he describes in connection with uranology, geology, and others. It, like the palaetiological sciences, is concerned with presuppositionless description, taxonomy and the explanation of the historical emergence of its objects.[69] In describing the individual varieties of phenomenology, Whewell is actually employing a general phenomenological method. Implicit in *The Philosophy of the Inductive Sciences* is the distinction between phenomenology as an object of this work and phenomenology as the method of this work. The described difference is rather like the distinction between logic as the object of logical discourse and the logical discourse (or metalogic), itself.[70] Because Whewell employs a variation of the very method he seeks to describe, it is difficult to extract any expression of his which provides an accurate rendition of what he perceives phenomenology's broadest ends to be. The best that can be done is to extrapolate the range of application which he assigns to his definitions and, by analogy, include all sciences as articulatable with phenomenological investigation.

If the requisite expansion of phenomenology is allowed, then phenomenology becomes a part of each science and aids each in clarifying its governing motifs and founding its theoretical apparatus. The ultimate end of phenomenology, therefore, is to provide unbiased descriptions of the states-of-affairs associated with facts and, on the basis of the governing motif of the associated science, to assemble these descriptions

---

[68]The point that we understand man, from within, better than we understand external physical realities is made well by Ludwig von Mises in *Epistemological Problems of Economics* (New York: NYU Press, 1973).

[69]Whewell is actually developing an elaborate "ontology" of science on the basis of its governing ideas, techniques, and structure.

[70]Logicians know well that there is no contradiction in employing logical methods to prove the consistency of other logical systems. Difficulties occur when a meta-language is confused with its objective language, just as Whewell's work would be invalidated if he did not claim for it a position above the things he was studying, hence the operative word in the title of his work is 'philosophy.'

in a taxonomy which provides the matter for etiology and theory. The proximate end to the achievement of this ultimate end is the clarification of the phenomena (the data of the governing motif), a task which is necessary in order to reduce the number of theoretical importations to a minimum.

5. The Whewellian Phenomenological Technique

Because there is an ambiguity in Whewell's explanation of phenomenology, there are two different but congruent ways of conceiving the Whewellian phenomenological technique. On one hand, Whewell seems to indicate that the methodological step he terms "the decomposition and observation of complex facts" is identical with phenomenology. It is this methodological step which contains only two substeps: (1) the decomposition of facts and (2) the measurement of phenomena. At other points in *The Philosophy of the Inductive Sciences*, Whewell seems to indicate that an additional substep, a substep belonging to the third methodological step (the colligation of elementary facts by means of conception), may be included as phenomenology. This substep is the induction of laws of phenomena, and, in the palaetiological sciences, it is identified with taxonomy. In the interest of comprehensiveness, and because Whewell--like the other six philosophical phenomenologists--believes that phenomena should dictate their own schemas of order, the methodological substep of taxonomy is included in the description of the Whewellian phenomenological technique.

By 'the decomposition of facts,' Whewell intends "the reduction of complex fact to 'elementary' facts which state relations among clear and distinct ideas as space, time, number, and force."[71] According to Whewell, the categories which determine the select relations are those determined by the governing motif of the science. The purpose of this reduction is to free the accepted facts from their conventional interpretation, to fragment them into their smallest constituents and then to observe their meaning freed from as many presuppositions as possible. Unfortunately, Whewell does not describe the peculiar intentionality which is to accompany this decomposition, although he does indicate that this form of analysis is to focus on elementary qualitative series which are apophantic for any observer. The precision of these analyzed observations is to be further sharpened by the casting of these observations into mathematical scales whenever a mathematical scale can be matched to an observation.

The coordination of observations with mathematical continua represents the second methodological step of Whewellian phenomenology. It is the step he calls "the measurement of phenomena" and consists of assigning scalar or vector descriptions to qualitative or quantitative variations in the analyzed phenomena. Thus, if one observes change in a phenomenon such as a change in color from scarlet to deep maroon, the proper phenomenological response is to associate this shading of color with the continuum of color values by which scarlet would represent one position, maroon another, and all intermediate qualitative values positions between these extremes. Other

---

[71]Whewell 1: 335.

examples of qualities with scalar description are temperature, brilliance and size. The correct response to a phenomenological decomposition is the discovery of a serial or variable order which enables the phenomenologist to describe the qualitative or quantitative properties of that phenomenon in terms susceptible to mathematical manipulation. This step, of course, presupposes that the phenomenologist has some acquaintance with mathematical methods. If might most accurately be called "phenomenometry."

Although Whewell gives contradictory impressions as to whether it is to be included as a part of phenomenology proper, or not, the next methodological substep in the Whewellian discussion of inductive method is taxonomy. About taxonomy, Whewell has much to say which is of value but not pliant to quick encapsulation. Nevertheless, some of his prescriptions may be sketched.

First, in providing a taxonomy based upon phenomenological decompositions and measurement, it is important to use the governing motifs of the science (under which the taxonomy is being constructed) as the principles of order. Classifications must not be arbitrary or result from purely capricious acts of comparison and reflection.

Second, a better taxonomy is distinguished from an inferior taxonomy by its being constructed on a system of order more likely to yield dependable predictions and generalizations of phenomena all the while being comprehensive enough to classify (as of yet undiscovered) phenomena. In Whewell's terminology, a good taxonomy is one in which its diagnoses insure its diataxes.

Third, taxonomies are to be constructed on principles of order which are essential and not accidental. One determines which of these principles are essential by studying which functions of the object are necessary to make it what it is. Application of Occam's razor insures that only those functions which are necessary to the chosen object are included as its defining characteristics.

According to Whewell, the motif under which these essential taxonomies are to be constructed is that of natural affinity. This motif implies that an individual is formed by environmental conditions in such a way that its functional features mirror the demands its environment makes upon it. Natural affinity also implies that classes of beings emergent from different environments (or causal contextures) will display similar functional features. It is on the basis of the functional features (without which the being would be inconceivable) that Whewellian taxonomies of affinity are to be constructed. In the Whewellian philosophy of the inductive sciences, the creation of a taxonomy completes phenomenology's involvement in the scientific enterprise. The remaining methodological steps are under the direct guidance of the particular science's etiology and theory.

CHAPTER VII

PEIRCE: PHENOMENOLOGY AS SEMIOTICS

1. The Peircean Phenomenology in Context

Though an American and reared according to educational principles which would be considered unorthodox even by today's standards, Charles Sanders Peirce was William Whewell's intellectual kin. Peirce had, in fact, read Whewell's works with a critical appreciation made possible by his own wide ranging interests and personal accomplishments. Like Whewell, Peirce was a polymath. Occasionally straying into relatively unbeaten paths such as Greek and Old English phonology, parapsychology and Egyptology, Peirce also made solid progress on main roads such as chemistry, astronomy, mathematics, geodesy, criminology, ancient history, Napoleonic biography, logic, philosophy and religion. Based upon what is known of his expansive genius, it would be no exaggeration to say that he might have made a success of himself had he chosen any career from that of mathematician to *dégustateur*.[1] Unfortunately, both his own erratic personality and the American university system, whose spirit was influenced more by German than English higher education, conspired to limit his immediate fame and influence. His *Photometric Researches*--still considered a classic of photometric astronomy--was the only book published in his lifetime. Even so, he employed a wide variety of other media to present his discoveries, media such as letters, magazine and encyclopedia articles, speeches and occasional pieces. It is in this incongruous body of works, and not in any systematic tome, that the religionist must seek the meaning of the Peircean phenomenology.

At its outset, this search immediately leads us to an obstacle: because phenomenology is incidental to Peirce's writings and, therefore, peripheral to many of these writings' central themes, any attempt to disclose a clear and unequivocal statement of Peircean phenomenology will be vain. Any construction of Peircean phenomenology's nuclear meaning is in danger of being torn asunder by major themes which seem to lend phenomenology discordant intentions.[2] And, though expositions like that of Feibleman

---

[1] A brief account of Peirce's bizarre upbringing and wide ranging interests can be found in "Charles Sanders Peirce," *Dictionary of American Biography*, ed. Dumas Malone, 10 vols. (New York: Charles Scribner's Sons, 1962) 7: 393-403.

[2] It should be observed that this perplexity is not unique to the theme of Peircean phenomenology, alone. Peirce, himself, admitted that he hardly found it possible to put his papers in any sort of systematic arrangement based upon their major themes. Moreover, the defects of *the* major attempt at the systematization of Peirce's works--the *Collected Papers*

and Murphey are notable for their ingenuity and clarity, they must be considered provisional, at best, because they do not pay phenomenology quite the attention it deserves for present purposes.

The only recourse, then, is a re-examination of the meaning of phenomenology in Peirce's writings. But because the texts of this study are a fragmented thematic field, the purpose of the present investigation is not to seek major themes but to seek out those secondary or tertiary themes which can serve as the material for substructuring and, thus, unifying Peirce's thoughts about phenomenology.[3] This means that the order of importance of the Peircean themes will be inverted and, instead of considering phenomenology to be thematically secondary, Peirce's writings will be considered as sites linked by a common phenomenological intent. Thus, the themes of phenomenology can be used as a means to order the heterogeneity of the various primary themes. This is made possible, first, by bringing together all the texts having to do with phenomenology and, second, by examining how the primary themes may be unpacked as consequences of the phenomenological intent. The result will be a presentation of the Peircean phenomenology which will have the effect of demonstrating the global relevance of phenomenology to the Peircean system.

2. The Peircean Phenomenology

Phenomenology, in the Peircean sense, "is the most primal of all positive sciences," 'positive sciences' meaning sciences directed to the discovery and description of factual knowledge, knowledge expressible in categorical propositions about adventitious experiences.[4] Phenomenology is first within this domain because it, alone, produces pure scientific description. Every other positive science presupposes phenomenology as methodologically foundational. Without rigorous factual description more abstract categorical propositions would be imprecise and ambiguous. The relation in which phenomenology stands to the other positive sciences disallows its foundation upon any

---

by Hartshorne and Weiss--are well-known. Hartshorne has even been said to have had nightmares about how his emendation and selection may have distorted Peirce's thought. This anecdote is part of the "folklore" surrounding the *Collected Papers* and was told to me by the late R.M. Martin some years ago.

[3]So far as I know, no one has linked the Peircean phenomenology to his system as a whole in the way I have. The fact that the Peircean phenomenological motif serves as a convenient means for substructuring the Peircean writings indicates, I think, the centrality of this motif to the Peircean corpus. By referring to my analysis as a substructuring of Peirce, I only indirectly follow Lazarsfeld's use for the word 'substruct.' Though Lazarsfeld applies this term to the sociological practice of discovering an attribute space and a reduction by which the attribute space can be deduced, my use of 'substructure' refers to the process by which I hypothetically make phenomenology a central theme of Peirce's thought and, then, observe the relations which emerge between phenomenology and other themes. In Peirce's case, this method proves very suggestive, if not productive. See Paul F. Lazarsfeld and Allen H. Barton, "Qualitative Measurement in the Social Sciences: Classification, Typologies, and Indices," *The Policy Sciences*, Daniel Lerner, ed. (Stanford: Stanford University Press, 1951) 153-192.

[4]Charles Sanders Peirce, *Collected Papers*, ed. Charles Hartshorne and Paul Weiss, 8 vols. (Cambridge: Harvard University Press, 1974) vol. 5: *Pragmatism and Pragmaticism* 39-40: 28. [The number(s) before the colon indicate(s) paragraph(s) and the number(s) after the colon pages within the volume.]

other factual science but not upon the class of sciences Peirce terms 'conditional' or 'hypothetical,' sciences whose distinguishing feature is that they employ abstract forms common to all science.[5] The distinction between the class of sciences which phenomenology founds and the sciences which found phenomenology is important because it places phenomenology squarely in the middle of the scientific architectonic. The hypothetical sciences precede the factual sciences because they are concerned, not with facts, but with abstract logical relations; they are sciences of pure possibility possessing ineluctable themes without which phenomenology, or any of the other positive sciences, would be impossible.

Of the hypothetical sciences, pure mathematics is supremely fundamental. It "meddles with every other science without exception."[6] But the converse is not true. Pure mathematics is not meddled in by any other science by virtue of the fact that its objects are of the highest generality: they are pure logical potentials which underlie all experience. Its practitioners are concerned with no matter of fact, they aim "to discover not how things actually are, but how they might be supposed to be, if not in our universe then in some other."[7] In that factual experience must be consistent with any such possibility, the sciences of factual experience must be founded upon the sciences of possible experience. Phenomenology as the first factual science must, therefore, be likewise founded.[8]

---

[5]Peirce, vol. 1: *Principles of Philosophy* 183-184: 78.

[6]Peirce *Principles* 245-252: 112-117.

[7]Peirce, *Pragmatism* 39: 28.

[8]Peirce believes that his articulation of phenomenology as the medium between the hypothetical and positive sciences enables him to transcend that "club-footed affair" which is the Hegelian phenomenology. In Peirce's estimation, Hegel errs in positing phenomenology as the *terminus a quo* of philosophical method, and, indeed, of all sciences, for such placement entirely ignores the significance of the sciences of the possible. By disregarding the possible and limiting phenomenology's object and method only "to what actually forces itself on the mind," Hegel limits phenomenology to the investigation of actual and not possible experience. He, thus, neglects a whole class of phenomena which have essential but not actual existence.

Neglected are those phenomena which exist as the necessary preconditions of thought: mathematical phenomena. Though not given to sensory experience because of their empty logical forms, mathematical phenomena possess a greater clarity and distinctness than factual phenomena. The mere experience of these essential phenomena means to be in immediate possession of their intelligiblity. Discovered, as they are, through conscious reflection and imagination, mathematical phenomena are wholly constituted by notions such as identity, reflexivity, consistency, truth and so on. Sensorially contentless, they are defined as hypothetical objects, the products of formal relations holding between logical possibilities. As apparition-like as they may seem to be, these phenomena structure the world order. Any factual phenomena--whether physical, metaphysical or aesthetic--can be described as a complex of logical relations holding between variables. All intelligible descriptions, in general, and applied mathematics, in particular, depend upon the properties of essential phenomena. No object, in fact, could be experienced were it not for the multitude of logical relations which structure it in relation to itself, other objects and the experiencing subject. Phenomenology in the Peircean sense, thus presupposes mathematical phenomena as irreducible. As such, they found experience naturally, but they can also be used as tools for the construction and interpretation of experience. In contrast to Peirce's concern about essential phenomena, Hegel's ignorance of mathematical realities lends the Hegelian phenomenology a thoroughly nominalistic and 'pragmatoidal" character.

In the thought of Hegel, mathematical phenomena are always subordinate to the dialectic. They can have no truly independent existence in such a system which does not respect the law of non-contradiction. Mathematical phenomena, thus become the mere products of conscious evolution worked out as the result of intellectual praxis. Peirce impugns this

2.1. The Peircean Phaeneron

The Peircean phenomenology is, thus, directed to a much wider range of objects than is the Hegelian phenomenology. Peirce makes this especially clear in the way he defines the key synonyms 'phenomenon' and 'phaeneron.' Phenomena are "to be understood in the broadest sense conceivable," that is, as "essentially different elements which seem to present themselves in what seems."[9] Phenomena are elementary; there is no going behind them. Moreover, they flesh in the content of the various percepts and, as such, possess both a peculiar mode of presentation and effect. Because they are never perfectly predictable, they forcibly intrude into consciousness as things alien to it, the effect of this intrusion being to evoke surprise in the observer. It is this surprise which most effectively demonstrates their otherness as well as the scissiparity of ego and non-ego, a scissiparity which is always characteristic of conscious experience. In every observation of phenomena, a moment of surprise occurs which is doubling of consciousness in which "the Ego," expecting a particular condition, is abruptly confronted with "the Non-Ego," a "strange intruder" in the form of an unexpected condition.[10] No experience is devoid of this diremption.

Peirce uniformly extends these descriptions of phenomena to phaenerons. Phaenerons are, among all things, the most "directly open to observation."[11] Identical to phenomena, they are "whatever seems to be before the mind *ipso facto*."[12] However, for the field of all phenomena, the universe of phaenerons, Peirce reserves the title 'the phaeneron,' which he defines as "the collective total of all that is in any sense present to the mind quite regardless of whether it corresponds to any real thing or not."[13] The features of the phaeneron are ubiquitous and accessible to any mind at any time; this fact makes phenomenology (phaeneroscopy) possible. Phenomenology, in short, is the study of the field of possible experiences present to any possible consciousness.

---

character as the reason for the worst abuses of the Hegelian dialectic. Certainly, it allows the Marxist interpreters of Hege. to disengage or misinterpret any historical or scientific datum which does not appear as the necessary result of tha historical dialectic presumed to schematize the single, practical path of mankind's evolution. Moreover, it becomes license for the Marxists to ignore any imaginative possibility which does not fit the straight jacket of thesis-synthesis-antithesis. Hegel and the Marxists discover a series of necessary stages or categories only by ignoring what militates against thei deduction of the categories: the fact that they are trivially exhaustive. In that they can be applied to everything, thei explanatory value becomes worthless. Because Hegel equates the possible with the historical dialectic--construing the two as the same limitation of Spirit--he narrows the meaning of historical possibility much further than is justified. Pure mathematics corrects this equation for its appreciation results in two realizations: first, that the logical meaning o possibility is certainly broader than can be *imaginatively* visualized and, second, that a description of historical evolution is not susceptible to simple encapsulation in the Hegelian evolutionary schema. Peirce's placement of phenomenology a dependent upon pure mathematics is intended to cure the Hegelian myopia. See Peirce, *Pragmatism* 37: 26.

[9]Peirce, vol. 2: *Elements of Logic* 197: 114.

[10]Peirce, *Principles* 320-324: 159-162.

[11]Peirce, *Principles* 286-288: 142-143.

[12]Peirce, *Principles* 288: 143.

[13]Peirce, *Principles* 284: 141.

Both the nature of phenomenological objects and the articulation of phenomenology in the scientific architectonic influence Peirce in his delineation of phenomenology's tasks. Peirce succinctly enumerates these tasks in his definition of phenomenology. Phenomenology, as viewed according to its tasks, is:

> . . . that study which, supported by the direct observation of phaenerons and generalizing its observations, signalizes several very broad classes of phaenerons; describes the features of each; shows that although they are so inextricably mixed together that no one can be isolated, yet it is manifest that their characters are quite disparate; then proves, beyond question, that a certain very short list comprises all of these broadest categories of phaenerons there are; and finally proceeds to the laborious and difficult task of enumerating the principal subdivisions of these categories.[14]

Though phenomenology has for its objects only the elemental components of the phaeneron--those elements which are indecomposable either logically or observationally--it leads to an ultimate analysis of experience which is neither argumentative, evaluative, or explanatory but which is purely descriptive.[15] Peirce radicalizes this proviso by maintaining that, in its first moment, phenomenology does not involve reasoning! Because reasoning results in conclusions which may be indubitable regardless of appearances, phenomenology does not primarily consist of reasoning. Phenomenology leads to no assertions except that things *seem* such and such a way. But since even minor assertions depend upon preceding reasonings about experience, phenomenology, ideally, should not even include assertions about the way things seem. "Phenomenology," in the ideal sense, "can only tell the reader which way to look and to see what he shall see."[16] Practically, however, phenomenology necessarily presupposes both assertions and reasonings, but these are to be minimized in that the phenomenological method limits their application to the description of elemental experiences and to the construction of systems of classification. Phenomenological method dictates that no unnecessary baggage is to be carried into the descriptive act. The phenomenologist must abstract himself "from any tradition, any authority, any reasons for supposing . . . such to be the facts, or nay fancies of any kind, and to confine himself to honest, single-minded observation of the appearances."[17]

2.2. Categorization in the Peircean Phenomenology

Nevertheless, Peirce is aware that phenomenology can never aid the sciences dependent upon it if its methods do not result in a body of descriptions possessing practical utility. Like Whewell, Peirce fully appreciates the need for a system of phenomenological classification, a taxonomy of phenomenological objects, a phenomenological ontology. But Peirce, in contrast to Whewell, conceives of this

---

[14]Peirce, *Principles* 286: 142.

[15]Peirce, *Pragmatism* 37-39: 26-28.

[16]Peirce, *Elements* 197: 114-115.

[17]Peirce, *Principles* 287: 142.

classification as analogous to philosophical categories and as not directly reliant upon the constructive methods of the natural sciences.

For Peirce, as for Aristotle, Kant, and Hegel, "a category is an element of phenomena of the first rank of generality."[18]   A category's generality is indirectly proportional to the number of coordinate categories occupying its level.   The more general a category, the fewer the number of coordinate categories; the more specific a category, the greater the number of coordinate categories.   Operative in the systematic arrangement of such categories are two apparently divergent, but actually convergent, philosophical intentionalities: one which is directed, with "minute accuracy," to the scrutiny of immediate appearance and one which is directed to establish "broadest possible generalization."[19]

Although each intentionality is to be operative at every level of generality, each is primarily responsible for a correlative categorical domain.   The intentionality which is directed to the specific scrutiny of phenomena results in the *particular* categories, categories which "form a series, or a set of series, only one of each series being present, or at least predominant, in any one phenomenon."[20]   The intentionality which is directed to generalization results in universal categories, each belonging "to every phenomenon, one perhaps more prominent in one aspect of that phenomenon than another but all of them belonging to every phenomenon."[21]   The particular categories are such that they characterize phenomena specifically; when a phenomenon is represented under a particular category usually it is not susceptible to representation under some other category.   In fact, particular categories tend to represent phenomena according to mutually exclusive elements.   Presumably, particular categories are series of qualities present as states of a phenomenal complex as that complex endures for a period of time. Universal categories, on the other hand, belong to all phenomena without exception, but their presence is capable of variation in that some universal categories more obviously found some phenomena than others, though every phenomenon depends upon some universal categories for its foundation, no matter how difficult the discernment of this foundation may be.   Universals, thus, function in Peirce's philosophy much like transcendentals do in other philosophical systems.   They apply indiscriminately to all phenomena at all times, regardless of exigencies, and they represent synthezing laws which shape thinking because they correspond to the "character" of the universe. Moreover, inasmuch as human thought is able to think these categories, it is able to partake in universal modes of action.[22]   Behind the tasks and definition of phenomenol-

---

[18]Peirce, *Pragmatism* 43: 30.

[19]Peirce, *Pragmatism* 43: 30.

[20]Peirce, *Pragmatism* 43: 30.

[21]Peirce, *Pragmatism* 43: 30.

[22]Peirce, *Pragmatism* 43: 30.

ogy stand both a criteriology of the categories as well as an aretalogy of the phenomenologist.

2.2.1. The criteria of categorization

For a category to be well-formed, Peirce stipulates that it must satisfy four criteria: it must be sufficient; it must be free from redundancy; it must clearly demonstrate its own relations to the other categories, whatever they are; and, finally, it must not be founded upon any axiology except insofar as that axiology is constitutive of it and is an inseparable part of its description.[23] The application of (at very least) three cognitive acts ensures that a category fulfills the above criteria. A category's sufficiency, its freedom from both redundancy and non-constitutive axiologies and its relations to the other categories is established once one establishes what can be discriminated, prescinded and dissociated from it. These mental acts represent a scale of possible relations between consciousness and its different objects.

Thus, if it is possible to discriminate one object from another, this means that those objects are distinguishable and disengageable in meaning alone. Logically, this means that any object may be discriminated from another providing that the second does not analytically found the meaning of the former. Anything having a different sense from another may be discriminated from it.

Precision, in contrast, is of a different order of consciousness than discrimination inasmuch as it does not apply to semantic modalities but, rather, to perceptual modalities. Precision, as Peirce defines it, is "the act of supposing . . . something about one element of a percept . . . without paying any regard to the other elements."[24] Thus, though color can be discriminated from space and space discriminated from color, color cannot be prescinded from space--since one cannot conceive of a chromic modality without extension. One can, however, prescind space from color since space can be defined as a tactile field as well as a visual field. Color is merely one more of space's modes of appearance and does not play a constitutive role in one's conceptualization of space.

Dissociation, the third act which insures the clear and distinct definition of the categories, has a broader field of application than either discrimination or precision but within that field is much less often actually applicable to objects.

> Dissociation is that separation which in the absence of a constant association, is permitted by the law of the association of images. It is the consciousness of one thing without the necessary simultaneous consciousness of the other.[25]

Dissociation is only possible when two conceptualized qualities do not call up associations. Dissociability defines the narrowest compass of distinguishability because

---

[23]Peirce, *Pragmatism* 37: 39.

[24]Peirce, *Principles* 549: 288.

[25]Peirce, *Principles* 549: 289-290.

it characterizes a consciousness of one thing which is absolutely devoid of a consciousness of another. Dissociation, therefore, belongs to an order of consciousness which might be termed "imagic" or "imaginational" and is an act which is possible when the objects distinguished are, in no wise, modalities of one another. In the case of dissociation, neither is space dissociable from color nor color from space since in the first instance color is an aspect of space while in the second instance space is an *a priori* condition of color. "Abstraction or precision, therefore, presupposes a greater separation than does discrimination, but less a separation than dissociation."[26]

2.2.2. The virtues associated with categorization.

Three "virtues" or faculties ought to be cultivated by the phenomenologist in order to regulate and facilitate the discovery of categories according to the above criteriology. The first is the faculty of seeing things as they are. It is "the faculty of seeing what stares one in the face, just as it presents itself, unreplaced by any interpretation, unsophisticated by any allowance for this or that supposed modifying circumstance."[27] This virtue, according to Peirce, most often characterizes the artist, who sees the colors as they are--often in minute gradations of hue and tone--and who chooses precisely the correct pigments to depict what he observes. The artist's penchant for accurate observation is the most valuable virtue for phenomenological description.[28]

The second virtue to be sought and husbanded by the phenomenologist is a "resolute discrimination which fastens itself like a bulldog upon the particular features that we are studying, follows it wherever it may lurk, and detects it beneath all its disguises."[29] This is the virtue of being resolutely monothematic; it is the concentration of the chessmaster who, excluding all outside interruptions, is able to keep his attention perfectly fixed on the move at hand and its implications for the rest of the game. A dogged resoluteness like that of the chessmaster makes it possible for the phenomenologist to reduce vast clouds of conflicting appearances to precise and elemental descriptions. Once one has perceived accurately and has followed those potentially illusive perceptions wherever they have led one, and once one has described one's perceptions with the virtuosity of an artist, one must be able to make essential generalizations about what one has described.

The third, and final virtue which ought to be the possession of the phenomenologist is "the generalizing faculty of the mathematician who produces the abstract formula that comprehends the very essence of a feature . . . purified from all admixture of extraneous and irrelevant accompaniments."[30] It is the mathematician's ability to generalize which

---

[26]Peirce, *Principles* 549: 290.

[27]Peirce, *Pragmatism* 42: 29.

[28]Peirce, *Pragmatism* 42: 29.

[29]Peirce, *Pragmatism* 42: 29.

[30]Peirce, *Pragmatism* 42: 30.

makes the abstraction of particulars into categories a precise matter. This faculty also enables a phenomenologist to engage in "abstractive observation," the imaginary construction of hypothetical states of affairs which enables him to determine what will be true of appearances even if he has only limited experience of their behavior. Without the generalizing faculty, the phenomenologist will find it impossible to take the final step toward scientific classification without abstractive observation.

Although Peirce never directly asserts the fact, it is evident upon examining his philosophy that both his criteriology of conscious acts and his phenomenological aretalogy are operative in his arriving at a vindication of his phenomenology. Indeed, his schematization of those categories which characterize all reality is itself an extension of the Peircean phaeneroscopy and results from the dialectic between the original intention behind the idea of phenomenology and the result of its application to the world. The resultant categories enable Peirce to develop a powerful phenomenological semiotics, a description and classification of different kinds of signs and the way these signs are related to the objects they represent.

2.3. The Peircean Cenopythagorean Categories

Peirce applies his phenomenological method to reality in order to discover the transcendentally formal and material categories of being. But although his attempt to discover transcendentally material categories yields no useful results, his attempt to discover transcendentally formal categories of being results in the discovery of universal logical principles "not merely . . . regulatively valid" but valid in their universal applicability as metaphysical truths.[31] Peirce terms the three logical principles the "cenopythagorean categories" of firstness, secondness, and thirdness.

These Peircean transcendental principles are characterized by peculiar epistemological and ontological relationships. Epistemologically, thirdness founds the possibility of the discovery of secondness and secondness, in turn, makes the discovery of firstness possible. In each case, the phenomenological scrutiny of each category takes place within thirdness which is essentially characteristic of thought, as will be explained later. Ontologically, the relationship is quite the reverse. Firstness is the ontological foundation of secondness and secondness ontologically founds thirdness. The significance of these epistemological relationships becomes evident when one examines how Peirce understands these categories.

2.3.1. The cenopythagorean category of firstness

Firstness signifies freshness, vivacity and freedom existing in uncontrolled variety and multiplicity without any determinations. If it could be made a pure object of consciousness—a possibility Peirce does not allow--it would be best represented by a single experience of feeling, a consciousness involving no analysis, comparison or process, no distinction between conscious states or acts but merely an experience "which

---

[31]Peirce, *Pragmatism* 43: 30.

in its entirety" is identical "in every moment of time as long as it endures."[32] Although the actual experience of firstness is only imaginable and, presumably, cannot be consumately reached by any conscious act, it is this pure experience which is what one transcendentally intends when one attempts to understand what is meant by a particular quality. The quality in itself is indecomposable and *sui generis*. However, when one begins to generalize about the communalities of monadic experience one arrives at a notion of quality as a class term, "a mere abstract potential," which is a sensorial possibility. It is in this sense that a partial identification between Peirce's notion of firstness and the class notion of quality is possible. Firstness applies most purely to the qualitative aspects of the world. "Quality is the monadic element of the world."[33]

2.3.2. *The cenopythagorean category of secondness*

Secondness, as a category, signifies struggle, resistance, duplication, causation, force, factuality and surprise as these are typical of oppositions between things or qualities.[34] If secondness could be made a pure object of consciousness, it would include every possible experience in which the subject could be purely distinguished from the object. It would express the pure relation between patient and agent resultant from the experience of other things happening not in control of one's ego.[35] This relation is best represented in those experiences when one is confronted from "outside," as it were, by an object which modifies consciousness according to some unexpected operation. When one experiences surprise, for example, an exaggeration of consciousness occurs which, according to Peirce, is typical of every variety of perception. Surprise results when a protention is met with an occurrence which is not expected. One expects to see a certain thing but, despite the expectation, one sees something quite different. Facticity, as experienced in consciousness and as abstractly intended, is another example of the dyadic nature of existence. A fact is experienced (and ideally intended) as something which, try as one might, cannot be banished from consciousness. It possesses a resistance which cannot be overcome by simple conscious alterations, and thus, it forces itself upon conscious recognition.

Peirce believes that two qualities typify every variety of secondness: resistance and effort. When we bump against a "hard" fact we register its otherness by applying effort to its resistance. Resistance and effort are present in every conscious operation

---

[32] Peirce notices that his conception of firstness has affinities with Kant's notion of the manifold of sense, since experienced firstness would be virtually identical with objectless experience. A monadic experience is objectless because contained in it is no comparison, no abstract "suchness" over and against which there might be other things. The intentionality associated with firstness is one which is particular without comparison; it is composed of pure natureless embodiments, parts, and features and without specification of its objective or subjective nature. Firstness is an idealization of what consciousness would be if it could forget the subject-object distinction completely and become a single uninterpreted sensation. See Peirce, *Pragmatism* 307: 152.

[33] Peirce, *Pragmatism* 426: 233.

[34] Peirce, *Pragmatism* 53-57: 38-40.

[35] Peirce, *Pragmatism* 52: 37-38.

we exercise whether these operations occur in the world of matter--in which case "our modification of other things is more prominent than their reaction on us" or in the perceptual world--in which case the effect of other things on us "is overwhelmingly greater than our effect on them."[36] Resistance and effort are important aspects to the experience of secondness because in lived experience they are measurements of the "durability" of one's ego and the strength of one's volition over and against the mindless force of other things. All interaction with the world of matter and persons results in a change in oneself, a change in other things and people or, as often, a change in both agent and patient. The practical test, therefore, of an idea or an action becomes its ability to produce the desired effect, a process which, though it is understandable only through consciousness' participation in thirdness, is possible only through the relative resistances and energies characteristic of the factual world. Unless one understands the characteristics which typify facticity as a pure form of dyadism, consciousness will be unable to construct instrumentalities by which dyadic relations may be utilized for predetermined ends. To ignore the irreducibly dyadic nature of existence is to be efficiently conditioned by what one has ignored. It is, also, to confuse the different categories of firstness, secondness and thirdness as these relate to facts.

The dyadism of facts, according to Peirce, is summarized, but not exhausted, by the following features: (1) facts are distinct; (2) facts occur accidentally or are the result of force; (3) facts have specific temporal and spatial locations; (4) facts are the sum of their consequences; (5) the existence of facts is proved by their resistance; (6) facts are determinable in their characteristics; (7) facts have subjects that express their existence; (8) all facts (as actions) entail reciprocal facts (as reactions); (9) the classification of facts takes place by dichotomies; (10) facts change only by variations in the qualities of their subjects not by annihilation or production; and (11) facts are existentially irreducible.

Since to be factual is essentially what it is to be dyadic, the different possible relations within dyads are expressive of the possible constitutions of facts. To understand these possible relations is to understand the characteristics of facts, as well.

Peirce compounds distinctions almost endlessly when he discusses the varieties of dyadic relations. First, he distinguishes essential dyadic relations from accidental dyadic relations by defining the former as dyads of compossible monads requiring nothing further than the presence of two qualities to effect a dyadic relation. Essential dyads are those in which the dyadic relation between monads is necessarily present when the two monads are present. Monads of this variety consist of qualities related by a species-singular distinction and a shared character. Thus, the relation is generally one of containment. Moreover, the experience of the constituent monads is sufficient to produce an experience of qualitative containment in every case, and this experience is not divorcible from the experience of the two monads so long as they are co present.[37]

---

[36]Peirce, *Pragmatism* 53-57: 38-40.

[37]Peirce, *Princples* 454: 247.

152

Accidental dyads, in contrast, derive an acquired mode of being--quality--from the interaction of their constituents. These dyads possess an additional property which is synthetic, not one of containment and not one analytically related to the mere presence of two monads. The oppositions existing within relations of this sort cannot be reduced to the difference between the experience of a universal and the experience of a particular. These oppositions, instead, contribute an entirely new character to the whole. Such relations are always experienced as the emergent, conjoint effects of their constituents, as effects which could not have been predicted on the basis of the dyad's constituents, if these constituents had been experienced individually.[38]

Accidental dyads are further divisible into two classes: that of inherential dyads and that of relational dyads. The former closely resembles the class of essential dyads in that the relation defining inherential dyads is approximately that of containment but a containment not of particular within species but of constitutive qualities within whole. The relation of containment characteristic of an inherential dyad is one approaching identity but never reaching it.[39] On the other hand, relational dyads are characterized merely in that neither constituent of the dyadic relation is a monad.

Although inherential dyads are not further divisible, relational dyads may be dichotomized according to whether they are: (A) dyads of identity and (B) dyads of diversity. The former are charactered by dyadic relations in which the constituents are "existentially one and the same" and the latter are characterized by constituents which are "existentially two and distinct."[40]

Dyads of diversity can be further dichotomized into two subclasses consisting of, on one hand, a class of relations characterized by the communion of two constituents resultant from the sharing of a single monad and on the other hand, a class of relations characterized by the sharing of a dyadic opposition or oppositions. The former are termed: (1) "qualitative dyads of diversity" because the diversity of the dyadic constituents is held together in relation by a shared quality. The latter are termed: (2) "dynamical dyads of diversity" because the relations existing between the constituents of this dyadic variety are typical of what, in the broad sense, may be termed "force."[41]

As was the case with the second class of all the preceding dichotomies, the class of dynamical dyads of diversity are susceptible to further binary subdivision. The result is two further subclasses: (a) materially unordered dyads and (b) materially ordered dyads. Both share common features in that the "matter" of their interrelations is the result of qualitative oppositions. However, the former is distinguishable from the latter in that the latter is the class of dyads in which the relations effected between

[38]Peirce, *Principles* 456: 247.

[39]Peirce, *Principles* 464: 250.

[40]Peirce, *Principles* 465: 250.

[41]Peirce, *Principles* 467: 251.

constituents are responsible for complementary, but distinct, interrelations. These complementary relations stand in relation to one another as reciprocals.[42]

Materially ordered dyads are, in turn, divisible into (i) formally unordered dyads, which imply no "existential or intrinsic distinction between the subjects as to which is first and which is second," and formally ordered dyads--which have an existentially intrinsic order. Insofar as two constituents are formally ordered, one of these constituent acts as the determiner (or agent) and the other acts as the determined (or patient). Moreover, the agent may be left relatively free or indeterminate with respect to conditioning by another. Thus, its character is relatively first, or monadic, though the constituent it conditions is characteristically altered and becomes second to it or dyadic.[43]

One final dichotomy defines the possible dyadic modalities. It is the bifurcation of the class of formally ordered dyads according to "the character of the dependence of one subject upon the other."[44] If the second constituent of a formally ordered dyad possesses monadic accidents which depend upon the first constituent (agent) of that relation, then the dyad is an actional dyad. If, however, the complete dyadic character of the patient is dependent upon the agent, then the relation and its constituents comprise a poietical or productive dyad.[45]

The above scale of dichotomizations exhausts the forms of dyadism as they occur in the world. Inasmuch as these forms represent the simple interactions between two qualities, a quality and a system of qualities, or two systems of qualities, they also define the different "mechanically" causal modalities which exist in the world. In his analysis of secondness, Peirce provides a taxonomy of force as force is conceived in the Hegelian system. In addition, Peirce lays the foundation for an analysis of the interaction between any *onta* which participate in secondness. It is not until Peirce brings the category of thirdness into the picture, however, that relationship between consciousness, firstness and secondness is elucidated and the foundation of a true phenomenology of consciousness and a phenomenological semantics is established.

2.3.3. The cenopythagorean category of thirdness

The cenopythagorean category of thirdness signifies transuasion, betweenness, nomology, generality and consciousness as these are each instantiations of a general antinominalistic principle actually operative in the world. The principle to which Peirce refers is a kind of teleological lawfulness which he understands to be the laws of nature which are not capable of mechanistic reduction to mere relations of secondness (or efficient causality) but actually imply a higher variety of interrelationship between onta, that of thirdness. It is thirdness, the mediation of firstness and secondness, which enables man to make sense out of appearances, to read appearances as signs of an

---

[42] Peirce, *Principles* 467: 251.

[43] Peirce, *Principles* 468: 251-252.

[44] Peirce, *Principles* 469: 252.

[45] Peirce, *Principles* 469: 252.

underlying, general order. Like Whewell, Peirce understands that the order in the universe can be sufficiently accounted for only if one recognizes "that the laws of nature are ideas or resolutions in the mind of some vast consciousness, who, whether supreme or subordinate, is a Deity relative to us."[46] In a passage which is reminiscent of Whewell's position on the interpretive aspects of science, Peirce suggests that his semiotics might well serve as a method for obtaining a disclosure of cosmological meaning, since he believes that the phenomena of the universe stand as signs expressing God's purpose.

> . . . [T]he universe is a vast representamen, a great symbol of God's purpose, working out its conclusions in living realities. Now every symbol must have, organically attached to it, its Indices of Reactions and its Icons of Qualities; and such part as these reactions and these qualities play in an argument that, they of course, play in the universe--that Universe being precisely an argument. In the little bit that you or I can make out of this huge demonstration, our perceptual judgments are the premises *for us* and these perceptual judgments have icons as their predicates, in which *icons* Qualities are immediately presented. But what is first for us is not first in nature. The premises of Nature's own process are all the independent uncaused elements of facts. . . . These premises of nature, however, though they are not the *perceptual facts* that are premises to us, nevertheless must resemble them in being premises. We can only imagine what they are by comparing them with the premises for us.[47]

The idea of thirdness possesses an inherent value in that it opens a channel to a universal science of interpretation. Inasmuch as man participates in universal thirdness by virtue of his consciousness and material being, the same formal relations of signification which operate within his social environment operate in the material world. Of course, man always interprets these relations from within consciousness since the world "which is present to us is a phenomenal manifestation of ourselves."[48] But this in no way dissolves the dichotomy between internal reality and external reality nor does it call the existence of an external world into question. This is because our consciousnesses are triadically related to the external world as signs of its existence. Our consciousnesses are related to the world, first, as signs to a conscious act of interpretation, second, as signs intentionally representing a field of objects to which an act of interpretive comprehension is directed and, third, as signs which share in a quality or aspect of the objects and which bring them into relations with one another.[49]

But the signal character of consciousness in relation to external objects is not unique. Consciousness also stands in reflexive relation to itself as a sign. Peirce rejects

---

[46]Peirce, *Pragmatism* 107: 69.

[47]The connection between the impetus to study the cosmos and the wish to play amaneuensis to the Divine is not an extraordinary one in Western thought. One's appreciation for the originality of this relationship in Peirce's thought is lessened further when one remembers that this connection exists in Whewell's philosophy, as well. Nevertheless, one should not rashly discount the significance of the Peircean conception of thirdness to the phenomenological enterprise merely because this conception is wedded to a theology or a proto-theology. See Peirce, *Pragmatism* 119: 75-76.

[48]Peirce, *Pragmatism* 283: 169.

[49]Peirce, *Pragmatism* 119: 75-76.

the possibility that immediate intuitions of conscious operations exist: every awareness of any conscious act is a mediate *cognition*. Thus, we have no direct experience of consciousness, no direct experience of the difference between the subjective elements of cognition, nor any power of introspection other than that derived from signs "external" to the conscious processes. In that cognitions mediate knowledge about cognitive processes--because it is necessary to think in order to observe--when we reflect, we necessarily form a sign which represents the conscious act we are attempting to observe. To reflect otherwise would be impossible for it would mean to have a cognition of cognitions, which is in no way related to previous cognitions; it would be to think without any interpretation; it would mean to interpret a sign which drew upon no previous concepts for its meaning. Therefore, in order to determine whether a cognition refers immediately to its object or whether it has been determined by a previous cognition, we must reason on the basis of previous conscious regularities which must always be interpreted as signs. Because no term has meaning if it conveys no cognition, or if it is incognizable in itself, "every thought must be interpreted in another."[50]

2.4. The Peircean Semiotics

A careful reading of the phenomena of consciousness opens the possibility that both consciousness and the cosmos can be understood. But before one can begin such interpretation, however, one must be familiar with the rules that cognitive and natural signs obey. One must possess an interpretive key enabling one to unlock a passage to the universal science of interpretation. In the Peircean philosophy, the hermeneutical key to the interpretation of the phaeneron results from the application of careful phenomenological description quite in the style of that which produced the cenopythagorean categories. This key consists of an elaborate taxonomy of signs and an intricate description of the formal relations implied by representations. The Peircean description of representation is the key which opens the passage to the Peircean semiotics and the Peircean science of meaning.

2.4.1. The Peircean notion of representation

Peirce describes representation as an "operation of a sign or its relation to the object for the interpreter of the representation."[51] As an essential triadic relation, representation cannot be reduced to dyadic relations or monadic qualities but exists, in its own right, as a *sui generis* relation of being. Within the relation of representation three components may be distinguished: (1) the representamen, "the concrete subject that represents," (2) the interpretant, "the mental effect or thought," and (3) the object, the thing for which the representamen stands.[52]

---

[50]Peirce, *Pragmatism* 119: 75-76.

[51]Peirce, *Principles* 540: 285.

[52]Peirce, *Principles* 253: 151.

156

Peirce relates these components as follows.

> A *representamen* is a subject of a triadic relation to a second called its object, for a third, called its *interpretant*, this triadic relation being such that the *representamen determines its interpretant to stand in the triadic relation to the same object for some interpretant.*[53]

The representamen does not act efficiently in every case so as to continue the string of significations infinitely. Rather its ability to determine the triadic relation is potential; it is a *power* to produce such other triadic relations though it does not necessarily do so.[54] What Peirce intends by this definition might better be explained with reference to Chart 6.

In relation to a representamen, a concept or idea stands as an interpretant (represented by the I's in the diagram), but the same interpretant can act as a representamen (represented by the R's in the diagram) in relation to *its* interpretants. In every case, there is an intention behind the representamen to use it to occasion an interpretant in order to represent an object. A sign is, thus, a trigger which awakens a relationship between a content of thought and a thing to which the sign is somehow related. The interpretant stands in such relation to its object that any occurrence of its related sign is sufficient to enable the mind to treat the interpretant as if, in some sense, *it were* the object.[55] Though an act of representation has an efficacy sufficient to prove its own reality, no such certainty is obtainable about its object. Although some complex of qualities is always the occasion for an act of representation, the interpretant may yield an idea which has no counterpart in reality.[56]

2.4.2. The kinds of representations

In considering the various kinds of representations, it is best to consider the broadest distinctions first and then proceed to examine the elaborate subclassifications of representations that Peirce has devised. The most general distinction between representations is between representations whose relations to their objects are constituted by communities of shared qualities (iconic representations), representations whose relations to their objects consist of correspondences of fact (indexic representations) and

---

[53] Peirce, *Principles* 541: 285.

[54] Peirce, *Principles* 564: 303.

[55] Peirce, *Elements* 274: 156.

[56] Peirce, Pragmatism 73: 50.

CHART 6

The Triadic Relation between a
Representamen, Interpretant and Object
According to Peirce

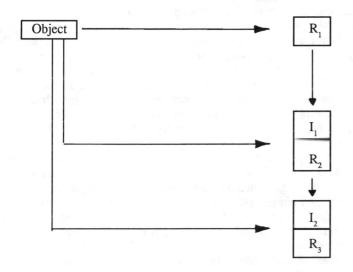

$$
\begin{array}{lcl}
R_1 & = & \text{Representamen 1} \\
I_1 & = & \text{Interpretant 1} \\
R_2 & = & \text{Representamen 2} \\
I_2 & = & \text{Interpretant 2} \\
R_3 & = & \text{Representamen 3}
\end{array}
$$

158

representations whose relations to their objects are merely imputed (synthetic representations).[57]

Peirce devises a second trichotomy of representations (signs) which can be cross-correlated with the first trichotomy. According to Peirce, the second trichotomy consists of (1) signs whose representational ability is governed by their qualitative character, (2) signs whose representational ability is governed by their relations to objects, and (3) signs whose representational ability is governed by their relations to interpretants.[58] Thus, the class of signs whose representational ability is governed by their qualitative character may be further trichotomized into (1a) *qualisigns* (signs which are qualities and require embodiment to be efficacious), (1b) *sinsigns* (existent things or events which, through their qualities or qualisigns, are efficacious as signs) and (1c) *legisigns* (laws, usually conventional, which signify through replicas or sinsigns).[59]

The class of signs whose representational ability is governed by their relations to objects may be further trichotomized into: (2a) *icons* (signs which, in representing objects, do not depend upon the objects' existence but represent by virtue of a qualitative similarity holding between the objects and themselves), (2b) *indices* (signs which represent by virtue of real effects induced in them by their object), and (2c) symbols (signs which refer to their objects nomologically, through "an association of general ideas" causing these signs "to be interpreted as referring" to existent objects).[60]

Finally, the third and last class of the second tripartition of signs, the class of signs whose representational ability is governed by their relations to interpretants, may be further trichotomized into: (3a) *rhemes* (signs which represent possible objects for their interpretants), (3b) *dicisigns* (signs which represent actual existents for their interpretants), and (3c) *arguments* (signs of law which represent the signal character of their objects for their interpretants.)[61]

Within each alternative of the second trichotomy of representations, the three respective subclasses are interrelated according to a general order of foundedness. The third subclass of each alternative (that is, 1c, 2c, and 3c, respectively) presupposes the respective second subclass (that is, 1b, 2b, and 3b) and the respective first subclass (that is, 1a, 2a, and 3a) as foundationally constitutive. In other words, for a legisign to be representative, it requires a sinsign and a qualisign as constitutive aspects of itself, and for a sinsign to be representative, it requires a qualisign as a constitutive aspect of itself.

---

[57]Peirce, *Pragmatism* 73: 50.

[58]Peirce, *Principles* 559: 297.

[59]Peirce, *Elements* 243-246: 142-143.

[60]Peirce, *Pragmatism* 74-76: 51-52.

[61]Peirce, *Elements* 250-252: 144.

Likewise, symbols require indices and icons, and indices require icons.   Arguments require both dicisigns and rhemes, though dicisigns require only rhemes.[62]

Moreover, the subclasses of the alternatives in the second trichotomy may be cross-classified according to the alternatives of the first trichotomy of representations. All of the first subclasses of the second trichotomy of representations can be classified as iconic representations, all of the second subclasses of the second trichotomy of representations can be classified as indexic representation, and all of the third subclasses of the second trichotomy of representations can be classified as synthetic representations.[63]

2.4.3. The 10 classes of signs

From the second trichotomy of signs, Peirce derives ten additional classes of signs. He believes that this derivation results in the only classes of signs which are actually existent: the nine classes of signs defined within the second trichotomy are construed as categorizations of possible semiotic components which have no pure, independent existence but function together, in combination, to form actually existent signs. How Peirce arrives at this derivation is not immediately obvious, though at least one solution has been proposed.[64]

Peirce arrives at a tenfold classification of signs because he recognizes that each alternative of the second trichotomy is related to the other two alternatives according to distinct relations of foundedness which make it impossible for a sign to exist without possessing semiotic aspects drawn from *each* of the three alternatives of the second trichotomy.   A sign cannot exist unless it has a qualitative aspect, an adjective aspect and an interpretive aspect.   Moreover, of these, the qualitative aspect is more fundamental than either the objective or interpretive aspects, and the objective aspect is more fundamental than the interpretive aspect.

---

[62]Peirce, *Pragmatism* 76: 52.

[63]At this point, one might be struck by Peirce's apparent duplication of categories, for if he has already defined iconic and indexic representations what can be his point of distinguishing icons and indices? The answer to this question becomes apparent when one considers the import of the first trichotomy. The first trichotomy of representations stands for distinctions between signs in terms of what one might call "adjectivity." This adjectivity is of use in characterizing the representations of the second trichotomy. Thus, the first subclasses constituting the second trichotomy have an iconic character even though only icons can be said to be essentially iconic. Similarly, only indices are essentially indexic, though both sinsigns and dicisigns are indexic in that they refer to correspondent facts. Symbols, alone, are symbolic essentially, but both legisigns and arguments are synthetic in that the objective relations they define between their various relata are imputed.

[64]The editors of the *Collected Papers*, Hartshorne and Weiss, provide an ingenious explanation for the derivation of only ten classes based upon rules which Peirce mandated to describe the triadic relations between semiotic possibles, semiotic existents and semiotic laws. Although this ingenious solution may, indeed, partly explain how Peirce arrived at the ten classes of actually existent signs, it ignores the relations of foundedness which Peirce describes as holding between the alternatives of the second trichotomy and which are equally important to an understanding of his derivation of the classes. See Peirce, *Pragmatism*, notes on pages 140-142.

(The various orders of foundedness holding between the alternatives of the second trichotomy are made lucid by Chart 7.[65])

Applying the foundational dependencies represented in the above lattice, one discovers that ten, and only ten, classes of actually existent signs emerge. These are: (1) *rhematic iconic qualisigns*, qualities which denote objects by common ingredients or similarities and which are signs of essence, (2) *rhematic iconic sinsigns*, objects of experience some of whose qualities determine the essence of an object, (3) *rhematic indexical sinsigns*, objects of experience which direct attention to the object by which they are caused, (4) *dicent indexical sinsigns*, objects of experience which, acting as signs, really provide information about their objects by being directly affected by them, (5) *rhematic iconic legisigns*, general laws or types which, when instantiated, possess qualities which produce ideas of objects sharing those qualities, (6) *rhematic indexical legisigns*, general laws or types which, when instantiated, are really affected by their objects so as to draw attention to their object, (7) *dicent indexical legisigns*, general laws or types having instantiations which are directly affected by their objects in such ways as to furnish information about those objects, (8) *rhematic symbolic legisigns*, laws of the association of general ideas and objects whose instantiations produce images which, in turn produce general concepts, (9) *dicent symbolic legisigns*, laws of the association of general ideas which actually (propositionally) connect the indicated objects in their existence with the general ideas which refer to them, (10) *argumentative symbolic legisigns*, laws which relate the components of dicent symbolic legisigns in such ways as to produce new dicent symbolic legisigns which are true.[66]

---

[65]Chart 7 represents a heuristic (of my own invention) for explaining why Peirce limited his classification of signs to 10. I think it clearly demonstrates the relations of foundedness he intended for each variety of sign.

In the diagram of the relational lattice, '1' signifies the first alternative of the second trichotomy of signs, '2' signifies the second alternative and '3' signifies the third alternative. Thus, '1a' signifies qualisign, '1b' signifies sinsign, '1c' signifies legisign, '2a' signifies icon, '2b' signifies index, '2c' signifies symbol, '3a' signifies rheme, '3b' signifies dicision and '3c' signifies argument. The direction of the various arrows indicate the direction of foundedness. The lattice is read by always beginning at the right (column 3) choosing a vertex and tracing a single segment which, without passing through any other vertices, will connect the first vertex with a vertex in the second column and then from that second vertex choosing a second segment which, without passing through any other vertices, will connect the second vertex with a vertex in the first column. The horizontal or diagonal relations, thus, represent foundational relations between semiotic aspects of alternative classes. These foundational relations are not isomorphic, however, but many to one. Within each class, however, a foundational order exists which is isomorphic, necessary, and vertical. Thus, within each column, the representations at the bottom of a column found the representations immediately above them. An example will make it clear just how the various signs are constructed. Take the series of *nexûs* 3b, 2c, 1c. By the rule stated above this series defines a sign. Within this aspectual series, 3b is founded upon 2c and 2c upon 1c. Moreover, 3b is founded upon its class predecessor 3a and 2c is founded on 2b and 2b on 2a and 1c is founded upon 1b and 1b on 1a. We may translate this as follows. The path 3b, 2c, 1c defines a sign called a dicent, symbolic legisign, it contains all triples of semiotic aspects upon which it is founded. Thus, it is constituted by a dicent, indexical, legisign, a dicent, indexical sinsign, a rhematic indexical legisign, etc. All varieties of representation follow this example in that they presuppose more fundamental representational triples as constituents. There are, however, no diagonals running from lower *nexûs* on the left of the lattice to higher *nexûs* on the right of the lattice because, by the nature of the signs which the *nexûs* represent, no representation within one class founds a higher level representation in another class without, first, being mediated by a higher level representation in its own class.

[66]Peirce, *Elements* 250-252: 144.

CHART 7

The Orders of Foundedness within
the Second Trichotomy of Signs
According to Peirce

1   2   3

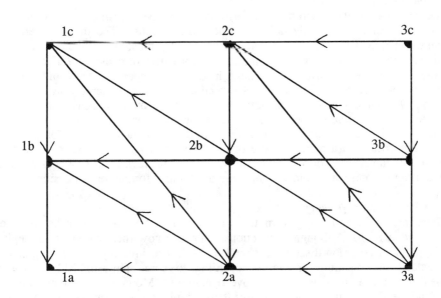

162

2.4.4. *The dimensions of rhematic symbolic legisigns*

Aside from possessing a characteristic signal structure, rhematic symbolic legisigns (r.s.l.s)--by virtue of their being symbols--also possess three dimensions which circumscribe the extent to which consciousness may expand or contract their application. These dimensions are breadth, depth, and information.

The *breadth* of a sign is the expansiveness of an r.s.l. with respect to its objects. Thus, an r.s.l. signifying a small class of objects has less breadth than one signifying a large class of objects. The *depth* of an r.s.l. is its expansiveness with respect to the common qualities it signifies in its object(s). Thus, an r.s.l. signifies a paltry class of properties has less depth than that which signifies a rich class of properties. Finally, the *information* of an r.s.l. is much like its horizon of possible uses; it is the sum of what is known of the symbol by its interpretant or the sum of all synthetic propositions which contain the r.s.l. as subject or predicate.[67]

The various mental operations on symbols may be classified according to the expansions or contractions they induce in these dimensions. The mental operation of *generalization* may be construed as an increase in the breadth of an r.s.l., a decrease in its depth and no accompanying change in its informative dimension. *Induction* results in an increase in breadth without a change in depth but upon the basis of an increase in conceivable (believed) information. *Abstraction* results in a decrease in the depth of a symbol, without a change in breadth, brought about by a decrease in conceived information. *Specification* produces an increase of both depth and information without any change in breadth. *Supposition* merely produces an increase in information, and determination results in a mere increase of depth, but *restriction* results in a decrease in breadth accompanied by a decrease in information. Finally, *descent* produces a decrease in breadth, an increase in depth and no change of the informative dimension.[68]

2.5. *The Pragmatistic Theory of Meaning*

These mental operations govern the way one uses language to make discoveries and to arrive at truth. Although conventions determine how rhematic symbolic legisigns *should* signify in common discourse, when one wishes to investigate their linguistic use or to extend the meaning of words according to some philosophical or scientific purposes, then one must employ the above operations. Moreover, any reasoning about words (and their meanings) which employs these cognitive operations successfully results in new knowledge of the world independently of dictionaries or other static repositories of knowledge. To think is not to use words as a reflex. Rather, it is to operate upon words according to new intentions and purposes which take the significations of words as given but extend these significations consistently, clearly, precisely, and verifiably in the pursuit of new knowledge. The meaning of a word is, thus, not a dead kernel. It is a living potential which is inexhaustible and expressive of a horizon of possible uses.

---

[67]Peirce, *Elements* 418: 253.

[68]Peirce, *Elements* 422: 255.

These possible uses are not automatically given in the word; only a very general structure of possible uses is implied. As Peirce points out, meanings, in general, are undepletable and closely analagous to pragmatic intentions. What "one *means* to do," expressed volitionally about acts in the world, and the *"meaning* of a word" are alike in that both express sought fulfillments.[69] But Peirce goes further in describing their similarity. Meanings, like acts, can be brought to fulfillment only if one can conceive of practical effects which will be the result of the meanings' being understood. For a meaning to be understood as different from another meaning, and for it to be fulfilled in that understanding, it must result in possible purposes behind some varieties of action. This is the *pragmatistic* theory of meaning and Peirce describes it thusly:

> To develop its [a concept's] meaning, we have, therefore, . . . to determine what habits it produces, for what a thing means is simply what habits it involves. Now, the identity of a habit depends on how it might lead us to act, not merely under such circumstances as are likely to arise, but under such as might possibly occur, no matter how improbable they may be. What the habit is depends on *when* and *how* it causes us to act. As for *when*, every stimulus to action is derived from perception; as for the *how*, every purpose of action is to produce some sensible result. Thus, we come down to what is tangible and conceivably practical, as the root of every real distinction of thought, no matter how subtle it may be; and there is no distinction of meaning so fine to consist in anything but a possible difference in practice.[70]

In the case of volitional acts, the actor determines the action's fulfillment by subjective criteria. Fulfillment is a subjective judgment relating to individual choice and purpose. But in the case of words, which are always the common property of some social group, meanings are never perfectly fulfilled but are indefinitely perfectible. The meanings of words are ideals which presuppose typical notions of the objects they intend. The historical meanings of words, insofar as they have developed continuously, are the data for the construction of the concepts which stand behind words. But insofar as the objects which these concepts interpret are, by nature, inexhaustible, the meanings of the words which designate them are always also provisional. The concepts related to meanings, and the meanings themselves, are always perfectible so long as knowledge of the objects to which the words refer is not exhausted. Thus, each meaning is associated with an open horizon of possible expansions of its intent, an open intentional horizon partially determined by its communal genesis and defined by the possible historical and technological dynamics of society.[71]

This notion of meaning leads Peirce to the espousal of the philosophy of pragmaticism, a philosophy which holds that all questions of meaning are to be decided upon the differences in action which they might possibly produce as defined within a community of shared meanings and action. Pragmaticism, thus, takes reality as the set of all possible meanings comprehensible within a society. In this sense, reality, as a *global* meaning, shares many traits with the individual meanings of words. Inasmuch

[69]Peirce, *Principles* 343: 174.

[70]Peirce, *Pragmatism* 400: 257.

[71]Peirce, *Pragmatism* 316: 189.

as reality is defined as the set of all intersubjective meanings, it, like individual meanings, possesses a relatively stable structure open, nevertheless, to possible futures and susceptible to constant re-evaluation and alteration within the society to which it belongs. Within the community, experiential reevaluations of reality result in unanimity when it is proven that conditions exist under which the new interpretation *could* possibly have practical implications for each member of the community. For a notion of reality to be validated it must be shown that the meaning of that notion could, potentially, have the same effect on every member of the community. Reality's meaning must be general and not private.[72]

Now, it is also possible to reverse the relationship between meanings and conscious behavior and to show that every purposive act points backward to a class of intersubjective meanings, each open to perfection and susceptible to "empirical" tests. These tests, as they are practiced in mundane life by the average societal member, are not rigorously scientific, but within their meaning, they hold the ideal of rigorous validation as an implicit intention. Thus, to test the meaning of an act or word intrasocietally, one must apply the standards of validation appropriate to that society. Relative to that society, such standards are a *scientific* test of meaning. Actions founded upon such "scientifically" established meanings, therefore, will be more certain and definite and better understood within the context of that society than those same meanings measured against standards drawn from outside the societal context.

Although he may not have consciously intended it, Peirce's pragmatistic interpretation of meaning makes it possible to study cultural constructions of reality according to a fruitful new method. One may begin either from actions, tracing the actions back to a field of meanings and shared intersubjective reality, or one may begin from meanings and attempt, after a study of the societal interpretation of reality, to discern the possible practical effects a meaning might have for a subject within that society. Thus, coupled with the Peircean semiotic, the Peircean pragmatics opens the way to a rigorous human science.

If one further introduces the Peircean cenopythagorean categories, one is able to extend the Peircean theory of meaning and signs to reality as a whole. Taking the categories of firstness, secondness and thirdness as irreducible aspects of experience it should then be possible to demonstrate how, by employing the Peircean semiotics and semantics as tools, that each philosophy or worldview is a particular structuring of the content of the various cenopythagorean data. It should also be possible to show the direction science must move in order to perfect the meaning of its concepts and, thus, perfect its description of reality. It was this general hermeneutic which Peirce was working toward when he wrote the articles interpreted in the body of this chapter. The ontological and semiotic taxonomies which result from his work testify to the precision of his phaeneroscopic method and promise fruitful applications in any discipline requiring a reliable hermeneutic.

---

[72]Peirce, *Pragmatism* 429: 286-287.

3. The Objects of Peircean Phenomenology

In one sense, the notion of phenomena which underlies the Peircean philosophy is the completion of all notions of phenomena up until the time of Husserl: Peirce provides a definition which in its comprehension is reminiscent of the semantic content with which '*phainô*' is charged in ancient Greek thought. In the Peircean conceptualization, 'phenomena' comes to a fruition intimated in the semantic potential of '*phainomena*' and developed through the definitions of Lambert, Robison, Hegel, Hamilton, and Whewell.

Peirce defines 'phenomena,' in its most expansive sense, as the field of all possible objects of consciousness. Within this field, the constitutive phenomena exist at different levels of complexity. Thus, there are phenomena which are the elements of experience, and there are phenomena which can be analyzed into constituent phenomena. Peirce generally accepts the hierarchy of phenomena first proposed in Lambert's phenomenology, but does not accord it a particularly significant role as a heuristic for philosophical investigation. Peirce is concerned, rather, with how phenomena present themselves to consciousness and how this mode of presentation is indicative of their natures.

Observation of phenomena yields three categories which serve to differentiate them: the cenopythagorean categories of firstness, secondness and thirdness. Phenomena classified into the first category are characterized by noncognitive experience because objectivity has no meaning with respect to them. They are better interpreted as ideal limits to the possibility of object-constituting consciousness, the sensorial contents of conscious acts before they are made the objects of consciousness. Phenomena typical of the second category are those which are characteristic of the subject-object dichotomy, a dichotomy which Peirce thinks arises from the confrontation between agent and patient or self and other. Typical phenomena falling under this category are what Peirce, somewhat misleadingly, terms "facts." Facts, according to the Peircean understanding, are anything experienceable which is distinct, efficacious, spatial and temporal, the ground of *all* its consequences, resistant, determinable, subjective, instigative, dichotomous, indestructible and ineducible. Finally, phenomena typical of the category of thirdness are characterized by the mediation of firstness and secondness. It is within this category that most phenomena associated with conceptualization occur because thirdness is the category of signification, a category defined by the triadic relation between an object (monadic, dyadic, or triadic), a representamen (the instrument of intention for representing the object) and an interpretant (the thought or concept which is the result of the representation.)[73] From these categories, and particularly on the basis of the category of thirdness, Peirce develops an elaborate semiotics, or theory of signs by which all experience can be classified, analyzed into its semiotic constituents and explained.

In distinguishing three transcendental categories under which all phenomena can be classified, Peirce (somewhat obscurely) echoes themes which are present in the

---

[73]See Chart 6.

phenomenologies of Lambert, Hegel, Hamilton and Whewell. All, in one manner or another, refer to the fact that conscious experience is necessarily consciousness of the subject-object dichotomy and that the subject-object dichotomy can be empirically observed in the conscious experience of otherness. According to each of these thinkers, subjectivity can never be defined without a reference to objectivity. Both subjectivity and objectivity--as poles of an epistemological relation between consciousness and the world--presuppose a heterogeneity between consciousness of the subject and the thing disclosed through a conscious experience of resistance. The content of this experience of resistance--it is very difficult to describe precisely--is that of an unintelligibility, opacity, or inertia which, initially, is unyielding to the intellectual, kinesthetic or sensory powers of the subject.[74] But it is in the struggle between the conscious will to know the object, or to achieve an object, that the separation between subject and object is most acutely recognized. The paradox is that through this struggle the nature of the object also becomes intelligible. Peirce, in a sense, vindicates the Aristotelian doctrine of the identity of subject and object in cognition. Aristotle's dictum about the mind becoming one with its object is true with these limitations: that the unity of subject and object is never more than an isomorphy and never occurs without the subject experiencing some resistance which discloses the scissiparity of subject and object.

Peirce's description of secondness is weak, however, in that he does not see that it is as expressive of the nature of consciousness as it is expressive of the nature of the object. In fact, this is the fundamental weakness of the Peircean phenomenology as a whole, for by concentrating upon the objective side of experience, Peirce misses the opportunity to apply his elaborate ontology and semiotics to mental phenomena. In fairness to the fragmentary character of Peircean phenomenology--it is developed sporadically in monographs, over a period of many years--it must be admitted Peirce recognized that mind, as a phenomenon characterized by thirdness, is *indeed* capable of being analyzed by the Peircean semiotics. Nevertheless, Peirce never engages in any extensive analysis of consciousness or its phenomena, except to describe its various instrumental operations and intentional contents. For this defect, the analyses of consciousness in the phenomenologies of Hamilton and Hegel provide valuable correctives.

4. The Ends of Peircean Phenomenology

The ultimate end of the Peircean phenomenology is to provide a schema for the classification and subclassification of phaenerons (or phenomena) which captures the ontological structure of the world. In its ultimacy, this end has no reference to the practical or immediate purposes to which the phenomenological method may be put. Rather, the explanation of reality is an end sufficient in itself. However, this is not to say that phenomenology cannot be used to achieve proximate ends. Indeed, Peirce employs the categories developed by phenomenology (1) to elucidate the nature of

---

[74]Peirce, *Pragmatism* 53-57: 38-40.

consciousness, (2) to explain representation and (3) to create an elaborate semiotics by which any human activity involving signification can be explored. He also understands the descriptions which emerge from the quest for a taxonomy of phenomena as regulative for the induction of the factual sciences and as illustrative of the logical possibilities of the hypothetical sciences. To put it somewhat differently, though phenomenology is not specifically directed to the ends of either the hypothetical or factual sciences, its descriptions can be employed to flesh in the manifolds of pure mathematics or to guarantee the observational sentences of empirical science. Nevertheless, for phenomenology either set of ends is unimportant; it operates according to a program of pure research into the phaeneron and the countless forms and categories of its manifestation.

5. *The Peircean Phenomenological Technique*

The Peircean phenomenological technique consists neither of the classification of the universe according to the conopythagorean categories of firstness, secondness and thirdness nor of the classification of signs by means of an elaborate semiotics. Rather, the Peircean phenomenological technique consists of those possible operations of consciousness which make both systems of classification possible.

Three conscious operations are of prime importance in effecting phenomenological analyses: (1) discrimination, (2) precision and (3) dissociation. Discrimination is an operation of consciousness upon meaning, precision an operation of consciousness on perceptions, and dissociation an operation of consciousness on ideas or imaginings. The first act is that whereby the consciousness is able to hold one objects's meaning in attention to the exclusion of another, an act which is possible when the object's meaning is not analytically founded by another. The second act is that whereby the consciousness is able to hold some element of a percept in attention without attending to the percept's other constituents, an operation which is possible as long as one does not attempt to prescind the quality from the *a priori* condition of its possibility. Finally, the third act is that whereby a neutral image can be distinguished from another without reference to that second image, an operation which is possible only if the two images are not associated in any way. Discrimination establishes the independence of meanings, precision the independence of perceptions and dissociation the independence of ideas or imaginings.[75] All three operations are employed in the discovery of categories which are sufficient, unique, distinct but not necessarily value-neutral. They may also be employed to distinguish phenomenal parts and wholes to reduce phenomena to their basic elements.

When phenomena are meanings--and are, thus, susceptible to analysis by the Peircean semiotics--a number of other mental operations may be called into service as instruments by which meanings are clarified. These are the operations of generalization, induction, abstraction, specification, supposition, determination, restriction and descent. These supplementary operations have considerable value since they apply to any

---

[75]Peirce, *Principles* 549: 288.

conceptual appearance which is associated with a word or a description. They make it possible to study a sign by the range of objects to which it applies (its breadth), the qualitative richness of the object it denotes (its depth), and the sum of its meaningful uses (its information). One compares the differences in meaning which the same sign signifies for different subjects by comparing these meanings with respect to the difference in the mental operations associated with each. If for subject A, sign S has meaning M_1, and for subject B sign S has meaning M_2, then a phenomenological comparison of M_1 and M_2 would demonstrate how one stands to the other according to each meaning's generality, inductiveness, abstractness, specificity, suppositiousness, determinateness, restrictiveness and declivity.

CHAPTER VIII

HUSSERL: PHENOMENOLOGY AS
EIDETIC METHOD

1. Organizational Preliminaries

The nature of the Husserlian phenomenology makes it necessary to organize this chapter according to slightly different principles than those uniformly employed in the six preceding chapters. Instead of describing the Husserlian phenomenology comprehensively, as has been done with its philosophical predecessors, it will be necessary to omit a complete discussion of this phenomenology and to substitute for it an expanded, critical treatment of its objects, ends and techniques. A change in treatment is demanded because the scope, richness and development of the Husserlian phenomenology cannot be described in a single chapter: its evolution spanned thirty-seven years and thousands of pages of dense philosophical text. In this chapter, the central features of Husserlian phenomenology will be presented, with special attention being paid to critical questions as they relate to the objects, ends and techniques of the Husserlian phenomenology.[1]

2. The Objects (Matter) of Husserlian Phenomenology

The Husserlian understanding of 'phenomena' is the most richly developed of all its philosophical antecedents. 'Phenomenon,' in its most general sense, means for Husserl any possible experience of consciousness. "In this sense, percepts, imaginative and pictorial presentations, acts of conceptual thinking, surmises and doubts, joys and griefs, hopes and fears, wishes and acts of will, etc., are just as they flourish in our consciousness, 'experiences' or 'contents of consciousness.'"[2] In his conception of the breadth of phenomenological objects, Husserl resembles Peirce, but unlike Peirce, he does not posit a world external to consciousness. For Husserl, consciousness and

---

[1]For a historical introduction to Husserlian phenomenology, in all its complexity, the reader is urged to consult the critical treatments of Spiegelberg and Farber listed in the bibliography of this work. A brief discussion of the periodicity in the development of the Husserlian phenomenology does occur, however, in section 3.1. of this chapter.

[2]Edmund Husserl, *Logical Investigations*, trans. J.N. Findlay, 2 vols. (London: Routledge & Kegan Paul, 1970) 2: 536.

possible consciousness exhaust the world. Whatever is not a possibility in consciousness simply cannot be thought in any sense. What cannot be thought possible cannot exist.[3]

Within this very broad field of phenomenological objects, Husserl discerns a very complex structure, any part of which may be an object of phenomenological analysis. At one extreme are the largest wholes which may be made the objects of consciousness, objects such as the world, "the totality of objects that can be known through experience."[4] At the other extreme are the most minute constituents of the individual ego's conscious acts. Between these two extremes, reality is structured and stratified according to an infinitely complex web of conscious acts and meanings, all of which are possible objects of the Husserlian phenomenological technique.

2.1. The Lebenswelt

In describing the matter (objects) of Husserlian phenomenology, it is necessary to begin with the Husserlian conception of the *Lebenswelt*. To some this might seem descriptively backward: Husserl developed his notion of Lebenswelt late in his career; it assumed centrality only two years before his death in 1938, and most scholars outside of the Husserlian inner circle were unaware of its importance until Merleau-Ponty undertook his study of the unpublished portions of *The Crisis of European Sciences*.[5] What, then, is the purpose of making such a late development the keystone of a discussion of the objects of Husserlian phenomenology? The question is not susceptible to a succinct answer which is, at the same time, adequate; to answer it adequately would mean to engage in a lengthy discussion and critique of the Husserlian philosophy of transcendental objectivity, a discussion and critique both of which are beyond the scope of this chapter.[6] Nevertheless, it is necessary to say something about such a controversial beginning.

In his early writings, and in the *Cartesian Meditations* in particular, Husserl characterizes the problem of explaining the monadic ego's relation to the intersubjective community, of which it is a member, as one of the most important problems phenomenology sets before itself for solution. His early solution is the analysis which comprises the fourth and fifth meditations, an analysis which is summarized at the end of the *Cartesian Meditations*: "The path leading to a knowledge absolutely grounded in the highest sense, or . . . a philosophical knowledge, is necessarily the path of universal self-knowledge--first of all monadic, and then intermonadic."[7]

---

[3]This derives from Husserl's equation of possible consciousness and reality. By possible consciousness he intends the complete horizon of potential experience, a horizon that includes logical as well as empiriological possibility.

[4]Edmund Husserl, *Ideas*, trans. W.R. Boyce Gibson (London: George Allen & Unwin, 1969) 52.

[5]Herbert Spiegelberg, *The Phenomenological Movement* (The Hague: Martinus Nijhoff, 1982) 144.

[6]My purpose here is not to engage in philosophical argumentation as an end in itself but only as a means to further the point of my work.

[7]Edmund Husserl, *Cartesian Meditations*, trans. Dorion Cairns (The Hague: Martinus Nijhoff, 1978) 156.

Originally, Husserl conceived the monadic ego as the absolute substrate for consciousness, that is he conceived it as a *solus ipse* having being for and in itself. Despite his denials, the character of Husserl's thought during his transcendental-idealistic phase is heavily colored by solipsism. He intends to explain the world by means of phenomenological analyses in which the whole world, including the world of intersubjectivity, is reduced to the conscious operations of the monadic ego. His goal is to develop a criteriology of knowledge on the basis of conscious alterations in the individual subject. But in the course of these meditations, Husserl confronts the impossibility of positing any self-sufficient subjectivity; he discovers that the ego can emerge neither independently of world nor independently of intersubjectivity: the ego is not an ego except in a community of egos. Husserl, thus, places himself in the paradoxical position of deriving the intersubjective constitution of the ego completely from within the experience of the ego, a task like that of explaining what a husband is without reference to either marriage or a wife.

Though the analysis of intersubjectivity which he proposes in the *Cartesian Meditations* is developed with rigor, Husserl clearly demonstrates his discomfort with the earlier formulations.[8] But it is not until the presentation of the *Lebenswelt* in *The Crisis of European Sciences* that Husserl is able to offer a more satisfactory, albeit more undeveloped, solution. In this last work before his death, he substitutes the *Lebenswelt* for the individual ego, thus transforming the former into the absolute substrate which genetically founds experience.[9] It is by this concept that Husserl makes a last ditch effort to save both the phenomenological reduction of the ego and the reality of intersubjectivity. The significance of this concept as Husserl's final formulation of the absolute substrate--as well as the intention to present the enduring discoveries of Husserlian phenomenology--make it necessary to present the *Lebenswelt* as the beginning point of the Husserlian discussion of phenomena.

It is difficult to provide an unequivocal description of what Husserl intends by the word '*Lebenswelt*' because he employs the term in a variety of senses. Its literal English equivalent is 'lifeworld,' and its most general sense is that of the pregiven manifold of all appearances, a totality possessing a determinate, but extremely rich, structure consisting of typical objects, possible objects and experiences. According to this general meaning, '*Lebenswelt*' most closely corresponds to the Peircean 'phaeneron'; however, within the general meaning of '*Lebenswelt*,' it is possible to identify at least four specific meanings which correspond to the different uses to which Husserl puts this word. Each of these four meanings is given a different designation by various scholars of Husserlian philosophy, though no single scholar seems to employ all of the same

---

[8]See Marvin Farber, *The Aims of Phenomenology* (New York: Harper & Row, 1966) 94 and Herbert Spiegelberg, *The Phenomenological Movement* 138-141.

[9]Edmund Husserl, *Experience and Judgment*, ed. Ludwig Landgrebe, trans. James S. Churchill and Karl Ameriks (Evanston: Northwestern University Press, 1973) 136-137.

designations.[10] Nevertheless, the regularity with which scholars discuss these four meanings in conjunction with the *Lebenswelt* allows their presentation as distinct connotations associated with distinct terms. Thus, the general term *'Lebenswelt,'* may be interpreted as covering the four following terms and their respective meanings: (1) *'Umwelt'* (surrounding or regional world), (2) *'Urwelt'* (primordial world), (3) *'Mittelwelt'* (mediate world) and (4) *'Wesenswelt'* (essential world). These terms denote distinct regions of the life world and taken together constitute it in its entirety.[11] [Chart 8 indicates the relations of these denotations to the lifeworld as a whole.] The term *'Lebenswelt'* is used by Husserl to refer to each of these connotations in ways that are distinguishable only by their contexts.

'Umwelt' is a general term covering a style of existence typical of a specific orientation toward the world and this orientation's accompanying *praxis*. The *Umwelt* (surrounding world) is that realm of experience which is relativized to a particular historical period, socio-economic class, scientific discipline, form of production, world-view, etc. It is a world populated by objects passively accepted within a particular form of life, and it possesses a form of experience whose structures (beliefs, suppositions, hopes, superstitions, intents, etc.) are pregiven and unquestioningly accepted by all those who live within it. Associated with each *Umwelt* is an ontology of the beings relative to the surrounding world, a catalog of their typical attributes and "an open horizon of anticipation" of further such attributes "which provides the ground for inductions and theories about the relative objects."[12]

The *Umwelt*, according to the Husserlian understanding, is the world most of us inhabit during our waking experience. It is the form of life characterized by acceptance of conventions, obedience to laws and predictability of behavior either in compliance with or reaction to accepted norms. It is a form of life in which participants are conditioned to follow established patterns. Conceptualization within it is mechanized and possesses established habits and means for the reactivation of typified concepts. Words are manipulated as mere cyphers, the primordiality of their meaning occluded and their phenomenological apodicity never brought to self-evidence. In short, the *Umwelten* are the worlds, as they appear real, pregiven and unquestioned, of the housewife, physicist, proletarian, aristocrat, priest, bureaucrat, criminal, or anyone living an "unexamined" existence.

Aron Gurwitsch characterized the *Umwelt* as follows:

---

[10]Husserl employs the terms *'Umwelt'* and *'Lebenswelt'* as does Gurwitsch. But that there is an implicit difference between the *Lebenswelt* and the *Lebenswelt*-as-reduced is evident from a number of texts throughout *Experience and Judgment* and *The Crisis of Euorpean Sciences*. Also, Husserl apparently maintains a tacit distinction between the *Welt* and the *Lebenswelt*, the former corresponding to what I call the *Wesenswelt*. Finally, the *Mittelwelt* is entirely my own creation but one which seems to be demanded by the other tacit Husserlian distinctions. See note 11.

[11]The *Wesenswelt* corresponds to the horizon of the *Lebenswelten*. The *Umwelten* are the relative worlds consisting of the *Urwelt* (corresponding to the noematic nucleus) and the individual *Mittelwelten* (corresponding to the noeses, and the noematic strata and their *Gegebenheitsweise*).

[12]Husserl, *Judgment* 332-333.

CHART 8

The Lebenswelt and Its Constituent Worlds

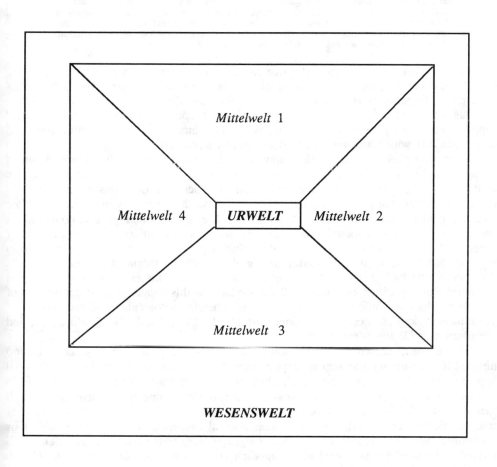

The Lebenswelt

As long as the pre-theoretical attitude prevails, all activities not only take place within the *Umwelt* and are oriented by the accepted traditional conceptions, but they are also pursued for the sake of living and for finding one's way within the *Umwelt*. All activities, including those of a cognitive or speculative nature, are motivated by and essentially related to, practical human interests. Practicality must not be construed in a crude utilitarian sense; it purports reference to human purposes and to the general welfare of individuals as well as the community. Notions like knowledge, error, truth, falsity, reality, appearance, etc., are here relative not only to nature and the structure of the *Umwelt* in question but also to a given specific situation, to needs and desires to be satisfied at the moment, to courses of action to be taken, to plans and desires to be carried out, etc. Cognitive and speculative activities remain confined within a finite horizon, the sense of finitude being defined by the relativities mentioned. At the level in question, neither the relativity nor finitude can obviously be disclosed and apprehended as such.[13]

From within the occluded and naive form of consciousness typical of the *Umwelt*, it is impossible to propose a critique of life or even to base life upon self-evident principles. Experience is so ubiquitously theory-laden (in the Whewellian sense) that there is no aspect of life which is not dependent upon a network of unchallenged suppositions, habits and customs as well as numerous lexical occlusions and sedimentations which are misconstrued as general meanings.

Husserlian phenomenology takes upon itself the task of disoccluding the sedimented meanings and structures of the *Umwelt* by investigating the relations between the passive constitution of the *Umwelt* and the primordial evidences for this constitution. This is to say that Husserlian phenomenology takes as its task the investigation of the *Umwelten* with the goal of analyzing the various forms of life, tracing their genetic constitutions and proving what is apodictic in them and what is tendentious.[14] It does this by accomplishing a reduction which separates what is pregiven to any consciousness from what is purely doxic or imported into the data without apophantic evidence. The instrument by which this reduction is accomplished is the Husserlian phenomenological technique (an exposition of which will follow later in this chapter). The application of the Husserlian technique results in two phenomenological residues and one phenomenological essence. The residues are (1) the *Urwelt* and (2) the *Mittelwelt*, and the essence is (3) the *Wesenswelt*.

The *Urwelt*, according to Husserl, results from a phenomenological reduction directed to separating theoretical importations into experience from the foundational appearances and conscious acts which characterize experience when it expresses life in its most fundamental form. The *Urwelt* is the world as one would live in it, if all meanings not founded upon apodictic evidence were suspended and if the criterion of true judgment were based upon phenomenological evidence, alone. The world, thus constituted, would be one in which every judgment were tested by direct experience and proved or falsified by an appeal to the apodicity of data which it involved. The *Urwelt* resulting would be that of humanity in its natural setting, which is to say it would be constituted by characteristically human strivings--as in the teleonomic structure of the

---

[13]Aron Gurwitsch, *Studies in Phenomenology and Psychology* (Evanston: Northwestern University Press, 1966) 404.

[14]The project of Husserlian phenomenology is not descriptive without being programmatic. Husserl, one must be aware, intends to perform a critique of all the sciences' foundations and, then, to ground them in apodictic evidence.

Aristotelian-Stoic five causes, for example--but these strivings would express themselves in forms of practice which would not be allowed to occlude the relations between judgment, meaning and practice.

Husserl recognizes that the *Urwelt* as *Lebenswelt* is an ideal: it is not to be achieved actually, but is a regulative construction by which phenomenology examines the evidential grounds for the various *Umwelten*. Each such *Umwelt* has attached to it an *Urwelt* which is the result of a phenomenological reduction which separates the unfounded forms of consciousness from the phenomenologically founded varieties. But since the individual *Urwelten* do not exhaust all possible varieties of phenomenologically lived existence, the correspondences and intersections between all the individual *Urwelten* comprises a single *Urwelt* as their primordial composite. It is life as it might be lived in this idealized foundational *Lebenswelt* which is the criterion for judging life in any of the individual *Umwelten*.

The *Mittelwelt*, by implication, is the theoretical surplus left when one accomplishes a phenomenological reduction to the *Urwelt*.[15] It consists of all doxic acts and concepts which have no phenomenological foundation but which are, as it were, the connecting tissue which holds the *Umwelt* together in consciousness but not in practice. Superficially, the *Mittelwelt* resembles the Marxist notion of ideological superstructure: just as the ideological superstructure of a society justifies the established productive forces on the basis of generalities which have no grounding in the concrete historical process so, too, the *Mittelwelt* is a tissue of ideas and doxa directed to explain the world in a way not grounded in apodictic evidences or phenomenological practice.[16] The theoretician as well as the simple, unreflective soul are alike in that each spends most of his conscious time in the *Mittelwelt*--the latter because he accepts the given order without having a clue as to how to effectively question it; the former because he lives at the very top of the scientific architectonic: his human project demands that he accepts the vast edifice of hypothesis and supposition which so tenuously supports him.

The *Wesenswelt* differs from the *Umwelt, Urwelt*, and *Mittelwelt* in that it is a positive result of perspectival variation, the method used by Husserl to disclose the essence of an object. It differs from other essences, however, in that it encompasses them and their perspectival horizons; it both grounds and limits their possibilities, though it, itself, finds a foundation in nothing more ultimate.

Though the *Wesenswelt* may be understood as the "horizon of all possible horizons," it should not be understood to be such in any reductionistic sense: it is neither the simple sum of all possible appearances nor the simple composite or extension of its possible parts or *onta*.[17] Unlike other essential wholes, it *is not* given to intuition in a simple synthesis of its components' possible horizons. Unlike other essences, it is given to the intellect, through unique protodoxa and preapprehensions, in the form of an

---

[15]The analogy is with the noematic and noetic residues which are bracketed from the noematic nucleus in a typical phenomenological reduction.

[16]The *Mittelwelt*, thus, corresponds to the theoretical component in existence.

[17]Husserl, *Judgment* 332-333.

unclarified but transcendental universe. As such, it is the precondition to the understanding of any variety of *Lebenswelt* as well as the universal context for the understanding of beings, meaning and existence.[18] The *Wesenswelt* is the ultimate transcendental because it is never given in its completion but is open toward the future. Yet within it, everything which is (or can be) manifests its peculiar form of typicality only by virtue of its being a part of its causal and structural contexture.[19]

But if the *Wesenswelt* is an essence in the Husserlian sense, it is an essence of a very specific kind: it is an essence of a higher level than the *eidê* which it composits. Unlike the essences which it encompasses, the *Wesenswelt* belongs to no species or genus; its essence is *sui generis* and simply exhausts the compossibility of the world.[20]

According to the Husserlian understanding, the world exists as a Peircean fact: it undeniably *is* (but might have been otherwise), though it is impossible from within the world to say what any other world might be like since Husserl includes all conceivability and possibility in the horizon of this present world. The *Wesenswelt* thus bears many affinities to the realm of abstract possibility which is the object of both the Peircean phenomenology and pure mathematics. In fact, Husserl draws a parallel between the *Wesenswelt* and the mathematical notion of the theory of manifolds. He describes their resemblance this way.

> 'Manifolds' are . . . compossible totalities of objects in general which are thought of as distinct only in empty formal generality and are conceived of as defined by determinate modalities of something-in-general. Among these totalities the so-called 'definite' manifolds are distinctive. Their definition through a 'complex axiom system' gives a special sort of totality in all deductive determinations to the formal substrate contained in them. With this sort of totality one can say a 'world in general' is constructed. The 'theory of manifolds' in the special sense is the universal science of the *definite* manifolds.[21]

Just as the theory of manifolds provides the structure of possibility for the definite manifolds but cannot, itself, be formulated except by making the definite manifolds consistent with one another in a metamathematical system, so too the *Wesenswelt* founds the possibility of individual *Lebenswelten*, but its own structure is not susceptible to specific elaboration except through the perspectival variation of these *Lebenswelten*. Even so, the *Lebenswelten* are related to the *Wesenswelt* as stocks of typifications which illustrate its structure but never exhaust its transcendence. It is this radical horizonality of the *Lebenswelten*--that is to say, their property of pointing beyond themselves to a horizon of horizons, the very property which distinguishes the *Wesenswelt* as one of the

---

[18] Husserl, *Judgment* 332-333.

[19] Husserl, *Judgment* 332-333.

[20] Joseph J. Kockelmans, *A First Introduction to Husserl's Phenomenology* (Louvain: Editions E. Nauwelaert, 1967) 195.

[21] Edmund Husserl, *The Crisis of European Sciences and Transcendental Phenomenology*, trans. David Car (Evanston: Northwestern University Press, 1970) 45-46.

meanings of '*Lebenswelt*'--that compels Husserl to identify the *Lebenswelt* as absolute substrate. The significance of this identification has yet to be made clear, however.

By 'absolute substrate' Husserl means in a general sense, an ultimate stratum of experience which is directly experienceable, immediately apprehensible, self-existent and not subject to essential determination by something more fundamental.[22] Although there are a number of absolute substrates in this sense--the transcendental ego being one example--Husserl, in his later writings settles upon the world as *Wesenswelt* as the *only* substrate *in the strict sense* of this phrase. Husserl describes this strict sense in *Experience and Judgment.*

> No individual body which we bring to givenness in experience is isolated and for itself. Each is a body in a unitary context which, finally and universally understood, is that of the world. Thus universal sensuous experience, conceived as proceeding in universal accord, has a unity of being, a unity of higher order; the existent of this universal experience is the totality of nature, the universe of all material bodies. We can also direct ourselves to this whole of the world and make it a theme of experience. . . . To be sure the world in the sense of the totality of nature is not to be encountered as substrate in a simple experience; its experience is therefore not a matter of something being simply displayed in substrate moments, in 'properties.' On the contrary, the experience of the totality of nature is founded in the prior experiences of individual bodies. But the totality of nature is also 'experience;' we can also direct our attention towards it . . . and also explicate it in its particularities in which it is being revealed. Thus, all substrates are connected together; if we move about the real world qua universe, none of them is without 'real' relation to others, and to all others, mediately or immediately.
>
> This leads to a *new understanding of absolute substrate.* A 'finite' substrate can be experienced simply for itself and thus has its being-for-itself. But necessarily, it is at the same time a determination . . . as soon as we consider a more comprehensive substrate in which it is found. Every finite substrate has determinability as being-in-something, and this is true *in infinitum.* But in the following respect the world is absolute substrate, namely, everything is in it, and it itself is not an in-something; it is no longer a relative unity within a more comprehensive plurality. It is the totality of existents; it is not 'in something' but is itself something total. Another absoluteness is also connected to this: a real existent . . . is subsistent in the causality of its alterations; and all realities which are causally connected and . . . make up relatively subsistent unities of pluralities are themselves again causally interlaced. This implies that *everything mundane,* whether a real unity or a real plurality, *is ultimately dependent; only the world is independent,* only it is absolute substrate in the sense of absolute independence; it does not subsist as a finite substrate does, namely, in relation to circumstances exterior to itself.[23]

Although Husserl tries to preserve the relative independence of the transcendental ego, once he makes the above admission he shifts the phenomenological project of his earlier career away from his obsession with the phenomenological reconstitution of the world within the consciousness of the monadic subject to the project of a phenomenological reconstitution of the world on the basis of intersubjective, practical intentions founded upon and revealed through the various *Lebenswelten*. Because even the attempt to reconstitute consciousness takes place according to the strictures of embodiment (and embodied intersubjectivity), it takes place within the *Wesenswelt*. As important to an understanding of subjective apodictic premises of existence are the apodictic existential premises which are pregiven in the lifeworlds we inhabit, premises

---

[22]Husserl, *Judgment* 132-136.

[23]Husserl, *Judgment* 137-138.

such as our embodiment, our selfhood (which is definable only in relation to others), and our predetermined membership in concrete communities of humans at a particular moment in history. In comparison to the independence of the world, the freedom of individual humans (even considered according to the independence of the transcendental ego) is thoroughly relative and quite limited.[24]

2.2. Object-Constituting Consciousness

Although the *Lebenswelt* is the total horizon within which all experience takes place, its general structure does not exhaust the phenomenological richness of the world. The other pole of the world's constitution is the subject, and though the existence of the *Lebenswelt* (as absolute substrate) is the primordial condition for the emergence of intersubjectivity--inasmuch as to be a member of a community is, first, to be enworlded and embodied--it is in the subject's conscious constitution of experience that the world gains its intricate texture and composition. However the horizonality of the world contributes to the general possibility and typicality of experience, it is the consciousness of the subject which fleshes in this general possibility. To come to a complete understanding of the Husserlian notion of phenomena, it is not enough to be familiar with the substructuring of that horizon, a substructuring which is equivalent to the collective experiences of the many subjects who inhabit the world. It is by means of the conscious acts of the subject that this substructuring occurs.

According to Husserl, experience (in its naively fundamental sense) is experience of the life-world.[25] At this level of naiveté, consciousness is unquestioning and unreflective; it accepts things as they appear in their typical modes of givenness and without recourse to criticism or scepticism; it accepts things as posited, as given according to their mere appearance and without any reflection upon the evidences which one might marshall to prove or disprove their meaning. It is the naive mode of consciousness which does not posit a difference between the inside or outside of reality as things are presented to consciousness, so they exist; consciousness' role in the construction of the world is almost completely ignored. The naively realistic model of the world is one which makes consciousness essentially passive, a wax tablet on which the efficacy of real objects forms impressions representative of the actual character of those objects. To have consciousness of an object according to this naive way of experiencing the world is to be a patient to an object which acts as a perfectly efficacious agent.

Over and against naive, everyday experience (and its complementary naively realistic epistemology), Husserl proposes a theory of experience and a corresponding epistemology which are more sophisticated in their recognition of the role consciousness plays in the construction of reality. The epistemology which Husserl proposes is one in which experience exhausts the content of consciousness so that there is no question of any possible objects, persons, qualities or things existing outside of it

---

[24]Husserl, *Judgement* 139.

[25]Husserl, *Judgment* 31-32.

Consciousness, in the Husserlian understanding, is the horizon in which any possible experience has a place. To ask what lies beyond it is to ask a question admitting no real sense because consciousness, itself, is the ground of *all* meaning.[26]

Now, according to Husserl, consciousness of the world and its objects is characterized by a general invariant structure, whenever consciousness is engaged. First, consciousness is always consciousness of an object; second, consciousness is always intentional; third, consciousness has a *noetic* component; fourth, consciousness has a *noematic* component; fifth, consciousness has a formal (morphic) component; sixth, consciousness has a material (hyletic) component; seventh, consciousness and its various components are susceptible to analyses according to the Husserlian logic of parts and wholes (mereology); and, eighth, consciousness is consciousness of essences.

2.3. Consciousness as Objectifying

By maintaining that consciousness is always consciousness of an object, Husserl disallows the possibility that there can be a conscious experience which is not of something; he denies that one can have a conscious experience devoid of the distinction between the conscious subject and an object to which the subject's conscious act is directed. One might think that because Husserl maintains this thesis, he has great difficulty in explaining those forms of consciousness which refer to objects which do not exist, such as hallucinations, for as everyone knows, a hallucination is an experience without a real object. Salamanders the size of terriers and spiders the size of doormats simply do not exist; how can they be the object of an experience? The Husserlian response to this question is that when a phenomenologist speaks of every experience having an object he means that every experience has an immanent object, an object which is contained within individual consciousness and has no necessary referent in the world beyond.[27]

---

[26] Anything which is not a possible object of consciousness can neither have meaning, be thought nor exist. Even when one attempts to think of things beyond consciousness, one is capable of doing so only by a trick of consciousness. Only by extending concepts developed within consciousness to the imagined objects is it possible to visualize them as beyond consciousness. Both the conceptualization of consciousness and what it means to be beyond consciousness are extensions of meaning developed within consciousness. Moreover, their supposed relationship--the state-of-affairs represented by the transcendental object and the sphere of consciousness thus conceptualized--are conceived imaginatively within a consciousness which encompasses them both. Thus, by saying that consciousness and experience are identical, Husserl makes consciousness the limit and the ultimate form of transcendence. No object of consciousness is more transcendental than consciousness. No variety of experience is conceivable apart from consciousness. Within consciousness the things of the world and the experiences of these things are constituted.

[27] But then, one might well ask "How does one distinguish hallucinations from real experiences of objects?" Since the Husserlian understanding of existence is one which makes existence intersubjective, the correct response to this question is to point out that the hallucinations of the alcoholic, though they purport to have an external reference open to the observations of other subjects, cannot be observed by others not similarly inebriated It would take a community of alcoholics (all of whom experience *coordinated* hallucinations) to constitute a *Lebenswelt* in which hallucinations seem to have external objects. Even then, any other intersubjective community which might come into contact with this association of alcoholics (and did not experience the coordinated hallucination) would pose a threat to their intersubjective reality. One possible Husserlian approach to explaining why hallucinations have a virtual object is to hypothesize that the hallucinations are a prestructuring of the hylectic data of experience: the ingestion of alcohol in large amounts causes a physiological alteration in the body which inhibits normal object-constituting experience, and a hyletic component having no corresponding object is chemically induced. Although this explanation is mere conjecture, it has a basis in Husserl's discussion of passive association. On this question of the constitution of intersubjective social reality, see Alfred Schutz,

2.4. Consciousness as Intentional

The Husserlian understanding of consciousness which makes all consciousness objectifying (but then interprets this objectification as immanent) is an understanding which directly affects the Husserlian interpretation of intentionality. In fact, it is the notion of an immanent object which primarily serves to differentiate the Husserlian understanding of intentionality from both that of the scholastics and that of his mentor Franz Brentano.

In scholastic thought, an intention is a real relation of consciousness which holds either between a being actually existing in the world or a being of reason existing in consciousness. In the first case, the scholastics call this relation a 'first intention' and used this technical term to refer to the relation by which consciousness comes into possession of knowledge of a thing by means of a *similutudo*, a likeness, which presents the being to the consciousness of the subject.[28] In the second case, the scholastics called this relation a 'second intention' and use this technical term to refer to a conscious relation between a first intention and consciousness, a relation which only derivatively arises from the being of an object but which is the instrument by which the mind grasps the meaning of the first intention according to categories and schemas of order which are of the mind's own making.[29] The first intention is a knowledge-producing relation which holds between the consciousness of the subject and a being as it actually is; the second intention is a knowledge-producing relation which holds between the consciousness of the subject and the first intention. Both varieties of intention are alike in that they presuppose an existent being--the first intention directly mediates this being; the second intention refers to that being through the mediation of the first intention--and they both take an object: the existent being for the first intention, the concept for the second intention.

Franz Brentano takes over the scholastic doctrine of intentionality but not without greatly modifying it. As Spiegelberg correctly points out, Brentano sharply emphasized that feature of the scholastic theory which makes intentionality object-taking.[30] For Bretano there is not "hearing without something heard, no believing without something believed, no hoping without something hoped."[31] Latent within Brentano's amplification of this scholastically conceived feature of intentionality is the distinction which Husserl makes so fruitful: the distinction between conscious acts and conscious contents.

"On Multiple Realities" in *The Problem of Social Reality, Collected Papers*, vol. 1 (The Hague: Martinus Nijhoff, 1962) 340-352.

[28]William A. Wallace, *The Elements of Philosophy: A Compendium for Philosophers and Theologians* (New York: Alba House, 1977) 23: 4: 64-65.

[29]John of St. Thomas, *The Material Logic of John of St. Thomas*, trans. Y. R. Simon, J. J. Glanville and G. D Hollenhorst (Chicago: University of Chicago Press, 1965) Q. 2, A. 2, 70-75.

[30]Spiegelberg, *Movement* 37.

[31]Spiegelberg, *Movement* 37.

Nevertheless, even in Brentano's modification of the scholastic theory, something still remains of the scholastic desire to make conscious relations refer to existent beings, and this residue is evidenced, particularly, in Brentano's abhorrence of fictitious entities and his insistence upon a minimalistic ontology.[32]

In comparison with either Brentano's or the scholastic descriptions of intentionality, the Husserlian notion represents a substantial development, particularly in the direction of an idealistic conception of consciousness. Spiegelberg illustrates Husserl's movement toward transcendental idealism by encapsulating the Husserlian description of intentionality in a definition which gives it five essential features, none of which have need of a referent beyond consciousness. According to Spiegelberg, Husserl's notion of intentionality is one which makes intentionality that aspect of any conscious act which (a) refers to a possible object of consciousness, (b) interprets pregiven mental materials as object-presenting, (c) establishes the identity of the objects of different intentional acts, (d) connects the various acts which produce its intuitive fulfillment and (e) constitutes the object meant.[33] That Spiegelberg is, indeed, justified in isolating these five characteristics as essential to the Husserlian doctrine of intentionality can be proven by examining chapter two of the fifth investigation in Husserl's *Logical Investigations*. There, Husserl provides his most extensive treatment of the problems associated with the old theories of intentionality, and he describes how his modified understanding of intentionality solves these problems and founds phenomenology.

Husserl begins his discussion of intentionality in the *Logical Investigations* by reflecting upon Brentano's contributions to his own theory. First, Husserl identifies the most important feature which he unreservedly borrows from Brentano's phenomenology. This is "that there are essential, specific differences of intentional relation or intention" and, furthermore, that the "manner in which a 'mere presentation' refers to its object, differs from the manner of a judgment; . . . the manner of a surmise or doubt; the manner of a hope or a fear, of approval or disapproval, of desire or aversion; of the resolution of a theoretical doubt . . . or of a practical doubt; of the confirmation of a theoretical opinion . . . , or of a voluntary intention."[34] Husserl recognizes this distinction between the intentional act of consciousness and the intentional content of consciousness to be Brentano's singular contribution to his own understanding of intentionality.

The second discovery of Brentano's phenomenology which Husserl adopts is the observation that mental phenomena are such only by either being directly presented to us or being founded upon presentations which have transcendental objects as their referents.[35] But Husserl does not accept this principle unreservedly. Rather, he rejects

---

[32]Spiegelberg, *Movement* 13-14.

[33]Spiegelberg, *Movement* 97-99.

[34]Edmund Husserl, *Logical Investigations*, trans. J.N. Findlay (London: Routledge & Kegan Paul, 1970) 2: 554-555.

[35]Husserl, *Investigations* 2: 558.

Brentano's association of presentation and external ontic reference on two grounds: first, this association leads to the conclusion that a real relationship holds between consciousness at one pole and the thing (as a thing in itself) at the other pole, and, second, it implies that because both the conscious subject and the object are united by a real relation, they are both equally real.[36] Over and against Brentano's understanding of presentation, Husserl proposes his own idealistic theory, one which admits the distinction between conscious contents and conscious acts but which interprets phenomenal presentations as explicable without reference to an ontic relation between knower and known.

According to the Husserlian understanding of intentionality, there is no question of an intention being a relation which holds between an external, real object and consciousness. Intentionality, in the Husserlian sense, merely implies that an object is "aimed at" in various conscious acts and is presented as intended; intentionality does not imply the existence of what is "aimed at" nor does it imply the separability of the object from the intentional relationship directed toward it and constitutive of it. Instead, the Husserlian notion of intentionality is one which makes an intentional act of consciousness "the full and sole presentation" of the object.[37] As Husserl puts it: "It makes no difference what sort of being we give our object, or with what sense or justification we do so, whether this being is real or ideal, genuine, possible or impossible, the act remains directed upon its object."[38] So radical is Husserl's rejection of the posited, ontic object of scholastic intentionality that he wishes to discard the relationality of intentionality completely. Knowledge is not to be understood on the basis of a model which makes it relational. Knowledge is the result of conscious production, and intentionality is to be understood as a form of production or constitution. There is no causal order between the extra-mental object and a conscious subject; there are only acts of consciousness and their internal contents and internal referents. One seeks in vain to find extra-mental objects of intentional experience. To posit them it to do metaphysics not phenomenology.

Even though Husserl rejects all varieties of intentionality which imply there is a conscious reference to an external, ontic object, he does admit that it is possible within the intentional act to distinguish the object according to the manner in which it is intended (the equivalent of the Fregean *Art des Gegebenseins*) from the object which is intended (the Fregean *Bedeutung*).[39] Although neither exists apart from consciousness, the latter represents the objective referent of the intentional act, and the former

---

[36]Husserl, *Investigations* 2: 558.

[37]Husserl, *Investigations* 2: 558.

[38]Husserl, *Investigations* 2: 559.

[39]Compare Husserl's discussion on pages 578 through 579 of the *Logical Investigations* with Frege's discussion of these terms' meaning in his article "On Sense and Reference" in *Translations from the Philosophical Writings of Gottlob Frege,* trans. Peter Geach and Max Black (Oxford: Basil Blackwell, 1970) 56-78.

represents the various individual conscious presentations (the Fregean *Sinn*) which *mean* the same object in different ways. Thus, whether one is sceptical, subservient or defiant with respect to God, these intentional acts are responsible for the altered presentation of the object (God) intended, but behind all the various conscious presentations of the object is the self-same object, whether it exists or not. It is this objectifying feature of intentionality which makes communication between subjects possible. Without objective referents shared in an intersubjective community, all talk would be at cross purposes. More fundamentally, it is doubtful that communication could even take place.

Though object-intentionality is the aspect of consciousness which is responsible for shared meanings, it is also the aspect of consciousness which makes the constitution of new objects possible. This constitution takes place as follows. When one experiences an object under a single mode of appearance corresponding to a single mental act, so long as it is possible for consciousness to posit the object under a different mode of presentation and a different conscious act, consciousness recognizes the intended object as transcending the single mode of intentionality. In fact, given within the first act of consciousness is, as it were, a thematic "ray" which reaches out from the first act to the second, uniting the intended object as the same intention for two different presentations. Husserl believes that it is characteristic of conscious presentation that it does in fact reach out in this fashion, which is to say he believes that all intentional acts presuppose a protentional moment, a moment which projects the original, dimly intended object into a second conscious act which in its presentation of the self-same object confirms the expectation of the original act. It is this aspect of intentionality which constitutes the object, because it is this protentional activity which always makes consciousness seek a richer object than that which is reducible to a single mode of givenness. A tree, as presented from a single viewpoint, is never taken as exhausting the object of that presentation. Space provides one of the positional horizons by which the intended object can be presented in a multiplicity of ways. Only the constant features of the object which refuse to be reduced to mere accidents of positional variation increase the richness of the intended object behind the presentations. The presented object, against its horizon of possible further presentations, against its horizon of possible perspectives or adumbrations, is intended by consciousness as transcendental. It is a part of the phenomenological method to suspend this protentional aspect of consciousness in order to separate adventitious presentations of meaning from the meanings which belong essentially to the object.

The only condition under which Husserl allows two different acts of consciousness to have an identical object intended in the same manner is when the two acts of consciousness present the object to consciousness "'with the same interpretive sense' or 'based upon the same matter.'"[40] When this happens--and only then--is there an identical presentation of the object. Husserl defines the test of this essential identity in what logicians call an extensional sense: "Two presentations are in essence the same, if

---

[40]Husserl, *Investigations* 2:578-579.

exactly the same statements, and no others can be made on the basis of either regarding the presented thing (either presentation being taken alone, i.e. analytically)."[41]

In Husserl's later works, the model of intentionality developed in the *Logical Investigations* is used as the means to construct more elaborate descriptions of consciousness' structures. From it, descriptions of the noema, noesis, noematic horizon, noetic horizon, phenomena, *hylê* and *morphê*, phenomenological parts and phenomenological essences are drawn out.

2.5. Noema and Noesis

Although Husserl employs the adjectives 'noematic' and 'noetic' in the *Logical Investigations*, he does so in a way which indicates only a partial understanding of their ultimate significance.[42] It is not until *Ideas* that Husserl uses these terms in a way that demonstrates their centrality to the phenomenological understanding of consciousness.

In the *Ideas* and in his later works, Husserl employs the term 'noesis' to denote the act of consciousness by which a meaning is intended. 'Noesis' covers all varieties of conscious acts which have it as their "essential nature to harbour . . . a meaning bestowing act."[43] It covers any act which has "effects of bringing out, relating, apprehending synoptically, and taking up the various attitudes of belief, presumption, valuation and so forth."[44]

According to the theory of intentionality developed in the *Logical Investigations*, the noesis may be understood as the *meaning*--in the verbal mode, that is conceived of as an act--of an intentional object colored according to particular conscious disposition. The noesis is the act-aspect of consciousness considered apart, but not as actually separable, from the content-aspect of consciousness. Therefore, corresponding to each noesis there must be a correlative content or noun aspect of meaning.[45] This correlative noun aspect is the content of the conscious meaning act, which is to say it is the meaning which is meant.[46] This content Husserl calls the 'noema' (the noun form of 'noesis').

Unfortunately, it is not an easy matter to say exactly what Husserl means by 'noema.' Originally, the view of Gurwitsch and of his school was the one which prevailed: they understood the noema to be "the concrete sensuous appearance, through

---

[41]Husserl, *Investigations* 2:578-579.

[42]There are only three references to the word 'noetic' and only one reference to the word 'noematic' in the 877 pages of the *Logical Investigations*.

[43]Husserl, *Ideas* 257.

[44]Husserl, *Ideas* 258.

[45]Husserl, *Ideas* 258.

[46]Husserl, *Ideas* 258.

which the object of perception is presented."[47]   As Hubert Dreyfus observes, it is this school of interpretation which has had the widest influence, and a string of Husserlian philosophers including Cairns, Schutz, Boehm, Fink, Solomon, Tugendhat and Merleu-Ponty have accepted it as normative.[48]   In opposition, a new school of interpretation has recently emerged in which the Husselian 'noema' is equated with meaning. This school is led by the Norwegian analytic philosopher Dagfinn Follesdal, and had its birth with the publication of his work *Husserl und Frege*.[49]   It is Follesdal's thesis that the Husserlian understanding of the noema can only be understood in the context of his intellectual dependence upon Frege, a dependence which makes the noema the correlate of the Fregean *Sinn*.

Despite the weight that the traditional position carries, when one examines Husserl's thought as it develops through its various phases, it is evident that Follesdal's interpretation of Husserl's understanding of the noema is closer to the mark than that of Gurwitsch. In his early work, it is evident that Husserl's original contemplation of the distinction between mental acts and contents occurs largely within the context of a discussion of meaning. Familiarity with the *Logical Investigations* makes this apparent. Moreover, the textual sites in *Ideas* in which 'noema' and 'meaning' are used equivocally are considerable.[50]   The weight of the textual evidence in favor of Follesdal's thesis is greater than that in favor of the Gurwitschian thesis, even though the latter is more influential. Nevertheless, it would seem to be possible to reconcile both interpretations by making Gurwitsch's thesis a particularization of Follesdal's in which noema as the meaning of sensuous appearance becomes a single variety of noemata, one type of meaning among many other varieties of meaning.[51]   However, since this reconciliation is beyond the purpose of this work, it will be reserved for another occasion.

According to Follesdal, the Husserlian noema can be characterized by the following twelve theses:

1.   The noema is an intensional entity, a generalization of the notion of meaning (*Sinn, Bedeutung*). . . .

---

[47]Hubert L. Dreyfus, "The Perceptual Noema," *Husserl Intentionality and Cognitive Science*, eds. Hubert L. Dreyfus and Harrison Hall (Cambridge: M.I.T. Press, 1984) 98.

[48]Dreyfus 98.

[49]Dafinn Follesdal, *Husserl und Frege* (Oslo: Aschehoug, 1958).

[50]Throughout the *Ideas* Husserl does, in fact, seem to use them as synonyms. This is explicit, for example, in his calling the noematic correlate of the noesis, the meaning (*Sinn*) of the act on p. 258 of *Ideas*. See Husserl, *Ideas* 258-262.

[51]One gathers that the unwillingness of Gurwitsch's school to accept this reconciliation has much to do with their own philosophical program. They view the phenomenological enterprise as *necessarily* beginning with an analysis of sensation and perception. From these the edifice of phenomenology will be built. However, they neglect later Husserlian developments such as the *Lebenswelt*, except as interpreted from the viewpoint of their program. Yet developments such as these seem to indicate that Husserl, at the end of his life, thought the phenomenological enterprise might progress at different analytical levels.

2. A noema has two components: (1) one which is common to all acts that have the same object, with exactly the same properties, oriented in the same way, etc., regardless of the "thetic" character of the act--that is, whether it be perceiving, remembering, imagining, etc., and (2) one which is different in acts with different thetic characters. . . .
3. The noematic Sinn is that in virtue of which consciousness relates to the object. . . .
4. The noema of an act is not the object of the act (i.e. the object toward which the act is directed). . . .
5. To one and the same noema, there corresponds only one object. . . .
6. To one and the same object there may correspond several different noemata. . . .
7. Each act has one and only one noema. . . .
8. Noemata are abstract entities. . . .
9. Noemata are not perceived through our senses. . . .
10. Noemata are known through a special reflection, the phenomenological re-flection. . . .
11. The phenomenological reflection can be iterated. . . .
12. This pattern of determinations, together with the "Gegebenheitsweise," is the noema. . . .[52]

Although all of these theses are self-explanatory for those familiar with Husserlian phenomenology, theses two, four, five, six, seven and twelve require ellucidation for the uninitiated. Theses ten and eleven, though requiring ellucidation, will be discussed in the section of this chapter having to do with Husserlian method.

By saying that every noema has two components, one component which is common to all intentional acts about the same object and another component which varies with the disposition of the conscious act (thesis two), Follesdal is indirectly referring to a distinction which Husserl makes in *Ideas* between the complete noema and the noematic nucleus, the former referring to the noematic nucleus plus its conditioning thetic strata, the latter referring to the sheer objective meaning of the intentional act.[53] It is the latter which is the meaning of the act in the objective intersubjective sense, the meaning which is shared by all those inhabiting a particular *Lebenswelt*. It is the coincidence between the thetic modalities of the conscious act which serves to define the noematic nucleus. The thetic modalities are arranged around the noematic nucleus like a stratified penumbra of different senses. These different senses (and associated thetic acts [*noeses*]) are the subjective constituents of the noema. Together, the noematic nucleus and noematic strata form the locus of meaning associated with a noesis. But the meaning of an act cannot be associated exclusively with either the noematic nucleus or strata. As Husserl puts it, "Meaning (*Sinn*). . . is *not* a *concrete essence* in the constitution of the noema as a whole, but a kind of abstract *form* that dwells in it."[54] The meaning, thus, is equivalent to the meaning of the "'object in its modal setting'--*as determined, namely, through the modes in which it is given*."[55] With these last two statements, Husserl draws his own phenomenological theory of meaning very close to the Fregean theory of meaning. Frege, like Husserl, postulates two aspects to every

[52] Dagfinn Follesdal, "Husserl's Notion of Noema," *Husserl, Intentionality and Cognitive Science*, 74-80.

[53] Husserl, *Ideas* 262.

[54] Husserl, *Ideas* 368.

[55] Husserl, *Ideas* 368.

meaning: a meaning's sense (*Sinn*) and a meaning's mode of presentation (*Art des Gegebenseins*).[56] The former corresponds to the noematic nucleus, and the latter corresponds to the thetic strata of the noema.

Theses four, five, six, and seven may be considered, together, in relation to one another. Thesis four is Follesdal's way of drawing a parallel between the Husserlian and Fregean semantics according to their respective theories of reference. Both Husserl and Frege distinguish the sense of a meaning from the meaning's actual object. According to Frege's theory, every meaning has a sense, a mode (or modes) of presentation and a referent (*Bedeutung*). Husserl, however, uses the terms '*Sinn*' and '*Bedeutung*' interchangeably to refer to meaning. Nevertheless, he does not conflate the distinct Fregean connotations of these terms. For referent (the Fregean *Bedeutung*) Husserl uses '*Gegenstand*,' to mean "object" or "that which stands over and against the subject."[57] Because the Husserlian object transcends the individual conscious act in which it is conceptualized, in no act of meaning is its own content confused with the object intended. Nevertheless, though the object may transcend specific acts of consciousness, the object does not transcend every form of consciousness in all its possible modes. The Husserlian object has a limited and peculiar form of transcendentality: it is an immanent object with respect to all forms of possible consciousness but a transcendent object with respect to particular conscious acts.

From the distinction between the noematic meaning and object, it follows that each object may have more than a single mode of presentation because every object transcends the individual conscious acts which present it to consciousness. But all of these modes of presentation have identical noematic nuclei which intend the same object. Therefore, to one object correspond many noema, but to many noema (having the same intention) corresponds only one object. Since it is the noesis, which is the *meaning* act which contains the noema as its content, it follows, also, that there can only be one noema for one act of meaning. Furthermore, there can be only one object for each act of meaning, though there may be many noeses concerned with a single object.

Thesis twelve represents Follesdal's condensation of Husserl's doctrine of perspectives as it relates to the noema. For Husserl, individual noeses and their corresponding noemata, though intending a transcendental object do not individually present the object as a whole. They merely represent incomplete perspectives or adumbrations of the object meant. To be sure, they point to a consistent series of determinations, but no single noesis or noema presents the object as wholly known.[58] Only when the potentially endless series of noeses and noemata are taken together (in a synthetic act which brings about the coordination of their various determinations) is something like the meaning of the transcendental object presented to consciousness. But, in a general sense, it is a limited series of determinations represented in a single

---

[56]Gottlob Frege, "On Sense and Reference," *Translations from the Writings of Gottlob Frege* 56-78.

[57]Dorion Cairns, *Guide for Translating Husserl* (The Hague: Martinus Nijhoff, 1973) 58.

[58]Husserl, *Ideas* 375.

act of consciousness (noesis) which is meant in the noema. These determinations in their peculiar thetic and perspectival embodiment--or, as Husserl would say, according to their mode of presentation (*Gegebenheitsweise*)--are the noema.[59]

2.6. Noematic and Noetic Horizons

Just as the *Lebenswelten* possess horizons of compossibility which diachronically trail off into past and future and which synchronically trail off toward the farthest reaches of the spatial world, individual noeses and their respective noematic contents possess similar horizons. In fact, it is the noetic and noematic horizons which substructure the horizons of the *Lebenswelten* as well as the *Wesenswelt* which is the horizon of horizons.

Husserl describes the horizons of noetic acts in the following way:

> . . . [To] everything and eventually to the whole world of things, with the one space and the one time, there corresponds the system of possible noetic events, of the possible experiences of individuals and community-units that relate to these events, experiences which, and parallel to the noematic manifolds . . . , contain in their own essence this peculiar feature of being related to the world of things through their import and posited meaning. In them accordingly there appear the relevant manifolds of hyletic data, with the appropriate "apprehensions", thetic act-characters, and so forth, which in their connected unity make up what we call *empirical consciousness* of this thinghood. Over and against the thing its unity stands an infinite ideal manifold of noetic experience of a quite determined essential content, over which . . . a proper oversight can still be kept, all the experiences arguing in this way that they are consciousness of "the same" object.[60]

Just as the noetic acts which intend a particular object are of infinite variety, so too the individual feature of the noematic meaning, the *Gegebenheitsweise* (or meaning associated with its mode of presentation) is of infinite variety as well. But the important thing to note is that the intentionality directed toward a particular object defines both the noetic and noematic horizons. Both horizons are founded upon a conscious intention of the object which transcends individual conscious acts and meanings. Moreover, though both the noematic and noetic horizons are infinite in the number of possible acts and contents they allow, there is an underlying substructure of typification which is intentionally associated with particular varieties of objects. This is to say that though an intended thing may have an infinite set of perspectives associated with it, this set has a phenomenological structure which is fixed in such a way that the perspectives vary infinitely but within the parameters described by the thing's typification. The thing's typification is a consistent coordination of all the thing's perspectives (or appearances) according to qualitative categories which are always

---

[59]Husserl, *Ideas* 272.

[60]Husserl, *Crisis* 31.

a part of the thing's presentation.[61] Every object of consciousness has its appropriate set of typical qualitative parameters within which it may vary infinitely and still remain the same thing. The qualities within these parameters are susceptible to mathematical description according to whether they can be associated with dichotomous, serial or variable orders.

Inasmuch as any experience of an object *means* that object within a set of typifications, some of whose instantiations are realized in the specific experience and some of whose instantiations are not realized but potentially realizable, each experience of a thing exists within the horizon of that thing's possible modes of presentation. Now, with respect to the temporal order in which the experience nests, it is possible to distinguish three components of an object's horizon of presentations. Thinkers of the Husserlian school designate these three components with greater or lesser clarity.[62] Though he does not provide neologisms for them, Husserl is aware of these horizontal distinctions (as is evidenced by his distinction between the thetic acts of protention, retention, and attention), protention being an anticipation of future presentation, retention being a remembrance of past presentations and attention (or apprehension) being a concentration on contemporary presentations.[63] Therefore, corresponding to the noematic and noetic components of an experience of an object, it is precise to distinguish between: (i) an antecedent noematic horizon, (ii) a copresent noematic horizon and (iii) consequent noematic horizon as well as (i*) an antecedent noetic horizon, (ii*) a copresent noetic horizon and (iii*) a consequent noetic horizon.

The distinctions between the various components belonging to the horizon of thing-experience are not exhausted by the temporal divisions of horizonality. Husserl also prescribes a distinction between the internal noematic horizon and external noematic horizon of a thing as well as the internal noetic horizon and external noetic horizon of a thing.[64] The internal noematic and noetic horizons are the field of all possible meanings and conscious dispositions which are typically associated with the thing, but the external noematic and noetic horizons are the field of all possible meanings and conscious dispositions which surround the things as their environment. For example, if one were to take the social organization, church, as a phenomenological object then one might describe the empirical typicalities which prescribe its general features. This component Husserl refers to as the "internal horizon" of the thing church. But if one

---

[61] An apple, for example, may be presented stereoscopically according to an infinite variety angles and chromatically according to an infinite variety of hues, but it is always presented to consciousness as three-dimensional, and it is always presented as colored either red, green, yellow, brown, etc. One never finds a one-dimensional apple or an apple without color.

[62] Otto Muck and Emerich Coreth, though in the Heideggerian line of descent from Husserl, develop the Husserlian notion of horizonality in a way which is complementary to Husserl's later understanding of it. See Otto Muck, *The Transcendental Method* (New York: Herder and Herder, 1968) 301-306, and Emerich Coreth, *Metaphysics*, trans. Joseph Donceel (New York: Seabury Press, 1973) 46-68.

[63] Husserl, *Judgment* 112-121.

[64] Husserl, *Judgment* 31-40.

were to describe the church within its complete social matrix, within its social environment which is the background for an aspect of its meaning, then one would describe its external horizon. Though a church might exist against a variety of possible external horizons, only one internal horizon makes it what it is.

Nevertheless, the possible external horizons of every object are not completely variable because they are horizons within the world and its typical style of existence, the *Wesenswelt*. In actuality, the number of possibilities within the external horizon of a thing are more limited than one might expect, since things have meaning only within the context of a field of other things (that is, within a world). Internal horizons, therefore, often depend upon a respective external horizon according to the relatively restrictive relations of foundedness. A historical object's internal horizon, for example, is much more dynamic and interactive in relation to its external horizon than are the internal and external horizons of a perceptual object. In the example of a historical object, there is a farrago of relevant noeses and noemata which are cogredient in its constitution.

To put it another way, historical objects are so complex and of such dependent constitution that the boundary between the horizon of their typicality and the horizon of their environment is often blurred. Because historical objects are the products of the historical *milieux* from which they emerge, they cannot easily be separated from their *milieux*. The noetic and noematic structures of *historical* objects are often dictated by the noetic and noematic structures of their surrounding historical world.

[Chart 9 describes the twelve possible varieties of horizonality as they characterize individual acts of consciousness. Charts 10 and 11 provide visual metaphors for the various varieties of horizon.]

2.7. The Husserlian Mereology

Inasmuch as noeses and noemata cofound one another--in that there could be no content of consciousness without an act of consciousness and no act of consciousness which is devoid of a content--there is no question of speaking of their *actual* separability. Even though they may be discriminated, in the Peircean sense, they cannot be prescinded from one another. The noemata and noeses form two necessary parts of all conscious acts.

When one considers the various horizons surrounding noeses and noemata, one discovers that different strictures on separability apparently hold. Inasmuch as particular horizons represent the possible alterations of a particular noema, these particular horizons are *both* able to be discriminated and prescinded from consciousness. However, the horizonality of noeses and noemata is discriminable but is *neither* prescindable *nor* dissociable. Unlike its particular instantiations, the general horizonality of consciousness is its constant and inseparable feature, though it may be fleshed in according to different possibilities.

Even when one examines the noema as discriminated from its respective noesis, one discovers relations of dependence and independence. The noemata of all conscious acts which intend a single object possess two parts: the pure noematic nucleus which is the objective intention of the self-same object and the various noematic substrata which represent its specific form of givenness in that conscious act. Though both can

CHART 9

The Varieties of Horizonality

Component of   Horizons
Consciousness:

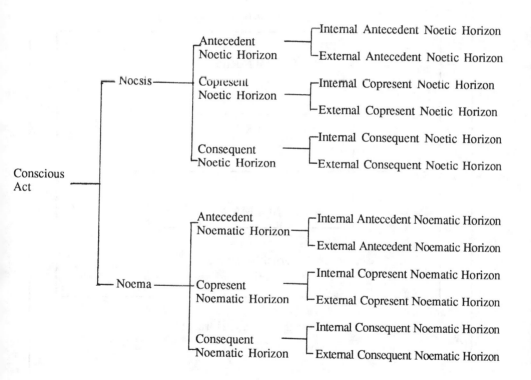

CHART 10

The Structure of the Internal and External Horizon
of a Conscious Act

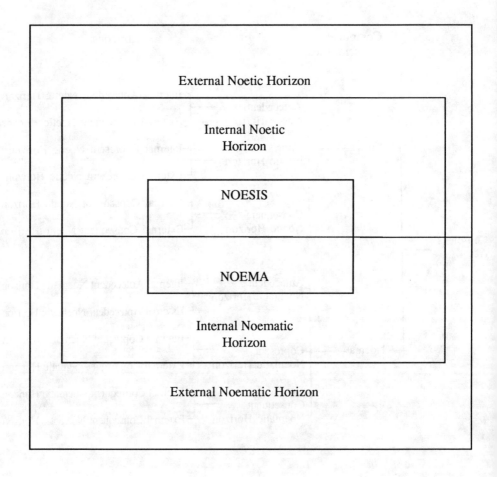

External Noetic Horizon

Internal Noetic
Horizon

NOESIS

NOEMA

Internal Noematic
Horizon

External Noematic Horizon

CHART 11
The Dynamic Relations Between
The Various Noetic and Noematic Horizons

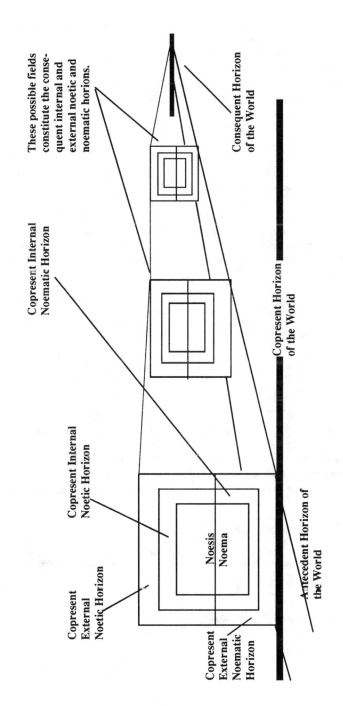

These possible fields constitute the consequent internal and external noetic and noematic horions.

Copresent Internal Noematic Horizon

Consequent Horizon of the World

Copresent Internal Noetic Horizon

Copresent External Noetic Horizon

Noesis
Noema

Copresent External Noematic Horizon

Copresent Horizon of the World

Antecedent Horizon of the World

be discriminated from the object, the former is not prescindable from the intention of the object. The latter, as a mere presentational residue, is. Moreover, both are prescindable from one another when not thematized as parts of a single act. However, when the conscious act (of which they are parts) is brought into play their prescindability evaporates. Obviously, behind the various structures of conscious activity, relations of dependence and independence, part and whole and mediateness and immediateness are always present. According to Husserl, these relations form the ultimate materially logical relations holding between *any* objects.[65] Inasmuch as consciousness can take its own acts as an object, these material relations are present in objects such as the noeses, noemata, noematic nuclei, etc. Inasmuch as consciousness can take as its objects Theravâda Buddhism, a subatomic particle or a parakeet, these material relations are present in these objects as well. It is not phenomenologically sufficient to reflect upon these various material relations in a way which is not rigorous, one must bring to them the apodicity of logical relations. It is rigor in the description of the material relations of things that Husserl's theory of parts and wholes ('mereology' from the Greek *meros* + *logia* = "science of parts") is designed to effect.[66]

Most important to an understanding of mereology is an understanding of the Husserlian definition of 'part.' It is defined as follows:

> We interpret the word 'part' in the *widest* sense: we may call anything a 'part' which can be distinguished 'in' an object, or, objectively phrased, that is 'present' in it. Everything is a part that is an object's real possession, not only in the sense of being a real thing, but also in the sense of being something really in something, that truly helps to make it up: an object in itself, considered from all contexts to which it is tied, is likewise a part. Every non-relative 'real' (*reale*) predicate therefore points to a part of the object which is the predicate's subject: 'red' and 'round', e.g. , do so, but not 'existent' or 'something'. Every 'real' (*reale*) mode of association, e.g. the moment of spatial configuration, likewise counts as a proper part of the whole.[67]

By 'whole' Husserl intends any object consisting of "a range of contents which are covered by *a single foundation* without the help of further contents."[68] This means that a whole exists in relative independence from superior wholes. But wholes are always defined by a conscious restriction which associates sets of specific contents with one another. Against the whole which is the world, all other beings are parts. In thematizing the world-whole, however, consciousness intends the greatest whole which

---

[65]Husserl, *Investigations* 2: 455-456.

[66]Husserl's axiomatic treatment of the theory of parts and wholes occurs in chapters one and two of "Investigation III" of the *Logical Investigations*. Considerations of economy prevent an extended treatment of Husserl's mereology here. However, it is necessary to present some of the fundamental principles of mereology, for without an understanding of this Husserlian discovery one cannot come to an accurate understanding of his theory of essences. See Husserl, *Logical Investigations* 2: 435-489.

[67]Husserl, *Investigations* 2: 437.

[68]Husserl, *Investigations* 2: 475.

can be given to consciousness. For the world, the possible internal and external horizons of all noeses and noemata are cogredient and foundational.

A part is, according to the above definition, any feature of a thing or object which, *in any sense*, can be discriminated. A whole is a content which though founded upon parts does not require further contents to found it. All things except the world--as the horizon of all horizons--are parts relative to some other whole.[69] It is possible to further distinguish the varieties of parts (and wholes) into four classes: (a) independent parts, (b) dependent parts, (c) immediate parts and (d) mediate parts.

Six propositions (or theorems) serve to define independent and dependent parts and wholes:

Theorem 1: If A is necessarily founded on M, then every whole of which A (but not M) is a part is founded upon M.[70]

Theorem 2: Any whole which includes a dependent moment (M_D) without including the foundation of that moment is itself dependent. Such a whole is dependent upon every subordinate independent whole in which M_D is contained.[71]

Theorem 3: "If W is an independent part of . . . F, then every independent part . . . of W is also an independent part of F."[72]

Theorem 4: If C is a dependent part of a whole W, then it is a dependent part of every whole of which W is a part.[73]

Theorem 5: A relatively dependent object is absolutely dependent, but a relatively independent object *may be absolutely dependent.*[74] (An object may be independent with respect to a more immediate whole but dependent with respect to a greater whole.)

Theorem 6: If A and B are independent parts of a whole W, then they are independent relative to one another. (If A were dependent on B, then there would be a part of W (that is, B) which would found A. Then, A would be dependent on W.)[75]

Now with respect to these different relations of dependency, it is further possible to distinguish relations of mediacy or immediacy. If something is part of a whole, anything which is part of it is also a part of the whole but only through the mediacy of the first part. The first part Husserl calls an immediate part and the second a

---

[69]Husserl puts it this way "[I]n the following respect the world is absolute substrate, namely, everything is in it, and it itself is not an in-something; it is no longer a relative unity within a more comprehensive plurality. It is the totality of existents; it is not 'in something' but is itself something total." See *Experience and Judgment* 137.

[70]Husserl, *Investigations* 2: 463.

[71]Husserl, *Investigations* 2: 464.

[72]Husserl, *Investigations* 2: 464.

[73]Husserl, *Investigations* 2: 464.

[74]Husserl, *Investigations* 2: 465.

[75]Husserl, *Investigations* 2: 465.

mediate part.[76] On the basis of the notion of mediation it is possible to distinguish: (a) immediate dependent parts, (b) mediate dependent parts, (c) immediate independent parts and (d) mediate independent parts. Both immediate dependent parts and immediate independent parts can have mediate dependent and independent parts as their constituent parts, but the theorems of dependency describe the relations which must obtain in these partitionings and subpartitionings.

Although Husserl seems, at places in the *Logical Investigations*, to distinguish the notion of foundedness from the notion of dependence by using the corresponding words with apparently different connotations, that there is no real difference between each can be seen by consulting his definitions of each. 'Dependence' means that a "content is bound by its nature to other contents," and that "it cannot be, if other contents are not there together with it."[77] Conversely, 'independence' means "that the existence of . . . [a] content, to the extent that this depends on itself and its essence, is not at all conditioned by the existence of other contents, that it could exist as it is, through an *a priori* necessity of essence, even if no-thing were outside of it, even if all around were altered at will."[78] The situations which Husserl envisions with respect to dependence and independence are the following. With respect to dependence, he imagines the content of a conscious act in which its various parts are inseparably related to one another. The situation which he envisions in his definition of independence, however, is one in which the noematic content of a conscious act is independent of its cogiven horizons as well as the possible background variations which may occur in those horizons. An independent content is one which always can be kept identical in conscious attention despite variations in the whole of which it is a part. In contrast, a dependent content or part is one which changes when the whole content (or object) changes or when the internal or external horizons are varied at will.

Husserl describes 'foundedness' or the 'foundational relationship' as "a relationship of necessary association."[79] Apparently, he makes an equation of 'dependence' and 'foundedness' at only one point in the *Logical Investigations*, immediately before he presents the six theorems which describe the relations of dependence between parts and wholes. Nevertheless, this equation is unequivocal. Husserl describes it this way: "The indefinite expression: A_0 . . . *is founded upon a certain moment*, plainly means the same as the expression: 'A_0 is non-independent'."[80]

It may seem a *trivial* point to demonstrate the equivalence between foundedness and dependency, except that only upon this basis is it possible to discover the essences of phenomena. The significance Husserl associates with the discovery of essences--this

---

[76]Husserl, *Investigations* 2: 469.

[77]Husserl, *Investigations* 2: 443.

[78]Husserl, *Investigations* 2: 443.

[79]Husserl, *Investigations* 2: 463.

[80]Husserl, *Investigations* 2: 463.

discovery being one of the major tasks of Husserlian phenomenology--lends the equation of dependency and foundedness its significance. Eidetic variation, the Husserlian method for the discovery of essences, depends implicitly upon what Husserl says about parts and wholes, dependence and independence and mediacy and immediacy. That the discovery of essences is dependent upon these relations, is clear from what he says about the isolability (or independence) of contents as well as what he says about the foundedness of contents. In both discussions, Husserl's casual references to essential laws makes it clear that the essential features of phenomena both found and are revealed through the various relations of part and whole. Considering isolability (independence) first, one finds that Husserl describes it this way.

> Isolability [independence] means only that we can keep some content constant in idea despite boundless variation--variation that is free, though not excluded by a law rooted in the content's essence--of the contents associated with it and in general given with it. This means that it is unaffected by the elimination of any given copresent contents whatsoever.[81]

Later, in the same investigation, when describing the difference between a loose aggregate of mental contents and a founded (dependent) content, Husserl describes foundedness as follows:

> A founded content . . . depends on the specific 'nature' of its 'founding' contents: there is a pure law which renders the Genus of the 'founded' content dependent on the definitely indicated Genera of the 'founding' contents. A whole in the full and proper sense is, in general, a combination determined by the lowest Genera of the parts. A law corresponds to each material unity. There are different sorts of whole corresponding to these different laws, or . . . to the different sorts of contents that are to serve as parts. We cannot at will make the same content at one time part of one sort of whole, at another time part of another sort. To be part, and more exactly, to be a part of some determinate sort (a metaphysical, physical, or logical part of whatever) is rooted in the pure genetic nature of the contents in question, and is governed by the laws which in our sense are a priori laws or 'laws of essence'.[82]

From these two passages--and from the Husserlian discussion of mereology *in toto*--one can, with some difficulty, draw the inference that to be an essence is equivalent to being (a) an object and (b) a whole which is independent of extraneous contents and yet necessarily dependent upon its constituent contents. An essence is, thus, the objective correlate of a noematic nucleus, whose meaning is dictated by the necessary relations of the object's foundedness. Put another way, an essence is an object which is a whole unto itself according to necessary laws of typification.

Aside from its value in providing the formal relations by which essences may be distinguished, the Husserlian mereology is also a useful tool for analyzing the various relations between any objects which appear as epiphenomena and not according to any essential necessity. It is actually in the dialectic between its two functions--as an instrument for the analysis of both epiphenomena and essential phenomena--that the Husserlian mereology proves its full worth.

---

[81] Husserl, *Investigations* 2: 443.

[82] Husserl, *Investigations* 2: 480-481.

2.8. Phenomenological Essences (Eidê)

Although the noematic nuclei of a number of noeses intending the same object are identical, and designate the object as a particular type of thing, this typification is empirical and not based upon the necessary properties which characterize the essence behind the thing. The empirical type, thus, represents a kind of object understood by means of the correspondences between its *actual* modes of appearance. But the ways an object actually appears are not identical with the ways it might possibly appear nor are they identical to the object's necessary phenomenological properties.

To have experienced only black swans and never to have experienced white swans might make one develop an empirical type of what it means to be a swan which includes blackness as one of its necessary qualitative parts (moments). But this would be incorrect from the point of view of an *essential* analysis of what it means to be a swan. An essential analysis would be one which roots the essence of a swan in a whole whose immediate parts are foundational. The result would be not a definition of swan which includes the specific possibilities black and white but which, as Husserl prescribes, includes the foundational genus of color (an abstract part) as a necessary part of its essence. The genera of its founding parts would be the eidetic generalities which found the laws which give the particular essence its necessary structure.[83]

The easiest way to think of what Husserl intends by the object he calls an 'essence' is to think of it, metaphorically, as a sort of algebraic function in which the variable places are held by individual quality modes and in which its mathematical structure represents the eidetic structure.[84] Just as the mathematical formula for a circle $X^2+Y^2=R^2$ can take an infinite series of X and Y values for each R, though retaining the general formula (read 'essence') for circularity, so too the essence of material thing, though prescribing generic characteristics of the thing which must always be present such as spatial extension, inertia, mass, etc., does not prescribe specifically what those values must be. The essence of material thing does not prescribe a particular mass, particular size, etc.

Nevertheless, Husserl does say that essences can operate at any level of generality so long as they represent the necessary features of the object intended. Therefore, essences such as that of George Bush, Jesus Christ, and the flagstone-at-the-foot-of-my-garden are not inconceivable. In Husserl's understanding they would be the necessary typifications of the phenomena George Bush, Jesus Christ, and the

---

[83]In this way, the investigation of an essence which is a higher composite whole implies that its founding contents themselves must be investigated, as well, at least in order to bring the higher essence to perfect apodicity. Practically however, this cannot always be done. Husserlian phenomenology would be in a sad state if no one attempted analyses of higher level essences until the phenomenological analyses of their founding genera were accomplished. Because of the potential inexhaustability of its objects, phenomenology would be little more than a science of perceptual analysis. Indeed the number of perceptual objects available for analysis might well stunt phenomenology, if it were to be directed solely to perceptual analyses. For phenomenology to be a progressive science of eidetic investigation, it must dabble in all levels of eidetic generality. Later, an articulation of its indubitable analyses will allow the various regional phenomenologies to assume the structure of a scientific architectonic.

[84]Although I had thought of this analogy independently, Robert Sokolowski provides an interesting and very lucid discussion of it in his *Husserlian Meditations* (Evanston: Northwestern University Press, 1974), 76-77.

flagstone-at-the-foot-of-my-garden. This should not seem particularly irregular for we all form typifications of personality and materiality in our everyday experience of the world.[85] The only difference between these typifications and eidetic typifications is that the former are founded upon empirical generalities never brought to the apodicity of intuition; the latter, though beginning in empirical data are brought to apodictic intuition by means of the phenomenological method.

Aside from the many regions of genera to which *eidê* belong as instantiations, are also susceptible to distinction as to whether they are exact or morphological essences. The former are those which are given perfectly to consciousness in non-sensuous forms. Examples of these are mathematical constructions such as circle, plane, dodecahedron, manifold, and so on. Morphological essences, in contrast, are the *a priori* structures of that which is given through the appearances of sensible, perceptible things such as children, trees, buildings, planets, etc.[86] These essences admit of various degrees of eidetic apodicity some of which may be brought to eidetic precision, others which cannot.

The goal of Husserlian phenomenological analysis is to eliminate the various accretions of consciousness which occlude the essences behind the experience of the world. From experience of objects, all extraneous contributions of the *Umwelt* must be eliminated before eidetic analysis can proceed. Once eidetic variation has been accomplished upon the controlled data with the result that the essences are denuded, then and only then, does one have a ground for the scientific study of that region of the world to which these essences belong.

3. The Ambiguity of the Ends of Husserlian Phenomenology

The Husserlian phenomenology poses particular problems for anyone hoping to accomplish its facile encapsulation. Unlike his phenomenological predecessors, Husserl does not take up phenomenology as a mere occasional work, as a task to be accomplished once and then forgotten. Rather, for Husserl the definition of phenomenology, as a task never finished and always capable of improvement, is life-long. This devotion to the revision of phenomenology has its disadvantages. Chief among them is that it makes it difficult to say exactly what the Husserlian phenomenology is and to what specifically it is directed. Derivatively, it becomes difficult to place Husserlian phenomenology in the architectonic of the sciences. Husserl's constant revision of phenomenology means that as he compounds definitions of phenomenology he also compounds the related aims. For every definition of phenomenology which entails a particular placement in the architectonic of the sciences

---

[85] An eidos is merely a rigorously founded model. In everyday life we form types of people, experiences and things but these are formed haphazardly and without the benefit of the Husserlian *epochê*. Everyday types are in no sense rigorous.

[86] Robert Sokolowski provides an illuminating discussion of the difference between exact and morphological essences in his book *Husserlian Meditations* 77-78.

there is an easily discoverable (but distinct) set of ends this phenomenology is to achieve. It is, therefore, possible to consider the ends and placements of the various versions of Husserlian phenomenology to be of one piece and to treat these linked aspects in a single section.

3.1. The Periodization of Husserl's Thought

Despite the numerous works written about the Husserlian phenomenology, there is surprising agreement about the periodization of Husserl's intellectual development. Since it is not the purpose of this work to present a history of the development of Husserlian phenomenology, but to come to some conclusions about its aims and placement, no new periodization will be proposed. Instead, the remainder of this section will be devoted to the periodizations of Spiegelberg and Farber which are not completely unproblematic descriptions of the various Husserlian phenomenologies and of these phenomenologies' respective aims.

Spiegelberg, in his attempt to describe the intellectual development of Husserl, divides Husserl's development of phenomenology into six periods: (1) a pre-phenomenological period (~1884-1900), in which Husserl's major concern was the derivation of arithmetic from psychological foundations; (2) the beginning of Husserl's actual phenomenological period (~1901-1905), in which Husserl defines phenomenology as the subjective correlate of pure logic directed toward a description of the ideal types of logical experience corresponding to the ideal logical laws; (3) the period in which phenomenology becomes "first philosophy" (~1906-1912) or the single science capable of providing an apodictic foundation for philosophy and empirical science; (4) the beginning of the period of transcendental phenomenology (~1913-1922) during which Husserl interprets phenomenology as the science which founds knowledge upon the transcendental reduction of the ego; (5) the period of the "system" of transcendental phenomenology (~1923-1933), in which Husserl attempted to work out the rudiments of a philosophical system in which civilization, intersubjectivity and a theory of the world would be grounded in the transcendental reduction of the ego; and, finally, (6) the period immediately preceding Husserl's death (~1934-1938), during which Husserl brings the *Lebenswelt* to the foreground as the preeminent object of phenomenological analysis.[87]

Marvin Farber proposes an alternative classification of the periods of Husserl's development of phenomenology, but more narrowly bases it upon Husserl's published output and its character than upon Husserl's complete intellectual history. Farber's periodization does, however, generally correspond to that given by Spiegelberg with the exception that Farber adds a period before--what Spiegelberg calls--Husserl's pre-phenomenological period.[88] Elsewhere, Farber conflates the more elaborate periodization of the Husserlian development of phenomenology and presents a simpler schema.

[87]Spiegelberg, *Movement* 84-147.

[88]Farber, *Foundation* 15-21.

Broadly speaking, four main periods are distinguished: (1) . . . [Husserl's] early period of interest in basic problems of mathematics, as well as in a psychological approach to logic; (2) the period of the "breakthrough" to phenomenology, which was at first called "descriptive psychology" and conceived as . . . neutral in its commitment . . . toward all metaphysics, without "presuppositions" of any kind--in short, as purely descriptive science; (3) the period of transcendental phenomenology, in which the reduction to pure consciousness of an individual knower is basic; and (4) the last period of the elaboration of a constitutive idealistic philosophy which is universal in its scope, and in which some attention is given to the concepts of life and historical culture.[89]

According to Farber, six distinct ends of phenomenology emerge from these developmental periods. Husserlian phenomenology is directed to (1) providing a critique of knowledge which founds logic, (2) providing descriptions of experience's essential structures, (3) providing a complete description of the mind's role in the constitution of experience, (4) providing "a unified theory of science and knowledge," (5) providing a ground for worldhood which is not based upon the usual naturalistic presuppositions, and (6) realizing "the ideal of a complete descriptive philosophy."[90] Although Farber does not associate these ends with specific periods in the development of phenomenology, they are susceptible to such association. Presumably, the first end of phenomenology may be associated with the first and second periods of Husserlian phenomenology's development. The second end of phenomenology is a constant objective of all periods of its Husserlian development as are ends five and six. The third objective of phenomenology, too, corresponds with all the Husserlian periods of development, but it more appropriately applies to the third, or transcendental period. Finally, the fourth end of phenomenology corresponds, in a direct fashion, to the fourth period of development.

Brief reflection upon the periodizations of Spiegelberg and Farber is sufficient to establish that within Husserl's development of phenomenology many of the ends of his predecessors are recapitulated. In fact, it is a general feature of the development of phenomenology that its ontogenesis recapitulates its phylogenesis; its systematization--at any one time--repeats its history. In taking up many of the problems of his predecessors, Husserl is compelled to allow his thought to follow similar orbits. That this is so follows from one of the fundaments of phenomenology (however it is defined): the structure of phenomena govern their presentation to consciousness. Insofar as the problems of phenomenological analysis may be treated as phenomena, their structures dictate a particular form of solution. The dictum which Marx proposes--in a very different context and with very different justification--is perfectly phenomenological in its grasp of this feature of experience: Man poses no question which is incapable of solution. That this is so follows from the preapprehension of meanings involved. To be a meaningful question is to be a question which prescribes an approach to its solution. In that the phenomenologists preceding Husserl--as well as Husserl himself--ask many of the same questions, they also come to many of the same conclusions regarding the definition, placement and ends of phenomenology.

---

[89]Farber, *Aims* 12.

[90]Farber, *Aims* 14.

From Farber's description of the ends of Husserlian phenomenology, and from the statements of Husserl, himself, it is possible to extract three general assertions of what Husserlian phenomenology is. Husserlian phenomenology is alternatively, a science, a philosophy, or a method.

3.2. The Three Meanings of 'Husserlian Phenomenology'

When viewed as a discrete set (or axiomatic system) of new propositions about the conscious constitution of the world, Husserlian phenomenology can, with some justification, claim the name 'science.' It does represent a body of certain knowledge which has utility in many established scientific fields. Moreover, it has as one of its ends the founding of the empiriological sciences in intuitive certainties, a project which, if it could be accomplished, would mean nothing less than justification of induction. But it is only in this sense that it can claim scientific status. In comparison, its claim to being a science is groundless because it has no characteristic domain of objects to which it is investigatively directed. The world, in all of its levels of complexity, is the object of Husserlian phenomenology. But just because it posits everything as its object, it can select no object which can serve to distinguish it from the other sciences. At best, it belongs as a school, or if viewed from its methodology, as a discipline within the philosophy of science because Husserl never achieves an adequate explanation of its value to the natural sciences. There is evidence that he begins this justification late in his career, and the major fruit of this last labor is *The Crisis of the European Sciences*. However, the real achievement of this project was frustrated by Husserl's death. With no such justification forthcoming, the Husserlian phenomenology can claim little more than a standing as a scientific metaphysics. As such, it belongs to the philosophy of science; it is not, however, a science.

When viewed as a style of thought, an intellectual way of being, or a love of wisdom, phenomenology has a legitimate claim to being a philosophy. But the same barriers to its considerations as a science prevent its equation with the philosophy or *first* philosophy.

It is well known that Husserl conceived his role of discoverer of phenomenology and teacher of the phenomenological method with a "messianic fervor" and as ectypical of the great thinkers in the Western philosophical tradition.[91] He believed himself the twentieth century heir-apparent to the line of philosophers stretching back to Plato, and he went so far as to equate phenomenology, implicitly, with the perennial philosophy.[92] He supposed that whatever was good and enduring in the Western philosophical tradition, reached fulfillment in Husserlian phenomenology with more rigor and justification than in its previous development. It was the messianic tone to Husserl's achievement which lent credence to his point that the practice of phenomenology was

---

[91]Spiegelberg, *Movement* 76-84.

[92]This is true of *The Crisis of European Sciences*, in particular.

like a religious conversion or a conversion to a new worldview.[93] His condemnation of the thought of his students who deviated slightly from his teachings had something of a religious devotion to dogma about it and served to corroborate his adoption of phenomenology as a way of life.

In his urging that devotion to truth is the *sine qua non* of phenomenology, Husserl was an exemplar of some of the West's most cherished myths regarding philosophers. But devotion alone is no compelling reason that phenomenology should be considered the only philosophy or first philosophy. Phenomenology can achieve this position only in competition with other philosophies, a competition whose outcome is measured by the fruitfulness of results. To date, very few philosophies have captured the position of paradigmatic (or first) philosophy for a long time. There is little reason to accord phenomenology either title except on grounds of productivity. Husserl's claims in this respect will, therefore, remain excessive until phenomenology fulfills its potential.

It is with respect to its third definition, as method, that Husserlian phenomenology comes into its own. It is only this claim, out of the three, which is not excessive. Moreover, it is this claim which allows phenomenology to save the various ends, which Farber describes, and to do so rigorously. But before this can be demonstrated, a distinction needs to be introduced.

3.3. Exploratory vs. Thematic Phenomenology

When one examines the way Husserl employs the phenomenological method, it is obvious that he does so with either of two very general aims in mind. On one hand, he uses it to uncover areas for future philosophical investigations. In this sense, the phenomenological apparatus is used for exploratory purposes as a means to disocclude problems for solution. Characteristic of this application of the phenomenological method are *Logical Investigations*, *Ideas*, and *Cartesian Meditations*. On the other hand, Husserl uses the phenomenological method to solve special problems which fall within another science's governing motif. Characteristic of this application of the phenomenological method are *Phenomenological Psychology, Formal and Transcendental Logic, The Phenomenology of Internal Time Consciousness, The Crisis of European Sciences*, and *Phenomenology and Anthropology*. The first variety of phenomenological investigations may be referred to as exploratory phenomenology. The latter variety of phenomenology may be referred to as thematic phenomenology.

According to either use, phenomenology is not sufficient both to ground itself and still claim to be presupposition-free. In its capacity as a method, themes must necessarily be imported from outside of the presuppositions behind its techniques. When the phenomenological method is employed in a free manner to general ends, its ultimate effect is to produce analyses which advance the problems it discloses. In its capacity to advance sciences, exploratory phenomenology--though requiring some grounding in the discipline under whose aegis it is employed--can be employed freely and without theoretical constraints. As thus applied, phenomenology effects a metatheoretical critique

---

[93]Spiegelberg, *Movement* 81-84.

of science, but it is always a metatheoretical critique which appeals to the internal criterion of the apodicity of appearance.

In its second capacity as thematic phenomenology, the Husserlian method should be employed as if the theoretical apparatus of the science were presupposed. In this case, the definition of the problem which is proposed by the science will become the definition accepted by phenomenology. In this case, phenomenology brackets the criticism of foundational presuppositions.

The component which unites both varieties of phenomenology is the application of the Husserlian *epochê* (about which more will be said below). In exploratory phenomenology, the *epochê* is not held back with respect to any object or experience within a demarcated field. Phenomenology is allowed to roam over the field in a relatively anarchistic fashion, its own presuppositions being the only criteria of judgment.[94] In thematic phenomenology, in contrast, phenomenology is a slave to the presuppositions of the science: the *epochê* is applied with a relativity which does not the science. Thematic phenomenology is phenomenally and eidetically reductive according to the aims of the science in which it is employed. It is radically descriptive within very narrow limits. It is not deconstructive nor reconstitutive of foundations.

Examples of legitimate objects for each variety of phenomenology allow one to clearly distinguish between their application. Exploratory phenomenology would have as its themes expansive subjects and objects such as: the nature of reality, physical law, philosophy, religion, etc. Thematic phenomenology, in contrast, would presuppose conventional definitions of those themes already established in the sciences. Its themes would be narrow subjects and objects such as: the content of hallucination which make hallucinations seem real, sensory efficacy and habit as these are related to animal faith, the phenomenological evidence for the teleonomic structure of ethics, a phenomenology of Christian prayer. Phenomenology, as it is concerned with the first set of themes, is actually productive of the definitions which would be employed in the second variety.

Interpreted as a method and as neither science nor first philosophy, Husserlian phenomenology could retain the general ends which Farber describes, but it would do so as a methodological part of the extant empiriological sciences and philosophy.

4. The Husserlian Phenomenological Technique

The Husserlian phenomenological technique is closely related to the ends of Husserlian phenomenology. Inasmuch as Husserlian phenomenology aims to be "an *a priori* science ('eidetic', directed upon the universal in its original intuitability), which appropriates, though as pure possibility only, the empirical field of fact of transcendental subjectivity with its factual . . . experiences, equating these with pure intuitable possibilities that can be modified at will and sets out as its *a priori* the indissoluble essential structures of transcendental subjectivity, which persist in and through all

---

[94]Husserl, *Ideas* 42-43

imaginable modifications," its accompanying technique reflects these intentions.[95] Phenomenology's method is directed, first, to reducing appearances to pure presentations, presentations which possess none of the unquestioned occlusions which mask their original apodicity. Second, it is directed to developing apodictically grounded concepts (essences) on the basis of the phenomenal reductions.

4.1. The Tasks of Husserlian Phenomenology

In other words, one can distinguish two major tasks that the Husserlian phenomenological technique is designed to accomplish: first, it is ordered to bring the phenomenologist to an apodictic understanding of appearances exactly as they present themselves to consciousness devoid of all preconceptions. Second, it is ordered to bring the phenomenologist to an understanding of the essential regularities and structures which exist within and through these appearances. The phenomenological technique is a technique whose objects are appearances and essences. But because the Husserlian phenomenology makes its discoveries within a realm of appearances defined by two absolute substrates the transcendental ego on one hand and the world on the other--its investigation of appearances rebounds between these two poles. Any phenomenological analysis is necessarily a phenomenological analysis of the contributions of the transcendental ego and the contributions of the world to the constitution of appearance.

If there were agreement as to exactly what the Husserlian phenomenological technique was, if it were possible to specify a precise number of steps to every phenomenological analysis, then the completion of this discussion of the Husserlian technique would be a simple matter. Unfortunately, there is no consensus as to what precisely the Husserlian phenomenological technique is. Scholars are generally in agreement that it always employs the *epochê* and that it results in the generation of essences after an initial reduction of phenomena, but about its specific steps and procedures there is wide-ranging controversy.

4.1.1. Lauer's interpretation of phenomenological technique

Quentin Lauer provides a most detailed (and hair-splitting) description of the phenomenological technique in his book *The Triumph of Subjectivity*. He discovers no less than six steps to phenomenological reduction: first, the psychological reduction which consists of the disengagement of psychological functions from the objective contents of thought; second, the eidetic reduction which results in the reduction of consciousness to consciousness of something; third, the phenomenological reduction which is the reduction of consciousness to the residue of conscious acts after the objects have been bracketed; fourth, the objective constitution of subjectivity within a community of intersubjectivity; fifth, the transcendental reduction which brackets the intersubjective and terminates in the transcendental ego as the ideal immanent terminus

---

[95]Husserl, *Ideas* 11-12.

of consciousness; and, sixth, the dynamic constitution of the subject in the flow of temporality-bound consciousness.[96]

The problem with this description is that it confuses Husserl's purpose in the *Cartesian Meditations* with his phenomenological project, in general.   What Husserl employs as a *modus operandi* in a single investigation is construed by Laurer as a prescription for *all* phenomenological analyses.   When taken seriously, Lauer's interpretation of Husserlian techniques quickly proves barren: it forces phenomenological method to move within tight circular analyses.   Moreover, Lauer's description of phenomenological method is flawed because it depends upon Husserl's idealistic phase and does not seriously consider those changes which took place in Husserl's thinking at the end of his life.   Completely absent form Lauer's discussion is any treatment of the reduction to the *Lebenswelt* construed as a positive revelation of the world.   This means that Lauer's understanding of the Husserlian method harbors the vain hope that the constitution of the world can proceed completely solipsistically within consciousness.

4.1.2. Kockelmans and Ricoeur on phenomenological technique

Against this anachronistic generalization of technique, the descriptions of Husserlian method provided by Kockelmans and Ricoeur provide partial, if not mutually consistent, correctives.   Kockelmans, although admitting that there is some truth in Lauer's distinction between the various steps of phenomenological analysis, argues that only one variety of transcendental reduction is clearly distinguishable from the psychological reduction. This Kockelmans calls, interchangeably, "eidetic reduction" and "the reduction of the world of culture to the original 'life world.'"[97] Otherwise, the relations between the various stages of the transcendental reduction are so closely related, so much of one seamless piece, that more is lost by distinguishing them as different reductions than is gained.[98]

Ricoeur carries this homogenizing tendency further and asserts that "Husserl never separated the transcendental reduction from that other reduction which he terms eidetic and which consists in grasping the fact (*Tatsache*) in its essence (*eidos*)."[99] Thus, the Husserlian transcendental ego is not the singular ego but the ego as essence.[100] Although it has a certain plausibility, Ricoeur's interpretation is at odds with that of Kockelmans because for Kockelmans eidetic reduction is associated with the disocclusion of the *Urwelt*, whereas for Ricoeur it is part and parcel of the transcendental reduction.

---

[96]Quentin Lauer, *The Triumph of Subjectivity* 51-56.

[97]Joseph Kockelmans, *A First Introduction to Husserl's Phenomenology* 167.

[98]Kockelmans, *Introduction* 167.

[99]Paul Ricoeur, *Husserl* (Evanston: Northwestern University Press, 1967) 178.

[100]Ricoeur 178.

4.1.3. Kóhak's pessimism about Husserlian phenomenological technique

Obviously, Lauer, Ricoeur and Kockelmans are all at odds about what it is to which the various Husserlian reductions refer. Moreover, this disagreement extends to the whole class of Husserlian scholars, the general result being that there is a pervasive malaise behind the various attempts to synthesize a Husserlian method. The despair which this sort of disagreement engenders is evidenced in the comments of Erazim Kóhak in his book *Idea and Experience*. There Kóhak prescribes the abandonment of any quest for a specifically Husserlian phenomenological technique. Husserlian phenomenology, he argues, is valuable not for its method but because of its perspective.[101] Kóhak describes the triviality of the Husserlian method as typical of methods in general.

> A method, conceived as a prescriptive "how-to," is crucial in crafts like pottery or filigree. There the skills, tools, and techniques are decisive, defining fields of endeavor. In the arts, the tools, and techniques, and procedures become distinctly secondary, subordinated to the artist's conception of his work. In a science, the method, in the sense of tools, techniques, and procedures, is wholly contingent on the task at hand. . . . Similarly, the challenge of phenomenology is not primarily methodological in the narrow sense of techniques and gimmicks. To reduce basic conceptions like phenomenological bracketing to the level of a gimmick distorts its significance no less than reducing the perspective of the natural sciences to a Five Step Method. Rather, phenomenology presents the challenge of an alternative metatheoretical framework. *The crucial phenomenological recognition is that reality is not material or mental but experiential, the reality of human praxis whose ultimate structuring is intentional and teleological. Thus, what we need to explain are not objects but experiences; and to explain means to grasp the intentional structure of an experience in principle, as a necessary pattern of subjective experience*, and only secondarily within a particular perspective, to find a cause.[102]

One can appreciate Kóhak's emphasis on the theoretical perspective of phenomenology without agreeing with him that the search for a phenomenological technique should be abandoned. To be able to keep the theoretical and methodological contributions of a discipline (or science) separate in one's consideration of its project is one thing, to argue that its method can be abandoned without altering its project--particularly when the project and method are so closely linked as in phenomenology--is quite another. Kóhak's position is symptomatic of a response to the confusion about Husserlian method which interprets perplexity as the basis for a new methodological program, a program which asserts the freedom of the philosopher over method. This seems extreme.[103]

---

[101]Erazim Kóhak, *Idea and Experience: Edmund Husserl's Project of Phenomenology in Ideas I* (Chicago: University of Chicago Press, 1987) 132-139.

[102]Kóhak, *Experience* 133-134.

[103]Twentieth century philosophy has stood about all of the autonomy of the philosopher it *can* stand. The assertion of this autonomy is either a mask for a lack of discipline or a license for superficiality as often as it is the promotion of a productive force in philosophy. Moreover, Kóhak's characterization of natural science as not being dependent upon a rigorous and defined method is shallow in its separation of theory from method. Contemporary natural science would be a worthless affair without a defined method. Even given the theoretical originality which is a *sine qua non* of the creative science, without a uniform canon of practicable methodological principles, there would be no empirical science, only fanciful metaphysical theories. To abandon the Husserlian technique, however one defines it, would be tantamount

4.2. The Steps in the Husserlian Phenomenological Technique

What, then, can be said about Husserlian method? Is there a regular series of steps which can be followed to produce a Husserlian phenomenological analysis? The simple answer to these questions is yes. Husserl certainly believes that he is employing a concrete technique of phenomenological analysis; he often employs this technique as a criterion for judging whether his students adopt the project of Husserlian phenomenology as their own.[104] Even though Husserl is aware that he has, according to Spiegelberg, provided "no adequate account of the reduction," toward the end of his life he insists "increasingly against his erstwhile associates and students that the phenomenological reduction and its correct understanding" are "indispensible for a real understanding of transcendental phenomenology."[105] The difficulty is that Husserl's various works are directed to different ends, thus the form of the phenomenological method--*contra* the opinion of Lauer--never seems to involve the same series of steps twice. Nevertheless, it does seem possible to describe what, in general, the techniques of phenomenological analysis are. Despite the substantial disagreement about what the phenomenological method *ought* to be, almost all are in agreement about the possibility of textually distinguishing (a) the *epochê*, (b) the reduction to phenomena and (c) the reduction to essences. The disagreement over the Husserlian method is really a disagreement about the regular substeps to each of the above procedures and not about these procedures *per se*. By understanding what Husserl means by each procedure, however, it may be possible to transform these disagreements into interesting *addenda* to a generalizable method.

4.2.1. The Husserlian epochê

'*Epochê*' is a term which Husserl borrows from the Greek sceptical philosopher Sextus Empiricus and which was also employed by the Academicians Arcesilaus and Carneades. Spiegelberg believes that the less sceptical context in which Arcesilaus and Carneades use this term--and not the more sceptical employment of Sextus Empiricus--defines the semantic potential for the Husserlian use. But this assertion is almost certainly incorrect.[106]

---

to adopting the attitude already prevalent in the study of religion: phenomenology, as a method, is anything one wishe it to be. With *that* radical assertion of freedom, one negates the possibility of coming to any consensus on what th phenomenological method *ought* to be.

[104]Spiegelberg, *Movement* 118-123.

[105]Spiegelberg, *Movement* 118-123.

[106]The only information available about the use of '*epochê*' in the thought of Arcesilaus and Carneades come through the secondary sources of Diogenes Laertius, Sextus Empiricus and Cicero. These sources agree substantially i reporting that both Arcesilaus and Carneades used the term epochê to describe a suspension of judgment which, whe applied to the *phantasia katalêptikê* (the apodictic or intuitive perception), demonstrated them to be chimera. It is in thi sceptical sense that Sextus Empiricus also uses the term. Spiegelberg's assertion that Arcesilaus and Carneades must hav used this term with a more positive connotation than Sextus Empiricus is based upon little more than the presumption tha the Academicans, because they in part accepted the Platonic philosophical project, were less sceptical. Because Husserlia

Since there is some confusion about the precise meaning of the Husserlian *epochê*, it is best to begin its explanation by saying what it is not. The *epochê* is not a denial of existence; it is not Cartesian doubt; it is not a conscious annihilation of what presents itself as appearance.[107] Rather, Husserl compares it to "a complete personal transformation, comparable in the beginning to a religious conversion, which . . . bears within itself the significance of the greatest existential transformation which is assigned as a task to mankind as such."[108] It is not so much a transformation in our experience of the world as it is a transformation of how we think about that world and our experience of it. Just as the religious convert inhabits the same world as his untransformed friends, just as they perceive the same mundane object, have the same mundane needs, etc., so too, the phenomenologist inhabits the same life world of his associates. But what he makes of this world, how he thinks about it, these things set him apart.

Less dramatically, and with more direct reference to his methodological concerns, Husserl defines the *epochê* as a mere suspension of judgment and willingness to take any positive position with respect to any object in order that whatever is self-evident in the object may be presented to consciousness. He describes what transpires in this suspension as follows:

> It is not a transformation of the theses into antithesis, of positive into negative; it is also not a transformation into presumption, suggestion, indecision, doubt. . . . *Rather it is something quite unique. We do not abandon the thesis we have adopted, we make no change in our conviction,* which remains in itself what it is so long as we do not introduce new motives for judgment, which we precisely refrain from doing. And yet the thesis undergoes a modification--whilst remaining in itself what it is, we set it as it were "out of action", we "disconnect", "bracket it". It still remains there like the bracketed in the bracket, like the disconnected outside the

---

phenomenology, in part, resembles the Platonic project, Spiegelberg apparently feels compelled to seek Platonic contexts for the use of the word *epochê*. In fact, however, the meaning of *epochê* as it was employed by Sextus Empiricus, Arcesilaus and Carneades is opposed to the Husserlian use, whether or not contexts are considered. Husserl believes the *epochê* to be a suspension of judgment that ultimately *results* in apodictic certainty. The suspended phenomenon is precisely that which is experienced as apodictic. But for the Greeks under no circumstance is the phenomenon the basis for scientific knowledge. It is with this reversal of meaning that Husserl defines his *critical* philosophy in opposition to the *sceptical* philosophers of the past.

Sextus Empiricus describes the philosophy of Arcesilaus as follows: "Arcesilaus . . . seems to me to have shared the doctrines of Pyrrho, so that his Way of thought is almost identical with ours. For we do not find him making any assertion about the reality or unreality of anything nor does he prefer any one thing to another in point of probability or improbability, but suspends judgment [*epochê*] about all." According to R. G. Bury, Carneades carried on the project of Arcesilaus. His philosophy can be summarized as follows: "Neither the sense nor the reason . . . can supply any infallible 'criterion': There is no specific difference between true 'presentations' and true: beside any true presentation you can set a false one which is in no wise different. . . . [Y]ou cannot distinguish the two impression from the false, or assert the one rather than the other [is] . . . produced by a real object." On the basis of these passages, Spiegelberg's opinion about Husserl's reliance upon Carneades and Arcesilaus for the notion of *epochê* would seem to be false. Spiegelberg should simply recognize the fact that though Husserl borrows the Greek term for 'suspension' he semantically transforms it. The *epochê* in the Husserlian system is the instrument for getting at truth but truth in a peculiar sense. The *epochê* is indispensible for determining the truth of essences. See Sextus Empiricus, *Outlines of Pyrrhonism*, trans. R. G. Bury (Cambridge: Harvard University Press, 1967) xxxiiii-xxxiv, 1: 232-235 and Philip Hallie, "Carneades," *The Encyclopedia of Philosophy*, vol. 2 (New York: Macmillan, 1972) 33.

[107]Husserl, *Ideas* 107-111.

[108]Husserl, *Crisis* 137.

> point to a definite but *unique form of consciousness*, which clamps onto the original simple thesis (whether it actually or even predicatively *posits* existence or not), and transvaluates it in a quite particular way. This transvaluing is a concern of our full freedom, and is opposed to all cognitive attitudes that would set themselves up as coordinate with the thesis. . . . We put out of action the general thesis which belongs to the natural standpoint, we place in brackets . . . this *entire natural world* therefore which is continually "there for us", "present to our hand", and will ever remain there, . . . [as] a "fact-world" of which we continue to be conscious, even though it pleases us to put it in brackets.[109]

The *epochê* which Husserl prescribes is a suspension of the pregiven world which does not negate the world but refuses to take a stand either in favor or against any of the presuppositions which confront us in the *Lebenswelt*.

Now, it is possible to employ the *epochê* to bring about a suspension of judgment about any object given to consciousness in its mode of givenness. Thus, it is possible to suspend, on one hand, the apparent habitual efficacy which makes us perceive a three dimensional red solid as an apple, and on the other hand, the series of presuppositions which make a particular religious affiliation plausable. In the first case, one identifies the associations, the history, the operations which make one associate the perceptual noema with the meaning of 'apple' and one suspends these from the perceptual noema. In the second case, one identifies the complete set of reasons which compel religious affiliation and one suspends these from the noematic meaning associated with the religion. Nothing, in fact, is changed in either noemata by this *epochê*, the only difference is that the judgments 'This is an apple' and 'These are the reasons I belong to this religious tradition' are suspended. One can, in effect, view the noematic content 'apple' on one hand and its perceptual noematic correlate on the other, just as one can view the noematic content 'Protestantism' on one hand and its doxic, noetic and noematic correlates 'the religion to which I am intellectually compelled to belong' on the other. According to Husserl, any conscious act or conscious content may be put out of play in this fashion with the intended result that the appearance in its mode of presentation be separated from the conscious dispositions, presuppositions sedimented meanings, etc., which generally attend and occlude it. When Husserl prescribes that the program of phenomenology must be one which returns to the things themselves for certainty, he prescribes a return to things as given by their bare presentations, without the interference of extraneous data, predispositions or associations.

Very simple appearances are susceptible to very simple bracketings, but as one ascends the scale of conceptual complexity it becomes more and more difficult to keep straight the various noematic and noetic structures and meanings which characterize objects. For this reason Husserl breaks the *epochê* into two varieties. When the *epochê* is directed toward the suspension of adventitious aspects of appearance, then it proceeds in the direction of the revelation of appearance as it is presented apodictically. This is the so-called *phenomenal* (or *phenomenological*) reduction. Its goal is to reduce an object to pure phenomenological data devoid of interpretation. However, when the *epochê* is directed, after completing a phenomenal reduction, to the bracketing of inessential properties of the object, while the quality forms of the thing are varied a

---

[109]Husserl, *Ideas* 108.

will, then one is engaged in eidetic reduction. The goal of this reduction is to produce a noematic meaning whose object is a necessary ideality.

4.2.2. The phenomenological reduction

The phenomenological reduction is directed to revealing the parts and wholes present in any content of consciousness. As such, it makes use of the Husserlian mereology but only to establish the relation of dependence-independence, mediacy-immediacy as these pertain to any object consciousness may take. Excluded from phenomenological reduction are the unnecessary components of the object (and its experience), components which are the habitual accretions of the surrounding lifeworld. To bracket phenomena means to negate the passive acceptance of the lifeworld and its meaning, to exclude its various fetishizations which give the phenomena adscititious forms. Those components remaining, after the phenomenal *epoché* is accomplished, will be given to consciousness as intuitively self-evident.

The phenomenological reduction is complete when, in consciousness, a content is obtained which is a whole and is necessarily dependent upon its constituent parts. This implies that the whole content is adequate (incapable of real increase or diminution), apodictic (intuitively indubitable), distinct (given self-evidently), and clear (refers unmistakably to the object intended).[110] In comparison, the eidetic reduction achieves completion when the above conditions are fulfilled and when the content of thought achieved is pure, that is to say when it contains no element of fact but when it is purely formal, analytic, and immediate.[111] All other contents which are not phenomenologically or eidetically reduced are characterized by being adumbrative, one-sided, susceptible of increase, empirical, inadequate, factual, practical, and habitual.

The eidetic reduction, in addition to employing the *epoché* to suspend the *specific* modalities of the perceived object involves the steps of *contemplative modalization* and eidetic variation. Before eidetic variation can be accomplished, the phenomenologically reduced content must be subjected to contemplative modalization.[112] This process may be generalized as follows.

First, the object is held in contemplative intuition which decides the limits of the object at hand. This is the lowest level of objectifying activity, and it precedes all explication.[113]

Second, explicative contemplation of the object is engaged and the intentional horizon of the object is activated. Husserl describes this activation in these terms.

> The object is present from the first with a character of familiarity; it is apprehended as a type already known in some way or other, even if a vague generality. Its appearance awakens

[110]Kockelmans 120-121

[111]Sokolowski, *Meditations* 57-85; and Husserl, *Ideas* 53.

[112]Husserl, *Judgment* 103-106.

[113]Husserl, *Judgment* 103.

> potential expectations . . . . [Interest] remains concentrated here on this one object . . . and strives to explain all that it 'is,' what it manifests of itself as regards *internal determinations*, to enter into its content, to grasp it in its parts and moments, and to enter anew into these by taking them separately and letting them display themselves--all within the synthetic unity which continually maintains itself 'on the basis of' the unity of the total apprehension of the object. *Explication is penetration of the internal horizon of the object by the direction of perceptual* [or conceptual] *interest.*[114]

At the second stage of modalized contemplation, one examines the possible modes of the object as these modes are implied in its internal horizon.

Third, the final stage of contemplative modalization occurs "when the interest is not satisfied with the explicative penetration into the internal horizon of the object but makes the objects which are copresent in the external horizon . . . thematic and considers the object in relation to them."[115] This stage is designed to disclose the relative determinations of the object, the object's possible ways of being in relation to other objects. This disclosure, however, does not reflect any change in the object's internal determinations unless these depend upon changes in its cogiven field.

Once the contemplative modalization of the object has been accomplished, one will be able to distinguish the immediately founding parts of the whole with regard to both its internal and external horizons. At this point, the eidetic reduction is engaged. The eidetic reduction is accomplished by taking each of the immediate founding parts of the object and subjecting them to imaginative rehearsal, first, by the random variation of the phenomenally reduced, but contemplatively modalized, object. This means that each of the separable qualities of the object will be varied at will, or in order (it matters not which), so that it becomes possible to grasp structural features of the object which are invariant through any imaginable change. After extensive variations of the conceptual content of the object are conducted, it will be possible to describe the parts of the object which make it what it is: namely, its general structural features. But a further imaginative variation is required as well. This involves the imaginative annihilation of the parts composing the object.

4.2.3. The essential reduction

The second step in eidetic variation is accomplished by the inclusion or exclusion of the discovered parts so as to determine whether or not they actually found the whole object. If the imaginative elimination of these parts makes the object incomprehensible, then they are essential to it.

When one completes the steps of contemplative modalization, imaginative variation and imaginative annihilation the result is an essence of the object, that is an object of a new type whose features are the necessary structures underlying its particular instantiations. Husserl maintains that essences can be constructed at any level of generality merely by attending to the abstractive level of the parts which found the object. Therefore, one could conceivably construct essences of (a) rational beings, (b)

---

[114]Husserl, *Judgment* 103.

[115]Husserl, *Judgment* 105.

man, (c) Napoleon and (d) Napoleon-as-strategist by varying the abstractive level of the objects intended. Because he maintained the possibility of constructing essences in this fashion, Husserl also commits himself to the theory that all conceivable objects form a vast taxonomy arranged according to species and genera, each level of which represents an eidetic generality greater in extent than the object immediately below it.[116] The eidos populating each level is equivalent to the Husserlian notion of the definite manifold.[117]

Once one grasps the fact that the complexity of Husserlian phenomenology is not a matter of the method--a method which consists only of the *epoché*, an application of the mereological relations and eidetic variation--but, rather, is dictated by the complexity of the objects and their complex meaning structures of noeses and noemata, then one is freed to employ the phenomenological method so long as one does justice to the objects on hand. The number of phenomenological reductions employed in any given case is, therefore, directly proportional to the noetic and noematic complexity of the objects involved. One would expect that a phenomenological analysis of an *Umwelt* would be much more complicated than, say, a phenomenological analysis of a perception. The former involves a whole series of strata of sedimented meanings, each of which must be understood, explored, bracketed and reduced before the *Umwelt* is disoccluded. The latter, in contrast, would involve a relatively simple suspension of thematic orientation. Nevertheless, the difficulty attendant upon any particular variety of phenomenological analysis should not lead one to believe that there is an absolute order to the phenomenological project. It is not mandated by Husserlian phenomenology that a phenomenology of perception must be developed before a phenomenology of conceptualization and that a phenomenology of conceptualization must precede a phenomenology of culture. Such a presumption is what has made the Husserlian phenomenology seem so discouraging. Instead, phenomenology is allowed to proceed on all eidetic levels of existence at the same time.

Because the noematic and noetic structures of the world may be bracketed and eidetically reduced at any level of complexity (providing one respects the appropriate part-whole relationships and attendant qualitative fillings) societies and social

---

[116]Sokolowski, *Meditations* 86-110.

[117]Sokolowski, *Meditations* 67-76. Ricoeur is correct in asserting that these two reductive movements are inseparably connected because phenomenological analysis is nothing if it is not directed to the discovery of essential certainties which result from initial phenomenal reductions. The phenomenal reduction is a mere prelude to the eidetic variation of the phenomenally reduced phenomenon.

Even so, the wide variety of objects which each variety of *epoché* may take means that the specific applications of each may be infinite. The six levels of phenomenological reduction which Lauer apparently discovers in *The Cartesian Meditations* should not, therefore, be construed as different varieties of phenomenological reduction but, rather, as applications of the two varieties of reduction to different objects. Lauer's steps two, four and five are merely examples of eidetic reduction related more or less closely to the phenomenally reduced objects in steps one, three, and six. In steps one, three, and six the *epoché* is employed according to the relations prescribed in the Husserlian mereology to produce deconstructed phenomena. In steps two, four, and five the deconstructed phenomena are varied while their adventitious properties are bracketed according to their various quality moments. This results in the *eidé* represented by the ideal types 'consciousness of something,' 'subjectivity' and 'transcendental ego.' It is with good reason that Ricoeur can describe the result of the *Cartesian Meditations* and its various phenomenological reductions as being one "not . . . described in its accidental singularity but rather as eidos ego." Only eidetically reduced phenomena can be the objects of science. See Ricoeur, *Husserl* 178.

organizations themselves may be taken as the objects of phenomenological analyses. These wholes will not be analyzed in terms of perceptual parts and contents but, rather, in terms of functional parts and contents--social structures and humans holding the places that color modalities would hold in perceptual objects. Higher-level phenomenological objects require an analysis which examines their immediate parts in a fashion appropriate to these objects' structures. It would make no sense to construct an *eidos* of the Roman Catholic Church by beginning with the perceptual presentations of a building or liturgy. The Roman Catholic Church as a religious and historical organization must be analyzed in respect to the functional parts which allow it to be characterized as such, that is to say according to whether it has a bureaucratic structure of a particular kind, an economic structure of a particular kind, a mission of a particular kind, and so on. The eidetic reduction of a social entity such as a church would consist of a definition which described those essential structural features which were invariant through time. In this way, any complex phenomenological object might be analyzed, providing that the perspective from which one attempted the analysis was kept pure from outside importations. Thus, the eidetic reduction of the Roman Catholic Church would be quite different according to whether one considered it a sociological object or an ecclesiological object. Ideally, both essences will be articulated but, at least initially, the motifs (or themes) of both analyses must be distinguished.

CHAPTER IX

A SYNTHETIC DEFINITION OF 'PHENOMENOLOGY'

1. Summary of Preceding Accomplishments

The purpose of the eight preceding chapters was to provide an accurate but thorough description of the multiplicity of meanings associated with the philosophical instantiations of 'phenomenology.' The word 'phenomenology' was chosen as the subject of this genetic analysis because it, unlike words such as 'phenomena,' 'phenomenal,' or even 'phenomenological,' signified the semantic fulfillment of an intention merely latent in the philosophical employment of nouns or adjectives denoting appearance. Whereas the terms 'phenomena,' 'phenomenal,' or 'phenomenological' demonstrate that it is semantically possible to delimit the world according to (a) appearances as objects and subjects, (b) appearances as qualifications of objects and (c) appearances as qualities or objects having regularities and a logic--indeed, a nomology--susceptible to recognition and study, none of these words in themselves exhaust the semantic field of which they are mere *tesserae*. In other words, none of them denotes a field of intellectual endeavor which has unique techniques especially adapted to the study of phenomena. 'Phenomenology' was the word chosen upon which to base a study of Husserlian antecedents because it implied an intentionality which encompassed both an awareness of the need for a special science of phenomena and an explicit purpose to delimit a new domain of scientific investigation. Finally, the investigation of the philosophical meaning of the single word 'phenomenology' has allowed the easy circumvention of an array of problems, such as deciding whether some philosopher was a phenomenologist though he never employed the term 'phenomenology.' Examination of only those sites where significant instances of 'phenomenology' occur has meant that it has been possible to avoid discussions and arguments to the effect that certain philosophers were *essentially* phenomenologists where textual evidence has been either suggestive, ambiguous or altogether lacking.

The application of this *modus operandi* has yielded seven different descriptions of the philosophical meaning of 'phenomenology.' These descriptions delimit seven diachronic semantic fields which seem, at many points, to be at odds with one another. It is the purpose of this chapter to synthesize a hortatory definition of phenomenology which resolves many of these oppositions and which is useful in the augmentation of religious phenomenology. This means that it is the *proximate* purpose behind this chapter to separate the common from the idiosyncratic in these definitions by investigating the points of articulation and communalities in the various concepts of phenomenology and their respective semantic fields. The *ultimate* purpose behind this chapter, however, is the synthesis of a hortatory definition of 'phenomenology' which will, in turn, delimit a transcendental semantic field encompassing everything of worth in the seven philosophical phenomenologies. This definition will be employed as a standard by which to judge whether the phenomenology of religion fulfills the general *will to phenomenology* expressed variously by Lambert through Husserl. Finally, it will be used to correct the excesses and inadequacies in the religious methodologies by bringing them into final methodological harmony.

Before presenting the synthetic definition of 'philosophical phenomenology,' a few clarifications of procedure are in order. First, the synthetic definition is not an adventitious synthesis, a mere conglomerate of accidental parts. Nor is this synthetic definition merely a combination of the least or greatest common denominators present in the described phenomenologies. Instead, it is a definition which is sensitive to the binding presuppositions which lie behind these phenomenologies and which were discussed at the end of each of the preceding historical chapters. It is a definition which includes presuppositions which are more comprehensive and fundamental than any one of these phenomenologies taken singly. Also, it is a definition which attempts to capture the semantic potential--and thus, the semantic nucleus--of 'philosophical phenomenology.'

Second, the presentation of this synthetic, hortatory definition of 'phenomenology' is one which follows an order reflecting the semantic nuclei of the following: (a) 'the objects of phenomenology,' (b) 'the ends of phenomenology,' (c) 'the placement of phenomenology,' and (d) 'the techniques of phenomenology.' Following these more general definitions, a single definition of 'philosophical phenomenology' combining these definitions is presented.

2. The Semantic Nucleus of 'Phenomena'

On the basis of the foregoing historical descriptions, it is possible to propose a definition of 'phenomema' which captures the important features of the meanings of 'phenomena' in the seven philosophical phenomenologies examined thus far. This definition has the import of being an aid to the definition of 'phenomenology' provided at the end of this chapter; it will enable the synthetic definition to comply with the criteria of definitional universality, comprehensiveness and articulatability.[1]

2.1. Definition of 'Phenomena'

On the basis of the preceding, it is possible to specify the salient and most general features of phenomena. A phenomenon is not a thing-in-itself but the complex product

---

[1]In the context of this discussion, these criteria prescribe the characteristics of good definitions. A general definition which is universal is a definition which covers all instances of those things which it is intended to denote. A comprehensive definition is a definition which is as descriptively rich in its enumeration of the qualities of its objects as is conceivable at its level of generality. An articulatible definition is one which is compatible with the semantic field with which it is associated; it is a definition which makes sense in terms of the concepts which are common to its discipline.

of (1) the *a priori* conditions of consciousness, (2) consciousness' attentional, mnemonic and imaginative powers and (3) an irreducible material principle (or structure) which, in its resistance to the *prise de conscience*, is indicative of an origin beyond consciousness. Phenomena disclose principles of order and structures which can most fundamentally be explained by the relations between parts and wholes. Phenomena stand in part-whole relations to one another and manifest these relations in every variety of object-constituting consciousness (including sensation, perception, conceptualization as well as the inner attentional modes by which consciousness observes its own moments). The complexity of phenomena is proportioned to the thought necessary to grasp it. Nevertheless, all phenomena are susceptible to decomposition both according to the contributions consciousness makes to them and according to their individual phenomenal structures. Thus, for example, a fact (in the Whewellian sense) can be effectively reduced to (1) its perceptual conditions, (2) the theoretical context in which those percepts are couched and (3) the conscious judgments which relate the percepts to the theoretical context. Such reductions ultimately stop at the level of qualia or sensations. Anything which appears before mind can be thus analyzed, but the more complex the phenomenon--as in the case of cultural objects--the more difficult the analysis and the greater the field of relevant data which must be brought to bear upon it. When the conscious contributions to a phenomenon are stripped away--as near as that is ever completely possible--the result is the structure (or form) which makes the phenomenon what it is. It is this analysis which the phenomenological method is designed to effect.

3. The Semantic Nucleus of 'the Ends of Phenomenology'

In proposing a synthetic definition of the 'ends of phenomenology' which captures the general movement of thought from Lambert to Husserl, it is important to stress the point that this trend makes phenomenology a part of the general system of the sciences. Even as a foundational science or method, phenomenology is not sufficient unto itself. In the cases when grandiose ends are proposed for phenomenology (as, for example, in the philosophies of Hegel, Peirce and Husserl), this end is still conceived as articulatable with the ends of dependent sciences. In each case, phenomenology is not described as a universal science whose methods encompass all other sciences. Rather, it is described as a foundational method or discipline which--though it proposes ultimate descriptions--is limited to the description and arrangement of phenomena, whether or not this description and arrangement are understood as grounds for compartmentalizing phenomenology as a separate discipline or including phenomenology as a methodological part of extant sciences. Nevertheless, the ends of dependent sciences do not influence phenomenology except to define the domain of objects capable of being reduced by phenomenological description. Dependent sciences contribute causal and theoretical terms to phenomenological analysis only at the risk of contaminating that analysis, for, as it is conceived by philosophers from Lambert to Husserl, phenomenology must be as presupposition-free as possible.

With these provisos voiced, it is possible to provide a synthetic definition of the ends of phenomenology. It has the following form.

3.1. Definition of 'the Ends of Phenomenology'

The ultimate end of phenomenology is to provide a body of descriptions and a systematic ordering of these descriptions upon which the factual sciences (in the Peircean sense) can base their inductions. In achieving this ultimate end, phenomenology has as its proximate ends: (1) the exhaustive diachronic and synchronic analysis of mental and physical phenomena and (2) the exhaustive arrangement of these phenomena into taxonomies expressive of the various governing motifs of the factual sciences. Phenomenological taxonomies mirror the diachronic and synchronic descriptions of phenomena by providing genetic and essential orderings which flesh in the governing motifs of the factual sciences. This means that, with respect to description and taxonomy, phenomenology is both a historical method as well as a method for discovering essential truths; it is concerned with describing the evolution of phenomena as well as providing systems of classification which make this evolution understandable according to principles of structure and order dictated by the phenomena themselves.[2]

4. Commonalities and Antinomies in the Descriptions of the Placement of Phenomenology

Inasmuch as all of the seven philosophers conceive of phenomenology as a foundation science, there is general agreement that it precedes other sciences both methodologically as a series of investigative tasks which must be prosecuted before dependent extra-phenomenological tasks can begin. It is a science whose techniques and accomplishments must develop before other dependent sciences can become sufficiently rigorous in their own right. Though this agreement establishes some very great commonalities between the conceptions of the placement of phenomenology, this agreement is unfortunately undermined, in part, by the different meanings the seven philosophers associate with the word 'science' as well as their different understandings of the role phenomenology must play in relation to the *a priori* formal sciences such as mathematics and logic.

4.1. Is Phenomenology a Science or a Method?

One meaning of 'science' is shared in the thought of Lambert, Robison, and Hamilton. By science they mean (what would now commonly be understood as) a method of study or a method of attaining certain knowledge and not a discipline or a particular branch of the sciences. This can be seen in the way Lambert makes phenomenology follow both logic and alethiology as a method which depends upon each for its criteriology. Robison's manner of construing phenomenology as the

---

[2]In describing the placement of phenomenology in the architectonic of the sciences, it is more convenient to disregard than to follow the form of the historical sections on the meaning of phenomenology. The *general* agreement between the seven philosophical phenomenologists about the placement of phenomenology in the architectonic of the sciences means that it is not necessary to discuss each philosopher's notion of this placement separately. All notions may, thus, be treated together, here, in a more succinct presentation than would otherwise be possible.

foundation of taxonomy and etiology makes it clear that neither taxonomy nor etiology are to be confused with scientific fields--such as physics or chemistry--but are, rather, general methods which transcend the individual scientific disciplines. Hamilton, likewise, places phenomenology before nomology (or rational psychology) and ontology (or inferential psychology), and, even though he conflates phenomenology with the empirical science of mental facts (interpreted as a form of history concerned with descriptions of cognitions, feelings and conative powers), he does not limit the application of phenomenological "science" to psychology, alone. Phenomenology, nomology and ontology are, together, to be transcendental methodologies which, when absorbed into complementary techniques of the individual sciences, give these sciences new precision and rigor. However, as methodologies which typify first science, or philosophy, psychological phenomenology, psychological nomology and psychological ontology have a disciplinary precedence as well.

Another meaning of 'science' is shared, for the most part, in the thought of Whewell and Peirce. For Whewell and Peirce, the word 'science' refers to extant disciplines unified under respective thematic concerns and having individual methodologies which, in part, resemble one another and, in part, differ from one another. For Whewell, there is no question of phenomenology being a science in the sense of a discipline. 'Science' he reserves as a word denoting the individual disciplinary areas such as physics, chemistry, geology and so on. 'Phenomenology,' on the other hand, denotes a method which has particular application within the so-called palaetiological (or historical) sciences. These include geology, paleontology, uranology, and so on. 'Phenomenology' also tacitly denotes the method Whewell employs in investigating the origins, methods and goals of the sciences. Insofar as *The Philosophy of the Inductive Sciences* is an exercise in the philosophical analysis of the inductive sciences, phenomenology as employed in these analyses becomes a part of metascience or philosophy. Its role there proves it, in fact, to be transcendental.

Although Peirce understands 'science' in the same fashion as Whewell, he makes phenomenology an independent discipline with a project of its own. In his architectonic of the sciences it is to stand between pure mathematics and the inferential sciences and to mediate logical forms supplied to the former by applying them to the data of observation. The results of this mediation will be descriptions and categories which will be of value to those sciences dependent upon apodictic observation. Thus, there can be a phenomenology of physics, a phenomenology of chemistry, a phenomenology of sociology and a phenomenology of religion because phenomenology is allowed to meddle at will in the subject matter of every discipline. But the converse is not necessarily true. The physics of phenomenology, the chemistry of phenomenology, the biology of phenomenology, if they existed, would most probably be scientific absurdities.

Finally, the meaning Hegel associates with 'science' makes it one which almost exclusively refers to philosophical disciplines since these, according to the Hegelian understanding, are the paradigms of certain knowledge. Phenomenology as a Hegelian science is foundational. Nevertheless, it does not found physics, chemistry, or biology but rather is the fundamental discipline on the basis of which logic, the philosophy of nature and philosophy of mind are developed. Phenomenology, as a discipline, is the first part in the "encyclopedia" of philosophical sciences.

What is one to make of the confusion about whether phenomenology is a science or a method? First, it should be noted that though philosophers have different ways of defining 'science' and phenomenology's inclusion or exclusion under the disciplines and methods which 'science' denotes, nevertheless, five of the thinkers--Peirce and Hegel being exceptions--make phenomenology a form of method. Husserl, in contrast to the other six, makes phenomenology both a method and a science. Phenomenology, interpreted as method, is a means to achieve clear insights into the nature of phenomena and to develop descriptions which provide the matter for other methods concerned with causal explanations and theory. Of the two philosophies in which phenomenology is interpreted exclusively as a science, the Hegelian description of phenomenology is sounder than Peirce's because Hegel, though not referring to phenomenology as method, at least understands its direction to be determined by the discipline of which it is the first part: philosophy. The phenomenological enterprise, for Hegel, is part and parcel of the Western philosophical enterprise (though he interprets this enterprise in an idealistic manner).

Only in the Peircean and Husserlian conceptualizations is phenomenology left to founder as a science without moorings. Because they define it as a science but then generalize its subject matter to include any phenomenon, they deprive it of any governing motif which can provide it a direction and a program. They deprive it of a project which would make it a discipline. The sheer lack of direction with which phenomenology is to produce descriptions is the chief argument against defining phenomenology as an independent discipline of scientific description.

4.2. Where can Phenomenology be Articulated?

When one considers the second point of contention about the articulation of phenomenology, one finds that the opposing camps are constituted along different lines. Of the seven phenomenologists studied, only Robison and Hegel do not see phenomenology as dependent in any way on logical, *a priori* categories, sciences, or methods. In contrast, Lambert, Hamilton, Whewell, Peirce and Husserl are firmly convinced that phenomenology, though a pure science of description, could not exist were it not for logical forms of consciousness which introduce principles of order into the data at hand. These *a priori* structures provide the possibility for the creation of sciences which have formally pure *a priori* relations as their objects. The exemplary, formally *a priori* science, for Lambert, is logic. Without logic, phenomenology would have no forms into which its descriptions could be cast to produce deductive certainties. In the terminology of Whewell, these sciences are aptly referred to as "formal sciences" and their methods of investigation and logic are the cornerstone of both the deductive and inductive sciences. Moreover, the Whewellian syzygies and the individual governing motifs are themselves formal *a priori* ideas. Without them a philosophy of inductive sciences--Whewell's *magnum opus*--would be impossible. Though revealed by phenomenological observation, the Whewellian ideas prove to be intuitive objects which found the possibility of any variety of knowledge, phenomenological or not. Finally, though both Peirce and Husserl conceive the relationship between pure mathematics (or in Husserl's terms "the theory of manifolds") and phenomenology to be a relationship between separate scientific disciplines, the way they conceive of the objects of pure mathematics makes it clear that phenomenology, whatever it is, could not exist were it not for the forms of pure possibility which mathematics elaborates. Were there not *a priori* forms of possible experience, were *anything* thinkable, then there would be no principles of order, and derivatively, no principles of knowledge. Even Hamilton, whose interpretation of *a priori* structures is psychologically reductionistic, understands that without some principles of preapprehension, the ordering and description of phenomena would be meaningless. Though he identifies these principles with conscious acts (psychologically conceived), these acts prestructure reality with a necessity which can be understood and controlled but never annihilated without also annihilating consciousness.

Both the phenomenologies of Hegel and Robison share the naiveté of supposing that one can produce neutral descriptions of phenomena without presupposing principles of conscious order and a science which studies these principles. In Robison's case, this naiveté is particularly apparent when he discusses the spatial and temporal coordinates which are admissible in describing phenomena. He demonstrates no awareness that (a) these may be *a priori* forms of consciousness and that they prestructure phenomena nor (b) that if they are not *a priori* forms of consciousness, they must be susceptible to a phenomenological analysis whose only outcome can be an irreducible residue such as seriality which, itself, is logical in nature. Robison's discussion of the parts of events is plagued with the same naiveté: without a preapprehended principle of order how can he make any sense of the notions of part and whole?[3]

In Hegel's phenomenology, the assertion that observationally neutral descriptions can be produced without reliance upon either *a priori* categories, more fundamental sciences or observational methods is worked out in a more sophisticated, but nonetheless uncritical, fashion. The assertion that Hegel does not found phenomenology upon *a priori* categories or *a priori* sciences does not mean that Hegel does not ascribe an *a priori* necessity to the evolution of spirit. In fact, the necessity with which Hegel charges the evolution of consciousness is unrivaled by any of the other philosophical phenomenologists. But this necessity is conceived ontologically: the moments of spirit's development are identical to the moments of consciousness. To understand one is to understand the other. Hegel does not see the necessity of founding discourse about this ontological necessity on prior logical categories; rather, he thinks that phenomenology itself represents a stage of conscious awareness at which the discovery of the reflexivity of understanding allows consciousness to disclose its necessary structures to itself. In other words, Hegel construes the evolution of consciousness as the *a priori* necessary ontological precondition for phenomenology as a particular form of consciousness. But phenomenology, according to Hegel, proceeds *a posteriori* in its investigation of consciousness. Because phenomenology must trace the evolution of consciousness, the discourse associated with such description must not be logically loaded but must be the perfect determination of the conscious forms studied. Phenomenological discourse is to be derived from ontological categories and is to contribute nothing to them. For Hegel, phenomenology describes what is, not what is possible. As Peirce aptly observes, the

---

[3]See the discussion at the end of Chapter III.

consideration of possibility is completely lacking in the Hegelian phenomenology. One could go further and say that the consideration of the ontological category of possibility is lacking in the Hegelian phenomenology by design: because Hegel is a proponent of the view that what is must be, there can be no room in his system for sciences of manifolds or pure mathematics which take precedence over phenomenology. The result of the Hegelian idealism is that phenomenology is put in the paradoxical position of being an observationally neutral form of scientific discourse about an *a priori* ontology of spirit.

This paradox, in part, explains Hegel's peculiar use of language and contradictions (oppositions) in *The Phenomenology of Spirit*. Language, which is conventional in form, is stretched to the breaking point in order to capture the complex moments of the Hegelian dialectic. Yet, in the end, one wonders whether the Hegelian project is radically successful in capturing the movement of spirit. Either he must obey the conventional rules of discourse at times, or else his phenomenology will be unintelligible.

Now, it is obvious that Hegel writes to convey the insights he has. But to convey insights, he must, at least in part, convey these insights in conventional discourse. Therefore, one must suppose that his discoveries are, in part, encapsulatable in conventional discourse, and derivatively, in conventional logic. But, if this is so, then Hegel must presuppose logical principles which preexist in common discourse before its conceptual analysis. Once this is admitted, it is difficult to understand how phenomenology can be foundationally free of logic and associated epistemological categories. Even if one concedes with Hegel that ontology should shape epistemology, and not *vice versa*, it is difficult to grasp how onta can be conceptualized without the logical preapprehension which is the condition for all knowledge. To pick and choose selectively among possible *a priori* conditions of experience in order to suit one's ontology, instead of recognizing their compulsiveness and explaining them in terms of that ontology, is to be quite as prejudiced as any philosopher who presumptuously compounds epistemological *a prioris*. It is accurate to say that one finds in Hegel's introduction to *The Phenomenology of Spirit* sufficient evidence of a disdain for formal logic to explain his placement of phenomenology as an absolutely first science.

4.3. The Semantic Nucleus of 'Phenomenology's Placement'

The immediately preceding discussion leads to two conclusions about phenomenology's placement in the architectonic of the sciences. First, it would not seem possible to consider phenomenology a scientific field sufficient unto itself because it is subject to no specific field of objects which serves to distinguish it from any of the other sciences. Phenomenology does, however, offer a new method by which the sciences may improve the rigor of their enterprises.

Second, phenomenology presupposes, at very least, a logical *a priori* as the foundation for its descriptions. Phenomenology, like all intelligible discourse, presupposes logical categories which ensure the univocity and consistency of its descriptions.

From these conclusions and the general intentions behind the discussions of the placement of phenomenology, it is possible to synthesize a hortatory definition of the placement of phenomenology among the sciences.

4.4. Definition of 'Phenomenology's Placement'

Phenomenology is a generalizable scientific method. As such, there is no question of it standing alone as a science; rather, it assumes a place in the general sequence of methods present in *all* sciences. Thus, there can be a philosophical phenomenology, a phenomenology of physics, a phenomenology of religion, etc. In this sense phenomenology is transcendental: it is methodologically applicable to all sciences.

To say that phenomenology assumes the same place in the general sequence of methods present in all the sciences means that phenomenology founds those general descriptions of method that go by the names of 'nomology' (that is etiology or the method of explanation) and 'ontology' (that is theory or the method of hypothetization). Inasmuch as each science presupposes logic as foundational, phenomenology--as a methodological part of each science--also presupposes logic. To insure the clarity and distinctness of its descriptions, phenomenology depends both upon logical categories and the science of logic.

5. The Semantic Nucleus of 'Phenomenological Technique'

The synthetic definition of phenomenological technique to be proposed here cannot rest upon a proof of the fruitfulness of some techniques and the disqualification of others. This is so not because it is impossible *in theory* to provide a proof of the viability of these techniques, but because it is impossible *practically* to do this. There are no universally applicable criteria by which to establish the superiority of one of these techniques over the others, because these techniques do not share identical goals. This means the bases for judging the relative worth of each method are incomparable. On the other hand, proving a phenomenological technique fruitful *without reference to another technique* is a relatively simple matter. One simply demonstrates that it is successful in managing appearances for the specific proximate end to which it is employed.

By this criterion, at least five phenomenologists have the right to claim their methods are fruitful. Hegel, Hamilton, Whewell, Peirce and Husserl all apply their phenomenological techniques with positive results. This is sufficient to establish their *qualified* fruitfulness. But when one wishes to determine which one of these techniques is *most* fruitful a problem arises. The impossibility of comparing the fruitfulness of these techniques is the impossibility of applying a single criterion to results generically different. The criterion one would employ to test the value of the Peircean cenopythagorean categories is not the same criterion one would employ to test the value of Whewellian natural taxonomies. One could judge the former by its ability to produce accurate inductions about a species of tree frog no more than one could judge the latter by its ability to produce descriptions of the necessary structures of appearance. It is obvious: different phenomenological techniques (applied to different objects to achieve different specific proximate ends) are not susceptible to simple comparative evaluations. To establish a homogeneous basis for evaluating the fruitfulness of techniques, one must begin with different techniques but apply them to the same data to achieve the same end. Only if this is done will the relative usefulness of phenomenological techniques for etiology and theory be comparable. Since none of the phenomenologies studied thus far are homogeneous with respect to objects and specific proximate needs, there is no basis for judging the relative fruitfulness of these methods.

If the synthetic definition of phenomenological technique cannot rest upon a selection of the procedures which are most fruitful in prosecuting the ends of phenomenology, then upon what principle of discernment can it depend? The answer to this question is simple. Without recourse to judgments of comparative value, the synthesis of a definition of phenomenological technique is accomplished by eliminating methodological redundancies, selecting technical felicities and joining all procedures of worth together in a consistent sequence and common program.

Among the notable redundancies in the descriptions of phenomenological technique are five (almost identical) explanations of how pure phenomenological description is to lead methodologically to taxonomic techniques such as diagnosis and diataxis. Robison, Hamilton, Whewell, Peirce and Husserl all agree that phenomenological description is to be continguous with taxonomy. However, they disagree whether this continguity should be one which is contained by phenomenological methods or whether this continguity is between description as a proper phenomenological technique and taxonomy as a proper etiological technique.

Under the interpretations of Robison, Hamilton, Whewell and Husserl, taxonomy is an inadmissible part of phenomenology, if causal relations are included as the objects of the taxonomic order. These thinkers interpret causality as a relation which cannot be reduced to appearance. As such, the idea of causality is a hypothetical contamination of the phenomenologically analyzed objects. Taxonomy is allowed inclusion in phenomenology only under the condition that it be of a type which relies on those principles of order which do not have hypothetical relations as their objects. In contrast, in Peircean thought there is no question of disallowing etiological taxonomic techniques as a part of phenomenology because causality is not hypothetical. Causality is a general principle expressive of secondness. Secondness--a form of experience represented by a cenopythagorean category--is an irreducible datum which is not a conscious construct added to experience. Peirce, therefore, allows taxonomies ordered according to causal characteristics to be a legitimate part of phenomenological description.

How is one to decide whether taxonomy is a part of phenomenology? Should one simply ignore Peirce's analysis and accept the majority interpretation? Certainly, an attempt to prove either that causality is founded upon irreducible experiences or that it is a hypothetical generalization imported into experience would be out of place here.[4] A compromise must be found which will admit the possibility that either position might be true without allowing the proof of either position to change the ultimate definition of phenomenological technique. The prudent solution is to allow phenomenology to include taxonomy only if the principles of order which found taxonomy are either necessary *a priori* categories of consciousness or necessary, *a posteriori* conditions of

---

[4]There is evidence that the experience of causation may be an irreducible experience and not merely a construct of consciousness. See, for example, Émile Meyerson, *Identity and Reality* (New York: Dover Publications, 1962).

experience. In this fashion, the synthetic description of phenomenological technique takes a middle path between a definition which includes all taxonomic techniques as phenomenology and a definition which excludes all taxonomic techniques from phenomenology.

Moving on to the technical felicities of the various phenomenologies, one finds that it is possible to differentiate the phenomenological techniques on the basis of whether they are directed to genetic analyses which are serial or dialectical in nature. Into the first camp fall the phenomenologies of Lambert, Robison, Hamilton, Whewell and Peirce, all of which--by virtue of their intent to create a method of description complementary to the natural sciences--are not primarily directed to analyses of consciousness' evolution; into the second camp falls the phenomenology of Hegel, which--by virtue of its almost exclusive concern with the historical development of ideas--is directed to the study of the intermittent conflict and resolution which typifies consciousness' evolution. The phenomenology of Husserl employs both serial and dialectical analyses inasmuch as his notions of *epoché* and eidetic reduction involve moments of the deconstruction and essential construction of reality.

The difference between these serial and dialectical methods is great but not so great as to be considered antithetical. In fact, if one grants each a legitimate domain of operations, one can bring them into supplementary relation with one another. Hegel, himself, provides the possibility for doing so by describing the first three procedures of his phenomenology in terms which make these steps the virtual equivalent of the descriptive techniques of Lambert, Robison, Hamilton, Whewell, Peirce and Husserl. Because Hegel describes these procedures in a particularly vague fashion, there is no reason that the more rigorous descriptive techniques of the other phenomenologists can not be articulated in the sequence of Hegelian procedures, thus, making the Hegelian dialectic a fourth part of a synthetic, but generalizable, phenomenological program. The value of effecting such an articulation of methods is obvious. This articulation results in a single phenomenological technique made stronger than its constituents by their complementary support of one another. Also, lateral, serial, and dialectical analyses of identical phenomena can be accomplished routinely, as parts of the same methodological program.

Only one task remains before it is possible to propose a synthetic definition of phenomenological technique: a conciliation between the descriptive techniques of Lambert, Robison, Hamilton, Whewell, Peirce and Husserl must be achieved. This is done as follows.

First, the Robisonian phenomenological technique must be put out of play because Robison achieves only the most meager development of those procedures which are to insure phenomenological description. Note is taken, however, of the importance Robison associates with the analyses of phenomenological parts and wholes, even though he does not provide a description of the sequence of steps by which such analyses are accomplished. In all other respects, the Robisonian discussion must be excluded from consideration because it describes phenomenological technique only in the vaguest manner.

Second, all of the Whewellian discussions of phenomenological description must be put out of play except for the discussions of the measurement of phenomena, diagnosis and diataxes. Only these procedures are retained because they represent the unique and undisplaceable contributions of the Whewellian philosophy of science to phenomenology. With the exception of these techniques, Whewell's definition of the techniques of phenomenological description is inferior to the rules of thumb provided by Lambert and Hamilton.

Third, the Lambertian technique of perspectival variation must be selected because it is an important heuristic demonstrating the way phenomenological description should proceed. Nevertheless, as described, it is little more than a suggestive technical metaphor. Its chief value lies in its being the conscious equivalent of experiment. It is a *Gedankenexperiment* in it most specific form: it is a technique for revealing the underlying structural principles of phenomena by mentally varying adventitious qualities. Nevertheless, its shortcomings are clearly evident as well: Lambert's discussion of the procedures by which one accomplishes perspectival variation does not include the specification of the individual conscious operations by which the subjective and objective adumbrations of the object are varied.

Fourth, the phenomenological techniques of Peirce and Husserl must be used to flesh in the six technical steps of Lambertian phenomenological description. The Hamiltonian techniques for the observation of consciousness--though relatively vague--are only employed when not supplanted by Husserlian techniques. The conscious operations which Peirce identifies provide the procedure for perspectival variation when this variation presumes objective analyses not covered by the Husserlian descriptions of conscious intentionality.

It is most effective to present the resultant technique, not in a lengthy definition but in a succinct schema which sketches the order of the proposed phenomenological method. The schema appears in Chart 12.

We can summarize the meanings of the preceding semantic nuclei in the following definition.

6. The Semantic Nucleus of the Philosophical Meaning of 'Phenomenology'

Phenomenology is a transcendental method of description compatible with all the sciences. Its ultimate end is to produce descriptions, essential taxonomies and essential phylogenies upon which its host sciences can base etiologies and theories. Leading to this ultimate end are two proximate ends: (1) exhaustive diachronic and synchronic analyses of mental and physical phenomena and (2) exhaustive arrangements of phenomenological descriptions into taxonomies and phylogenies whose principles of order are dictated by the *a priori* forms of consciousness and the governing motifs of the host sciences.

Phenomenology's object consists of the field of phenomena. Phenomena are the complex products of (1) *a priori* conditions of consciousness, (2) attentional, mnemonic

Chart 12

Constituent Procedures for a
Synthetic Phenomenological Technique

Procedures:	Constituent Steps:

1. **PURE OBSERVATION AND DESCRIPTION** [*Purpose*: To provide comprehensive unprejudiced diachronic and synchronic descriptions of phenomena]

1.1 Observe without interpretation.

1.2 Describe without hypothetical importations

1.3 Associate serial or variable orders with qualities of appearance. [phenomenometry]

----

2. **DIALECTICAL DECON-CONSTRUCTION OF IDEATIONAL APPEARANCES** [*Purpose*: To deconstruct ideational appearances to trace their morphogenetic history]

2.1 Trace the emergence of an appearance to its first synthesis.

2.2 Deconstruct it according to the thesis and antithesis which gave rise to it.

2.3 Deconstruct its productive thesis and antithesis according to the same dialectic, and so on, *ad terminum*.

2.4 Describe the history and emergence of the ideational appearance according to its morphogenetic development (as well as on the basis of the synchronic descriptions provided in procedures one and two).

2.5 Associate dichotomous, serial or variable orders with the morphogenetic evolution of essences.

3. PHENOMENOLOGICAL
REDUCTION,
ESSENTIAL OBSERVATION
AND DESCRIPTION
[*Purpose*: To provide
descriptions of the
essences of phenomena
which distinguish true
appearances (invariant
objects) from false
appearances (accidental
properties)]

3.1 Fix appearance positionally or
or mentally [From procedures 1 & 2]

3.2 Vary conscious conditions of
appearance. (Rehearase the possible
relations the appearance may have to
consciousness; for ideational
appearances, use the Peircean mental
operations and Husserlian eidetic
variation).

3.3 Vary objective conditions of
appearance with respect to each
conscious condition. (Rehearse the
qualifications of the object for each
possible relation of consciousness;
use Peirce's operations for ideational
appearances in conjunction with
Husserlian method of eidetic
variation.)

3.4 Describe all conditions of
phenomena (on the basis of
procedures 1 & 2).

3.5 Match conscious conditions and
apparent alterations as well as
independent conditions and apparent
alterations.

3.6 Distinguish alterations in appearance
from unconditional components using
Husserlian mereological relations.

3.7 Describe unconditional component of
appearances (essence).

3.8 Associate serial or variable orders
with the essential qualities of
phenomena.

4. TAXONOMY [*Purpose*: To transform the descriptions developed in procedures one through three into orders expressive of the generic and specific natures of the appearances, according to the governing motifs of the host science]

4.1 According to the descriptions developed in procedures 2 & 3, provide diataxes for the phenomenological essences.

4.2 Arrange essential descriptions of contemporaneous phenomena into a taxonomy based upon Husserlian mereological relations and Whewellian relations of affinity.

4.3 Arrange the serial descriptions and the morphogenetic histories of phenomenological essences into a phylogeny.

[At this point, the results of phenomenological analyses are taken over as data by the etiological and theoretical portions of that science under whose governing motifs the phenomenological analyses were conducted.]

and imaginative alterations and (3) irreducible structural characteristics (phenomenological essences). Phenomenological method is directed primarily, to disclosing the latter.

Phenomenology's formal principles consist of *a priori* conditions of consciousness, the governing motifs of the sciences and the mereological relations between phenomena. These are employed in the analysis and ordering of its field of objects.

Phenomenology consists of four phenomenological procedures: (1) pure observation and description, (2) dialectical deconstruction, (3) phenomenological reduction, essential observation and description, and (4) taxonomy. These, in turn, are constituted by the methodological steps described earlier in this chapter. Finally, phenomenology's agential aspect consists of researchers whose natural tendency to biased observation has been ameliorated by instruction in fairness, love of truth, humility and abstractive incisiveness.

The synthetic definition of phenomenology encapsulated above is superior to the seven phenomenologies which gave rise to it. According to the criteria of definitional economy, it surpasses each historical phenomenology with respect to universality, comprehensiveness and articulatibility. Only by the criterion of simplicity does it seem to be inferior to the historical definitions of phenomenology. But this inferiority is inconsequential because (a) though the historical phenomenologies possess simpler techniques they also possess vaguer techniques and (b) the criteria of methodological economy are proposed as concomitant, not independent, criteria. Since it is impossible, here, to decide the comparative fruitfulness of the various phenomenological methods, this criterion must be put out of play. This leaves only the criteria of universality, comprehensiveness, articulatibility and simplicity as the grounds for comparison. Given that the synthetic definition of phenomenological method is more universal, more comprehensive, more methodologically rigorous, and better articulatible than previous philosophical definitions, and given that a simple vague definition of phenomenology is not superior to a complex precise definition, the synthetic definition of phenomenology, proposed above, is superior to both the historical definitions of 'phenomenology' and to any definition of 'phenomenology' proposed on the basis of general similarities.

CHAPTER X

THE RAMIFICATIONS OF
THE PHILOSOPHICAL MEANING OF 'PHENOMENOLOGY'
FOR THE SCIENTIFIC STUDY OF RELIGION

1. The Meaning of 'Phenomenology of Religion'

Two facts help simplify the task of describing what 'phenomenology of religion' means. First, phenomenologists of religion, though eager to adopt and transform methodologies from other areas such as anthropology and philosophy, demonstrate a startling naiveté in their theoretical interpretation, combination and reconciliation of these often opposing methods. It has been said, with not a little justification, that the philosophical phenomenologist is like the baker who spends all his time fiddling with his recipe and no time baking his cake. It is equally accurate to say that the *phenomenologist of religion* is like the baker who spends all his time baking bad cakes without a recipe.[1] The philosophical origins of the phenomenology of religion are indubitable, as has been clearly shown by George James, but whether phenomenologists of religion have accurately grasped what is demanded by these methods is dubitable. Certainly, the theoretical justifications for the methodologies they adopt lack integrity. But it is precisely because they do not labor at the theoretical justification of the phenomenology of religion that it is easier to describe their conceptions of phenomenology. Second, the differences which exist in the various conceptions of religious phenomenology have been amply documented by others.[2] To repeat these descriptions in great detail would be unnecessarily repetitious.

For both of the above reasons, the description of the phenomenology of religion presented in the next section will consist of a list of summaries expressing distinct aspects of the objects, ends, placement and techniques of religious phenomenology as these are described by phenomenologists of religion. This means that instead of presenting the phenomenologies of religion, individually, thus repeating the propositions they share about common objects, aims, methods, etc., the following discussion will present each proposition about the objects, aims, methods, etc., of phenomenology of

---

[1] I owe the first metaphor to Richard Kieckhefer of Northwestern University who employed it as a critique of religious phenomenology. The second metaphor is my rejoinder to his critique.

[2] See the introduction and bibliography of his work for references.

religion only once with the name of its author and the names all of its adherents following it in parentheses.[3]

2. The Objects, Ends, Placement, and Techniques of the Phenomenology of Religion

2.1. The Objects of Phenomenology of Religion

With respect to the objects of phenomenology of religion, most religious phenomenologists perceive their subject matter to be religious acts, concepts, beliefs, and customs as these may be grouped under the general heading of religious anthropology and religious cultus.

The following representative propositions describe the various objects of the phenomenology of religion as well as the theoretical interpretation which the phenomenology of religion attaches to them. They are characterized by different levels of generality.

(01) The "accurate definition of the character of religious phenomena" is best left to philosophy. (*C. de la Saussaye*)[4]

(02) ". . . '[A]ppearance' [in the religious sense] refers equally to what appears and to the person to whom it appears; the phenomenon . . . is neither pure object, nor the object, that is to say, the actual reality, whose essential being is merely concealed by the 'appearing' of the appearances. . . . The term 'phenomenon', still further, does not imply something purely subjective, not a 'life' of the subject. . . . " The actual reality is dealt with by metaphysics and the subject is dealt with by psychology. (*Van der Leeuw*)[5]

(03) "The 'phenomenon' . . . is an object related to a subject, and a subject related to an object; although this does not imply that the subject deals with or modifies the object . . . , nor (conversely) that the object is somehow or other affected by the subject. The phenomenon . . . is not produced by the subject, and still less substantiated or demonstrated by it; its entire essence is given in this . . . appearance to 'someone.'" (*Van der Leeuw*)[6]

---

[3]In each case, the author's name will appear first, italicized. Other adherents to fundamentally the same position will be named in sequence following the author's name.

[4]Chantepie de la Saussaye, *Manual of the Study of Religion* (London: Longman, Green & Co., 1891) 67.

[5]G. Van der Leeuw, *Religion in Essence and Manifestation*, 2 vols. (London: George Allen and Unwin, Ltd., 1964) 2:672.

[6]Van der Leeuw 2: 672.

(04) "The appearance . . . subsists as an image. It possesses backgrounds and associated planes; it is 'related' to other entities that appear either by similarity, by contrast, or by a hundred nuances that can arise here: conditions, peripheral or central position, competition, distance, etc. These relationships . . . are always perceptible relation ships, 'structural connections.' They are never factual relationships nor causal connections,. . . . Such a relation, . . . whether it concerns a person, a historical situation or a religion, is called a type, or an ideal type." (*Van der Leeuw*)[7]

(05) "The richest material . . . for the phenomenology of religion is supplied by religious acts, cult and custom; with regard to many nations and periods, it is the only mirror that reflects something of their religious ideas and sentiments." (*C. de la Saussaye*, Kristensen, Van der Leeuw, Bleeker, Smart)[8]

(06) "The subjects of Phenomenology of Religion may be classified into three groups: the conceptions or doctrines we find in . . . religions about the world, about man, and about the practice of worship . . . , in other words, religious cosmology, religious anthropology, and cults." (*Kristensen*, C. de la Saussaye, Van der Leeuw, Bleeker, Smart)[9]

2.2. The Ends of the Phenomenology of Religion

When one surveys the variety of ends associated with phenomenology of religion one finds general agreement. The phenomenology of religion must study religion as it is revealed through various essences and phenomena. The proximate end of this investigation is access to the inner meanings of religious symbols, myths, and concepts, but this is not phenomenology's ultimate end. The phenomenology of religion is, after all, a methodological part of the science of religion. As such, it is concerned with a form of understanding which transcends the mere wish to understand religious things as believers understand them, a wish which has no direct relation to scientific endeavor. The agreed upon end of the phenomenology of religion is that of understanding individual religions as manifestations of an underlying order of experience having its own laws and qualities. Under this interpretation, religions become instantiations of a general form of human experience. Although some of the phenomenologists use a private, not generally accepted, technical vocabulary to make this point, the communalities of the ends of religion are unmistakable. The phenomenology of religion has as its ultimate end, the arrangement of sympathetically interpreted religious phenomena in taxonomies which reveal their common forms of development.

---

[7]Van der Leeuw 2· 672

[8]C. de la Saussaye, *Manual of the Study of Religion* 69.

[9]W. Brede Kristensen, *The Meaning of the Study of Religion* 7.

234

The following propositions describe the various ends of the phenomenology as well as the various regulative principles which condition these ends. They are characterized by different levels of generality.

(E1) The end "of the science of religion is the study of religion, of its essence and its manifestations." (*C. de la Saussaye*, Kristensen, Van der Leeuw, Bleeker, Smart)[10]

(E2) An end of phenomenology is "to arrange the principle groups of religious conceptions in such a way that the most important sides and aspects should appear conspicuously from out of the other material." (*C. de la Saussaye, Kristensen*, Van der Leeuw, Bleeker, Smart)[11]

(E3) An end of the phenomenology of religion is "to classify and group the numerous and widely divergent data in such a way that an overall view can be obtained of their religious content and the religious values they contain." (*Kristensen*, C. de la Saussaye, Van der Leeuw, Bleeker, Smart)[12]

(E4) An end of the phenomenology of religion is "to understand . . . religion . . . according to [its] own inner meanings and structure, leaving aside . . . all judgment upon them." (*Kristensen*, C. de la Saussaye, Van der Leeuw, Bleeker, Smart)[13]

(E5) An end of the phenomenology of religion is "to gain an overall view of the ideas and motives which are of decisive importance in all of History of Religions." (*Kristensen*, C. de la Saussaye, Van der Leeuw, Bleeker, Smart)[14]

(E6) An end of the phenomenology of religion is "to answer the question of what we understand by the concept [i.e., sacrifice, purification, God, holiness, etc.] . . . and what is common to its various forms." (*Kristensen*, C. de la Saussaye, Van der Leeuw, Bleeker, Smart)[15]

---

[10]C. de la Saussaye, *Manual of the Study of Religion* 7.

[11]C. de la Saussaye 7.

[12]Kristensen 1.

[13]Kristenson xx-xxi.

[14]Kristenson 1.

[15]Kristenson 4.

(E7) It is not an end of the phenomenology of religion to build a "rational and systematic structure in the science of religion"; this is impossible because the "purely logical and rational does not indicate the way we must follow because in Phenomenology we are constantly working with presumptions and anticipations." (*Kristensen*, Van der Leeuw)[16]

(E8) An end of the phenomenology of religion is to seek phenomenal structure "which is neither merely experienced directly, nor abstracted either logically or causally, but which is understood"; it is to seek a significant "organic whole which cannot be analyzed into its own constituents, but which can from these be comprehended," to seek "a fabric of particulars, not to be compounded by . . . addition, nor . . . deduction, but . . . only understood as a whole." (*Van der Leeuw*)[17]

(E9) An end of the phenomenology of religion is to discover the *theoria* of religious phenomena, '*theoria*' being understood as "the religious implications of the various aspects of religion which occur all over the world. . . ." (*Bleeker*)[18]

(E10) An end of the phenomenology of religion is to discover the *logos* (*logoi*) of religious phenomena, '*logos*' being understood as the "hidden structure of different religions . . . showing that they are built up according to strict inner laws." (*Bleeker*)[19]

(E11) An end of the phenomenology of religion is to discover the *entelecheia* of religious phenomena, '*entelecheia*' being understood as "the course of events in which the essence is realized by its manifestations." (*Bleeker*)[20]

(E12) It is not an end of the phenomenology of religion merely to provide "pure description of religious phenomena," it must also explain their "significance and structure." (*Bleeker*, C. de la Saussaye, Kristensen, Van der Leeuw, Pettazzoni, Smart)[21]

---

[16]Kristenson 10.

[17]Van der Leeuw, 2: 672-673.

[18]C.J. Bleeker, *The Sacred Bridge* (Leiden: E.J. Brill, 1963) 14.

[19]Bleeker 14.

[20]Bleeker 14.

[21]Bleeker 5-6.

(E13) The following are ends of the phenomenology of religion: the structural description of religions in a social milieu at a particular time; the typological description of religious concepts, doctrines, myths, ethics, rituals, experiences and institutions; the typological comparison of individual features of specific religious traditions; "internal structural explanations"; and dialectical-phenomenological studies which make use of methods drawn from other disciplines. (*Smart*)[22]

2.3. The Placement of Religious Phenomenology

About the placement of the phenomenology of religion there is less agreement between phenomenologists of religion. Although the earlier workers in the field (Chantepie de la Saussaye and Kristensen) recognized and even approved of the interdependence between the phenomenology of religion, history of religion and philosophy of religion, the tendency of later religious phenomenologists was to compartmentalize phenomenology so that it had little, if nothing, to do with other disciplines even within the science of religion. Still, most phenomenologists recognize the fact that phenomenology of religion employs the data of the history of religion, though they are not willing to admit that either discipline dictates terms to the other. That phenomenology of religion shapes the historical-religious research by proposing suggestive research problems, or that the philosophy of religion develops the concepts of phenomena or essences for the phenomenology of religion, are not popular views of correct phenomenological protocol for contemporary religious phenomenologists.

The following propositions describe the various conceptions of the placement of the phenomenology of religion in the architectonic of the sciences.[23]

(P1) The phenomenology of religion is a transition discipline between the history of religion and the philosophy of religion. (*C. de la Saussaye*, Kristensen)[24]

(P2) "The phenomenology of religion is most closely connected with psychology insofar as it deals with the facts of human consciousness" because "the outward forms of religion can only be explained from inward processes." (*C. de la Saussaye*)[25]

---

[22]Ninian Smart, *The Phenomenology of Religion* (London: The Macmillan Press, 1973) 47.

[23]See the preceding discussion in this work of an understanding of the way philosophical phenomenologists conceive of the placement of phenomenology.

[24]C. de la Saussaye 8.

[25]C. de la Saussaye 67.

(P3)   There is a mutual dependence and "narrow correlation between history or religions and phenomenology of religions." *(Van der Leeuw*, C. de la Saussaye, Kristensen, Bleeker, Van der Leeuw, Smart)[26]

(P4)   The phenomenology of religion should keep itself as clear as possible from the contamination of "a certain philosophy or psychology for fear of being forced to accept the theoretical implications of these concepts." *(Bleeker)*[27]

(P5)   The "phenomenology of religion is an empirical science without philosophical aspirations." *(Bleeker)*[28]

(P6)   The phenomenology of religion has nothing to do with the history of religion. *(Pettazzoni)*[29]

2.4. The Techniques of Religious Phenomenology

Finally, the least agreement about the meaning of 'phenomenology' is found when one examines the various phenomenological methods. Of all the notions of religious phenomenological method, the method of Van der Leeuw (VT1) is perhaps the best conceived. It is a definition which unites the felicities of most other methods without contradiction, and, by better comprehending the extensive scope of phenomenological investigation, possesses none of the others' blind spots. Bleeker's method (BT1), too, contains much to recommend it, particularly in his specification of the steps of a modified eidetic reduction. However, Bleeker's method (BT1) is more restrictive than Van der Leeuw's because it is designed to exclude all reference to history and yet be a purely empirical affair! The difficulty with this intent is that it undermines the very means by which phenomenology of religion operates as an empirical science: by its dependence on history. In comparison, the phenomenological method of Van der Leeuw is the saner approach to phenomenological method because it recognizes the need to test phenomenologically developed essences and descriptions by external, empirical sciences of meaning such as archaeology and philology.

The following propositions describe the various techniques which phenomenologists of religion employ or recommend. They are expressive of different levels of methodological precision.

(CT1) The phenomenology of religion creates classifications of ethnographic and historical material based upon significant morphological (qualitative) and

---

[26]Van der Leeuw 2: 686.

[27]Bleeker 7.

[28]Bleeker 7.

[29]Raffaele Pettazzoni, *Essays on the History of Religions* (Leiden: E.J. Brill, 1954) 217.

genealogical features but without homogenizing the heterogeneous or heterogenizing the homogeneous features of religion. (*C. de la Saussaye*)[30]

(KT1) The phenomenology of religion "takes facts and phenomena out of their historical setting which it encounters in different religions, brings them together and studies them in groups . . . [in order] to become acquainted with the religious thought, idea or need which underlies the group of corresponding data." (*Kristensen*)[31]

(KT2) The phenomenology of religion "studies identifiable categories which reach across traditions" by "distinguishing essential from inessential appearances. . . ." (*Kristensen*)[32]

(KT3) The phenomenology of religion examines religious phenomena from within consciousness; it demands that the phenomenologist forget himself, put himself in the believer's place and sympathetically understand "how the believer conceives the phenomena." (*Kristensen*)[33]

(VT1) The phenomenological method consists of the following steps: (a) the phenomenologist assigns tentative names to phenomena to signify initial impressions of similarity; (b) the phenomenologist interpolates the phenomena into his life by employing an intentional, methodical surrender to the believer's experience of the phenomenon; (c) the phenomenologist, though he surrenders to the phenomena, brackets commitment to, as well as explanatory and theoretical thinking *about*, the religious phenomena; (d) the phenomenologist clarifies what was observed on the basis of essential structural features; (e) the phenomenologist interprets the *logos* (or meaning) of the data revealed through steps (a) to (d); and (f) the phenomenologist tests the disclosed meaning by comparing it to the results of philological and archaeological research. (*Van der Leeuw*)[34]

(BT1) The phenomenology of religion proceeds by penetration into the thought of religious believers by means of their thought forms; this penetration is achieved through (a) a complete devotion to its objects, (b) the exclusion of historical surroundings in favor of ideological connections (the severing

---

[30]C. de la Saussaye 8.

[31]Kristensen 1.

[32]Kristensen 2.

[33]Kristensen 17.

[34]Van der Leeuw 2: 674-677.

of facts from their historical context and their recombination into meaningful classes), (c) the suspension of judgment and preconceived notions and (d) the employment of eidetic vision to search for the essentials of phenomena by comparing analogous religious phenomena side by side. (*Bleeker*)[35]

(BT2) The 'phenomenology of religion' "means both a scientific method and an independent science." (*Bleeker*)[36]

3. Discussion of the Continuities between the Various Objects, Ends, Placements and Methods of the Phenomenology of Religion

The long series of propositions listed above gives one some notion of the great variety of ways in which phenomenologists of religion have conceived of their task. This is not to say, however, that there is not a common core to the meaning of 'religious phenomenology.' Chantepie de la Saussaye, Kristensen, Van der Leeuw, Bleeker and Smart are, at points, in substantial agreement about the objects, ends and placement of religious phenomenology.

But if the communalities between the various understandings of religious phenomenology serve to define a general approach to the study of religious phenomena, they do so with a precision far short of the hortatory synthetic definition introduced in the preceding chapter. In fact, in many respects the various religious phenomenologies hide their definitional inadequacy behind prodigious historical labors. This is because, in most cases, the phenomenologies of religion are not obedient to any clear rules about how to construct essences, how to bracket phenomena phenomenologically, or how to achieve the sympathy necessary to identify oneself with the mental life of the believer. Although Van der Leeuw, of all the phenomenologists to date, has done the most to introduce serious methodological considerations into the phenomenology of religion, even his methods are vague at many points. Though his understanding of phenomena resembles some of the notions of philosophical phenomenologists, his method of extracting essences from phenomena is virtually unintelligible. So great is his fear that the phenomenology of religion will aspire to the logical and analytical methods of formal sciences that he proposes a definition of 'phenomenological essence' incapable of being understood much less of being used in a taxonomy of religions. One is led to speculate that the phenomenologists of religion who, at present occupy a no man's land between the history of religion and the philosophy of religion, feel so threatened by the encroachment of either discipline on their territory that they prefer methodological obscurantism to a clear-cut procedure.

---

[35]Bleeker 2-3, 8-9.

[36]Bleeker 10.

Despite the threat that phenomenologists of religion may feel about the encroachment of historical or philosophical methods (P4, P5, P6), and despite the siege mentality which results in their rejection of methods or concepts drawn from other disciplines, there are a number of surprising continuities between the various definitions of 'religious phenomenology' and the hortatory definition of 'philosophical phenomenology.' There is, for example, little opposition between the definitions of 'phenomena' employed in the phenomenology of religion and that proposed in the synthetic definition of 'philosophical phenomenology.' Religious phenomena stand to the complete field of phenomena described by philosophical phenomenology as a subspecies having their own specific character, a character connected with the religious variety of experience. There are even continuities between the way philosophical phenomenology describes the essential features of phenomena and the way Van der Leeuw describes the essential features of religious phenomena (02, 03, 04). Van der Leeuw's abstract analysis of the essence of religious phenomena provides the theoretical backdrop against which the structural features of the concrete varieties of religious phenomena--the cosmological, the anthropological and the cultic phenomena--can be described. Taken as a phenomenon, any religious datum can be characterized by the complex relations of objectivity and subjectivity which Van der Leeuw describes as being neither entirely objective nor subjective, neither entirely the result of an external reality not the product of the subject's constitution. This is not to say, however, that it is in principle impossible for there to be wholly subjective and objective aspects of a given appearance. These aspects are precisely what the phenomenological method is supposed to reduce in order to yield the uninterpreted phenomenon. This is what Van der Leeuw means when he says in (03) that a phenomenon's "essence is given in its appearance to someone."

There are continuities between the self-proclaimed ends of religious phenomenology and the ends of philosophical phenomenology, as well. Just as the end of philosophical phenomenology is to establish exhaustive taxonomies of mental and physical phenomena based upon rigorous analyses of these phenomena, religious phenomenology is "to classify and group . . . widely divergent data in such a way that an overall view can be obtained of their religious content and the religious values they contain."(E3)

Although Kristensen (according to E7) is under the impression that the presumptions and anticipations involved in religious phenomenology prohibit the phenomenology of religion from becoming a "rational and systematic structure in the science of religion," it is precisely upon the apodicity of the intentionality associated with such modes of consciousness that Husserl proposes to build a science of consciousness. If presumption and anticipation can be analyzed and understood, then they can be controlled to produce the certain descriptions of the mental life of religious individuals as this mental life is actually experienced. The Husserlian project of eidetic and phenomenological reduction is simply a philosophical method designed to discover the necessary structures behind all forms of consciousness and then, after understanding these structures, to control them for the purpose of scientific description. Even without the promise of a Husserlian science of consciousness, it would be difficult to understand how presumptions and anticipations are necessarily in opposition to a rational and systematic structure. If there are essences of religious phenomena, then there are essences of the forms of thought associated with religious presumptions and anticipations. There is no reason their structure and nomology is any less rational than that of any other physical phenomena.

From the point of view of philosophical phenomenology, most of the religious phenomenologists' assertions about the placement of religious phenomenology are correct, except when these exclude the involvement of other disciplines such as history of religion or philosophy of religion. According to the hortatory definition of 'phenomenology,' any phenomenology besides exploratory phenomenology subserves the motifs of the science of which it is a part. Phenomenology of religion, in that it is a part of the science of religion, must accept the concepts and data of this discipline whether they be a part of the philosophy of religion or history of religion. Religious phenomenology, therefore, may not have philosophical aspirations, but it cannot remain phenomenology without depending upon some philosophical conceptions, since even its origin was dependent upon philosophy, as James has shown.[37] Although there is sense in trying to keep the phenomenology of religion clear of unnecessary metaphysical presuppositions, philosophical presuppositions and concepts underlie virtually every concept of method known. To refuse to do philosophy because one fears philosophical importations is to do bad philosophy; the retreat from the attempt to ground the phenomenology of religion on sound philosophical concepts and presuppositions can only lead to its grounding upon unrecognized presuppositions and unexamined philosophical concepts.

Finally, there are continuities between the hortatory definition of phenomenological technique and phenomenological technique as defined by religionists. Even though Bleeker adamantly insists that he uses Husserlian terms in an equivocal fashion, his phenomenological technique and the phenomenological technique of Van der Leeuw demonstrate the influence of the Husserlian notions of phenomenological and eidetic reduction.[38] Even so, the intent associated with Bleeker's phenomenological technique (BT1) is much the same as Husserl's. Since, Bleeker does not flesh in the means by which the phenomenologist is to be sympathetic, is to suspend judgment and is to apply eidetic vision except in the most unsubstantial fashion, even with the danger of philosophical contamination, it is difficult to see how phenomenology of religion could fail to benefit from the Husserlian approach to eidetic and phenomenological reduction. The Husserlian technique would be of similar value to Van der Leeuw's method, as well, for though Van der Leeuw conceives of the phenomenological technique correctly, at least according to its general outline, his explanations of the various constituent steps are vague.

---

[37]George James, "Phenomenology and the Study of Religion," *The Journal of Religion* 65, Number 3 (July 1985): 311-335.

[38]The very terms they use, such as 'eidetic vision,' '*epoché*,' or 'suspension of judgment,' indicate this kinship.

4. The Contribution of the Hortatory Definition of 'Phenomenology' to the Phenomenology of Religion

The original purpose of this work was to synthesize a definition of 'phenomenology' which would prescribe how that word was to be used, generally, to denote the various philosophical phenomenologies and, by methodological transitivity, the phenomenology of religion. The scope, sensitivity and completeness of this definition have been demonstrated in the preceding chapter. What remains is a discussion of the contributions of this definition to the augmentation of phenomenology of religion. Aside from the beneficial univocity of meaning which would be gained if the hortatory definition were adopted as normative, the phenomenology of religion would gain a clearer definition of its methodological project. It has been demonstrated above that the hortatory definition of 'phenomenology' and the religious definition of 'phenomenology' are in greatest agreement about the objects and ends of a science of phenomena. It is, therefore, particularly with respect to methodological precision that the phenomenology of religion is in need of the greatest augmentation. Taken in turn, the most important positive contributions of the hortatory definition to the phenomenology of religion amount to the following.

First, in describing the objects of phenomenology as consisting of *a priori* structural principles and *a posteriori* experiential principles, the hortatory definition of 'phenomenology' reopens the question of whether or not there are *a priori* material principles which are implicit in the objects of religious phenomenology. In other words, beside insisting that phenomenology of religion must allow that its objects are structured by *a priori* formal principle (the logical relations of part and whole, for example), it also opens the possibility that the governing motifs of religion also include *a priori* experiential contents, religious experiences, emotions, sensibilities, and so on, which are the universal possessions of mankind. Rudolf Otto raised the possibility that such material givens do exist, but the investigation of these has become undeservedly *passé*. Accepting the postulate of the intentional unity of mankind--a postulate without which the Husserlian phenomenology would be impossible--one might well find that there are doxic intentionalities and emotive intentionalities (as well as hyletic contents) which are common to mankind. Why should there not also be specifically religious intentionalities which are given and irreducible? The hortatory definition of phenomenology leads, by way of Husserlian analyses, to the search for an analysis of such religious intentionalities under the auspices of the phenomenology of religion.

Second, in its description of phenomenological method, the hortatory definition of 'phenomenology' prescribes a procedural sequence which is unrivalled in its breadth and precision. Although the phenomenology of religion accepts this *general* methodological sequence, the meanings it associates with the terms 'taxonomy,' 'description,' 'essence,' 'structure,' and so on, are considerably more vague than those proposed by philosophical phenomenology. At issue are two distinct classes of terms: (1) terms referring to phenomenological procedure and (2) terms referring to scientific concepts. The hortatory definition of 'phenomenology' prescribes specific procedures for the phenomenological method, and the specific definition of these procedures has the effect of making associated regulative concepts richer and more precise than those employed in the phenomenology of religion. Because of this, there is no reason that the phenomenologist of religion should not adopt both these procedures and concepts. What the phenomenologist of religion has to gain by adopting the procedures of philosophical phenomenology is obvious.

All of the phenomenologists of religion are agreed that one of the ends of religious phenomenology is to understand the meaning structures associated with religious cosmology, anthropology, cultus, and so on. They also agree that what is involved in such an understanding is a methodological application of sympathy as well as a suspension of judgment and an eidetic reduction of some sort. In each case, however, the precise means by which one accomplishes each of these acts is not described. The only clue one has to the workings of these methods comes from their application to religious data, and these applications are not always unequivocal. Moreover, even if one is dimly able to grasp the means for accomplishing an eidetic reduction (interpreted in the religious methodological sense), one discovers that this means is guided by few regulative concepts. It is not as though there is any regularity to any of the religious methodological techniques. Religious phenomenological techniques such as eidetic reduction, the *epochê*, and so on, seem to be accomplished whimsically, according to different procedures at different times.

The hortatory definition of phenomenology is directed to remedy the situation by clearly prescribing those procedural steps entailed by the phenomenological method. One can use Chart 12 as a map of the various phenomenological techniques and the various preceding historical chapters as glosses on the meaning of each constituent procedure. Thus employed, the chart of synthetic phenomenological techniques and the preceding historical chapters can lend new conceptual precision to methods already employed by phenomenologists of religion. Among the methodological procedures particularly salient for a phenomenology of religion are: (a) the technique of phenomenological reduction, (b) the technique of perspectival variation, (c) the technique of eidetic reduction, (d) the technique of eidetic variation, (e) the technique of dialectical analysis and (f) the technique of Husserlian mereological analysis. Accompanying these procedures are regulative concepts which guide their investigations. The important regulative concepts are the following: (a*) the Husserlian concepts of *Lebenswelt, Mittelwelt, Wesenswelt, Umwelt,* and *Urwelt* which are used in conjunction with the phenomenological reduction, (b*) the Husserlian concepts of noema, noesis, noematic nucleus and eidos which are used in conjunction with eidetic reduction and (c*) the Whewellian notion of affinity which is used in conjunction with *diataxis*. To understand these regulative concepts is to understand what the phenomenological techniques are designed to effect, because both procedures and concepts are of one piece. Therefore, if the phenomenologist is intent upon understanding a religious practice as it nests within its cultural and historical milieu, (then in philosophical phenomenological terms) he is interested in the *Lebenswelt* associated with that practice, and he is given access to that *Lebenswelt* by means of that phenomenological reduction. From his vantage point from within the historically relativized *Lebenswelt* (or *Umwelt*), the religious phenomenologist may investigate, by employing further phenomenological reductions, the ideologies of that lifeworld (the *Wesenswelt*) or the invariant features shared between that lifeworld and our own (the *Urwelt*). It is this last investigation (the investigation of *Urwelt*) which provides the actual foundation for a sympathetic understanding of the religious individuals because it is the *Urwelt* that reveals the species being (to use a Marxist phrase) which we all share. For the phenomenologist of religion to move toward the definition of phenomenological essences the regulative concepts of noesis, noema, eidos, and so on, must be employed in conjunction with the method of mereology, perspectival variation, eidetic reduction and eidetic variation. Once the religious phenomenologist has completed the description of these essences, then he can employ the Husserlian mereology and the Whewellian notion of affinity, in conjunction, in order to locate that essence according to taxonomic and phylogenetic relations.

The two above contributions to the phenomenology of religion represent only the most important augmentations of religious phenomenology suggested by the historical discussions of phenomenology contained in this work. One could use this work as a guide to new methods for the study of religion and probably increase the fecundity of religious science in the process. Nevertheless, the above augmentations represent only those immediately suggested by the hortatory definition of phenomenology which was synthesized from the various historical meanings of phenomenology.

No further claim about the value of the idiosyncratic features of any particular phenomenology is made. The augmentations which emerge from the hortatory definition of phenomenology have force because they are based upon general features implicit in the major formulations of phenomenology. The phenomenologist of religion is urged, nevertheless, to make use of the individual methodologies in any way he chooses, providing he understands that these sometimes deviate from what has been proposed as the general phenomenological project.

5. Concluding Remarks

The purpose of this book was to produce a general meaning of 'phenomenology' which transcended the various individual phenomenologies and yet captured what was common to all. It was supposed that, because phenomenologists of religion were in a great state of confusion about phenomenology's meaning, that such a definition might have value in helping redefine its project. Both a hortatory definition of the meaning of 'phenomenology' and some suggestions as to how this definition can augment religious phenomenology have been presented. But for phenomenologists of religion to take either the proposed definition or proposed augmentations seriously, a considerable relaxation of the distrust they feel toward philosophy and the philosophy of religion must occur. This work, inasmuch as it is directed toward clearing up some of the ambiguity surrounding 'phenomenology of religion,' can also be interpreted as an argument for a *détente* between the phenomenologists of religion and philosophical phenomenologists as well as a reminder that it is incumbent upon the phenomenologists of religion to begin to reflect philosophically about their task. The reception this work receives remains to be seen. For a newcomer to the field of religious methodology to present a hortatory definition of 'phenomenology' and then to urge religious phenomenologists to reflect philosophically about their project may seem presumptuous. But no matter how presumptuous they may seem, both exhortations have importance. As C. J. Bleeker expressed it,

> Some people . . . doubt whether an exposition of the phenomenological method is of great value. Historians of religion usually get impatient when they are forced to read lengthy treatises on the principles and methods of their work. Nobody will blame them. However, they must admit that it is extremely useful to be now and then reminded of one's proper task.[39]

---

[39]Bleeker 11.

BIBLIOGRAPHY

Adorno, Theodor W. *Against Phenomenology*. Trans. Willis Domingo. Cambridge, Massachusetts: The MIT Press, 1983.

Aristotle. *Metaphysica*. Trans. Sir David Ross. Oxford: Oxford University Press, 1972.

_____. *The Physics*. 3 vols. Trans. Philip H. Wicksteed and Francis M. Cornford. Cambridge: Harvard University Press, 1970.

_____. *The Works of Aristotle*. 2 vols. Chicago: Encyclopaedia Britannica, 1952.

Baird, Robert D. *Category Formation and the History of Religion*. The Hague: Mouton & Co., 1971.

Barfield, Owen. *Saving the Appearances: A Study in Idolatry*. New York: Harcourt, Brace & World, Inc., 1976.

Barton, Allen H. "The Concept of Property-Space in Social Research." In *The Language of Social Research*, 40-53. Eds. Paul F. Lazarsfeld and Morris Rosenberg. Glencoe, Illinois: The Free Press, 1955.

Becker, Howard. "Constructive Typology in the Social Sciences." In *Contemporary Social Theory*, 17-46. Eds. Harry S. Barnes, Howard Becker, and Frances B. Becker. New York: Russell & Russell, 1940.

_____. "Culture Case Study and Ideal-Typical Method: With Special Reference to Max Weber." *Social Forces*, March 1934: 399-405.

Bellah, Robert N. "Religious Evolution." *American Sociological Review* 29 (June 1964): 358-374.

Berger, Gaston. *Phénoménologie du Temps et Perspectif*. Paris: P. U. P., 1954.

Berger, Peter L. *Invitation to Sociology: A Humanistic Perspective*. New York: Doubleday & Company, Inc., 1963.

_____. *The Sacred Canopy*. New York: Doubleday & Company, Inc., 1969.

_____. *The Social Construction of Reality: A Treatise in the Sociology of Knowledge*. New York: Doubleday & Company, Inc., 1969.

Bettis, Joseph Dabney, ed. *Phenomenology of Religion*. New York: Harper & Row, 1969.

Blanché, Robert. *Axiomatics*. London: Routledge & Kegan Paul, 1965.

Bleeker, C.J. "Comparing the Religio-Historical and the Theological Method." *Numen* 18 (1971): 9-29.

_____. "The Future Task of the History of Religion." *Numen* 7 (1960): 221-234.

_____. "*In Memoriam* Professor Dr. W. Brede Kristensen." *Numen* 1 (1954): 235-236.

_____. "The Phenomenological Method." *Numen* 6 (1959): 1-15.

248

_____. "The Relation of the History of Religions to Kindred Sciences, Particularly Theology, Sociology of Religion, Psychology of Religion and Phenomenology of Religion." *Numen* 1 (May 1954): 141-155.

_____. *The Sacred Bridge: Researches into the Nature and Structure of Religion.* Leiden: E.J. Brill, 1963.

Bloombaum, Milton. "A Contribution to the Theory of Typology Construction." *Sociological Quarterly* 5 (1964): 157-162.

Bochenski, I. M. *Contemporary European Philosophy: Philosophies of Matter, the Idea, Life, Essence, Existence, and Being.* Trans. Donald Nicholl and Karl Aschenbrenner. Berkeley, California: University of California Press, 1969.

_____. *The Logic of Religion.* New York: New York University Press, 1965.

_____. *The Methods of Contemporary Thought.* Trans. Peter Caws. New York: Harper & Row, 1968.

Bologh, Roslyn Wallach. *Dialectical Phenomenology: Marx's Method.* Boston: Routledge & Kegan Paul, 1979.

Cairns, Dorion. *Guide for Translating Husserl.* The Hague: Martinus Nijhoff, 1973.

Carman, John B. "The Theology of a Phenomenologist." *Harvard Divinity Bulletin* 29, number 3 (April 1965): 13-42.

Carnap, Rudolf. *Introduction to Symbolic Logic and its Applications.* Trans. William H. Meyer. New York: Dover Publications, 1958.

_____. *The Logical Syntax of Language.* Trans. Amethe Smeaton. London: Routledge & Kegan Paul, 1971.

Carr, David. *Phenomenology and the Problem of History.* Evanston: Northwestern University Press, 1967.

Carré, Meyrick H. *Realists and Nominalists.* Oxford: Oxford University Press, 1967.

Casey, Edward S. *Imagining: A Phenomenological Study.* Bloomington: Indiana University Press, 1976.

Chisholm, Roderick M. ed. *Realism and the Background of Phenomenology.* New York: The Free Press, 1960.

Chantepie de la Saussaye, P.D. *Manual of the Science of Religion.* London: Longmans, Green, and Co., 1891.

Collingwood, R.G. *An Essay on Philosophical Method.* Oxford: The Clarendon Press, 1970.

_____. *The Idea of History.* Oxford: Oxford University Press, 1956.

Compact Edition of the Oxford English Dictionary. 2 vols. Oxford: Oxford University Press, 1979.

Corduan, Winfried. *Handmaid to Theology: An Essay in Philosophical Prolegomena.* Grand Rapids, Michigan: Baker Book House, 1981.

Coreth, Emerich. *Metaphysics*. Trans. Joseph Donceel. New York: The Seabury Press, 1973.

Cotter, A. C. *Logic and Epistemology*. Boston: The Stratford Company, 1930.

Deaville, James. "Translation of the Phenomenological Section of Johann Lambert's *Neues Organon*." Commissioned translation, 1984 (Handwritten manuscript)

Dhavamony, Mariasusai. *Phenomenology of Religion*. Rome: Gregorian University Press, 1973.

Dictionary of American Biography. Ed. Dumas Malone. 1962 ed., s.v. "Charles Sanders Peirce."

Douglas, Mary and Edmund Perry. "Anthropology and Comparative Religion." *Theology Today* 41, number 4 (January 1985): 410-427.

Dreyfus, Hubert L., ed. *Husserl, Intentionality, and Cognitive Science*. Cambridge, Massachusetts: The MIT Press, 1982.

Duhem, Pierre. *To Save the Phenomena: An Essay on the Idea of Physical Theory from Plato to Galileo*. Trans. Edmund Doland and Chaninak Maschler. Chicago: The University of Chicago Press, 1969.

Durkheim, Émile. *The Rules of Sociological Method*. 8th ed. Trans. by Sarah A. Solovay and John H. Mueller. New York: The Free Press, 1966.

Eccles, Sir John C. *The Human Mystery*. Gifford Lectures 1977-1978. London: Routledge & Kegan Paul, 1984.

_____. *The Understanding of the Brain*. New York: McGraw Hill, 1977.

Eliade, Mircea, and Kitagawa, Joseph M., eds. *The History of Religions: Essays in Methodology*. Chicago: The University of Chicago Press, 1959.

Encyclopaedia Britannica, 3rd ed. s.v. "Philosophy," by John Robison. 1798.

Encyclopedia of Philosophy, 1972 ed., s.v. "Carneades," by Philip Hallie.

Encyclopedia of Philosophy, 1972 ed., s.v. "Arcesilaus," by Philip Hallie.

Euclid. *The Thirteen Books of Euclid's Elements*. Trans. with introduction and commentary by Sir Thomas L. Heath. 3 vols. New York: Dover Publications, 1956.

Farber, Marvin. *The Aims of Phenomenology: The Motives, Methods, and Impact of Husserl's Thought*. New York: Harper & Row, 1966.

_____. *The Foundation of Phenomenology: Edmund Husserl and the Quest for a Rigorous Science of Philosophy*. Albany, New York: State University of New York Press, 1968.

_____. *Philosophic Thought in France and the U.S.* New York: University of Buffalo Press, 1953.

Fichte, J. G. *The Science of Knowledge*. Ed. and trans. Peter Heath and John Lachs. Cambridge: Cambridge University Press, 1982.

Frege, Gottlob. *The Foundations of Arithmetic*. Trans. by J. L. Austin. Evanston: Northwestern University Press, 1968.

_____. *Translations from the Philosophical Writings of Gottlob Frege*. Eds. Peter Geach and Max Black. Oxford: Basil Blackwell, 1970.

Garraghan, Gilbert J. *A Guide to Historical Method*. New York: Fordham University Press, 1948.

Glassner, Barry. *Essential Interactionism: On the Intelligibility of Prejudice*. London: Routledge & Kegan Paul, 1980.

Green, Henry A. "Gnosis and Gnosticism: A Study in Methodology." *Numen* 24 (1977): 95-134.

Gurvitch, Georges. *The Social Frameworks of Knowledge*. Trans. Margaret A. Thompson and Kenneth A. Thompson. New York: Harper & Row, 1971.

_____. *Studies in Phenomenology and Psychology*. Evanston: Northwestern University Press, 1966.

Hacker, Helen Mayer. "Arnold Rose's ' Deductive Ideal-Type Method'." *American Journal of Sociology* 56 (January 1951): 354-356.

Hamilton, William, Sir. *Lectures on Metaphysics and Logic*. 2nd ed. Eds. Rev. H. L. Mansel and John Veitch. 2 Vols. Edinburgh: William Blackwood and Sons, 1851.

Harris, Marvin. *Cultural Materialism: The Struggle for a Science of Culture*. New York: Random House, 1979.

Hayek, F. A. *The Counter Revolution of Science: Studies on the Abuse of Reason*. Indianapolis: Liberty Press, 1979.

Hegel, G. W. F. *The Phenomenology of Mind*. Trans. J. B. Baillie. New York: Harper & Row, 1967.

Heidegger, Martin. *The Basic Problems of Phenomenology*. Trans. Albert Hofstadter. Bloomington: Indiana University Press, 1982.

_____. *Being and Time*. Trans. John Macquarrie and Edward Robison. New York: Harper & Row, 1962.

Hirsch, E. D., Jr. *Validity in Interpretation*. New Haven: Yale University Press, 1967.

Hiz, Henry, ed. *Questions*. Dordrecht: Reidel, 1978.

Höffding, Harald. *The Philosophy of Religion*. Trans. B. E. Meyer. New York: Books for Library Press, 1971.

Hultkrantz, Ake. "The Phenomenology of Religion: Aims and Methods." *Temenos* 6 (1970): 68-88.

Husserl, Edmund. *Cartesian Meditations: An Introduction to Phenomenology*. Trans. Dorion Cairns. The Hague: Martinus Nijhoff, 1973.

_____. *Cartensiansche Meditationen und Pariser Vorträge*. The Hague: Martinus Nijhoff, 1950.

_____. *The Crisis of European Sciences and Transcendental Phenomenology*. Trans. David Carr. Evanston: Northwestern University Press, 1970.

_____. *Erfahrung und Urteil. Untersuchungen zur Genealogie der Logik.* Hamburg: Claassen & Goverts, 1954.

_____. *Experience and Judgment.* Ed. Ludwig Landgrebe. Trans. James S. Churchill and Karl Ameriks. Evanston: Northwestern University Press, 1973.

_____. *Formal and Transcendental Logic.* The Hague: Martinus Nijhoff, 1978.

_____. *Formale und transzendentale Logik. Versuch einer Kritik der logischen Vernunft.* Halle: Niemeyer, 1929.

_____. *Ideas.* Trans. W. R. Boyce Gibson. New York: Humanities Press, Inc., 1976.

_____. *Ideen zu einer reinen Phänomenologie und phänomenologischen Philosophie. Erstes Buch: Allgemeine Einfuhrüng in die reine Phänomenologie.* The Hague: Martinus Nijhoff, 1954.

_____. *Die Krisis der europäischen Wissenschaften und die transzendentale Phänomenologie. Eine Einleitung in die phänomenologische philosophie.* The Hague: Martinus Nijhoff, 1954.

_____. *Logical Investigations.* 2 vols. Trans. J. N. Findlay. London: Routledge & Kegan Paul, 1970.

_____. *Logische Untersuchungen.* 2 vols. Halle: M. Niemeyer, 1900-1901.

_____. *Phenomenology and the Crisis of Philosophy.* Trans. Quentin Lauer. New York: Harper & Row, 1965.

_____. *The Phenomenology of Internal Time-Consciousness.* Ed. Martin Heidegger. Trans. James S. Churchill. Bloomington: Indiana University Press, 1964.

Ihde, Don. *Experimental Phenomenology: An Introduction.* New York: G.P. Putnam's Sons, 1977.

Ingarden, Roman. *The Cognition of the Literary Work of Art.* Trans. Ruth Ann Crowley and Kenneth R. Olson. Evanston: Northwestern University Press, 1973.

_____. *The Literary Work of Art.* Trans. George G. Grabowicz. Evanston: Northwestern University Press, 1973.

James, George A. "Phenomenology and the Study of Religion." *The Journal of Religion* 65, number 3 (July 1985): 311-335.

John of St. Thomas. *The Material Logic of John of St. Thomas: Basic Treatises.* Trans. Yves R. Simon, John J. Glanville and G. Donald Hollenhorst. Chicago: The University of Chicago Press, 1965.

_____. *Outlines of Formal Logic.* Trans. Francis C. Wade. Milwaukee: Marquette University Press, 1955.

Katz, Jerrold. *Semantic Theory.* Evanston: Harper & Row, 1972.

Kishimoto, Hideo. "An Operational Definition of Religion." *Numen* 8 (1961): 236-240.

Kobler, John F. *Vatican II and Phenomenology: Reflection of the Life-World of the Church.* Dordrecht: Martinus Nijhoff, 1985.

252

Kockelmans, Joseph J. *A First Introduction to Husserl's Phenomenology*. Louvain: Editions E. Nauwelaerts, 1967.

Kockelmans, Joseph J. ed. *Phenomenology: The Philosophy of Edmund Husserl and Its Interpretation*. New York: Doubleday & Company, Inc., 1967.

Kohák, Erazim. *Idea and Experience: Edmund Husserl's Project of Phenomenology in "Ideas I."* Chicago: University of Chicago Press, 1978.

Koyré, Alexandre. "Manifold and Category." *Philosophy and Phenomenological Research* 9, number 1 (August 1948): 1-20.

Kristensen, W. Brede. *The Meaning of Religion: Lectures in the Phenomenology of Religion*. The Hague: Martinus Nijhoff, 1960.

Kubinski, Tadeusz. *An Outline of the Logical Theory of Questions*. Berlin: Akademie-Verlag, 1980.

Kuhn, H. "The Phenomenological Concept of 'Horizon'." In *Philosophical Essays in Memory of Edmund Husserl*. Ed. M. Farber. Cambridge, Massachusetts: 1941.

Kung, Guido. *Ontology and the Logistic Analysis of Language*. Dordrecht: D. Reidel Publishing Co., 1967.

Kuyper, Abraham. *Principles of Sacred Theology*. Trans. J. Hendrik de Vries. Grand Rapids, Michigan: Baker Book House, 1980.

Laertius, Diogenes. *Lives of the Philosophers*. Trans. and Ed. A. Robert Caponigri. Chicago: Henry Regnery Company, 1969.

Lambert, Johann Heinrich. *Neues Organon: Oder Gedanken über die Erforschung und Bezeichnung des Wahren und der Unterscheidung von Irrtum und Schein*. 2 vols. Leipzig: Johann Wendler, 1764.

Landgrebe, L. "The World as a Phenomenological Problem." *Philosophy and Phenomenological Research*, 1, number 1 (1940): 35-58.

Lauer, Quentin. *Phenomenology: Its Genesis and Prospect*. New York: Harper & Row, 1965.

_____. *The Triumph of Subjectivity: An Introduction to Transcendental Phenomenology*. New York: Fordham University Press, 1978.

Lazarsfeld, Paul F., and Barton, Allen H. "Qualitative Measurement in the Social Sciences: Classification, Typologies, and Indices." In *The Policy Sciences* 155-92. Eds. Daniel Lerner and Harold D. Lasswell. Stanford, California: Stanford University Press, 1951.

Leonard, Henry S. *Principles of Reasoning: An Introduction to Logic, Methodology and the Theory of Signs*. New York: Dover Publications, 1967.

Levinas, Emmanuel. *The Theory of Intuition in Husserl's Phenomenology*. Trans. Andre Orianne. Evanston: Northwestern University Press, 1973.

Liddell, Henry George and Scott, Robert. *A Greek-English Lexicon Based on the German Work of Francis Passow*. New York: Harper Brothers, 1846.

Locke, John. *An Essay Concerning Human Understanding*. 2 vols. London: J. M. Dent, 1961.

Lonergan, Bernard. *Method in Theology.* New York: Herder and Herder, 1973.

Losee, John. *A Historical Introduction to the Philosophy of Science.* 2nd ed. Oxford: Oxford University Press, 1980.

Luckmann, Thomas, ed. *Phenomenology and Sociology.* New York: Penguin Books, 1978.

Luijpen, William A. *Phenomenology and Metaphysics.* Pittsburgh: Duquesne University Press, 1965.

Lyons, John. *Introduction to Theoretical Linguistics.* Cambridge: Cambridge University Press, 1968.

McCormick, Peter, and Elliston, Frederick, eds. *Husserl: Shorter Works.* Notre Dame, Indiana: University of Notre Dame Press, 1981.

McKinney, John C. *Constructive Typology and Social Theory.* New York: Appleton-Century-Crofts, 1966.

McKnight, Edgar V. *Meaning in Texts: The Historical Shaping of a Narrative Hermeneutics.* Philadelphia: Fortress Press, 1978.

McMurtry, John. *The Structure of Marx's World-View.* Princeton: Princeton University Press, 1978.

Maritain, Jacques. *Distinguish to Unite or The Degrees of Knowledge.* Trans. Gerald B. Phelan. London: Geoffrey Bles, 1959.

_____. *Existence and the Existent: An Essay on Christian Existentialism.* Trans. Lewis Galantiere and Gerald B. Phelan. New York: Doubleday & Co., Inc., 1961.

_____. *Philosophy of Nature.* Trans. Imelda C. Byrne. New York: Philosophical Library, 1951.

Marrou, Henri. *The Meaning of History.* Trans. Robert J. Olsen. Montreal: Palm Publishers, 1966.

Merleau-Ponty, M. *Phenomenology of Perception.* Trans. Colin Smith. London: Routledge & Kegan Paul, 1962.

Meyerson, Émile. *Identity and Reality.* Trans. Kate Loewenberg. New York: Dover Publications, 1962.

Miller, Izchak. *Husserl: Perception and Temporal Awareness.* Cambridge, Massachusetts: The MIT Press, 1984.

Monier-Williams, M., Sir. *Sanskrit-English Dictionary.* Oxford: The Clarendon Press, 1976.

Muck, Otto, S. J. *The Transcendental Method.* Trans. William D. Seidensticker. New York: Herder and Herder, 1968.

Muller-Thym, Bernard J. "Of History as a Calculus Whose Term is Science." *The Modern Schoolman* 19, number 3 (March 1942): 41-47.

Nota, John H., S. J. *Phenomenology and History.* Trans. Louis Grooten. Chicago: Loyola University Press, 1967.

O'Dea, Thomas F. *The Sociology of Religion.* Englewood Cliffs, New Jersey: Prentice Hall, Inc., 1966.

254

Ohman, Suzanne. "Theories of the 'Linguistic Field'." *Word: Journal of the Linguistic Circle of New York* 9, number 2 (August 1953): 123-134.

Oxtoby, Willard Gordon. "*Religionswissenschaft* Revisited." In *Religions in Antiquity: Essays in Memory of E. R. Goodenough.* Ed. Jacob Neusner. Leiden: E. J. Brill, 1968.

Paci, Enzo. *The Function of the Sciences and the Meaning of Man.* Trans. Paul Piccone. Evanston: Northwestern University Press, 1972.

Parmenides. *Parmenides: A Text with Translation, Commentary, and Critical Essays.* Trans. and ed. Leonardo Taran. Princeton: Princeton University Press, 1965.

Peirce, Charles Sanders. *Collected Papers of Charles Sanders Peirce.* Eds. Charles Hartshorne and Paul Weiss, 8 vols. Cambridge, Massachusetts: Harvard University Press, 1979.

Percy, Walker. *The Message in the Bottle.* New York: Farrar, Straus, and Giroux, 1979.

Pepper, George B. "A Re-examination of the Ideal Type Concept." *The American Catholic Sociological Review* 24 (Fall, 1963): 185-201.

Peters, F.E. *Greek Philosophical Terms: A Historical Lexicon.* New York: New York University Press, 1967.

Pettazzoni, R. *Essays on the History of Religions.* Leiden: E. J. Brill, 1954.

Pfänder, Alexander. *Phenomenology of Willing and Motivation.* Trans. Herbert Spiegelberg. Evanston: Northwestern University Press, 1967.

Plato. *The Collected Dialogues.* Eds. Edith Hamilton and Huntington Cairns. Princeton: Princeton University Press, 1971.

Popper, Karl and Eccles, John C. *The Self and Its Brain: An Argument for Interactionism.* London: Routledge & Kegan Paul, 1977.

Przelecki, M. *The Logic of Empirical Theories.* London: Routledge & Kegan Paul, 1969.

Pummer, Reinhard. "Recent Publications on the Methodology of the Science of Religion." *Numen* 22 (1975): 161-182.

_____. "*Religionwissenschaft* or Religiology?" *Numen* 19 (August and December 1972): 90-124.

Reat, N. Ross. "Insiders and Outsiders in the Study of Religious Traditions." *Journal of the American Academy of Religion* 51 (September 1983): 459-76.

Ricoeur, Paul. *Husserl: An Analysis of His Phenomenology.* Evanston: Northwestern University Press, 1967.

Rose, Arnold M. "A Deductive Ideal-Type Method." *American Journal of Sociology* 56 (July 1950): 35-42.

Royko, Mike. "Educt, Reduct and Other Muck." *The Chicago Tribune*, 6 August 1985.

Sartre, Jean-Paul. *Being and Nothingness.* New York: Philosophical Library, 1956.

_____. *Critique of Dialectical Reason.* Trans. Alan Sheridan-Smith. London: NLB, 1978.

_____. *Imagination: A Psychological Critique.* Trans. Forrest Williams. Ann Arbor: University of Michigan Press, 1962.

_____. *Search for a Method.* Trans. Hazel E. Barnes. New York: Random House, 1963.

_____. *The Transcendence of the Ego.* Trans. Forrest Williams and Robert Kirkpatrick. New York: Farrar, Straus, and Giroux, 1957.

Saussure, Ferninand de. *Course in General Linguistics.* Trans. Wade Baskin. New York: McGraw-Hill, 1959.

Schutz, Alfred. *Life Forms and Meaning Structure.* Trans. Helmut Wagner. London: Routledge & Kegan Paul, 1982.

_____. *The Phenomenology of the Social World.* Trans. George Walsh and Frederick Lehnert. Evanston: Northwestern University Press, 1967.

_____. *The Problem of Social Reality: Collected Papers 1.* Ed. Maurice Natanson. The Hague: Martinus Nijhoff, 1962.

Schutz, Alfred, and Luckman, Thomas. *The Structure of the Life-World.* Trans. Richard M. Zaner. Evanston: Northwestern University Press, 1973.

Searle, John R. *Intentionality: An Essay in the Philosophy of Mind.* Cambridge: Cambridge University Press, 1984.

Sextus Empiricus. *Outlines of Pyrrhonism.* Trans. R. G. Bury. Cambridge: Harvard University Press, 1967.

Sharma, Arvind. "An Inquiry Into the Nature of the Distinction Between the History of Religion and the Phenomenology of Religion." *Numen* 22 (1975): 81-95.

Sharpe, Eric J. *Comparative Religion: A History.* London: Duckworth, 1975.

Smart, Ninian. "Beyond Eliade: The Future of Theory in Religion." *Numen* 25 (August 1978): 171-183.

_____. *The Phenomenon of Religion.* London: The Macmillan Press, 1973.

_____. *The Science of Religion and the Sociology of Knowledge: Some Methodological Questions.* Princeton: Princeton University Press, 1973.

Sokolowski, Robert. *Husserlian Meditations.* Evanston: Northwestern University Press, 1974.

Spence, N. C. W. "Linguistic Fields, Conceptual Systems and the *Weltbild.*" In *Transactions of the Philological Society.* New York: 1961.

Spiegelberg, Herbert. *The Phenomenological Movement: A Historical Introduction.* The Hague: Martinus Nijhoff, 1982.

Stephenson, William. "A Statistical Approach to Typology: The Study of Trait-Universes." *Journal of Clinical Psychology* 6 (January 1950): 26-38.

256

Strasser, Stephan. *Phenomenology and the Human Sciences: A Contribution to a New Scientific Ideal.* Pittsburgh: Duquesne University Press, 1974.

Taylor, A. E. *Aristotle.* New York: Dover Publications, Inc., 1955.

Thiselton, Anthony C. *The Two Horizons: New Testament Hermeneutics and Philosophical Description.* Grand Rapids, Michigan: William B. Eerdmans Publishing Company, 1980.

Thévenaz, Pierre. *What is Phenomenology?* Trans. James M. Edie. Chicago: Quadrangle Books, 1962.

Thomas Aquinas, Saint. *Commentary on Aristotle's Physics.* Trans. Richard J. Blackwell, Richard J. Spath, and W. Edmund Thirlkel. London: Routledge & Kegan Paul, 1963.

_____. *Commentary on the "Posterior Analytics" of Aristotle.* Trans. F. R. Larcher. New York: Magi Books, Inc., 1970.

_____. *The Division and Methods of the Sciences.* 3rd ed. Trans. Armand Maurer. Toronto, Canada: The Pontifical Institute of Mediaeval Studies, 1963.

_____. *Truth.* 3 vols. Chicago: Henry Regnery, 1952.

Toulemont, René. *L'Essence de la Société Selon Husserl.* Paris: P. U. Press, 1962.

Ullman, Stephen. *The Principles of Semantics.* Oxford: Basil Blackwell, 1963.

van der Leeuw, G. *Religion in Essence and Manifestation.* Trans. F. E. Turner. London: George Allen and Unwin, Ltd., 1964.

Veatch, Henry Babcock. *Intentional Logic.* Hamden, Connecticut: Archon Books, 1970.

Voegelin, E. "On the Origins of Scientism." *Social Research* 15 (1948): 462-494.

Volpe, Galvano Della. *Logic as a Positive Science.* Trans. Jon Rothschild. London: NLB, 1980.

von Hildebrand, Dietrich. *What is Philosophy?* Chicago: Franciscan Herald Press, 1973.

von Mises, Ludwig. *Epistemological Problems of Economics.* New York: New York University Press, 1976.

Waardenburg, Jaques. *Classical Approaches to the Study of Religion: Aims, Methods and Theories of Research.* 2 vols. The Hague: Mouton, 1973.

_____. "Religion Between Reality and Idea." *Numen* 19 (1972): 128-203.

Wallace, William A. *The Elements of Philosophy: A Compendium for Philosophers and Theologians.* New York: Alba House, 1977.

Weber, Max. *The Methodology of the Social Sciences.* Trans. and eds. Edward A. Shils and Henry A. Finch. New York: The Free Press, 1949.

Whewell, William. *The Philosophy of the Inductive Sciences Founded Upon Their History.* 2 vols. New York: Johnson Reprint Corporation, 1967.

Whitehead, Alfred North. *Modes of Thought*. New York: The Free Press, 1966.

Wojtyla, Karol. *The Acting Person*. Trans. Andrzej Potocki. Dordrecht: D. Reidel, 1979.

_____. *Sources of Renewal: The Implementation of Vatican II*. Trans. P. S. Falla. San Francisco: Harper and Row, 1980.

Yinger, J. Milton. *The Scientific Study of Religion*. London: The Macmillan Company, 1970.

Zuesse, Evan M. "The Role of Intentionality in the Phenomenology of Religion." *Journal of the American Academy of Religion* 53 (March 1985): 51-73.

Znaniecki, Florian. *Cultural Reality*. Chicago: The University of Chicago Press, 1919.

INDEX OF NAMES

INDEX OF SUBJECTS

Diairesis (division): its role in the Platonic dialectic, 18, 19

Dialectics: Aristotelian assessment of, 19-20; Hegelian notion, 62-63; Platonic notion, 16-19; in the synthetic phenomenological method, 225, 227, 230

Dialektikê (dialectics): equated with *epistêmê* in Plato's thought, 17-19. *See also* **Dialectics.**

Diataxis: and the construction of taxonomies according to Whewell, 118-119; in the synthetic philosophical technique, 229

Discrimination: its role in categorization according to Peirce, 147, 167

Dissociation: its role in categorization according to Peirce, 147, 167

E

Eidetic reduction: Husserlian, 211-214

Eidetic variation: and eidetic reduction, 211; and the Husserlian theory of parts and wholes, 196-197

Eidos/eidê (idea, form, essence): exact vs. morphological essences, 198-199; opposed to *doxa* in Plato's thought, 17; as phenomenological essences in Husserl's thought, 198-199

Encyclopedicists: 44, 45, 75

Epistêmê (certain knowledge, science): relation to *dialektikê* in Plato's thought, 17; relation to *logos* in Plato's thought, 16; relation to *apodeixis* in Aristotle's thought, 19-21

Epochê (suspension): in eidetic reduction, 210-213; Husserlian notion, 51-52, 204; its meaning according to Arcesilaus and Carneades, 208, 208-209n.106; not Cartesian doubt, 209; relation to phenomenological reduction; 210; as suspension of judgment and the pregiven world, 209-210

Error: Lambertian notion of, 26-27

Etiology (aitiology): Hamiltonian notion takes mind as necessary precondition, 80-82; relation to the Peircean cenopythagorean categories of secondness and thirdness 150-155; Robisonian notion unmetaphysical, 45-4; Whewellian motif of causation founds it, 125-128

Experience: according to Husserl, conscious variety intentional, 180-184; noetic and noematic components of, 184-188; and the Peircean cenopythagorean categories, 149-155; physical, psychological and moral varieties according to Lambert, 27-30; structured by Whewellian syzygies, 105; its total horizon is the *Lebenswelt*, 170-178; *Umwelt, Urwelt, Mittelwelt* and *Wesenswelt* are its different realms, 172-176

F

Facts: related to secondness, according to Peirce, 150-153, 165; in the Whewellian syzygy of theory and fact, 108-109

G

Gegebenheitsweise (manner of givenness): 172n.11, 188

Gegenstand (object): 187

Governing motifs: Whewellian notion vs. axioms and definitions, 114-115; causation, 125-129; classification (in phenomen-ology), 116-125; conciliance, colligation and simplicity, 129-134; distinguishing features of, 115-116

H

History: affinities with phenomenology: according to Hamilton, 89; according to Hegel, 65-68; according to Husserl, 188-190; according to Whewell, 102-103, 115-116

Synthetic definition: criteria of good, 216, 216n.1; of 'ends of phenomenology,' 218; of 'phenomena,' 216-217; of 'phenomenological technique,' 225, 227-229; of 'phenomenology's placement,' 223

Syzygies, Whewellian: ideas and sensations, 109; induction and deduction, 107-108; matter and form, 111-112; necessary and empirical truths, 106-107; reflexion and sensation, 109-110; subject and object, 110-111; theory and fact, 108-109; thoughts and things, 106

T

Taxonomy: impossibility of the palaetiological sciences without this motif, 116; Peircean system of signs an example of, 155-162; part of the synthetic definition of 'phenomenology,' 223-230, 243-244; product of the Husserlian mereology, 190-197; second part of scientific method according to Robison, 49-50

Theologia (science of things divine): 15, 21

Theôria (contemplation, reflection, speculation): 22

Theory: Whewellian notion, 129-135. *See also 'Theôria.'*

Truth: Hegelian notion, 50; Lambertian notion, 26-27, 36-37

U

Umwelt (surrounding world): 172, 172n.10, 172n.11, 174, 175, 199, 213, 243

Urwelt (primal world, original world): 172, 172n.11, 173, 174, 175, 243, 244

W

Weltbild (world picture): 6, 9

Wesenswelt (essential world): 172, 172n.10, 172n.11, 173-178, 188, 243

TORONTO STUDIES IN RELIGION

This series of monographs and books is designed as a contribution to the scholarly and academic understanding of religion. Such understanding is taken to involve both a descriptive and an explanatory task. The first task is conceived as one of 'surface description' involving the gathering of information about religions, and 'depth description' that provides, on the basis of the data gathered, a more finely nuanced description of a tradition's self-understanding. The second task concerns the search for explanation and the development of theory to account for religion and for particular historical traditions. The series will, furthermore, cover the phenomenon of religion in all its constituent dimensions and geographic diversity. Both established and younger scholars in the field will be included and will represent a wide range of viewpoints and positions, producing original work of a high order at the monograph and major study level.

Although predominantly empirically oriented the series will also encourage theoretical studies and even leave room for creative and empirically controlled philosophical and speculative approaches in the interpretation of religions and religion.

TORONTO STUDIES IN RELIGION will be of particular interest to those who study the subject at universities or colleges but will also be of value to the general educated reader.

DATE DUE
